Post-Colonial Globalisation

With the globalist project immersed in conflicts and adversity, *Post-Colonial Globalisation* offers an insight into the actors who animate it and the power dynamics which run through it. Using the law as the prism through which these are examined, and fusing historical with contemporary perspectives, the book contributes to understanding the crisis in which we find ourselves as a moment of both existential danger and an opportunity.

This book is in two parts. The first part charters capitalism's historical progression to globalism through the lens of the act of taking. Taking has risen to institutional prominence as a core concept in the legal lexicon of foreign investment protection to denote deprivation of private property. *Post-Colonial Globalisation* advances a broader notion of taking as a tool of social criticism. From enclosures, to colonial settlement to an empire of unequal exchanges, to contemporary land grabs, private property, now so vigorously protected against taking, was itself born out of taking. The second part focuses on the ecological dimension of neoliberal globalisation and its hallmarks of unlimited growth and excessive extraction. It has negatively impacted the climate, the earth and its human and non-human inhabitants to the point of putting their continued existence at risk. Central to this is the deification of property. Our understanding of proprietary relations and the rights they confer must be revisited if our interface with the planet is to be reconfigured. The emerging doctrine of rights of nature offers one route which may lead us in this direction. The two parts complement each other. One looks at taking by members of the human species from each other. The other looks at taking by the human species from nature.

This book is aimed at anyone who wishes to gain insight into the current crisis, including students, academics, NGOs and policymakers.

Yonit Manor-Percival is a practicing solicitor and lectures at the School of Law, School of Oriental and African Studies, University of London.

Janet Dine is Professor of International Economic Development Law at the Centre of Commercial Law Studies, Queen Mary University of London.

Post-Colonial Globalisation

Law, Power and Actors in the 21st Century

Yonit Manor-Percival and Janet Dine

Routledge
Taylor & Francis Group
LONDON AND NEW YORK

Designed cover image: © Getty Images

First published 2024
by Routledge
4 Park Square, Milton Park, Abingdon, Oxon OX14 4RN

and by Routledge
605 Third Avenue, New York, NY 10158

Routledge is an imprint of the Taylor & Francis Group, an informa business

British Library Cataloguing-in-Publication Data
A catalogue record for this book is available from the British Library

ISBN: 978-1-138-23016-3 (hbk)
ISBN: 978-1-138-23017-0 (pbk)
ISBN: 978-1-315-38678-2 (ebk)

DOI: 10.4324/9781315386782

Typeset in Times New Roman
by Apex CoVantage, LLC

To Daniel, Gil and Behnaz with all my love and to all those who struggle with humility and gratitude.

Yonit Manor-Percival

To my husband Keith, my children Rob and Liliana, Helen and Simon and Liz and my grandsons Tim and Nick with love. I am so blessed that my family understands the climate emergency.

Janet Dine

Contents

Figures

Preface

This book is the product of years of collaborative teaching and writing. During this time, consequential processes and events, some more palpable than others, have been transforming the globalised landscape. As these processes and events intensify, the globalisation to which we have grown accustomed and which has guided much of our teaching is being transfigured by its unintended consequences. Notable among them are the coming on stage of new centres of power and the construction of an alternative organisational, financial and institutional infrastructure, home to new interstate alliances. In response, rivalries (real, perceived or manufactured) erupt, forging a plenary topography in which openly declared economic wars and military campaigns criss-cross economic interdependency and integration. A Global South narrative of multipolarity that is based on equal sovereignty, harmonious co-existence of differences, cooperation and common prosperity competes with the dominant discourse of a rule-based order designed and policed for the benefit of all under the auspices of a benevolent and exceptional US empire. In the words of Hilary Clinton speaking at the 2016 Democratic National Convention, 'America is great because America is good'. Yet, in both the halls of governance and the streets of Africa, Latin America and Asia, public statements and contestations about neocolonialism, exploitation, imperialism and the prerogative of shaking them off are making a comeback.

Transformations make for times of flux and disorder. New arrangements are coming to the fore whilst the old ones are extant. This melange, too young to reap the benefits of a longer historical view, breeds confusion, fearfulness and, in turn, passionate debates. It should come as no surprise that we were no exception. Our collaboration has become an arena of factual, analytical and theoretical contentions. We differed in both our observations of what is unfolding as well as how it is to be understood. Yet, beyond disagreements, we continued to share the key conviction that capitalist, alternatively neoliberal globalisation has produced adverse outcomes and that addressing its counterindications and contradictions has become an existential emergency. It is with this in mind that this book was written. It was to bring together a shared purpose with divergent perspectives, making for a wider canvass for the reader to contemplate.

Amidst the upheaval of changes, contestations and fluidity of power structures, at least for now, the actors which inhabit the globalised space – states, corporations, population and non-human ecological systems – have remained unchanged. The law continues to provide the institutional framework within which their interactions are configured. The relative longevity of this format endows globalisation with a temporal unity in which past, present and future bleed into each other in a mixture of continuities, inflections and interruptions. The first part of the book examines the present through the lens of past events and the processes of dispossession by which property came into being. It speaks to the proposition that time is essentially indivisible so that the past continues to animate the present and is pivotal to shaping the future. We need to recover our memory if we are to formulate new visions and open our mind to those who share our bed yet have different dreams. It is to this bed – the planet, our only home – that the second part of the book is dedicated. This part focuses on the present but has its eye on the future. Where we stand vis-à-vis our non-human bedfellows has been shaped by our addiction to a particular juridical formation of property relations, an addiction which has its roots in the past and which by now threatens our continuing existence. It must be revisited if we are to survive.

This book would not have been written without the support, expertise and talent of others.

Acknowledgements

Special gratitude is extended to Dr Corinna Mullin, Dr Rachel Chamber and Professor David Margolis for their encouragement and the comments and ideas they so generously shared with me. Elizabeth Campbell was by my side, observing, remarking and holding my hand throughout the ups and downs of writing. Special thanks also to Alastair Percival who tirelessly read and commented on each and every draft, always patient and never losing his belief in me, to Daniel and Behnaz Percival for their support, to Gil Percival for sharing with me the secrets of simplicity and to Audrey Bomse for her friendship and encouragement. Last but not least, I owe a debt of gratitude to the writers and thinkers who created a pool of knowledge and analysis from which I derived inspiration and greatly benefited.

Yonit Manor-Percival
London, December 2022

Special gratitude is also extended to colleagues and friends Peter Muchlinski, Nick Bernard, Michael Blecher, Beate Sjafell and her team in the SMART (Sustainable Market Actors for Responsible Trade) project in Oslo University. I have dedicated this book to my near family, I love them dearly.

Janet Dine
London, December 2022

Introduction

This book is in two parts, each written by one of its two co-authors. Each focuses on a different but complementary perspective of the globalist project. In the first section, Yonit Manor-Percival charters capitalism's historical progression to globalism through the lens of the act of taking. The act of taking has risen to institutional prominence as a core concept in the legal lexicon of foreign investment protection. It denotes dispossession. The boundaries of this dispossession are, however, circumscribed. First, what is being taken is limited to private property reconfigured as foreign investment and mostly concentrated in the hands of a few corporate proprietors. Second, the protagonists include only these proprietors in their moment of deprivation on the one hand and the state in the role of the perpetrator on the other. Yonit Manor-Percival broadens the parameters within which the idea of 'taking' is examined. She approaches it as a family of terms used also as a tool of social criticism and covering a plethora of actors and their interactions. This includes the part played by these same proprietors in the production of dispossession. The breadth of the term when used as a tool of social criticism is rendered all the more striking by the narrowness of its legal parameters. It is particularly striking considering that private property in its narrow legal sense emerged out of taking in its enlarged, social sense. Its birth signified the historical transition from glorification of the act as heralding the advent of civilisation to its denigration as compensable infringement of rights. In the process, appropriators were reimagined as an injured party.

In the second part, Janet Dine focuses on the ecological dimension of neoliberal globalisation and its hallmarks of unlimited growth and excessive extraction. Neoliberal globalisation, argues Janet Dine, equates unbridled capitalism. It has negatively impacted the climate, the earth and its human and non-human inhabitants to the point of putting their continued existence at risk. She cites Pope Francis who described it as 'the dung of the devil'.[1] Thus, the two parts of the book complement each other. One looks at taking by members of the human species from

1 Pope Francis, 'Unbridled Capitalism Is the "Dung of the Devil", Says Pope Francis' (*The Guardian*, 10 July 2015) <https://www.theguardian.com/world/2015/jul/10/poor-must-change-new-colonialism-of-economic-order-says-pope-francis> accessed 28 July 2022.

DOI: 10.4324/9781315386782-1

each other. The other looks at taking by the human species from nature. In both instances, the prism used is that of the law and its role in conceptualising, defining and ordering social relations and their consequences. Within the prism of the law, the emphasis is on property and property relations as the lynchpin of capitalist civilisation. Together, the two parts seek to contribute to understanding the crisis in which we find ourselves, the actors who animate it and the power dynamics which run through it.

The law is a suitable prism through which to undertake this endeavour because it penetrates discursive surfaces to reveal their hidden realities. It provides an insight into power structures and the systemic allocation of benefits and privileges which sustains them. Legal rules, principles and doctrines legitimise these structures and allocations. They demarcate the boundaries within which legality is negotiated. They provide the institutional framework which locks in norms, practices and strategies so that they may not be easily deviated from. All of which makes for clarity rarely found elsewhere. It is telling, for example, that taking as a legal concept capable of invoking a compensatory regime is dedicated to the protection of foreign investors, movers and shakers of the globalist project. By contrast, other forms and instances of taking remain without route to either compensation or restitution. Chattel slavery is a glaring example. Upon its abolition in the United Kingdom, former slave owners were held to be entitled to compensation for the loss of their property. Not so the slaves whose untold suffering and labour were deemed of no compensable value. This is notwithstanding that labour is conceptualised in liberal doctrine as tradeable private property possessing market value, and that its free expropriation from the slaves has enriched and changed the course of entire economies.

The role which the law plays in systemic ordering is underscored by the fact that two of our protagonists – corporations and states – are legal constructs. The corporation comes into existence by the operation of a juridical fiction which conceives it as a person. This abstraction operates to distance it from the material realities and consequences of its presence in the world of property. States are abstracted by the operation of international law. It confers on them a legal personality possessing sovereign competences and monopoly over legislation and coercion. Principles such as sovereign equality and non-intervention draw a curtain of formalism over the realities of their place in a hierarchical world of nations. As will be seen in the second part, our third protagonist – nature – is in the process of acquiring a juridical personality. In jurisdictions, such as New Zealand, where this transformation has been institutionalised, property rights over nature gave way to rights of nature. Through them, it acquired the standing to claim in its own name and the ability to secure remedies which go directly to its benefit. The practicalities of where, as between the world of property and the world of nations, this novel legal person will reside is as yet unclear.

Janet Dine suggests that implementation of the doctrine of rights of nature requires that property rights be transformed and their primacy eroded. Their deification, she argues, blinds us to their adverse consequences. The legal construct of ownership with the power to exclude as its defining attribute is in essence a political tool used to include some, keep others out and subjugate nature. Following Tony Arnold, she advances a concept of property as a web of interests rather than relationship with either things or people. The concept of a web of interests is helpful, she contends, because it facilitates recognition of the interconnectedness of everything. Guidance should be sought from indigenous cultures pertaining to both property and nature.

As to the practicalities of implementation, it will fall to our fourth protagonist, human populations, to act on behalf of nature and to represent its interests. Nature, Janet Dine proposes, will exercise its newly acquired agency via the cross-border communities which inhabit it. This is because Nature it is impervious to territorial constraints. Rivers flow, forests grow and mountains range across jurisdictions. The obstacle this presents for the implementation of the doctrine at the national level featured in the 2017 Indian Supreme Court's deliberations about the rights of the river Ganges and its Yamuna main tributary. Janet Dine's proposed solution is in answer to the court's conclusion that the territorial nature of state sovereignty renders implementation of the doctrine impractical. The earth, its inhabitants and its climate, she posits, form a new sphere of the commons. No one state or individual can fashion a solution. Interstate collective action is both necessary and possible. However, this requires the dismantling of the edifice of power, law and political economy within which humanity was reimagined as an itemised, self-obsessed, self-interested, competitive yet miraculously entirely rational *homos economicus*. Is it doable? Considering that legal mechanisms have been devised and are employed to adapt our world of national borders to the expansive compulsions of capital, there is no reason why the same cannot be done for nature.

Yonit Manor-Percival disagrees. She would argue in response that there is a reason why treaties are successfully concluded to create enforceable exceptions to international law and, through them, accommodate and protect capital. There is a reason why no such treatment is extended to anyone else. The explanation is to be found in the recesses of the capitalist logic and its laws of motion. The construct of *Homo economicus* and the ecology of power, law and political economy which nourish it are the product of this logic. No significant or enduring change is feasible in a system of social relations that is moved by the capitalist compulsions of commodification, endless accumulation and competition. For a true change to take place, a different way of organising society and its methodology of production is needed. This disagreement points to important differences in approach.

Janet Dine's proposed solution is premised on the view that neoliberalism, originator of the current ecological malaise, is an aberration of capitalism, representing its extreme and degenerative form. On this view, capitalism is but a generic term for a commercial society. As such, it hosts a plethora of systemic possibilities and options. It is capable of assuming different versions, some better than others. Neoliberalism is but one of these versions. Therefore, it is rectifiable and may be reformed by regulatory and legislative means. It may be tamed, constrained and rendered less destructive through state discipline and supervision. It also follows that the law has emancipatory potential and constitutes a route to meaningful and enduring changes. Legislation and legal actions facilitate reforms from within. The institution of private property can be transformed within systemic confines through conscious action.

By contrast, Yonit Manor-Percival approaches capitalism from the perspective of a historically distinct and unique system of social/production relations, not to be confused with non-capitalist commercial societies. The compulsions of endless accumulation, life lived through the market and capital as mediator of survival are specific to capitalism and are immutable. Invariably, these essential compulsions will reassert themselves, pushing back reformative efforts as if fighting an existential threat. The failure of social democratic movements and their co-option into the capitalist logic is but one example. Neoliberal globalisation is not degenerate capitalism. Rather, it represents its restructuring going forward. It is victorious capitalism at ease, sufficiently confident to take on its purest form. As to liberal law, it was created to legitimise and facilitate, not restrain, capitalist accumulation. Therefore, legislative reforms and legal actions have little, if any, true emancipatory potential. On the contrary, they sustain the system by smoothing away its rough edges and disengaging critics from collective action. They bury the support which the law extends to capital under a narrative that – in the words of the eminent historian E. P. Thompson – the law evolves 'by its own impartial logic' and 'true only to its own integrity'. Thompson was moved by the deadly trials which sprung out of the Black Act of 1723 to describe this narrative as the 'greatest of all legal fictions'.[2] It is a fiction which lends institutional support to another one. That is, the fiction that the compulsion to enter the market and live through it is a form of liberty.

Yonit Manor-Percival's view that liberal law has been the creature of capitalist social relations from inception is apparent from her narration of the act of taking. A historical perspective provides a vantage point from which can be gleaned the way liberal law was used to justify, legitimise and enable the enclosure of land in England, the appropriation of land and resources in the colonial encounter and the extraction and transfer of wealth in the post-colonial empire of capital. It also illuminates the theoretical and material origins of the property created through these processes and its repositioning as the object of protection. The means of production were taken, vested in a class of people and transformed into private property. The dispossessed were commodified as waged labour, aka human resources. In other words, the juridical formation of private property was born out of agrarian capitalism nourished with dispossession. The English countryside provided the conditions for a successful gestation period. Thereafter, property was shaped by its capitalist genes in conjunction with formative experiences amassed as it followed its capitalist parent across colonial and imperialist landscapes.

This bloodline, argues Yonit Manor-Percival, speaks to the existence of a positive correlation between state law and capitalism. In the words of Hayek's fellow neoliberal, jurist Ernst-Ulrich Petersmann, 'The common starting point of the neoliberal economic theory is the insight that in any well-functioning market economy

2 E. P. Thompson, *Whigs & Hunters: The Origin of the Black Act* (Breviary Stuff Publications 2013) 146.

the "invisible hand" of the market competition must by necessity be complemented by the "visible hand" of the law'.[3] A feature of this visible hand is its adaptability. It tracks, responds and adjusts to the mutations, changing needs and crises of the invisible one. It ensures that transformations are unlikely beyond 'all kinds of patchwork' that do not impair capitalism's ability to incessantly accumulate.[4] The problem is that social and ecological abuses cannot be eliminated 'without hurting capital and profit in the least'.[5] If the survival of ecological systems is a precondition for the survival of natural people, extraction, accumulation and expansion are preconditions for the survival of juridical ones. The two are irreconcilable with so-called green deals fast becoming a new frontier for neocolonial extractivism and capital accumulation. The pressure which the West is exerting on South Africa to implement a quick transition from coal to renewable energy is accompanied by financial support destined to increase the debt burden shouldered by this already heavily indebted country. The deal comprises borrowing in foreign currency at a high interest rate and against a weakening rand and a strengthening dollar. The credit is conditional on the deployment of US and European multinationals to carry out the transition. This is in addition to the intensification of mining necessitated by the technological responses to the climate emergency and the exploitation, dispossession, immiseration and ecological destruction which go with it.

Beyond technology-based solutions, a narrative of sustainability, legal contortions and a flurry of international agreements, the bottom line is simple. The survival of humanity requires that taking and associated reliance on consumption cease. By contrast, an end to or even a reduction in taking and consumption pose an existential threat to capitalism. Janet Dine believes that the climate emergency might jolt capitalism out of its neoliberal trajectory and people out of their selfish slumber. By contrast, Yonit Manor-Percival views both the climate emergency and the egocentric *Homo economicus* as the products and outcomes of capitalism. Therefore, a different way of organising society is necessary if these are to be remedied. In this regard, the book offers the reader two contradictory perspectives to reflect upon and further explore.

Summary

In the first part of the book, Yonit Manor-Percival argues that property, now so vigorously protected against taking, was itself born out of taking. Private ownership, an avatar of capitalist social relations, was produced through processes of dispossession and privatisation. Once property was produced, placed and ordered in private hands, subsequent taking outside institutionalised boundaries was delegitimised. Put differently, discursive structures, including legal ones, were developed

3 Quinn Slobodian, *Globalists: The End of Empire and the Birth of Neoliberalism* (HUP 2018) 7.

4 Fredrick Engels, 'From the Preface to the German Edition of 1890' in Karl Marx Fredrick Engels (ed), *The Communist Manifesto* (Pathfinders Press 1987) 27.

5 Ibid

to first sanction and enable taking, and then prohibit and penalise that same practice. This continuum of possession and dispossession, legitimisation and delegitimisation took on different forms over time. Yet, invariably, it was governed by the logic of capital. From the beginning in the English enclosures, the injunction was to appropriate and improve. The term 'improve' in its original sense meant to make a profit, increase the value of something. It was this labour of improvement which was to transform 'idle' possession into the higher state of ownership. It was to inform England's agrarian capitalism as it spread to the New World in a tidal wave of genocidal taking by colonial settlement. Later, as capitalism evolved to become a worldwide system, improvement through labour was reimagined as development through investment.

At all times, the uniqueness of land made it a prime target. Land is unique, *inter alia*, by virtue of being a source of life. It is indispensable to human life, be it nomadic, agricultural or industrial. Therefore, its commodification in private hands foreclosed the main route through which the dispossessed could escape their transformation into waged labour. Thus, the narration of the continuum of possession and dispossession begins with the taking of land in the English enclosures and settler colonialism. It concludes with land grabs as its contemporary, globalised incarnation. This leads seamlessly to the second part with its focus on the ecological consequences of these practices.

The first part opens with a theoretical framework centred on Marx's and Hayek's insights into the law, the social ordering of market societies and the structural nature of the flows of gains and losses they produce. The two men stand in opposition to each other both methodologically and ideationally. However, they also come together. Notably, the Hayekian analysis of the principles governing market societies bears out what Marx identified centuries ago as the essential nature of capitalism and its laws of motion. Hayek posited as true and proper those same social relations which Marx singled out as unique to capitalism. His enthusiasm for market societies as representing just conduct that is contingent on a limited role for the legislator is a testament to the genius of Marx. Three characteristics of liberal law are then teased out. They are the drawing and enforcement of boundaries, adaptability and violence.

This theoretical prelude is followed by an overview of the act of taking as a sociopolitical concept set against its analysis as a legal concept, integral to the foreign investment protection regime. Expropriation – direct and indirect – is singled out for interrogation. Its evolvement is explored along lines of expansion and conflation on the one hand and constancy and continuity on the other. Expansion was facilitated by vague drafting and adjudicative discretion. Together, vagueness and discretion created the conditions under which the scope of impugned state conduct could be enlarged. For example, the decision not to define investment in the ICSID Convention and the non-exhaustive nature of the list of qualifying assets in the majority of international investment agreements meant that the meaning of investment for the purpose of establishing a tribunal's subject-matter jurisdiction could be kept hazy and open-ended. Haziness enabled 'investment' to expand. It now may include contract rights, purely financial assets and portfolio investment.

In turn, expansion had jurisprudential implications. The foundational principle of territoriality was weakened and the requirement of a contribution to the host country's economy was sidelined. This is notwithstanding that, not so long ago, that same requirement was advanced as a rationale for the internationalisation of state contracts – the first lap in the race to a contemporary protection regime. As to conflation, the hitherto different concepts of confiscation and nationalisation have been subsumed by that of expropriation. By now, posits Sornarajah, the law relating to taking is best described as the law on expropriation.[6] With nationalisations becoming rare, the concept of indirect expropriation as a route to a cause of action rose to prominence. All the while, the regime remained constant in its focus on foreign investors and their investments as its sole objects of protection. Similarly constant is the asymmetry in the distribution of rights, obligations and standing to claim. Also explored in this section is the way expropriation interfaces with both sovereignty and populations.

Thereafter, the discussion takes on a historical perspective as it moves on to the English enclosures and the colonial encounter. The rationale of taking by colonial settlement is examined through the writings of the theologian Francisco de Vitoria and those of John Locke, an enlightenment philosopher. Vitoria's preoccupation was with the public domain of sovereign title. Locke sought to theorise the origins of private title to property. Yet, in their different ways, Locke and Vitoria both provided nested layers of reasoning within a single rationale of empire. A single rationale was possible because of the intimacy which the world of nations shares with the world of property. It was evidenced by the collaboration between the state and the English aristocracy in ensuring the success of enclosures. In the colonies, declarations and rituals of sovereignty were a precursor to the taking of land by settlers.

At this juncture, the historical account is paused to enable a brief examination of the judicial formation of property. Property is explored from the perspectives of its abstraction, the debate surrounding its conceptualisation in liberal law, its interface with the state and its roots in ownership of the body. This starting point of self-ownership links property to liberty and the right to life, with the law in charge of their hierarchical ordering. The colonial setting injected a racialised dimension, painting property rights the colour white.

The narration then takes a leap to the 20th and 21st centuries and taking by wealth transfer within a framework of integrated, globalised and monopolised circuits of capital. Taking by transfer is characterised by the transition to the informality and invisibility of control by economic means, notably unequal exchanges and indebtedness. Unequal exchanges are defined and explored through the lens of free trade and foreign investment as informed by their 19th-century legacies. In conclusion, the first part of the book takes the discussion to the political economy of land grabs, often referred to in the literature as the new enclosures. Modern-day land grabs, by contrast to their predecessors, do not necessarily implicate physical

6 M. Sornarajah, *The International Law on Foreign Investment* (3rd edn, CUP 2010) 433–4.

removal but may manifest themselves in the integration of formerly subsistence farmers into the globalised circuit of capital. Additionally, modern-day land grabs are governed not only by national law, but also by international law in its so-called transnational form as a foreign investment protection regime.

The second part of the book opens with reflections on the rule of law and the severance of property and contractual principles from ethics. The value of the planet is overshadowed by the prominence of belief in strong property rights. The discourse which surrounds property rights impacts on the well-being of the planet because it is grounded in assumptions about the superiority of humans and their entitlement to dominate other forms of life. Scientific evidence of the gathering dark clouds of environmental emergency makes it of paramount importance that the system of property rights be reformed. Yet, doubts created by scientists with close ties to industry hinder the mobilisation of public opinion. This is coupled with the intensification of free market principles, deepening social inequality, the adverse effects of corporate activities and the commodification and monetisation of the environment. All of these stand in the way of a substantive change.

The discussion then proceeds to consider possible solutions. It begins with a critical examination of the UN 2030 Agenda for Sustainable Development followed by an enquiry into the Gaia theory and its erasure of human exceptionalism. It is suggested that the Gaian model offers ways of resolving distributional issues and delivering social justice. It can also serve as the overall worldview within which the legal doctrine of rights of nature may be accommodated. The world of Gaia and the world of strong property rights, it is argued, are not as contradictory as they appear at first blush. This is because the rhetoric of absolute property rights is illusory. Absolute rights, understood in terms of the absence of social constraints, do not exist in reality. The view of property as rights over people (rather than things) demonstrates that ownership gives rise to a spectrum of rights and obligations. Both are embedded in social expectations. The remainder of this part is dedicated to an account of the transition from property rights to animal rights and from there to rights of nature. The jurisprudence which so far has developed out of the doctrine of rights of nature is explored through legislation and case law from New Zealand, India and Colombia.

1 The globalist project

In times of crisis

At the time of writing, a sense of malaise is permeating the post-colonial globalist project. The pledge of historically unprecedented prosperity is losing its shine as globalised supply chains struggle with disruptions, worldwide spiralling inflation is bedfellow to stagnation and worsening food and energy shortages are read into the near future. Standards of living are declining in the Global North and the spectre of famine is looming over the Global South. The UN World Food Program puts the number of people in the Global South currently under this threat at over 50 million, with riots and instability spreading across numerous countries in consequence. In what economist Samir Amin termed 'apartheid on a global scale', both the North and the South witness deepening inequalities. Poverty intensifies and spreads as great wealth correspondingly accumulates and concentrates.[1] Trust in the US dollar as a safe haven fractures under the weight of economic wars of attrition and arbitrary confiscations of the gold and foreign exchange reserves belonging to the enemy of the day.

A weakened US-led monetary and financial order is but one symptom of a broader disintegration. Potentially devastating eruptions of interstate conflicts are brewing under the geopolitical outer crust as the Eurasian and Atlantic-European tectonic plates of political economy pull away and diverge. Their separation tracks the construction of a 'Berlin Wall of sanctions'.[2] As Russian trade flows to Europe and the US are being blocked, the country is re-orienting its economy towards the East. The bulk of its sanctioned oil and coal is being absorbed by China and India. In turn, trade-tariffed China exports manufactured goods to Russia, including those hitherto imported by Russia from the West. In the first three months of 2022, Russia-BRICS countries' trade turnover has gone up by 38%, reaching up to US$45 billion.[3] Russia, having been locked out of the US SWIFT bank-clearing system, is setting up with Türkiye a new bank which will employ block chain

1 Samir Amin (tr), *Ending the Crisis of Capitalism or Ending Capitalism?* (Pambazuka Press 2011) 6.

2 Michael Hudson, 'Ukraine a Trojan for Germany's US Dependence' 3 June 2022 <https://michael-hudson.com/2022/06/ukraine-a-trojan-for-germanys-us-dependence/> accessed 4 July 2022.

3 The BRICS countries are Brazil, Russia, India, China and South Africa.

DOI: 10.4324/9781315386782-2

technology to integrate the two financial systems. Russia is similarly integrating with the Chinese financial system. Importantly, both countries have responded to the sanctions-based economic war waged on them by focusing on self-sufficiency in their supply chains as import substitution policies are making a comeback. This wall of estrangement, argues Hudson, also delineates divergent economic philosophies and political consciousness.[4] On one side is the economic model of de-industrialised and financialised neoliberal capitalism under US leadership. On the other is an industrial mixed economy evolving into socialism under Chinese leadership in alliance with resource-rich Russia and its growing manufacturing base. The predicted eruptions are therefore no longer between US/NATO and countries at the fringes of the American empire, but with economically and militarily powerful protagonists. NATO Strategic Concept 2022 refers to the Russian Federation as 'the most significant and direct threat to Allies' security', whilst China is classified as their systemic challenge.[5] Michael Pompeo, former US secretary of state, in a July 2022 speech to the Hudson Institute talked about the imperative of preventing the formation of a 'Pan-Eurasian colossus incorporating Russia, but led by China'.[6]

Not so long ago, envisioned was a unitary world of nation-states tied together by a mutually beneficial web of dependencies. It was to be managed by them within a US-led institutional and organisational framework and in reliance on transnational capital's wealth creation expertise. Renato Ruggiero, the first director-general of the World Trade Organisation, pledged historically unique prosperity. 'The potential for eradicating global poverty in the early part of the next [21st] century', he said, was 'a Utopian notion even a few decades ago, but a real possibility today'.[7] This state of well-being was sure to follow because, as the philosopher Robert Nozick advocated, world resources were put in the hands of those best equipped to make efficient use of them. That is, the property owners, people of independent means whose role was said by Hayek to be indispensable to the preservation of civilisation. That was the promise. The reality turned out to be a hierarchical interstate edifice governed by colonial legacies and opaque practices of imperialist wealth extraction and transfer. States and class-power differentials are controlled by a combination of economic strategies and warfare supported by globally orchestrated security apparatuses. Recurrent economic crises hit the globalised shores whilst an exhausted planet signals that it has reached the end of its capacity to

4 Hudson (n 2); Michael Hudson, *The Destiny of Civilization: Finance Capitalism, Industrial Capitalism or Socialism* (ISLET 2022) 25–44, 85–106 and generally. For a table comparing industrial with financial capitalism see pp. 43–4.

5 NATO, 'NATO Strategic Concept 2022' June 2022 <https://www.nato.int/nato_static_fl2014/assets/pdf/2022/6/pdf/220629-factsheet-strategic-concept-en.pdf> accessed 4 July 2022.

6 Hudson Institute, 'Transcript of Pompeo Speech on Ukraine and a Global Alliance for Freedom' 24 June 2022 <https://www.hudson.org/research/17914-transcript-of-pompeo-speech-on-ukraine-and-a-global-alliance-for-freedom> accessed 9 July 2022.

7 Ha-Joon Chang, *Bad Samaritans: The Guilty Secrets of Rich Nations & The Threat to Global Prosperity* (Random House Business Books 2007) 23 citing from R. Ruggiero, 'Whither the Trade System Next?' in J. Bhagwati and M. Hirsch (eds), *The Uruguay Round and Beyond – Essays in Honour of Arthur Dunkel* (The University of Michigan Press 1998) 130.

accommodate and adjust to human presence and activities. Are we seeing the end of the post-colonial globalist project? Is this chaos signalling its terminal phase?

Malaise is hardly new to the globalist project. Following a quarter of a century of growth in the wake of World War II (1945–1970), a proclivity for cataclysm may be said to have become its all too familiar feature. From endless local wars, to the energy crisis and stagflation of the 70s, to the banking crisis and recession between the 80s and early 90s, to the global recession of 2000–01 and the financial collapse of 2008, crises seem to follow one another with the regularity of a well-run bus service. Their precise beginnings and endings are elusive, as is the way in which they may or may not interrelate. In the 1990s many were unsure whether the downturn of the 1970s was ever resolved. As the current wave of immiseration threatens to engulf a growing number of people worldwide, analysts question whether the 2008 financial collapse was ever remedied. Sociologist William Robinson points to a series of 'lesser jolts to the global economy', such as the 1995 Mexico peso crisis, the 1997–99 meltdown of the Asian financial markets, the dot-com bust and the 2000–01 recession as 'preludes' to the 2008 breakdown.[8] By 2018 he remarked, 'we are living through times of a dire global crisis'.[9] Others, like Amin, observe a single process rather than a series of disparate events. It began in the 1970s and went on to fashion the 21st century. Where we are now is thus 'part of the unfolding of the long crisis of an ageing capitalism'.[10] Intervening periods of restructuring, reorganisation and expansion add to the confusion. In between downturns, statistics about growth, assets appreciation, greater liberalisation and stock markets at dazzling heights paint a picture of renewed wealth and vigour. By reference to them, the preceding crisis appears to have dissipated and to have become a best-forgotten past interruption.

But has it? Robinson distinguishes between cyclical and structural crises. The former recur every ten years or so and last for some 18 months. Examples are the recessions of the early 80s, 90s and 2020s. The latter get their name from the fact that their resolution requires systemic restructuring. These occur every 40–50 years. One example is the economic stagnation of the late 19th century, resolved through a new wave of colonialism and imperialism. Another is the Great Depression of the 1930s addressed through a 'class compromise' of Fordism-Keynesianism and distributive policies. Going global was the structural answer to the stagnation of the 70s. Wealth accumulation was put on steroids by means of an ideology of self-regulating markets translated into neoliberal policies and so-called flexibility in the management of labour. This was supplemented by far-reaching digitalisation of the economy and a Fourth Industrial Revolution as a technology-based response to the recession of the 1980s.[11]

8 William I. Robinson, *The Global Police State* (Pluto Press 2020) 27.

9 William I. Robinson, 'Introduction' in Peter Phillips (ed), *Giants: The Global Power Elite* (Seven Stories Press 2018) 15.

10 Amin (n 1) 3.

11 Robinson (n 8) 16–17, 33–9.

It is not only beginnings and endings that are elusive. Similarly, the full impact and significance of these waves of boom and bust are rarely entirely understood. In this, they blend into the opacity of relationships, processes of inclusion and exclusion and the invisibility of power that is characteristic of the 'empire of capital' and its principal methodology of rule by economic means.[12] One quandary which seems to arise with each crisis is whether it signifies an irreversible, systemically terminal cessation or merely a spontaneous, market-generated corrective pause. An example is the 'chaos/turbulence' of the 70s and 80s, which Giovanni Arrighi took 'to signal the breakdown of the system as instituted under US hegemony . . . a key component of a possible but by no means certain future reconstitution of the system on new foundations'.[13] Seen from Arrighi's perspective of historically recurrent cycles of hegemonic transitions, the financialisation associated with the 'going global' response is said to have the hallmarks of a terminal phase.

Financialisation, the tendency to valorise capital through money rather than through commodities, is invariably disruptive. Violent swings between ups and downs and periodic destruction of the profitability attained through trade and productive investment destabilise the trajectory of expansion. Finance replaces trade and productive investment at the commanding heights of the economy as corporate entities increasingly rely for their profits not on the exchange of the commodities they produce, but on the rent extracted from their abstraction as financial instruments. The bulk of society's material base no longer comprises the means of production but rent-yielding financialised assets. Examples are real estate, stock and debt. In particular, debt attracts compound interest, causing its volume to inflate incessantly and irrespective of the productive economy's ability to service it. A financialised economy resembles a Ponzi scheme in that it is sustained not by production but by an indefinite stream of credit created through systems of accounting. Banks take from the future money yet to come into being, lend it in the present and look to future production to finance the payments which will give it materiality. Sooner or later, however, as the volume of made-up credit grows, production is unable to catch up and waves of bankruptcies and foreclosures follow. As we shall see, the same applies to globalised indebtedness. Particularly since the 70s, lending to the Global South as a mechanism for rent extraction, bondage and control has become central to imperialism by economic means.[14] Other features of financialisation include short-termism and related de-industrialisation. Revenues are channelled into rent-yielding financial assets to the detriment of longer-term investment in productive ones. The public domain is captured so as to extract monopoly rent

12 Ellen Meiksins Wood, *Empire of Capital* (Verso 2003); see also David Chandler, *Empire in Denial: The Politics of State-Building* (Pluto Press 2006).

13 Giovanni Arrighi, *The Long Twentieth Century: Money, Power and the Origins of Our Time* (Verso 2010) 80; see also Giovanni Arrighi and Beverly J. Silver (eds), *Chaos and Governance in the Modern World System* (Contradictions of Modernity Series University of Minnesota Press 1999).

14 See pp. 175–87.

from privatised infrastructure and diminish the government's ability to plan and exercise regulatory control.[15]

Against this backdrop of diminishing public control, finance managers turn instability into profitable speculations. In this they are aided by access to inside information and the capacity to manipulate markets. When speculations turn sour, at least for those banks deemed too big to fail, there is the option of a government bailout. The cheque for 406 billion euros, which German Chancellor Angela Merkel handed over to the country's banks in 2009, 'was barely enough to cover their trades in U.S.-based toxic derivatives.[16] John Stuart Mill likened rent extraction to making money while asleep. When combined with rescue policies, an essentially risk-free path to fortune accumulation opens up.[17] Consequently it is not in speculators' interest to restore production or control volatility.

Financialisation and the corresponding decline of the productive base thus offer one historically based lens through which the current crisis of the US-led post-colonial globalist project may be viewed. It signifies 'not just the maturity of a particular stage of development of the capitalist world-economy, but also the beginning of a new stage'.[18] As early as five years ago, Alastair Crooke, British diplomat and founder and director of the Conflicts Forum, predicted the end of financialised globalisation and, with it, the denouement of the world as we know it.[19]

Given that financialisation phases assume different patterns, this one may or may not prove terminal. However, the current malaise has additional historically unprecedented dimensions. Reproduction and expansion are hitting also against ecological and systemic limits, about which more later.

The globalist project and capitalism

The crises of the 19th century and the 1930s speak to the fact that upheavals are not exclusive to either the post-colonial period or the globalist project. Both crises came later. Therefore, a better insight may be gained by employing a wider lens directed at the project's underlying system of social relations. That is the capitalist system and, on a Marxian analysis, its inherent proclivity to fall into periodic, ultimately terminal dysfunctionality. Economist Richard Wolfe points out that since the capitalist system first emerged in England on or about the 17th century, it crashed on average every four to seven years wherever in the world it had settled. To this day, none of the efforts to stop its in-built instability have proved

15 Hudson (n 4) 27, 28–9, 30–1.

16 Yanis Varoufakis, *Adults in the Room: My Battle with Europe's Deep Establishment* (Penguin Random House 2017) 25.

17 On risk-free banking pursuant to bailouts by the International Monetary Fund see Janet Dine, *Companies, International Trade and Human Rights* (Cambridge Studies in Corporate Law CUP 2005) 100–2.

18 Arrighi (n 13) 88, 240–1.

19 Alastair Crooke, 'The New Times' (*Open Lecture*, October 2016) <https://www.youtube.com/watch?v=WjnxmdOI84E> accessed 25 June 2022.

successful.[20] Seen through this lens of the underlying social relations and their instability, the post-colonial globalist project is but a comparatively late episode on a continuum of capitalist maturation which may or may not signal the arrival of the next 'great transformation'.

The globalist project

The post-colonial globalist project engages multiple disciplines and schools of thoughts rich with perspectives, definitions and controversies.[21] Here, however, we confine ourselves to two of its less contentious, yet distinctive dimensions. First is the transnationalisation of capital. Networks of capital may not be exclusive to the globalist project and may be traced back to 19th-century colonialism or even earlier. However, the depth and intensity of their transnationalisation and the technological revolution which underpin and enable them all point to a mutation that is both qualitative and structural. Capital's historical trajectory towards liberation from political authority, national moorings and the constraints of national borders is said to have come of age in the post-colonial period.

In a state of transnationalisation, production can no longer be disaggregated along territorial boundaries. It cannot be measured or assessed and analysed purely by reference to national economies and the trade and investment flows which pass between them.[22] Instead, globalised financial flows and supply chains cross borders in patterns of both division and integration. One the one hand, primary sites of production and extraction (located mainly in the Global South) are separated from primary sites of consumption and accumulation (located mainly in the Global North). On the other hand, they are linked by chains of value that are originated and transported by transnational, border-crossing corporate networks. These corporate networks go by different names, such as multinational enterprises and transnational corporations. The diversity of terms and definitions employed to describe them testifies to their ontological complexities to which we return later. For now, it suffices to make a couple of general comments. First, many of the major multinationals are headquartered in the Global North. From there they spread to the Global South through a web of equity and contractual ties. By contrast, the direction of travel of the surplus value so produced is from the South to the North. Second, overall power has remained centralised in Global North headquarters. Under their baton, production, distribution, investment and finance are orchestrated extraterritorially.

20 Richard Wolfe, 'Crises of US Capitalism: Pandemic, Crash and Secular Decline' (*Oxford Economic Society*, 23 November 2020) <https://www.youtube.com/watch?v=p_Axv2h7SIs> accessed 9 July 2022.

21 For definitions and discussion see for example Charles Tilly, 'Globalization Threatens Labor Rights' (1995) 47 *International Labor and Working Class History* 1–23 at 1–4; Anthony Giddens, *The Consequences of Modernity* (Polity Press 1999); Ankie Hoogvelt, *Globalization and the Post-colonial World: The New Political Economy of Development* (2nd edn, Palgrave Macmillan 2001) 120–43.

22 Intan Suwandi, *Value Chains: The New Economic Imperialism* (Monthly Review Press 2019) 42.

Through this methodology of business organisation, 'dominant companies are able to retain their exclusive access to innovations and other technological know-how while putting pressure on their dependent suppliers to provide flexibility in production'.[23] Moreover, it means that, notwithstanding the transnationalisation of production and finance, the cultural and governance structures in the networks' interior tend to preserve their national characteristics and alliances. It is against this backdrop of power in the North, production in the South and South to North transfer of surplus value that multinationals are said by critics to be networks of new imperialism by economic means.[24]

Thus, transnationalisation is predicated on worldwide integration of production and financial systems, the creation of a worldwide, single (if variegated) labour market and the concentration of power in the hands of members of a transnationalised corporate elite with its centre in the Global North. Integration is enabled, *inter alia*, by technological advances, legal infrastructure and geopolitical interventions. In the ordinary conduct of the business of empire, economic interventions are mediated by the Bretton Woods organisations, known collectively as international financial institutions (IFIs).[25] In proximity to the IFIs and in communion with them (as well as with national governments) are private, informal and largely secretive policymaking forums, such as the Trilateral Commission, the Group of 30, the Atlantic Council and the Bilderberg Group. Their members constitute a global power elite referred to in the literature as transnational capitalist class (TCC). They comprise corporate executives, politicians, professionals and consumerist elites and 'operate in oligopolistic clusters around the world'.[26] They are the ones 'who decide whatever is decided'.[27]

The stated aims of the IFIs are to reduce poverty, spread progress and supervise financial stability. This is achieved through implementation of what came to be known on or about 1989 as the 'Washington Consensus'. The term denotes a collection of policy prescriptions to include fiscal discipline, removal of subsidies, tax

23 Suwandi (n 22) 34.

24 Ibid generally; Jingzhong Ye, Teodor Shanin et al., 'BRICS Countries, Extractivism, Expolary Economies and Alternative-Oriented Struggle' (2016) BICAS Conference Paper No. 22 presented at the 4th International Conference of BICAS China Agricultural University of Beijing 6 and generally.

25 Other than the Bretton Woods organisations – the World Bank and the International Monetary Fund – the IFIs also include the Bank for International Settlements, a bank of central banks. Some include also the World Trade Organisation among the IFIs. However, its remit is trade rather than finance. Following the failure to create an international trade organisation at Bretton Woods, the World Trade Organisation was finally established in January 1995.

26 Phillips (n 9) 25; the study of elites was first introduced in 1956 by C. Wright Mills in his book *The Power Elite* (new edn OUP 2000); see also Leslie Sklair, *The Transnational Capitalist Class* (John Wiley and Sons 2000); William I. Robinson, *A Theory of Global Capitalism: Production, Class and State in a Transnational World* (The Johns Hopkins University Press 2004); David J. Rothkopf, *Superclass: The Global Power Elite and the World They are Making* (Little, Brown Book Group 2009); William K. Carroll, *The Making of a Transnational Capitalist Class: Corporate Power in the 21st Century* (Zed Books 2010).

27 Mills (n 26) cited in Phillips (n 9) 23.

reforms, the freeing of interest and exchange rates, free trade and foreign direct investment, market liberalisation, privatisation of state industries, deregulation and the all-important secure property rights.

The IFIs pursue their stated aims by opening up national economies to migratory capital and ensuring responsiveness to its needs. They instil discipline in the interstate system and manufacture subservience, primarily by means of indebtedness. They dispense non-negotiable prescriptions for economic 'do and don't'. The objective is interstate uniformity and the creation and enlargement of spaces governed by the precepts of capital. In what some refer to as 'a race to the bottom' and others view as a globalised class war to mirror globalised capital, one important aim is reduction in the cost of labour. Policies that are reductive of workers' rights habitually form part of the structural adjustments on which access to credit is contingent. Renowned economist Michael Hudson is among those who argue that the IFIs were established by the US to institutionalise its hegemony and promote its national interests and, integral to this, the interests of its corporations.

This intimacy between capitalism, the globalist project and US state/corporate hegemony suggests that the crisis of one may prove also a crisis of the others.[28] This view is supported by recent phenomena, such as the return of the social democratic 'pink tide' to Central and Latin America, and the establishment of what came to be known as a multipolar world order. New economic powerhouses and new geopolitical cooperative arrangements are forming. The volume of transactions undertaken in local currencies is growing. In particular, the trading of oil in national currencies challenges the petrodollars, a major source of US domination and prosperity. In central banks' coffers, US treasuries are being substituted for gold reserves. Alternatives to the US-designed SWIFT system of international payments are introduced in response to sanctions. On the organisational side, the influential BRICS group of emerging economies presently constitutes 41% of the world population, some 25% of global GDP and 16% of global trade. The group is set to expand with the addition of Iran and Argentina. Egypt, Türkiye, Saudi Arabia and others are also knocking on the door.[29] The New Development Bank is expanding and has now moved to its permanent headquarters in Shanghai. Unlike the US-dominated IFIs, its founding members, the five BRICS countries, share equal voting rights. Equality in voting rights is based on the equal distribution of initial capital contributions. The eight-members-strong intergovernmental Shanghai Cooperation Organisation (SCO) is similarly set to expand. Iran, until 2021 an Observer State, has now acceded to full membership. Four other Observer States, Afghanistan, Iran, Belarus and Mongolia, have expressed interest in following

28 Arrighi (n 13) 277–309; Amin (n 1) 11–13.

29 Global Times, 'More Countries Are Knocking on BRICS' Door a Sign the World Needs Fairer Governance Than West-Dominated One' 16 July 2022 <https://www.globaltimes.cn/page/202207/1270661.shtml> accessed 18 July 2022. The original BRICS nations are Brazil, Russia, India, China and South Africa.

suit.[30] Also in 2021 Egypt, Qatar and Saudi Arabia joined the SCO's six Dialogue Partners (Armenia, Azerbaijan, Cambodia, Nepal, Sri Lanka and Türkiye). Hudson emphasises the importance of the SCO to the emerging multipolar order, placing it above that of the BRICS cooperation forum. 'The Shanghai Co-operation Organisation', he wrote, 'is the only group that has the critical mass . . . to be able to create an alternative to dollarized neoliberal imperialism'.[31] Thus, former US Secretary of State Henry Kissinger's doctrine that whoever controls the money controls the world appears to come under threat from those who control energy, other natural resources and production.

The onset of multipolarity may be a particularly powerful instance of contemporary divergence. Nevertheless, it is not the first. An earlier example is the forum of Non-Aligned Nations, which sought to break away from external dirigisme in the 60s and 70s. Its 120 members avoided taking sides in the Cold War of the day. Instead, they focused on advancing the interests and aspirations of developmental nations in line with five principles: mutual respect for territorial integrity and sovereignty, non-aggression, non-interference, equality, mutual benefit and peaceful co-existence. By means of UN General Assembly resolutions, they introduced a set of international law innovations known as the New Economic Order (NIEO). In the main, the NIEO comprises the Permanent Sovereignty Over Natural Resources (PSNR) resolution of 1962 and the Charter of Economic Rights and Duties among States (CERDS) resolution of 1974. The aim was to reform international law and, through it, challenge the mandate era's narrative of European-led progress.[32] At least in part, the PSNR was in response to the Atlantic Charter of 1941. The Charter, concluded by industrialised countries, defined natural resources as 'the raw materials of the world'.[33] The new states, where much of the world's natural resources are located, responded by asserting the permanence of their sovereignty over them. At least from an economic perspective, this attempt at a breakaway ultimately proved

30 The SCO is a permanent intergovernmental organisation originally founded in 2021 by China, Russia, India, Kazakhstan, Kyrgyzstan Pakistan, Tajikistan and Uzbekistan. Its main stated goals are contained in its charter, the SCO's constitutional document. They include strengthening trust and neighbourliness among member states as well as political, economic and cultural cooperation.

31 The Analysis News, Michael Hudson in Conversation with Patrick Bond, 'Is China's Trade Predatory or for Mutual Benefit?' 28 March 2022 <https://theanalysis.news/is-chinas-trade-predatory-or-for-mutual-benefit-hudson-and-bond-pt-2-2/> accessed 4 April 2022.

32 Anthony Anghie, *Imperialism, Sovereignty and the Making of International Law* (Cambridge Studies in International and Comparative Law, CUP 2004) 4.

33 Nico Schrijver, *Sovereignty over Natural Resources: Balancing Rights and Duties* (Cambridge Studies in International and Comparative Law Series, Cambridge University Press 1997); The US-UK joint declaration known as the Atlantic Charter provided the blueprint for many of today's agreements, including the Agreement on Tariffs and Trade (GATT); see also Anghie (n 32) 212; to the extent that the division of wealth between the Global North and South can be characterised as the technological advances of the first and the natural resources of the latter, it is interesting to note the difference between the principle of humanity's free access to natural resources with international law principles relating to intellectual property rights as expressed, for example, in the TRIP agreement. The characterisation of resources as belonging to humanity as a whole can be found also in the narrative of the mandate era. Anghie (n 32) 212.

unsuccessful because the nations involved 'lacked the diversification and self-sufficiency to become independent'.[34] Nevertheless, the movement's five principles have survived to form part of a Global South-led multipolar paradigm.

That the law was selected as a terrain of struggle is no coincidence. Desired structures of political economy are conferred permanence through their juridification. In the context of the globalist project, Claire Cutler adds to the web of national and international laws a layer of transnationally revived medieval merchant laws. That is, laws developed by a 'mercatocracy' operating both locally and globally. A main feature of transnational merchant laws (*lex mercatoria*) is their universalisation, achieved 'through the unification and harmonization of national commercial legal orders'. *Inter alia*, it 'blurs the distinction between public and private commercial actors, activities and law'.[35] *Lex mercatoria* may be found in the governing law clauses contained in privately negotiated contracts. However, its prime example is said to be the legal regime of foreign investment protection, considered in some detail later in the book. Foreign investment protection merges state-made investment laws with public international law, international treaty law, principles governing commerce and the mechanism of private commercial arbitration. Its purpose is to shield capital from the political vagaries of state sovereignty and enable it to exit its jurisdiction in pursuit of compensation. In particular, the World Bank Group includes the International Centre for the Settlement of Investment Disputes (ICSID), an arbitral forum in which foreign investors claim against states for infringing their property rights. This includes their legislative undertakings. ICSID claims to be 'autonomous', meaning that it floats in the transnational space, delinked from national courts. Whereas enforcement of commercial arbitral awards goes through the national court of the seat of enforcement, ICSID awards assume the force of a judgement upon issuance and are directly enforceable. Failure to discharge an award amounts to a breach of treaty and revives the diplomatic protection suspended by the ICSID Convention.[36]

Thus, the law is adapted to mirror the transnationalisation of capital and the power structures which animate it. It provides an integrated infrastructure acting as

34 Hudson (n 4) 221.

35 A. Claire Cutler, *Private Power and Global Authority: Transnational Merchant Law in the Global Political Economy* (Cambridge Studies in International Relations CUP 2003) 5, 108–25, 180–236. For more about transnational law see for example Terence C. Halliday and Gregory Shaffer (eds), *Transnational Legal Orders* (CUP 2915); Peer Zumbansen (ed), *The Many Lives of Transnational Law: Critical Engagements with Jessup's Bold Proposal* (CUP 2020); Peer Zumbansen (ed), *The Oxford Handbook of Transnational Law* (OUP 2021).

36 Diplomatic protection is part of the international law doctrine of state responsibility. Under international law a state is responsible for an injury caused to an alien by the state's wrongful act or omission. Diplomatic protection is the procedure employed by the state of nationality of the injured person to secure protection of and reparations for the injured person. It applies to both natural and juridic person. John Dugard, 'Diplomatic Protection' (2021) *Oxford Public International Law* <https://opil.ouplaw.com/view/10.1093/law:epil/9780199231690/law-9780199231690-e1028> accessed 16 July 2022; Draft Articles on Diplomatic Protection 2006 <https://legal.un.org/ilc/texts/instruments/english/commentaries/9_6_2001.pdf> accessed 16 July 2021.

guarantor of stability, certainty and predictability and a route for globalised capital to escape states' political authority. In this way, favourable conditions for the penetration and incorporation of foreign capital into national economies are maximised. Notably, in this newly constructed system of law-making, the NIEO resolutions have been marginalised. They are rarely advanced in arguments, if at all. General Assembly resolutions do not have the force of law. However, considering that they articulate the will of the majority of the world's states, their force as a source of international law must surely exceed that of international/transnational law said to have been formulated by privately appointed arbitrators.

The second and related dimension of the post-colonial globalist project is the concentration and centralisation of wealth in the hands of a transnational corporate elite. Monopolistic concentrations span a growing number of industries and countries, primarily by means of worldwide mergers and acquisitions (M&As). Through them, the productive process is internalised to be performed by different corporate or divisional units operating within a single multinational entity. It is estimated that some 75% of world trade has been so internalised. M&As are now also used to diversify into formerly unrelated new areas of products and services. This relatively novel strategy of expansion and monopolisation is facilitated by technological advances and innovations in business organisation. The aim is to attain complete market dominance. Amazon's hold over the entire spectrum of retail is a prime example. The investment management multinational Blackrock handles multiple types of assets across the globe. Since 1993, consolidation has reduced the number of defence firms from 107 to five. In the field of agribusiness, Monsanto merged with Bayer, Kraft with Heinz and Dow with DuPont. Over 80% of the pesticides world market is now controlled by five corporations. The 187 media outlets which existed in America 25 years ago have been whittled down to a mere six. Over 75% of the global grain trade is in the hands of four corporations: ADM, Bunge, Cargill and Dreyfus. Pharmaceutical companies too have been merging at an accelerated rate in recent years. By 2018, the largest four firms had 75% market share. Amazon sells 74% of all e-books and 64% of all printed books purchased online.[37] This trajectory of concentration applies also to members of the TCC. Between 2016 and 2017, the number of people who hold as much wealth as half of the world population has gone down from 62 to 8.[38]

Concentration is enhanced by interconnectedness produced through informal alliances, such as cross shareholdings and interlocking boards of directors. They are formed also with rivals. Blackrock, for example, circumvents competition by owning shares in competing entities. Interlocking boards cause the number of people involved in key corporations to decrease. Carroll's study of the consolidation of 'transnational corporate-policy networks' between 1996 and 2006 revealed a drop in the average number of board members from 20.2 to 14 during this period.

37 Open Markets, 'Monopoly by the Numbers' <https://www.openmarketsinstitute.org/learn/monopoly-by-the-numbers> accessed 9 June 2021.

38 Phillips (n 9) 21 and generally; see also Robinson (n 8) 11–16 and generally.

Concentration and interconnectedness, in turn, consolidate the ties which bind together members of the TCC and consolidates the class consciousness necessary for political solidarity.[39]

Together, concentration, internalisation and interconnectedness signify cooperation and planning rather than the competition stated to be at the core of the capitalist mode of production. Control over technological knowledge, labour, price-making and superprofits is vested in a shrinking number of dominant multinationals and the TCC behind them.[40]

By way of a footnote, M&As also provide a route by which corporations avoid risk and circumvent existential threats. Corporations can be made to disappear for a while and then reappear again, once the threat has dissipated. Alternatively, they may take on a restructured form to become unrecognisable to the naked eye. An example is the agribusiness firm Monsanto. In the face of anti-globalisation campaigns and consumer boycotts, it disappeared behind a merger. It then reappeared again as a separate entity, only to merge again, this time with Bayer. This latest merger came about against the backdrop of multiple claims against Monsanto for loss and harm to health occasioned by the use of Roundup, its best-selling weed killer.

We need to speak about capitalism

Thus, globalised capitalism is distinguished by the plenary reach and integration of ever larger in size but smaller in number worldwide networks of corporate oligopolies. They are its modern-day missionaries. They spread the cult of property, efficiency, markets, consumption and accumulation as they penetrate and reshape collective and individual landscapes. Consequently, capitalist imperatives span the globe, adorned by the paragons of universalism, naturalism and inevitability. Capitalist imperatives re-colonise in whole or in part ostensibly independent post-colonial nation-states. They are nursed in a historically unique empire of rule by economic means. In turn, rule by economic means is sustained by an underlay of extra-economic means and renovated methodologies of appropriation. Kwame Nkrumah, Ghana's first prime minister and president, called the imposition of economic prescriptions a state of neocolonialism. Its defining feature is that 'the State which is subject to it . . . has all the outward trappings of international sovereignty. In reality its economic system and thus its political policy is directed from outside'.[41] Capitalist imperatives also shape who we are, our relationship with each

39 Phillips (n 9) 26 referring to Carroll (n 26). Interlocking boards occur when a member of one company's board also serves on the board or within the management of another.

40 See for example Paul A. Baran and Paul M. Sweezy, *Monopoly Capital: An Essay on the American Economic and Social Order* (Penguin Books 1973) 29, 80, 162 and generally; Suwandi (n 22) 29–30, 32, 80–90; for multinationals monopolisation, anti-competitive practices and regulatory responses see Peter T. Muchlinski, *Multinational Enterprises & the Law* (3rd edn OUP 2021) 89, 428, 437–43.

41 Kwame Nkrumah, *Neo-colonialism: The Last Stage of Imperialism* (Panaf Books 1970) ix.

other as well as our interface with non-human forms of life. The planet's exhaustion may therefore be reframed as having less to do with humanity *per se* and more with the intensity and destructiveness of capitalist exploitation, an obsession with taking which leaves little room, if any, for reciprocity and the respite necessary for regeneration. At issue is not globalisation in and of itself, but the capitalist imperatives which mould it.

To assist in clarifying the sense in which the term capitalism is used, we propose at this juncture to briefly examine what it is and then apply its imperatives to the post-colonial globalist project. We undertake this task at risk of simplification since the object of our enquiry is complex. Much of our account of capitalism follows the insight provided by Marx, the object of extensive and lively polemics. We therefore confine ourselves to its basic and less controversial tenets. The definition advanced by Wood provides a helpful starting point: 'Capitalism is a system in which goods and services, down to the most basic necessities of life, are produced for profitable exchange, where even human labour-power is a commodity for sale in the market, and where all economic actors are dependent on the market'.[42]

It follows that capitalism is first and foremost a mode of production. As such, it possesses certain unique characteristics which distinguish it from other historical modes of production. These characteristics may be identified by reference to questions, such as what is being produced, the purpose and method of production and the manner in which products circulate. What is being produced is commodities. Commodities represent the abstraction of concrete goods and their replacement as the elementary unit of wealth. Specific to capitalism is the fact that commodities are produced not for the satisfaction of needs, but for sale. The purpose of the sale is to start a new cycle of production. In other words, the commodity is not sold for its use value. The proceeds of sale are not expended on the purchase of another commodity and the satisfaction of wants. Rather, they are harnessed as capital. This makes capitalism an exceptionally dynamic system for the creation of wealth. Its more controversial aspect pertains to the question of who gets to have this wealth. This is addressed later and in the account of the formation of capitalist property in the first part of the book. What and whose act of taking is legitimate and what and whose act of taking is conversely punishable? This is the question.

Marx defined capital as value used to generate more value, commonly referred to as profit.[43] Money is capital's first form and the medium through which it circulates. Capitalism could not take its place at the table of human history until such time as the circulation of commodities gave rise to money relations. Yet, not all money is capital. Money is capital when it is expended to buy something for the purpose of selling it again. When it is invested. Marx expressed this as an M-C-M formula. Money transformed into commodities, transformed back into money. By

42 Ellen Meiksins Wood, *The Origin of Capitalism: A Longer View* (Verso 2002) 2.

43 Broadly, value is the labour required to produce the commodity which determines its exchange value with other commodities; see also note 17 in chapter 2 and the first paragraph under the section 'Capitalist Characteristics and the Globalist Project' in this chapter.

this process money becomes capital. It is spent only in order to get it back. When money is used for the satisfaction of wants, the act comes to an end upon purchase of the desired thing. Where money circulates as capital, the aim is circulation in and of itself. Through its endless repetitions or renewals, capital self-valorises and expands. The circulation of capital is therefore uniquely without limits, making endless accumulation one of capitalism's most defining features and its existential objective. 'In fact, the production of goods and services is subordinate to the production of capital and capitalist profit'.[44]

Subordination to the endless production of capital and capitalist profit calls for life on the move. Competition causes the rate of profit to decline as markets become crowded. Conversely, competition also ends up producing monopolies/oligopolies as weaker or smaller participants are taken over by stronger or bigger ones. Either way, a search is on for virgin markets where new investment opportunities exist and the profit rate may be restored. Thus, capitalism is a system of frontiers that are forever in a state of motion and advancement. Conquest of one frontier's purported wilderness signals the birth of another. Moreover, conquest has its own specific logic of power. Arrighi distinguishes between the logic of power or mode of rule which guides capitalist expansion and the territorial logic which underpinned pre-capitalist expansion. In the latter, power was identified with enlargement of the territories and populations acquired and brought under control. Wealth was merely 'a means or a by-product of the pursuit of territorial expansion'. By contrast, in capitalist expansion, power is identified with command (secured through property rights) over resources. Acquisitions of territories and populations are 'a means and by-product of the accumulation of capital'. This difference in systemic logic informs state formation. Pursuant to the territorial logic, control over territories and populations is the objective, whereas control over wealth creation is the means. Pursuant to the inverse capitalist logic, 'control over mobile capital is the objective, and control over territory and population is the means'.[45] Wealth is the route to power rather than power being the route to wealth.

It follows that for capital with its existential need for mobility, boundaries are obstacles. They are to be overcome in the turbulence of what Marx identified and the political economist Joseph Schumpeter termed 'creative destruction'.[46] Boundaries may or may not be geographic. New frontiers, and through them new markets, may be found internally as in the privatisation of public services hitherto deemed

44 Wood (n 42) 3.

45 Arrighi (n 13) 34, 35.

46 Referring to the 'perennial gale of creative destruction', Joseph Schumpeter, an economist of the Austrian School, first coined the term in his 1942 book *Capitalism, Socialism Democracy*. The term describes the messy nature of capitalist progress, the way capitalism – a method of economic change that can never be stationary – incessantly revolutionises itself structurally from within, incessantly destroying the old and creating the new. The term derives from Marx's analysis of the methods (economic crisis, war) by which production is destroyed and a new round of wealth accumulation is enabled. Unlike Marx who saw this inherent motion as ultimately self-destructive, Schumpeter saw creative destruction as natural and necessary for growth.

part of the commons. Spaces formerly freely available for use by populations and/or under state control fall under the command of capital. Alternatively, borders are crossed into new geographical territories. Colonial expansion, argue Alexander Anievas and Kerem Nisancioglu, enabled English capitalism to survive the limits of domestic production by which it otherwise would have been constrained.[47] Philosopher Michel Foucault traces the early seeds of the globalist project to the 18th century. It was then, he argues, that for the first time Europe 'has the entire planet for its horizon'. For the first time, Europe saw the world as its own economic domain, a space of competitive production and exchange, a global market to be internationally organised and juridified, integral to the continent's uninterrupted enrichment and an underwriter of its perpetual peace.[48] Early indications of the project of converting the 'entire planet' into a European domain may be found in the less than orderly colonial taking of and settling in the lands of others. With the passage of time, as capitalism established itself and matured, settler colonialism evolved into more orderly and juridically institutionalised gunboat imperialism. The world as a European domain was taking shape. Amin traces to the second half of the 19th century the move towards imperialism by economic means. The trigger was a period of economic crisis and stagnation which began in 1837. In response, new monopolies reinforced existing colonial conquests and profits were inflated by the rent extracted from cheap labour.[49] This period signalled the formation of multinational enterprises in their contemporary form and is discussed in further detail in chapter 6.

Herein lies the problem. The globalist project signified the germination and maturation of these early seeds. Yet, the planet is finite, as are the interstate system's legally defined territories. Accumulation may be endless, but not so new frontiers. From this flow at least two dimensions of the current crisis, the singularity of which distinguishes it from earlier ones. Moreover, potentially, they put it beyond re-stabilisation.

These two dimensions are associated with two types of limits. One is systemic. The other is ecological. As to the systemic limit, the incorporation of the former Soviet Union, China and India into globalised circuits of capital may be seen as the last three significant attempts at expansion. Yet, the absorption of China and Russia remains partial with potentially either different outcomes or a breakaway. Sovereignty over resources and markets has not been surrendered to transnational capital lock, stock and barrel, prompting Pompeo to warn that an ambitious Russia 'will become a Juggernaut, dominating fossil fuels'.[50] The two countries have moved to strengthen their alliance and advance an alternative world order. Their current direction of travel seems to have taken a turn away from incorporation into

47 Alexander Anievas and Kerem Nisancioglu, *How the West Came to Rule* (Pluto Press 2015) 152.

48 Michel Foucault, *The Birth of Biopolitics: Lectures at the College De France 1978–1979* (Palgrave Macmillan 2008) 56–7, referring to Kant's 1795 writing on perpetual peace, specifically to his chapter 'On the Guarantee of Perpetual Peace'.

49 Amin (n 1).

50 Hudson Institute (6).

the globalised networks of financialised monopoly capitalism, suggesting a different form of globalisation. Consequently, says Hudson, they are being perceived as an existential threat 'to the global expansion of U.S.-centred *rentier* wealth'. It is necessary that they be deterred from 'socializing their financial systems, land and natural resources, and from keeping infrastructure utilities public to prevent their being monopolized in private hands and siphoning off economic rents'.[51] With uncertainty hanging not only over Russia and China, but also over other members of the SCO and the BRIOCS nations, '[t]here are no longer any new territories of significance to integrate into world capitalism and new spaces to commodify are drying up'.[52] In the interior of nation-states, privatisation has already gone through the first line of candidates, such as health, education, utilities, housing and land. It now includes also the law, policing and war-making.[53] Consequently, there is not much left of the commons to be turned into spaces dominated by capitalist imperatives. In the face of systemic limits, capital is propelled towards financial speculations as the route to restored/augmented rates of profit. The implications of this have been considered earlier.

With regard to the planet's ecological limits, as globalised capitalist accumulation is hitting against them, the survival of humanity itself comes under threat. In the face of rising earth temperatures, the Intergovernmental Panel on Climate Change (IPCC) has warned that the impact of climate change may well exceed the human species' capacity to adapt or mitigate it. UN Secretary-General António Guterres described the IPCC 2021 report as 'a code red for humanity. The alarm bells are deafening, and the evidence is irrefutable: greenhouse gas emissions from fossil fuel burning and deforestation are choking our planet and putting billions of people at immediate risk'.[54] The process of desertification, for example, now spans more than 100 countries, and land degradation is predicted to rise from 75% of the earth to 90% by 2050. East Africa is in the grips of a drought. In the Brazilian Amazon, the rate of deforestation has been exceeding the rate of carbon capture by the remaining trees since 2016. Cash crops such as tea and coffee are affected by climate change. Low-lying islands are at risk of being submerged by rising sea water levels. The list goes on. Biodiversity is lost at an alarming rate, and human disruption to the balance of the nitrogen cycle in both aquatic and terrestrial ecosystems is pervasive. Some scientists conclude that in all these respects the tipping point has already passed. The planet tells us that it can no longer accommodate what Marx described as its expropriation. That is, its appropriation without reciprocity and without the opportunity to regenerate and restore balance. In the

51 Hudson (n 4) 221.

52 Robinson (n 8) 18.

53 The reference to the privatisation of the law is reference to *lex mercatoria* and arbitration, a mechanism for dispute resolution which is based on a private agreement between the parties to deal with their disagreement outside the jurisdiction of national courts.

54 Fiona Harvey, 'Major Climate Change Inevitable and Irreversible – IPCC's Starkest Warning Yet' (*The Guardian*, 9 August 2021) <https://www.theguardian.com/science/2021/aug/09/humans-have-caused-unprecedented-and-irreversible-change-to-climate-scientists-warn,> accessed 1 June 2021.

second part of this book, Janet Dine points out that we close our eyes to this limit at our existential risk.

Associated with these two dimensions is the crisis of overaccumulation. Enormous amounts of capital are amassed as the cost of labour goes down and productivity is enhanced through technological innovations of the productive process. Strategies of tax avoidance produce idle capital secretly stagnating in tax haven jurisdictions. Standing in the way of resolution are not only the ecological and systemic limits alluded to earlier, but also the underconsumption attendant on immiseration, globalised austerity policies and inequality. For a while, the flow of cheap products from China masked inflationary trends and held underconsumption at bay. With the fracturing of the globalist project, both inflation and underconsumption are assuming structural dimensions. Thus, capital's ability to be true to itself is constrained. It is prevented from doing that which it must do to survive.

Capitalist characteristics and the globalist project

Commodities circulate by means of market exchange. That is, impersonally and without direct social organisation. A feature of market exchange is the abstraction of a product's specific and concrete use value as equalised exchange value. Two different use values in a relationship of exchange are abstracted as exchange value. So much of one commodity equals so much of another. Two commodities may differ concretely but are nevertheless of equal value. The equalised nature of this exchange gives rise to a problem. No new value is created. Therefore capital, in order to expand, needs to purchase a commodity, the consumption of which does create new value. This commodity is labour-power. Wages represent that portion of the value created by labour which is necessary for its survival and reproduction. The rest (surplus value) is captured and put into capitalist circulation.

It follows that profits are generated in the course of the productive process. Therefore, for the capitalist to survive, production must be cost effective and competitive. It further follows that the lower the wage, the greater labour's productivity in exchange for this wage (efficiency) and the greater the competitive advantage. Hence, an important constituent of the globalist project is corporations' ability to offshore production to countries where wages are low, down to bondage and child labour.

Scanning the world in search of cheap labour necessitates freedom of movement coupled with at least a degree of certainty about the cost to be shouldered upon border crossing. These are maximised through interstate competition over foreign investment (aka 'race to the bottom') and the promotion of market-based political economy on a plenary scale. As observed earlier, central to the creation of a monoculture are IFI's conditionalities and a treaty-based regime of foreign investment protection. Mainstream investment treaties impose no obligations on foreign investors or their home states. These are reserved for the host. Consequently, beyond possibly a general obligation to comply with the host county' laws, on the whole there are no provisions regarding, for example, terms and conditions of employment or the indigenisation of management. This international architecture of essentially free rein for foreign investors is supplemented by risk-distancing corporate laws. Risks associated with the operation of non-resident overseas subsidiaries is distanced from the parent and its assets.

Prominent among the mechanisms of risk-distancing is the doctrine of the corporate veil found in most jurisdictions. The term refers to the principle that a corporation is a juridical person. It is separate from its shareholders whose liability in the event of insolvency is limited to the value of their shares.[55] When applied to groups of companies, this principle fragments the group into a collection of independent units. They may be bound together by equity links, but each is a separate legal person. The starting point is therefore that the shareholding company has no claim to the assets of its subsidiary, nor is it responsible for its losses or any harm it has caused. Fragmentation also means that where, as in supply chains, the group's corporate units are linked to each other by a contract, on the whole, this contract is deemed to have been entered into at arm's length between separate and independent parties. The management and control, which underpin the group's commercial integration and make it into an organisation, are thereby made to vanish.

A third veil which flows from the principle of corporate personality when applied to multinational enterprises is jurisdictional. The different units of the multinational enterprise are located in different states and exist pursuant to their laws. Therefore, each has the nationality of and is subject to the laws of the country of its incorporation; alternatively, its main place of operation. Insofar as states' jurisdiction is territorial, at least as a starting point, the jurisdiction of their courts does not extend to the corporate units established beyond their borders. This enables multinationals to practice jurisdictional arbitrage, including worldwide labour arbitrage.[56]

Liability for unlawful exploitation of labour may be controlled through group structuring. The directly exploiting subsidiary may be kept short of assets available for compensation or be made to disappear altogether whilst its parent is likely to prove beyond reach. Liability may also be distanced by building indirect control

55 See the limited liability law enacted by the state of New York in 1811 and the Limited Law Act 1855 in the UK.

56 The concept of arbitrage originates from the fields of economics and finance. It refers to the practice of taking advantage of the price differentials which exist between markets by entering into matching deals and capitalising on the price difference. For global labour arbitrage in value chains see Suwandi (n 22) 21–31 and generally. For jurisdictional arbitration by corporations see for example Janet Dine, 'Stopping Jurisdictional Arbitrage by Multinational Companies: A National Solution?' (2014) 11(2) *European Company Law*, University of Oslo Faculty of Law Research Paper No 2014–20 <https://papers.ssrn.com/sol3/papers.cfm?abstract_id=2471501> accessed 8 June 2022; a line of recent UK case law indicates a tendency to relax the conditions in which the jurisdictional veil may be sidestepped by the application of tort law. See for example *Vedanta Resources and another v Lungowe and others* [2019] UKSC 20; *Okpabi and others v Royal Dutch Shell Plc and another* [2021] UKSC 3; a case involving slavery-type labour exploitation now going through the English court is *Josiah and Others v British American Tobacco Plc & Others* [2021] EWHC 1743 (QB).

into supply chains. The production process is sourced out to local suppliers to be performed by them in accordance with the multinational's instructions. These instructions then percolate to the factory floor where they fashion working conditions. In other words, the dependency and power differentials built into the local suppliers' relationship with their multinational buyers mean that, in practice, multinational buyers exercise much influence over what transpires in their commodity chains. Interviews conducted by Intan Suwandi with executives of Indonesian suppliers produced statements such as 'multinationals are always looking for the most competitive supplier', they 'would observe, control how you work' and 'we only follow their lead'.[57] Yet, from a legal perspective, multinationals and their dependent suppliers are deemed independent parties to a contractual arrangement said to have been negotiated at arm's length. To date, attempts at legislative reforms proved weak. The responsibility for events of slavery in supply chains imposed on multinationals pursuant to the UK Modern Slavery Act 2015 is as yet limited to reporting. On 23 February 2022, the European Commission adopted a proposal for a directive intended to impose on multinationals a legally enforceable obligations of due diligence. Whether member states will consent to the proposed directive and, if so, how it will be implemented through national legislation remain to be seen.

In sum, subject to certain restrictions on mobility, such as the location of resources in extractive industries, corporations can turn their backs on their workers as they outsource production to the cheapest available next location. They can do so with the aid of a legal infrastructure of free movement, risk-distancing and direct protection. Where wages rise and better working conditions are mandated in the new location, capital may exit again and move to the next centre of cheap production. In turn, this exerts pressure on conditions in the location left behind and beyond, including the Global North. As 'the world's workers are brought into competition in a single market', the deterioration in wages, work conditions and workers' capacity to protect them thus assumes worldwide dimensions.[58] Hudson points to an additional mode of labour exploitation practiced by financial and other forms of rentier capital. This time, the target is not the wage earned, but rather the way it is spent. The aim is 'to maximise the obligation of labor to pay its wages for debt service and to buy basic needs that are monopolized to produce monopoly rents'. Industrial and financial modes of value extraction from labour exist in harmony. Indebtedness creates 'an employment "marketplace" in which losing one's job leaves workers in a precarious economic position'. This locks them into current jobs and inhibits resistance and unionisation. 'The result is what former chair of the U.S. Federal Reserve, Alan Greenspan called the "traumatized worker" syndrome'. Through this syndrome, rent-seeking exploitation indirectly enhances the profits of industrial capital.[59]

57 Suwandi (n 22) 42, 68, 98.

58 Giovanni Arrighi and Beverley J. Silver, 'Introduction' in Arrighi and Silver (n 13) 10.

59 Hudson (n 4) 26–7.

Thus, production for exchange in the market masks the social relations on which it is founded. On the face of it, purchases appear a simple exchange of a commodity for money. Yet, behind it lies a less visible network of social relations and class interactions. According to Marx, primary among them is the antagonism between the owners of the means of production and the workers, owners of their labour. This is because another defining feature of a capitalist mode of production and a precondition for its formation is the separation of direct producers from the means of production. For capitalist social relations to form, it is necessary that a class of free labourers comes into existence. These are propertyless people who have no access to the means of survival and reproduction except through the sale of their labour for a wage. Facing them is another class of people, those who own the means of production as their private property. The institution of private property is thus central to capitalist social relations and the power structures which underpin them. As John Adams, US president in late 18th century, has put it: 'The balance of power in a society accompanies the balance of property and land'.[60] This property-power nexus and the manner of its balancing underpins the class antagonism identified by Marx, rendering it structural and the source of ongoing struggle. As alluded to in the introduction, questions arise as to whether such struggle can reach a fair resolution through reformative action within capitalist social relations or whether an altogether new way of social organisation is required. If the latter, how should the transition take place? Were transformation to take place, should it involve, as in the case of the Chinese model, at least to begin with, the harnessing of capitalist elements for their wealth creation potential? Dine adds the voice of Nature to this debate. The property-power nexus in its neoliberal incarnation, she argues, spills over to all corners of the web of life, negatively impacting not only class relations but also the interface between human and non-human ecological systems. In reality, the two are indivisible.

These questions are thrown into relief and are becoming particularly pressing against the backdrop of a globalist project in a deepening and potentially terminal crisis. Much of the struggle associated with these questions takes the form of a contest over the state. This is because it is the state which mediates the distribution of property and associated balance of power in the society. For a while and at least superficially, it seems to have been overwhelmed and captured by corporate might. Yet, as the globalist project fractures and contestations surge, particularly in the Global South, the nation-state seems to have found its voice and to be reclaiming its position as a lynchpin of popular aspirations. It is to this that we now turn our attention.

Capital and the state

Casting our eyes back to the heydays of the globalist project, even on the neoliberal case, the supportive role fulfilled by states was conceived as indispensable. The

60 Charles Francis Adams (ed), *The Works of John Adams, Second President of the United State* (Vol. 9 Books for Libraries Press 1969) 367 cited in Nicholas Blomley, 'Law, Property, and Geography of Violence: The Frontier, the Survey, and the Grid' (2003) 93(1) *The Annals of the Association of American Geographers* 122.

Geneva School made this point when it argued that the market does not and cannot take care of itself. It needs the protective arm of the state behind it. According to the jurist Ernst-Ulrich Petersmann, this starting point of the neoliberal economic theory stipulated that in 'any well-functioning market economy the "invisible hand" of the market competition must by necessity be complemented by the "visible hand" of the law'.[61] Yet, it cannot be any law. According to Hayek, for the 'free system' to function properly, state-made legal rules 'must be such that the market will work tolerably well'. Most importantly, fraud and violence are to be prevented, property must be protected, contracts must be enforced and the 'equal rights of all individuals to produce in whatever quantities and to sell at whatever prices they choose' must be recognised.[62] In other words, at issue is not the existence or size of a state, but what *kind* of a state. From capital's perspective, a good state is one which creates the conditions for the market to operate freely. It shields private property, allows the freedom to contract and enforce contracts subject to the requisite of preserving social order.

Hayek's depiction of the interface between the world of states and the world of property is subject to passionate debates. Yet, the disagreements are mostly about where the boundaries are to be drawn and the extent and nature of the space allocated to each. Less questioned is the underlying premise that, at least as a starting point, state and capital/property are separate. They are in close proximity, yet differentiated. This premise can be read into Cutler's proposition that transnational law blurs the boundaries between the private and the public spheres. Clearly, for boundaries to be blurred, it is necessary that they exist in the first place. Polanyi theorised this separation as a process of disembedment. The economy was disembedded from society and society was then subordinated to it. Hayek described it as a distinction between the man-made order where the legislator resides and the self-generating order created through spontaneous adaptations to changing circumstances (society/markets).[63] Wood called it political devolution, a time when 'the "moment" of coercion was cut off from the "moment" of appropriation'.[64] The economic and civil spheres were severed from the realm of politics and placed firmly in the individual sphere. The split was veiled using discursive structures constructed around notions of freedom to contract, to exchange and to labour.

Notwithstanding these scholarly differences, all acknowledge that first, the division does exist, and second, it is a structural arrangement specific to capitalist social relations. In feudalism, argues Wood, the unity of appropriation and coercion meant that, 'the lord's coercive power – at bottom, his military power – is also

61 Cited in Quinn Slobodian, *Globalists: The End of Empire and the Birth of Neoliberalism* (HUP 2018) 7.

62 F. A. Hayek, *The Constitution of Liberty* (Routledge 1960) 200.

63 F. A. Hayek, *Law, Legislation and Liberty: A New Statement of the Liberal Principles of Justice and Political Economy* (Routledge 1982) 36–41.

64 Larry Patriquin (ed), *The Ellen Meiksins Wood Reader* (Historical Materialism Book Series Vol. 40 Brill 2012) 19 <https://cominsitu.files.wordpress.com/2016/01/the-ellen-meiksins-wood-reader-2012.pdf> accessed 20 October 2022.

his power to exploit'. In capitalist social relations, by contrast, 'from the beginning, the relations between the capitalist class and the state has been distinctive, with capitalists using their property to exploit propertyless workers, whilst the state maintains social order at arm's length from capital'.[65] She situates this 'beginning' in the enclosures movement which swept through the countryside of early modern England. The emerging centralised English state struck a bargain with the aristocracy. Pursuant to this bargain, the ruling feudal elite submitted to the common law and renounced its political obligations in exchange for strong and vigorously protected property rights.

As shall be seen from the discussion in chapter 4, the state stuck to its side of the bargain. The success of the privatisation-by-enclosures project would not have been possible without it first turning a blind eye to its unlawfulness as matter of existing statutes such as the Charter of the Forest, and then extending to it legislative and judicial support. Much later, in the 21st century, the privatisation of Greece's national assets would not have been possible without Germany and France closing their eyes to the prohibition on funding member governments' debts contained in the EU founding treaty. To circumvent this prohibition, part of the loans which were to constitute Greece's so-called bailout was laundered through the International Monetary Fund (IMF). In turn, this required the IMF to close its eyes to its own prohibition on lending to a bankrupt government in the absence of prior debt restructuring. The other and greater part of the funds to be advanced was redesigned as loans from individual member states rather than the EU itself. Thus, most of the burden of bailing out German and French banks via the pretence of bailing out Greece fell 'onto taxpayers from nations even poorer than Greece, such as Portugal and Slovakia'.[66] The money was wired to the banks, but the debt was added to Greece's already negative balance sheet, instigating a boot-sale of assets hitherto held in common and now made available for taking by capital.

This binary of partition on the one hand and proximity and interdependency on the other fosters systemic contradictions and contestations. The jurisdictional veil referred to previously is one example of these contradictions. On the one hand, the territorial nature of a state's competence to legislate (prescriptive jurisdiction) and to enforce its laws (enforcement jurisdiction) serves capital well. It facilitates arbitrage and obstructs liability for matters such as unlawful exploitation, tax avoidance and harm to people and Nature. On the other hand, at least formally, territorial limits render it impossible for the state to guarantee the conditions which its restless corporation may encounter upon border crossing. The state is restrained from acting as guarantor by international law foundational principles of equal sovereignty and non-intervention. Nevertheless, states can bypass this obstacle and come to the rescue as members of the IFIs, promoters of economic liberalisation, and the World Trade Organisation, promoter and legal guarantor of free trade. Additionally, they conclude international investment agreements in which the host state commits to

65 Wood (n 12) 16.
66 Varoufakis (n 16) 27.

indulging a future foreign investor with privileges. In all these instances, states exercise their competences in favour of property. They curb the scope of their sovereignty and impose limits on their ability to respond to the demands of what Arrighi and Silver term 'subordinate groups'.[67] Another example of a contradiction is the ability of corporations to avoid direct human rights obligations on the ground that they have no personality in international law and are not bearers of the duties it imposes. These fall on states. Yet, when it comes to the protection of private investment, corporations are accorded *locus standi* to claim under international law, facing respondent states as if they were their equals.

As to contestations, the state becomes an arena for struggle as each of the workers and proprietors/appropriators look to harnessing its protective hand to the task of advancing its interests. It is a struggle over location of boundaries and priority of interests. What is a good state and who is to decide? In particular, as capital grows in power and workers correspondingly lose power, corporations seek to shape and enlarge the parameters of the legislated protection on which they depend. They do so through incursions into the realm of political authority. In part, such incursions are visible as when corporations take over the state's social functions and turn them into new markets for rent extraction. In part, they are opaque as when corporations, using their economic dominance and lobbying budgets and expertise, covertly usurp political power. They become the invisible power behind ostensibly democratic processes of governance, law and policy formation. Thus, insofar as corporations reign over *dominium*, the world of private property, they also seek control over *imperium*, the world of nations, political authority and sovereignty. Property and statecraft are partitioned, but, as observed by Nkrumah, in practice, they are also intertwined so that one cannot be shaped without intervention in the other.[68] In what some identify as a state of neo-feudalism, globalised economic networks are increasingly becoming also power networks. According to French historian Fernand Braudel, this quest for political power to supplement economic authority is immanent to capitalism. 'Capitalism only triumphs when it becomes identified with the state, when it is the state'.[69] As against it, labour seeks to shape the political sphere through grassroots activism, trade unions and participation in party politics.

Whether a capitalist state can be anything other than a guarantor of capital and a vehicle for its worldwide expansion is contested. Wood, as we saw, views the state as an institutional framework tasked with attending to capital's needs and securing its property rights. This was the bargain from the outset: centralised sovereignty

67 Arrighi and Silver (n 58) 10. Arrighi and Silver's use the term 'subordinate group' particularly by reference to labour.

68 For a discussion on the role of the law in relocating the boundaries between public and private authorities see Rodney Bruce Hall and Thomas J. Biersteker (eds), *The Emergence of Private Authority in Global Governance* (Cambridge Studies in International Relations CUP 2002); Cutler (n 35).

69 Fernand Braudel, *Afterthought on Material Civilization and Capitalism* (John Hopkins University Press 1997) 64.

in exchange for sheltered property, appropriation in exchange for coercion. The fact that a corporation is owned by the state, she argues, does not exclude it from the ranks of the appropriators since it too engages in the exploitation of labour, operates in competitive markets and is moved by capitalist compulsions.[70] The contrary argument is that ownership does matter. Through it, the state retains a measure of political authority over its economic actors. This includes the capacity to dispense instructions in the public interest, decide what is to be done with the surplus of profit and even withdraw the corporation from the market altogether. The corporations, the means of production, profits and assets are not private. They are integrated into the state and, through it, form part of the nation's collective assets. A premise of this argument is that the state itself is a collective entity. It belongs to its citizens and acts as a transmitter and caretaker of their needs. It is a guarantor of their well-being. Global South states provide examples. In Ecuador and Bolivia, constitutional processes were used to institutionalise the doctrine of rights of Nature, a novel concept of development and the recognition of multiple forms of property relations. In El Salvador, grassroots campaigns and ecological concerns led to this small country being the first to have banned all forms of metallic mining. This year, in the economic powerhouse of Zhejiang province, China introduced the first pilot scheme for the implementation of its ecological, material and spiritual 'common prosperity' policy. The policy is designed to redress uneven development, reduce inequality and reshape the distribution of income. Targeted are the disorderly expansion of capital, monopolistic concentrations, speculation and the cost of privately provided education, housing and potentially health. The policy is said to herald a new phase in China's path to a socialist civilisation.[71] The aim is to restore social and ecological harmony. Attempts by corporations and the TCC behind them to jump on the bandwagon by channelling resources through foundations and non-governmental organisations were rebuffed as unwelcomed incursions into the realm of the state's political authority exercised in fulfilment of its social functions.

The difference between these two perspectives is exemplified by two contrasting views of the welfare system. According to one, the welfare state represents a progressive evolution in the state's recognition of its obligations towards the well-being of its citizens and the need to shield them from the vagaries of capital operating in competitive markets. It is constructed in performance of the state's care obligations and in response to labour's demands and struggles. The contrary view is that welfare provisions are the means by which the state keeps alive a reserve army of workers available for when capital may need them. This leaves private economic actors free to augment the surplus value they harvest from their labour force by tailoring its size and cost to the minimum necessary. They can do so safe in

70 Wood (n 12) 16.

71 Michael Dunford, 'The Chinese Path to Common Prosperity' (2022) 12(1) *International Critical Thought* 35 <https://www.tandfonline.com/doi/full/10.1080/21598282.2022.2025561> accessed 20 June 2022.

the knowledge that the state will ensure the survival of discarded or superexploited labour in contemplation of future need. The state, to support the institution of property and the interests of the propertied, must also take care of the propertyless. This necessitates a balancing act. A minimum wage is legislated to afford workers a degree of protection against superexploitation and to introduce a measure of stability and legitimacy into their relationship with capital. At the same time, the minimum wage is kept sufficiently low to ensure that the cost of labour does not disturb the basic arrangement which frames state-capital relationships. Welfare provisions must suffice to keep body and soul together and 'remove labour from the danger zone'.[72] However, they must not go so far as to circumvent the market as the only route to survival. They must not enhance labour's bargaining power, thereby putting an upwards pressure on wages. Seen from this perspective, the genealogy of welfare provisions goes back to the Poor Laws of 16th-century England and their culmination in the workhouses of the 1834 Poor Law Reform. The Poor Laws were the 'first systemic, national and state-regulated "welfare" programme in response to the apparent threat to social order arising from the expropriation of direct producers and a growing population of "masterless men"'.[73] Particularly the 1834 workhouses represented a harsher *laissez-faire* philosophy towards social order. It posited pauperism among able-bodied men as a moral failing for which no relief was to be made available except through employment in the dreaded workhouse. Also on this view, the current trajectory of restricting access to welfare and degrading its quality may be seen as an indication that, with the introduction of robots and digitalised technologies into the productive process, future increase in the need for labour is not anticipated. Moreover, improvements in surveillance and control technologies offer an alternative route to the preservation of worldwide social order.

Paradoxically, the view of the state as caretaker has been incorporated into the neoliberal discourse. Private economic actors must be supported because they generate the wealth which then naturally trickles down to the rest of the population. Ultimately, it is said, private wealth production benefits all. The interests of private economic actors, populations and the good state are thereby aligned. The good state withdraws from the market in contemplation of its citizens' well-being since the capitalist appropriation of the value produced by labour is in labour's own interest. As we shall see, this view that the dispossessed benefit from their own dispossession goes back to the theory of capitalist property rights in the writings of John Locke. It is also to be found in the narrative which justifies the extensive legal privileges accorded to multinational enterprises pursuant to the investment protection regime. Yet, the exponential increase in the concentration of capital and corresponding enlargement and intensification of worldwide poverty tell a different story. Ever greater wealth is accumulated in the hands of fewer beneficiaries

72 Karl Polanyi, *The Great Transformation: The Political and Economic Origins of Our Time* (Beacon Press Boston 1957) 73.

73 Wood (n 12) 18–19; Polanyi (n 72) in particular 73, 82–4, 143.

whilst the number of losers grows. In defiance of gravity, wealth trickles up rather than down.

The tension which permeates the interface between state and property occasionally changes the dynamics which shape the interior of their alliance. In particular, the replacement in the 19th century of the royal charter with an administrative procedure of incorporation as originator of corporate rights, duties and privileges may be seen as a transformative moment. Both are state-granted concessions. Yet, they differ substantively. Pursuant to the royal charter, the ultimate power over the company's fate was vested in political authority. Incorporation (1811 in the US and 1844 in England and Wales) represented a move towards privatisation. The state relinquished its power over the fate of the company, bar certain legal/regulatory instructions as to the way it is to be governed. The corporation became a juridical person whose fate was relegated to the economic sphere. A zone of free enterprise was created in which state power was to make room for market competition as arbiter of success or failure. Monopolies were no longer politically granted but were to be created through market mechanisms. They lost the territorial feature which defined them as managers of the colonies to become commodities-based. The corporation's rights and obligations now emanated from its legal personality, away from the whims of a political handout. In return, the corporations relinquished the sovereign powers formerly granted to the joint stock charter company for the purpose of governing the colonial project, and which modern multinationals are at pains to recapture.[74]

The post-colonial globalist project is said to have once again recast the interior of the state-property alliance. This time, the change is associated with globalisation's primary features of transnationalisation, concentration and rise of a TCC. Whether the impact of these processes amounts to a transformative moment is subject to debate. At issue are the presence and significance of changes to the balance of power between the two protagonists. On one view, multinational corporations' explosive growth and maturation as networks of both accumulation and power has put them beyond the reach of sovereign competences. In particular, their de-territorialisation through processes of integration and worldwide internalisation of production and finance has reduced the nation-state's influence and has marginalised the role it historically played. The territorial nation-state is no longer either a source of power or a source of opposition to capital. Even when its power was suppressed by the propagation of free trade in the 19th century, says Arrighi, suppression was only partial. Ample room was left for sovereign delinking.[75] Now, by contrast, capital is delinking itself from the sovereign. It is 'subject to no state authority'.[76] Instead, as argued by Cutler, it creates its own laws. On this view, corporate elites operate in a transnational space where they are allied to nobody and owe loyalty to no one

74 For the difference between royal charter companies and present-day multinational enterprises see for example Arrighi (n 13) 73–5.

75 Arrighi (n 13) 67–8.

76 Ibid 75.

other than their own economic imperatives of expansion and profit maximisation. US jurisprudence uses the language of corporations being 'at home' for the purpose of its courts being able to establish general personal jurisdiction over them.[77] However, beyond the legal technicalities of presence in the jurisdiction, corporations call no state their home. 'The emergence of this free enterprise system – free, that is, from the constraints imposed on world-scale processes of capital accumulation by the territorial exclusiveness of states – has been the most distinctive outcome of US hegemony'.[78] Michael Hardt and Antonio Negri conceptualise this outcome as the constitution of a new global empire, one that is devoid of territorial centres of power and control. According to them, globalisation produced a spatial totality in which nation-states' sovereignty has been replaced with boundless sovereignty that is situated everywhere and nowhere. The juridical pronouncements which emanate from it 'tend to project a single supranational figure of political power'.[79] The territorial state has been disempowered to become a shadow of its former self. Charles Tilly attributes the reversal of labour rights' former trajectory of expansion to the incapacitation of the state as mediator.[80] As capital went global and its power congealed, it reconstituted 'its social power by breaking free of nation-state constraints to accumulation, to do away with the Fordist-Keynesian arrangement, and to beat back the tide of revolution in the Third World'.[81] Moreover, supranational private authority, particularly in its financialised form, pillages the state.

The contrasting view (followed here) is that at all times the nation-state has remained central to the post-colonial globalist project. It has not and cannot decline into irrelevancy as a source of capitalist power, alternatively as a source of opposition to and constraints on its ability to shape the world in its own image. The two are intertwined and cannot be disaggregated. The state continues to play its traditional roles as a protector, facilitator and guarantor, discussed previously. It uses its coercive force and legislative competence to underwrite market conditions. In the face of systemic crises, disruptions and labour's contestations, it ensures supply of the oxygen of stability or, at least, seeks to do so. At the time of writing, the prospect of a countrywide rail strike in response to declining wages and standard of living moved the UK government to announce legislation which will permit corporations to supress strikes by taking on agency workers. Capital cannot shoulder these legislative and coercive functions, nor would it make financial sense to do so. As it is, labour pays for much of the cost of its own coercion. To a large extent, coercion is financed through a stream of tax receipts generated from that portion of the surplus profit which capital allocates to labour in the cause of its survival

77 *Goodyear Dunlop Tires S.A. v Brown* [2011] 131 S. Ct. 2846; *Daimler Chrysler AG v Bauman* [2013] 133 S. Ct. 1995; Howard M. Erichson, 'The Home-State Test for General Personal Jurisdiction' (2013) 63 *Vanderbilt Law Review En Banc* 81. The concept of personal jurisdiction refers to a court's power to adjudicate the rights and obligations of a litigant within its jurisdictional reach.

78 Arrighi (n 13) 75.

79 Michael Hardt and Antonio Negri, *Empire* (HUP 2000) xii, 9, 239.

80 Tilly (n 21) 14–22.

81 Robinson (n 8) 25; Arrighi and Silver, 'Introduction' (n 58) 7–8.

(income tax). Moreover, the relative invisibility of corporate incursions into the political/legal sphere facilitates a narrative which demonises the state. The state stands in plain sight, so that popular anger about the hardships of poverty, inequality, evictions and unemployment are easily directed at it.

> It is always the fault of the government. Whatever goes wrong. You may be fired by a capitalist, but you are angry at the politician. You may be pushed out of your home by the bank which lent you the money to buy your home, but you are angry at the politician.[82]

With regard to expansion, the establishment of the nation-states system pursuant to the Treaty of Westphalia in the 17th century provided the structural framework through which capitalism could become a worldwide system. Thereafter, according to the historian and sociologist Max Weber, the competition and struggle for power in which states engaged 'created the largest opportunities for modern western capitalism . . . The separate state had to compete for mobile capital, which dictated to them the conditions under which it would assist them to power.'[83] It was this competition for mobile capital which produced the 'memorable alliance between the rising states and the sought-after and privileged capitalist powers'.[84] That is to say, from the beginning, the state was both dependent on capital and a conduit of its enlargement, facilitating it both at the point of departure and at the point of arrival. European states, faced with the competitive pressures exerted by Britain's capitalist transformation, encouraged capitalist development at home.[85] It would have been impossible for private economic actors to engage and prevail in the colonial encounter without the military prowess of the European state behind them. For Arrighi, it was states' gunboats rather than the artillery of cheap commodities that ultimately were the 'true "midwife" of the subordination of China to the imperatives of the "endless" accumulation of Western Capital'.[86]

As to the globalist project, the IFIs and the World Trade Organisation are creatures of its member states. International investment agreements are entered into between states. The investor awaits in the wings as an ostensibly passive beneficiary until such time as it moves centre stage to assert a breach of treaty and claim compensation. Yet, but for the agreement entered into between states, such an appearance would not have been possible. These agreements may be classified in academic circles as transnational law. Nonetheless, they come into existence through state action. With the exception of ICSID, awards are enforced by national

82 Wolfe (n 20).

83 Max Weber (tr), *General Economic History* (Collier 1961) 247–9 cited in Arrighi (n 13) 12.

84 Marx Weber, *Economy and Society* (California University Press 1978) 353–4 cited in Arrighi (n 13) 13.

85 Wood (n 12) 23, 118–42.

86 Giovanni Arrighi, 'China's Market Economy in the Long Run' in Ho-fung Hung (ed), *China and the Transformation of Global Capitalism* (The Johns Hopkins University Press 2009) 24 citing from Karl Marx, *Capital* (Foreign Languages Publishing House 1959) 751.

courts. Further, a corporation cannot enter a new territory without the sovereign's say-so. Insofar as this say-so has been extracted under the pressure of IFIs conditionalities, the IFIs are made up of states. Therefore, the ability to fashion a state's conduct cannot be said to be exclusive to multinationals. It also reflects interstate power structures and patterns of domination.

The concepts of 'home' and 'host' states in and of themselves point to capital's national bonds. Whether as a matter of commercial considerations or in compliance with a requirement contained in most national laws, foreign investment habitually enters the host state's territory through a locally incorporated subsidiary. As we saw, this subsidiary is a separate legal person possessing the nationality of the state of its incorporation. It follows that the state in receipt of the investment, the so-called host state, is in fact a home state. It is home to the corporate person through which the investment is channelled. Its conceptualisation as a host speaks to the fact that multinationals do maintain and are identified by reference to primary national attachments. Such attachments may succumb to the pressure of competitive markets, profit opportunities and potential liabilities and may be concealed by the operation of the law. Nevertheless, when in need, corporations will turn to their home state for assistance in matters such as the opening up of new markets and access to resources through loans, aid and, when all else fails, military and political interventions.

Thus, the transnationalisation of capital is inconceivable without the state's supportive and protective hand. If anything, the vast amount of money corporations spend on ensuring that they can dictate the terms of this support and protection evidence that they have not abandoned, nor would they want to abandon, their alliance of mutual dependency with the state. In fact, argues Wood, [i]t may be that . . . global capital is more dependent on the territorial state than any an imperial power has ever been before'. More than ever, '[t]he world today, in fact, is . . . a world of nation-states'.[87] Crooke predicts that the globalist project's trajectory of disintegration will be accompanied by a counter-trajectory of states' empowerment. As globalised and financialised networks of private economic actors cease to produce the growth which hitherto legitimised their power and privileges, populations will turn increasingly to the state as an expression of their collective will and a guarantor of their well-being.[88]

87 Wood (n 12) 15, 20.
88 Crooke (n 19).

Part one

Taking

A historical perspective

2 On law and order

An outline of a debate

The origins, history and functions of the law are the subject of much debate. Legal theorists grapple with issues such as its role as mediator of social relations, the processes which determine its norms, the rights and the obligations it creates, the objectivity of its logic and the part it plays in the organisation of power. A broad observation which cuts across disagreements is that structures and processes external to the law partake in its formation. In the words of F. A. Hayek, a grandee of the neoliberal movement, the principles which shape the development of the law 'inevitably come in part from outside of the law'.[1] As to what this 'outside' consists of, for Hayek, the most defining input comes from the power of ideas about 'what is right and proper'.[2] Economics is but one, non-decisive factor. This focus on ideas about what the law ought to be is at the heart of liberal legal philosophy. It is premised on a conception of the law as a discreet system of socially essential rules that are at a distance from custom or morality and distinct from the exercise of force. As part of what Marxists call legal fetishism, statements are made that the law is a prerequisite for the formation and conduct of social life. Its authority and legitimacy shield property and citizens from infringement of rights and prohibited violence. A government acting under the rule of law must never coerce or punish unless in the course of its enforcement and pursuant to due process. In the context of positivist law, the quest for the realisation of desired goals (justice) was overtaken by emphasis on methods and procedures (legitimacy). In the words of Walter Benjamin: 'If natural law can judge all existing law in criticizing its ends, so positive law can judge all evolving law only in criticizing its means. If justice is the criterion of ends, legality is that of means'.[3] Legal concepts are analysed and

1 F. A. Hayek, *Law, Legislation and Liberty: A New Statement of the Liberal Principles of Justice and Political Economy* (Routledge 1982) 69.

2 Hayek (n 1) 69, 70.

3 Walter Benjamin, 'Critique of Violence' in Peter Demetz (ed), *Walter Benjamin Reflection: Essays, Aphorisms, Autobiographical Writings* (Schocken Books 1986) 278.

DOI: 10.4324/9781315386782-4

justice is understood on the basis of 'assumptions about the legitimate authority of the power exercised through the institutions of a modern legal system'.[4]

By contrast, from a Marxist perspective, the defining input comes from material conditions and class struggle. Much of Marxist jurisprudence interrogates the structures of power and domination which both produce and are validated by liberal ideas about the rule of law. Marxists question liberal logic and disrupt the beliefs and values by which notions about right and wrong are buttressed. In this respect, Marx's engagement with legal theory, fragmented and controversial as it is said to be, cannot be isolated from his analysis of the organisation of power.[5] Legal rules mirror the dominant ideology, itself a reflection of the role performed by the owners of the means of production in the relations of production, their shared experiences and their perceptions of where their collective interest lies.[6] The law is neither conspiratorially oppressive nor the discreet, detached and independent institution which liberals make it out to be. It does not provide objective rules of due process for the exercise of political power. For Marxists, law is political in and of itself.

Marxists are not alone in attributing a political function to what in liberal legal theory is an autonomous institution. The French philosopher Michel Foucault used a traffic metaphor to describe the internal dynamics of what he conceptualised as a juridical-ecopolitical ensemble. Through this ensemble power is organised and truth is imparted. Discourse (understood as a system of meanings) determines the type of transport deployed whilst the law functions as a 'highway code' to manage its circulation.[7] As such, the law mirrors the power structures of the day and the mode of their retention. Yet, it also has a productive force, constructing subjectivities and regulating their interactions. The history of the discourses which circulate throughout society and its institutions 'is coupled, from the start, with the history of law'.[8]

The proposition that the law circulates and that it possesses at least some productive power is also shared by some Marxists. At issue is the degree of economic determinism to be read into Marx and Engels's writings. In the Marxist conception of history, people enter into relations of production that correspond to the stage of development of the forces of production. The totality of these relations forms the economic structure of a society and its material base. Out of the material

4 Hugh Collins, *Marxism and the Law* (OUP 1984) 1.

5 For a sample of works on the Marxist theory of law see for example Maureen Caine, Alan Hunt, *Marx and Engels on Law* (Academic Press 1979); Collins (n 4); Evgeny Pashukanis, *The General Theory of Law and Marxism* (Routledge 2001); Karl Renner, *The Institutions of Private Law and Their Social Functions* (Routledge 2009); Paul O'Connell and Umut Ozsu, *Research Handbook on Law and Marxism* (Edward Elgar Publishing 2021).

6 Collins (n 4) 43.

7 Michel Foucault, *The Birth of Biopolitics: Lectures at the College De France 1978–1979* (Palgrave Macmillan 2008) 162. By 'discourse' Foucault meant a system of meanings which entails rules, practices and strategies and which describes as well as constructs the object it talks about.

8 Foucault (n 7) 35.

base grows a superstructure, being the mesh of beliefs, ideas, institutions and laws which inform common sense. At the same time, at the material base, consciousness is generated by social experience and interaction and is determined by people's class or production relations. In opposition to those in the Marxist camp, which hold that the economic base is the sole dawn of history and the law is only its by-product, others maintain that the base and the superstructure are co-constitutive. Ideas which sprout out of experiences and interactions at the material base produce conscious actions which in turn impact on the base. On their reading of Marx and Engels, the law does not merely reflect the relations of production. It is also a site of contestation and class struggle productive of legal reforms. These, in turn, can modify the material base. In the course of ongoing interactions between consciousness and material conditions, material conditions may be changed by deliberate action and in turn alter consciousness.[9] 'On the one hand, the logic of a given mode of production will throw up distinctive social forms and social arrangements of which the law is one. On the other hand, the class struggle will be expressed through, and impacted upon, by the law'.[10] Thus, the law does not remain within the confines of the superstructure but has its own dynamics, its own laws of motion and relative autonomy from the base.[11] As argued by E. P. Thompson when writing about the English enclosures and the Black Act of 1723, the law also descends from the heights of the superstructure and is absorbed in the day-to-day acts through which civilisation is realised.[12]

This simple sketch is no more than an outline of what is a large and complex debate. It serves as a prelude to the more detailed (but admittedly still partial) discussion that follows. Marx and Hayek are among the main shapers of contemporary consciousness. They stand in opposition to each other, not least in matters pertaining to the dispossessive process which delineates winners from losers. Yet, Hayek and Marx also come together in the objects of their enquiry, such as the interface between the construction of social orders and the objective of human survival. Notably, the Hayekian/neoliberal analysis of the principles governing market societies bears out what Marx identified centuries ago as the essential nature of capitalism and its laws of motion. The political, social and juridical project which Hayek posited as true and proper mirrors the social relations which Marx singled out as unique to capitalism. Hayek's elevation of market societies to the status of just conduct that is contingent on a limited role for the legislator is a testament to the genius of Marx.

9 Collins (n 4) 37.

10 Robert Knox, 'Marxist Approaches to International Law' in Ann Orford and Florian Hoffman (eds), *The Oxford Handbook of the Theory of International Law* (OUP 2016) 306 at p. 309.

11 B. S. Chimni, *International Law and World Order: A Critique of Contemporary Approaches* (2nd edn CUP 2017) 440–550; for a view of the rule of law as a human good see the Marxist historian Thompson (n 2) 202–12; see also for example Nicolas Poulanzas, *State, Power, Socialism* (Verso 2014).

12 E. P. Thompson, *Whigs & Hunters: The Origin of the Black Act* (Breviary Stuff Publications 2013) particularly 202–10.

Marx and Hayek

Of particular interest for present purposes is the Marxist observation that the law has evolved in tandem with the 'rise, extension and systemization' of individual ownership and the regulatory response this necessitated.[13] The method of analysis employed by Marx in coming to this conclusion is known as historical materialism. John Bellamy defines materialism as a 'theory of the nature of things'. It has its beginnings in Greek philosophy, notably Epicurus, in whose work Marx had great interest. Materialism is premised on claims that the origins and development of whatever exists is dependent on a level of physical reality which is independent of and precedes thought.[14] It follows that historical materialism refers to history understood in material terms so that its ultimately determining element 'is the production and reproduction of life' or the production and reproduction of the means of survival.[15]

Thus, Marxism first looks to past patterns of social change in order to understand the forces of history and, through this, catch a glimpse of the future. The aim is 'to discover how men had reacted to their conditions and to identify the causes of instability which eventually led to successive transformations of that society'. Second, the examination of prior civilisations rejects metaphysical explanations as well as those derived from thought, values and ideals. It is in the world itself, in the material conditions of life and the totality of social relations, including legal ones, that the key to unlocking the enigma of past and future historical progression is to be found. Accordingly, examination of capitalist property rights is not confined to legally formalised relations with a thing. Rather, they are rooted in and represent a specific type of social relations, one which reached its capitalist form upon the demise of communal ownership and then of feudalism.

With the rise of capitalism, status and privilege were replaced by the market as mediator of the appropriation of value and by the law as mediator of relationships.[16] The process which brought this about, particularly in relation to the law, was one of distancing. Distancing engendered double existence in which man 'lives in the *political community*, where he regards himself as a *communal being*,

13 Knox (n 10) 309.

14 John Bellamy Foster, *Marx's Ecology* (Monthly Review Press 2000) 2.

15 Chimni (n 11) 440.

16 Marx's concept of value is variously interpreted in Marxian scholarship. Fred Moseley identifies three main aspects of value alluded to in Chapter 1 of *Das Capital*: the substance, magnitude and form of appearance of value. Substance is the common property of commodities being the abstract labour required to produce them and which determines their exchange value with other commodities. Magnitude is the quantity of the substance of value. That is, the quantity of socially necessary labour time contained in them. The form of appearance is the observable phenomena of prices and money. Fred Moseley, 'Abstract Theory of Value and Money in Volume 1 of Capital' (The Franke Lectures in the Humanities, Yale University 28 October 2020) <https://www.youtube.com/watch?v=9OuQtocg81c> accessed 30 March 2022; Karl Marx, *Capital* (Wordsworth Editions Ltd 2013) 17–127; see also Fred Mosely (ed), *Marx's Theory of Money: Modern Appraisals* (Palgrave Macmillan 2005); for a non-Marxian perspective of value see for example Mariana Mazzucato, *The Value of Everything: Making and Taking in The Global Economy* (Penguin Books 2019).

and in *civil society* where he acts simply as a *private individual*'.[17] As a private individual, his liberty is that of a 'man regarded as an isolated monad, withdrawn into himself'.[18] Civil society's loss of direct political character and its fragmentation into a collection of itemised individuals opened the way for the law to replace status as mediator of relationships. The law as mediator determines the limits of individual liberty 'just as the boundary between two fields is marked by a stake'.[19] As famously articulated by Henry Maine, the 19th-century British jurist and legal historian: 'The movement of progressive societies has hitherto been movement from *status* to *contract*'.[20] Contract law provides a medium through which the relationship of capitalists and labour is constituted. It enables them to meet each other as purportedly free and independent proprietors of commodities – one owns the means of production and the other owns the labour of her body. Given that civil society is the mechanism through which the material basis is being reproduced, 'the role of political society' is 'simply to preserve civil society'.[21] In other words, in the context of capitalist social relations, the function of communal political life and, by extension, the law is to guard the apolitical sphere of the individual.

This vision of capitalist social relations as straddling two spheres is found also in neoliberal ideology, in particular its European version and Hayek's teachings about what constitutes a true and proper order. To Margaret Thatcher, former British prime minister and a protagonist in neoliberalism's transition from an ideological movement to a political project, Hayek was an inspiration. Yet, according to Quinn Slobodian, he was also misunderstood. The perceived wisdom is that neoliberalism is an ideology of self-regulating markets. Not so, says Slobodian. For neoliberals of the Geneva school, the market does not and cannot take care of itself. 'The core of twentieth-century neoliberal theorizing involves what they [the neoliberals – my comment] called the meta-economic or extra-economic conditions for safeguarding capitalism at the scale of the entire world'.[22] In other words, behind the invisible hand of the market lies the visible, protective hand of the state. It is therefore necessary that the state be captured and its functions tailored to respond to the needs of capital as it roams the planet, ceaselessly accumulating in a market-based globalised space of free trade and investment. This vision calls for restrictions on state sovereignty and a redesign of the state's legislative competence in favour of regulating the deregulation of economic activities.

As seen earlier, Marx's 'two societies' observation forms part of his analysis of what capitalism is. Hayek's version of this observation forms part of his analysis of what is right and proper – what capitalism should be if it to survive challenges to its legitimacy, attain its true nature and expand on a plenary scale. In line with Hayek's

17 Karl Marx, 'On the Jewish Question' in Robert Tucker (ed), *The Marx-Engels Reader* (Norton & Company 1978) 26 at p. 34 (emphasis in the original).

18 Marx (n 17) 42.

19 Ibid 42.

20 Sir Henry Summer Maine, *Ancient Law* (Henry Holt and Company London 1861) 151.

21 Knox (n 10) 310.

22 Quinn Slobodian, *Globalists: The End of Empire and the Birth of Neoliberalism* (HUP 2018) 2.

belief in the centrality of ideas, his starting point is the truth about how social processes come about. Only once such truth is established, law can be of benefit. At the core of this truth is the distinction between two types of orders (alternatively systems, structures or patterns). The two co-exist and integrate. Yet, each is different from the other and is governed by its own rule of law. What Hayek understood by the concept of 'order' is pertinent, since much flows from this understanding. Order is 'a state of affairs' in which multiple and various elements are so related to each other that acquaintance with only part of them suffices to form correct or likely to be correct 'expectations concerning the rest'.[23] In other words, an order is not necessarily deliberately made. Nor is it necessarily fully understood. Such is the self-generating structure of relationships that is society. It is governed by universal rules of just conduct. Just conduct refers to individual acts and practices deemed successful because they increased the chances of group survival. Society is produced by 'individual elements adapting themselves to circumstances'. It is thus born out of human action yet is not humanly designed. It involves no outside agency and has no purpose other than its own preservation or restoration. Its hallmarks are spontaneous self-growth and complexity of interactions.[24] The complexity may be such that 'no mind can comprehend them all'.[25] There is no knowable future. In the talk Hayek gave in 1974 when accepting the Nobel Memorial Prize in economics, he alluded to the *Limits to Growth*, a 1972 computer simulation of exponential economic and population growth in the face of finite and dwindling resources. Reminiscent of some present narratives, Hayek dismissed this report as a pretence of knowledge, an 'illegitimate argument made under the mantle of science'.[26] Thus, pivotal to Hayek's understanding of a true social order, and by extension functional law, is the limits of human capacity to grasp the totality of the many different and fluid ways by which the individual elements of society affect and influence each other as they change and adapt. Applying the metaphor of flying geese formations, their patterns may be predicted but not so a goose's individual behaviour.[27] Thus, cognizant of the limits of power that come with the limits of knowledge, like the farmer or gardener who cultivates his plants where he knows and can control some of the determining circumstances, 'the wise legislator will probably attempt to cultivate rather than to control the forces of the social process'.[28]

By contrast, the second order, the one where the legislator resides, is everything that the market/society is not. It is an artificial, directed and deliberate construct. It comprises concrete and preconceived man-made rules installed to serve a purpose known to their maker. This order is a powerful tool because it can be adapted to the wishes of its organisers. However, first, the scope of its operation is limited to a small number of concrete and particularised tasks such

23 Hayek (n 1) 36.
24 Ibid 41.
25 Ibid.
26 Slobodian (n 22) 225.
27 Ibid 228.
28 F. A. Hayek, 'Degrees of Explanation (1955)' in F. A. Hayek (ed), *Studies in Philosophy, Politics and Economics* (Routledge 1967) 19 cited in Slobodian (n 22) 226.

as preserving peace, keeping out the enemy, providing certain services and, crucially, enforcing the society/market's rules of just conduct. Second, the actions undertaken by its rule-making organisations are coordinated by the more comprehensive, spontaneous overall order into which they are integrated. Third, where these organisations intervene in the market beyond the execution of a finite number of undertakings, the result is authoritarian rule and the ascendency of vested interests rising on the tide of mobilised consent. All of which would prevent the adaptations required to maintain the prevailing standard of living. Thus, the government's role is to translate spontaneous rules into binding legislation so as to guarantee that no such interference takes place and individuals can engage with the market society freely. In the words of Hayek's fellow neoliberal, the jurist Ernst-Ulrich Petersmann, 'The common starting point of the neoliberal economic theory is the insight that in any well-functioning market economy the "invisible hand" of the market competition must by necessity be complemented by the "visible hand" of the law'.[29] Over 30 years earlier, in 1950, Nazi jurist Carl Schmitt articulated a somewhat similar idea when he proposed that there was not one world, but two. One was the world of nations which, borrowing from Roman legal terminology, he called the world of *imperium*. The other was *dominium* – the world of property.[30]

Many among the critics of neoliberalism view it as an instance of systemic degeneration. Words such as 'predatory' and 'unfettered' capitalism imply a distortion capable of reform. As seen previously, there is much in neoliberal ideology to suggest that, rather than a deviation, it voices and seeks to actualise as a true order what Marx understood to be the essential nature of capitalist social relations. This includes the separation between the political/communal sphere and the civil realm of itemised individuals. The former follows and guards the latter's ongoing journey of adjustments necessary for the reproduction of society's material basis, or in Hayek's words, standards of living. Hayek acknowledges that inequality and the sacrifice of some members of society are integral to his true and proper order. However, by now, the depth and spread of immiseration on the one hand and wealth concentration on the other are historically unprecedented. Moreover, insofar as the neoliberal mutation corresponds to the essential logic of capital, arguably, its transformation is unlikely beyond transitory 'all kinds of patchwork'. Social abuses cannot be eliminated 'without hurting capital and profit in the least'.[31] On this view, the answer lies in the fundamental reorganisation of society, its mode of production and the relations it gives rise to.

Features of capitalist law

The remainder of this section will look at three features of the law which flow from the capitalist/liberal order in which it is situated and which guided the shifts in the

29 Slobodian (n 22) 7.
30 Ibid 10.
31 Engels (n 4) 27.

legal treatment of the act of taking. They are adaptability, the drawing of boundaries and violence.

Adaptability

The function of the law is one of adaptation, Antonio Gramsci, Marxist theoretician and founder of the Italian communist party, observed from his prison cell. Through it, the 'civilization' and morality of the masses are being constructed and reconstructed so that they may correspond to the development of and changes in the economic structure and the class of people who preside over it.[32] Put in terms of classical Marxist theory of historical transformation, as the forces of production grow and the relation of production are recast, so does the superstructure – legal and otherwise. Through it, the recast relations of production are embedded in popular consciousness and made to appear normal and inevitable. This need for responsiveness to shifts in the material reality means that the law must be free 'from every absolute'.[33] If one is to read 'property rights' into 'relations of production' as do Jon Elster and others, then the changes to which the law must adjust track the way property is conceptualised and distributed.[34] In the context of the replacement of feudalism with capitalist social relations, the sea change was its liberation from political and societal associations and its vesting in the civil domain of the individual body and her labour. Thus, the abstraction of labour as private property so that it may be sold by its owner for a wage went hand in hand with the rise of market-mediated and exchange value-driven social relations.

In the third section later, the focus is on these changes as they unfolded in England and, thereafter, were transported to and imposed on colonised populations. However, the same applied to Germany of the 19th century. In an important moment in the development of German capitalism, legal instruments such as the Theft Act 1837 were introduced to formalise and legitimise the private expropriation of common land, hitherto 'executed without cover of appeal to legitimacy'.[35] Formerly lawful taking of forest products by the peasantry was mandated unlawful and the peasant was reimagined as a thief for doing that which she had been doing for centuries.[36] This adaptation engaged both the substance of the law and the procedure of its enforcement. In particular, public punishment was supplemented with private compensation payable to the forest's newly declared proprietor. The criminal was to be reformed through the '"improvement of the percentage of

32 Antonio Gramsci, *Selections from the Prison Notebooks* (Lawrence and Wishart 1971) 195, 242, 258.

33 Gramsci (n 32) 246.

34 Jon Elster, *An Introduction to Karl Marx* (CUP 1986) 106; Brian Leiter, 'Marx, Law, Ideology, Legal Positivism' (2015) 101 *Virginia Law Review* 1179 at 1180.

35 Peter Linebaugh, *Stop, Thief: The Commons, Enclosures and Resistance* (PM Press 2014) 56.

36 Linebaugh (n 35) 45.

profit" devolving to the forest owner'.[37] The young Marx referred to this instance of adjustment as one in which the immortality of the law was sacrificed and the idea of the state degraded.

Turning to Hayek, as we saw, the wise legislator confines herself to the cultivation and protection of the spontaneous interactions on which group survival depends. This self-generating order consists of 'perpetually shifting relationship of exposure to stimuli'. Therefore, it necessitates an ongoing flow of responses and adaptations.[38] Since legislation emanates from governments situated in the other, man-made order, it lends itself to purposely designed responses. It thus provides a powerful (if limited in scope) tool for converting voluntary social responses into binding rules known as laws under which citizens act. As such, laws 'constitute an adaptation of the whole of society to its environment and to the general characteristics of its members'.[39] In the face of differences in expectations and the inevitable dissatisfaction of some, experience determines the most expedient arrangement of contractual and property rights. In tandem with price signals, such legal arrangements transmit the information necessary to guarantee the preservation of the social order nationally and transnationally.

One such arrangement is the legal regime designed to protect foreign investors' property – tangible, intangible and abstracted as value. In this adaptation, discussed in more detail later, taking as a legal concept was transformed from a progressive act of improvement that is productive of property into a punishable transgression that is injurious to property. It clarified whose expectations and needs are to be satisfied and whose are to be sacrificed at the altar of Hayek's standards of living or Marx's endless accumulation of capital.

Boundaries

Another main preoccupation of liberal law is the drawing and enforcement of boundaries, both internal and external.

Boundaries are internal in the sense that they delineate the areas where the law may legitimately intervene and where it may not. Looming large among them is the line which separates individuals' private spheres from each other and from Marx's political community or Hayek's order of the organisation. At issue is the liberal concept of individual liberty which the law demarcates 'just as the boundary between two fields is marked by a stake'.[40] Hayek alludes to this function of the law as prevention of coercion, alternatively freedom under the rule of law. Coercion is understood as the forcing of one person to act in a manner that is willed by and serves the purpose of another. It comprises measures which interfere with 'legitimate expectations' (a terms which has made its way into the lexicon of foreign

37 Ibid 47.
38 Slobodian (n 22) 223.
39 F. A. Hayek, *The Constitution of Liberty* (Routledge 1960) 138.
40 Marx (n 17) 42.

investment protection), infringe rights and curb the ability to autonomously shape one's own sphere.[41] The drawing of this boundary is complex since its outcomes are unavoidably uneven and necessarily unequal. Fulfilment of some expectations entails the frustration of others. That which is a privilege to some is deprivation to others. In the face of this problematic, says Hayek, guidance is to be drawn from the law. Specifically, guidance is to be found in the laws governing property and contracts. These laws in their advanced form are founded on David Hume's 'three fundamental laws of nature . . . *stability of possession, of transference by consent and the performance of promises*'.[42] They are abstract and impersonal in the sense of being equally applicable to all and detached from their consequences. In this way, legal rules convey to the citizen the assurance of freedom.

The rules which delimit the individual and communal spheres extend to the ordering of both material objects and a range of rights. Their principal methodology is the disaggregation of the material environment and the rights attached to it into that which belongs to one and that which belongs to another. The private property produced in consequence and the protection afforded to it against intervention deemed improper constitute an essential condition not only of liberty but also of civilisation itself. 'A people averse to the institution of private property', Hayek wrote, 'is without the first element of freedom'. 'Nobody', he continued, 'is at liberty to attack several property and to say at the same time that he values civilization. The history of the two cannot be disentangled'.[43] This idea of property-as-civilisation is integral to liberal political philosophy and will be returned to later. For present purposes, it suffices to draw attention to the possibility, intimated by Hayek, that whilst a legal regime of private property purports to secure individual freedom, it simultaneously also curbs it. In particular, it inhibits the expectations, thoughts, speech and acts deemed disruptive to the sanctity of property. Those who oppose private property have no claim to civilisation. This argument was advanced, for instance, in the context of the debate about the abolition of the institution of chattel slavery.

The linkage between private property and civilisation brings us to the outer limits of liberal law or what we may call its external boundaries. The law's external boundaries separate law-based spaces inhabited by the 'civilised' from the non-law-based chaos inhabited by the 'savage'. As Blomley puts it: 'Law itself requires the construction of a constitutive outside with reference to, and against which, it sets itself apart'.[44] In the context of European colonial expansion, such constitutive outside was conceptualised in terms of absences, specifically the absence of a civilisation of property. Article 38(1)(c) of the Statute of the International Court

41 Hayek (n 39) 122, 123.

42 David Hume, *A Treatise of Human Nature* (New Ed Dover Publication Inc 2004) 374; cited in ibid 138.

43 Sir Henry Summer Maine, *Village Communities in the East and West* (Henry Holt and Company New York 1880) 230; cited in ibid 123.

44 Nicholas Blomley, 'Law, Property, and Geography of Violence: The Frontier, the Survey, and the Grid' (2003) 93(1) *The Annals of the Association of American Geographers* 121 at p. 123.

of Justice (ICJ) 1945 counts among the sources of international law (IL) 'general principles of law recognized by civilized nations'. The provision reflects the classical IL view that the equality attendant on admission into the family of nations was contingent on meeting a standard of civilisation. The standard turned on the protection extended to life, liberty and the property of aliens and the extent to which such protection adhered to the requirements of a rule of law as designed by the Europeans. This was underpinned by a civil–savage dichotomy pursuant to which European statehood was deemed uniquely civilised with the power and entitlement to draft the rules of admission.

This dichotomy served as handmaiden to a colonial project the savageries of which were in need of legitimisation. Genocidal taking of life and land were justified under the rubric of improvement and related private ownership, hallmarks of civilisational progress. The dead, expropriated and dispossessed were deemed savages lacking in capacity. By the 19th century, jurist James Lorimer divided humanity into three categories: first, the civilised Western state-organised societies with their commitment to the rule of law and the protection of personal liberties; second, the barbarous humanity which developed state formations, yet their governance fell short of European standards; third, savage humanity comprising simple people who lacked any semblance of organised rule. The latter were entitled only to humane treatment whereas the partially civilised qualified for partial recognition. Members of the first category had the right to dominate those of the second and colonise those of the third.[45] This taxonomy was grounded in concepts of natural law which continued to be applied to non-Europeans even after IL had transited to positivism. The language of natural law served to underscore the inferiority of the 'savage'. It also 'performed a leading role in helping to normatively coordinate and propagate logics of private property'.[46]

In the face of ongoing transformations and related need for continuous adaptations, legal boundaries may be kept vague. Vagueness may diminish certainty and predictability. Yet, it also assists in securing desired outcomes, circumventing undesired ones and, where necessary, facilitating expansion. According to Thompson, a consensus existed among 18th-century English lawmakers that the state's existential rationale was to safeguard property and its associated liberties. Against this backdrop, the 1723 Black Act dealing in offences against enclosed land 'was so loosely drafted that it became a spawning-ground for ever-extending legal judgements'.[47] In a more recent iteration, the broad language which typifies standards of

45 James Lorimer, *The Institute of the Law of Nations* (William Blackwood and Sons 1883); for a discussion of the standard of civilisation see for example Andrew Linklater, 'The Standard of Civilisation in World Politics' (2016) 5(2) *Human Figurations* <https://quod.lib.umich.edu/h/humfig/11217607.0005.205/-standard-of-civilisation-in-world-politics?rgn=main;view=fulltext> accessed 28 May 2019; Gustavo Gozzi, 'The Particularistic Universalism of International Law in the 19th Century' (2010) 52 *Harvard International Law Journal* 73.

46 Tarik Kochi, 'Dreams and Nightmares of Liberal International Law: Capitalist Accumulation, Natural Rights and State Hegemony' (2017) 28(1) *Law and Critique* 23.

47 Thompson (n 12) 1, 2.

treatment contained in international investment agreements (IIAs) is conducive to the production of a capacious jurisprudence. Tribunals are able to apply discretion and expansive interpretations to the construction of standards of customary IL.

Insofar as one accepts the proposition that the law can be a site of contestation, vagueness may also facilitate the unlocking of legal boundaries' emancipatory potential. Put in Hayekian terms, the creation of boundaries and their ongoing adjustments foster a continuous flow of losers and winners. Thus, boundaries incessantly produce new sites where frustrated expectations may morph into dissent. Consequently, violence is needed to maintain order and stability in the face of challenges by the newly excluded and marginalised. It was the legal violence visited on the peasantry as part of 19th-century Germany's transition to capitalism that triggered young Marx's interest first in economics and then in socialism.

Violence

To the liberally minded, the suggestion of proximity between violence and the law seems counterintuitive. Liberal narratives posit violence and the law as antithetical. Violence is pictured as located in an uncivilised wilderness which lies beyond the law. The rule of law is said to move human society in the direction of freedom and equality, away from oppression and the tyranny of status and privilege. This understanding persists despite the prevalence of legal concepts such as enforcement and punishment and despite the recurrent representations of violence as legally sanctioned in Western political and juridical thought. The word 'enforcement', pointed out Algerian-born French philosopher Jacque Derrida, contains within it the possibility of the use of force. For John Locke, hailed as the father of liberalism, an essential condition of political power is the law's prerogative to impose the death penalty. Legal philosopher John Austin viewed legal rules as sovereign commands backed by credible threats of punishment. Together they form a relationship of power and obedience in which morality is sidelined. In the context of 17th-century debates, natural rights were conceptualised as comprising also obligations and punishment. Indeed, awareness of punishment for unlawful acts was said to separate the human from non-human forms of life. In the words of John Selden, an English follower of Hugo Grotius, the Dutch jurist associated with the founding of IL: 'The idea of a law carrying obligations irrespective of any punishment annexed to the violation of it . . . is no more comprehensible to the human mind than the idea of a father without a child'.[48] For Hobbes, punishment was essentially natural. The pain it induces is integral to the chain of consequences triggered by human action when undertaken in breach of the laws of nature. For Grotius, punishment was not only innately human, but also a matter of justice. 'The powers of Mercy must be limited', he opined when commenting on rebellion against European conquests, so

48 Cited in Talal Asad, *Formations of the Secular: Christianity, Islam, Modernity* (Stanford University Press 2003) 131.

'that her actions may be just; and when wickedness becomes excessive, punishment as it were unavoidably arises out of justice'.[49]

Accepting that law shares a common space with violence opens the door to the possibility of tracking the multifaceted forms it may take. It may be literal, or it may be latent, comprising 'imaginings and threats of force, disorder and pain'.[50] It may manifest itself in action or in discourse aimed at persuasion and the manufacturing of consent. Its interface with the law flows in two directions: on the one hand, violence enables the relocation of legal boundaries and the restoration or preservation of order and stability in the face of disruptions. On the other hand, violence itself needs the legitimacy which the law can best provide.

Walter Benjamin's observation regarding the interface between means and ends extends also to the role violence plays in the making and preservation of legal orders. It is a fundamental dogma of jurisprudence common to both natural and positivist law, says Benjamin, that 'just ends can be attained by justified means, justified means used for just ends'.[51] Violence is legitimate when it is exercised for a legitimate purpose. Benjamin objects to this dogma, *inter alia*, because it does not allow for a critique of violence. Any critique would necessarily be confined to the purpose for which it is employed. On his analysis, the relationship between law and violence has two characteristics. First, it is the means by which law or a new legal order is instituted and preserved. Second, domination is the aim of all law-making. 'Law-making is power-making, assumption of power, and to that extent an immediate manifestation of violence'.[52] With regard to the first characteristic, Benjamin distinguished between law-making and law-preserving violence. The distinction, though, is not absolute and in some instances (e.g. policing) may be suspended. Nor is each category sequestered. Rather, law-making and law-preserving bleed into each other. The former is typically situated outside a legal order; it is extra-legal. The validity of the just ends which are its justification does not depend on a system of positive law. Just ends are self-standing and have no need for the cover of law-based legitimacy. It is when victory is attained and a peace ceremony held that a new, historically acknowledged law is constituted and law-making violence morphs into a law-preserving one. Thus, the peace ceremony between the victor and the vanquished is an instance of domination inherent in all law-making: violence in the name of power is exercised under the guise of equality before the law. The primacy of obedience now takes over and the main aim is to 'divest the individual, at least as a legal subject, of all violence, even that directed only to natural ends'.[53]

49 Cited in Domenico Losurdo, *Liberalism: A Counter-History* (Verso 2011) 22–3.

50 Austin Sarat and Thomas R. Kearns, 'Introduction' in Austin Sarat and Thomas R. Kearn (eds), *Law's Violence* (University of Michigan Press 1992) 1–23.

51 Benjamin (n 3) 278.

52 Ibid 295.

53 Ibid 283; see also Onur Ulas Ince, 'Between Equal Rights: Primitive Accumulation and Capital's Violence' (2018) 14(6) *Political Theory* 885 at 900. <SSRN: https://ssrn.com/abstract=2971324 or http://dx.doi.org/10.2139/ssrn.2971324> accessed 23 February 2022.

My narration of the act of taking begins in England at a time when the appropriation of common land was unlawful but nevertheless legitimated. Private commercial interests conceptualised as progress, improvement, efficiency and public interest provided the necessary just ends. They served to warrant the violence which accompanied a profound social transformation involving loss of rights, deprivation of the means of subsistence, the obliteration of ancient legitimacy, large-scale killings and a novel understanding of property. It was when the boundary between victors and vanquished, winners and losers acquired sufficient material permanence that Parliament turned to the task of using law-making to endorse newly constituted boundaries. In an act of domination undertaken under the guise of equal rights – 'rich and poor are equally forbidden to spend the night under the bridges' – a new juridical order was installed. This pattern was then exported to Scotland and Ireland, England's first colony. It continues till today, for example, in the ongoing plunder of the commons (aka privatisations). First, a reality of inefficiency, backwardness and dissatisfaction is constructed, legitimised and propagated through defunding policies and narratives which fetishise individual choices and market forces as fountains of progress and freedom. The plunder then attains permanence through law-making. This time law-making includes an 'invitation to foreign capital to colonize' the former commons and have them incorporated into a globalised legal order. A mesh of domestic and treaty laws guarantee subordination and protect against attempts at reversal.[54]

Conclusion

This section offered a theoretical prelude to the enquiry into the act of taking by reference to both the neoliberal worldview about what capitalist social relations should be and the Marxist analysis of what they are. In both instances it is accepted that these relations are mediated by the law in one way or another. The law, in fulfilment of this role, must be light on its feet. It must be alert to the changes which animate the material base and the forces and relations of production. Boundaries are erected with sufficient vagueness to facilitate their redrawing and violence in its different manifestations forms part of its *modus operandi*. Its rule is backed by claims to objectivity, impartiality and equality. Yet, on the neoliberals' own case, its application necessarily produces winners and losers. This inequality is said to be justified by the fact that the law is impersonal. It merely adheres to contractual and property principles which best serve societal order and survival. The premise of equality and impartiality means that no account is taken of class structures and power differentials. This theme is developed in the next section which looks into the meanings of taking; in particular, its conception in the legal regime of foreign investment protection.

54 Guy Standing, *Plunder of the Commons: A Manifesto for Sharing Public Wealth* (Pelican Books 2019) x.

3 Perspectives of taking

Introduction

The 'act of taking' is treated here as an umbrella concept covering a range of protagonists and their interactions. Examples of terms used include nationalisation, appropriation, expropriation, confiscation, exploitation, dispossession, theft, grabbing, extractivism and, at least on some views, taxation. The meaning ascribed to each of these terms may be shaped by their context, such as the discipline within which the word was formed, the worldview it seeks to express as well as its historical and cultural provenance. In what follows, a sample of this family of concepts is briefly explored through a socioeconomic lens. This is followed by an enquiry into its use as a legal category in the regime of foreign investment protection. The aim is to illustrate the diversity of meanings associated with the act of taking when used as a tool of social criticism, set against the narrowness of its legal parameters. When used as a tool of social criticism, it tends to implicate multiple actors and objects of taking. When used as a legal category, it is collapsed into a single taker – the state in the exercise of its legislative, regulatory and *eminent domain* powers. The sole object of protection is private property configured as foreign investment. Taking as a legal category is confined to internationally proscribed state conduct and the pecuniary redress available to investors. These confines remain constant. Yet, within them, the scope of state responsibility and the reach of investors' protection mutate and expand. A side effect of this elasticity is its impact on established legal principles. Juridical constraints and treaty limits are all too often swept away by the force of ambiguous norms, arbitral discretion, power structures and ideological compulsions.

Taking as a socio-political concept

The Historian Peter Linebaugh depicts expropriation as the primary gate through which capitalism enters to take its place at the table of human history. Its hallmark is the violence of primary (alternatively, 'primitive' or 'original') accumulation. Primary accumulation refers to the forcible detachment of people from the means of subsistence through the enclosure or privatisation of resources previously held in common. It is the process through which the reservoir of capital and labour is

DOI: 10.4324/9781315386782-5

first created. 'The violence of primary accumulation is a history of expropriation', writes Linebaugh.[1] It leads to the formation of two mutually dependent classes. They are located on either side of a poll of exploitation through which each produces and reproduces the other. On one side is the wage earner who has lost her direct access to the means of survival. Consequently, she has no option but to sell her labour piecemeal to survive. On the other side is the capitalist whose capital self-valorises through the appropriation of the wage earner's unpaid-for portion of labour. Thus, says Linebaugh, it is necessary for the gate of expropriation to first open for those of exploitation to follow. Expropriation and exploitation are co-constitutive. 'Expropriation not only prepares the ground so to speak, it intensifies exploitation'. Tools and land are taken from the commons and transformed into tradeable commodities. They become what Marx termed constant capital. Constant capital then interacts with waged labour (variable capital) in a dynamic of exploitation.[2]

On this view, expropriation represents moments of violent taking, of forcible dispossession and dislocation. In his 'Between Equal Rights', Ince talks about extra-legal, or what he terms 'capital positing', violence employed to expropriate productive assets and conscript them to the service of an emerging or expanding capitalist order. In these moments, the conditions for exploitation are produced and reproduced and, in Polanyi's words, one's habitation in the world is transmuted into fluid and interchangeable wealth.[3] Thus, expropriation is located in the political terrain. It is the storm which produces private property. Exploitation on the other hand is embedded in economic relations. It is the ensuing façade of orderly calm which enables peaceful accumulation.[4] However, argues Ince, in mature, globalised capitalism the difference between the two has become blurred. Accumulation 'takes place as much through predatory strategies of expropriation and appropriation as through (or even instead of) investment in productive capacity and employment of labor'.[5]

Philosopher and political scientist Nancy Fraser offers her own perspective of the expropriation-appropriation-exploitation triad. She supplements what she calls Marx's two-tiered model of appropriation and exploitation with a layer of ongoing moments of expropriation. Expropriation is not limited to primary accumulation. Rather, it is continuous, broader and racialised. It is differentiated by the manner in which capacities and resources are taken and the discreet characteristic of the

1 Peter Linebaugh, *Stop, Thief: The Commons, Enclosures and Resistance* (PM Press 2014) 68.

2 Linebaugh (n 1) 73, 77 and 82 respectively; Linebaugh identifies in Marx's writings four gates of exploitation of labour being the extension of the working day, the division of labourers, the mechanisation of work and the composition of reproduction.

3 Onur Ulas Ince, 'Bringing the Economy In: Hannah Arendt, Karl Marx and the Politics of Capitalism' (2016) 78(2) *The Journal of Politics* 411 and at 415.

4 Ince (n 3) 415.

5 Onur Ulas Ince, 'Between Equal Rights: Primitive Accumulation and Capital's Violence' 14 (2018) 16 *Political Theory* 885 at 900. <SSRN: https://ssrn.com/abstract=2971324 or http://dx.doi.org/10.2139/ssrn.2971324> accessed 23 February 2022.

group produced in consequence. Central to this distinction is the fact that exploitation of the expropriated is not mediated by an employment/wage contract. The expropriated, having been reduced to the status of lesser beings, are deemed to be devoid of a separate legal personality and thus the capacity to enter into contractual relationships. They are manifestly dependent and unfree. Conversely, the merely exploited are at least formally free. Domination over them is mediated by an employment/wage contract. They are the lucky ones. They enjoy the status of citizens-workers and possess the independent legal personality necessary for them to enter into a contractual relationship for the sale of their labour.

Expropriation, argues Fraser, is particularly important in times of crisis. It functions to suppress the cost of labour with the aim of reaching zero. Both appropriation and expropriation involve exploitation in the sense that surplus value created by labour is transferred to capital. However, in the case of expropriation, this is achieved through brute confiscation from which both the option of negotiations and the pretence of freedom are absent. Confiscation may be blatant, as in the case of slavery and child labour, or 'may be cloaked by a veil of commerce' as in the case of predatory loans.[6] It is associated with practices of early capitalism such as colonial conquests, enclosures and chattel slavery, as well as contemporary ones such as corporate land grabs, dispossession by debt and prison labour. Fraser joins Linebaugh in positing expropriation and exploitation as co-constitutive: 'The subjugation of those whom capital expropriates is a hidden condition of possibility for the freedom of those whom it exploits'. Expropriation makes visible 'the violence and theft concealed behind the orderly façade of contractual relations and market exchange'.[7] Together, the two form a harmoniously calibrated nexus of capitalist expansion, with the boundaries between them becoming increasingly hazy as transnational capital homogenises the post-colonial world.

Sociologist William Robinson explains this haziness and blurring of the lines by reference to the ongoing process of capitalist restructuring and the formation of a new, globalised capital-labour relationship. He points to a number of transformations which have recast the power balance in this relationship in favour of capital. One is the digitalisation of the economy and the Fourth Industrial Revolution, being a technology-based response to the crisis of the 1980s. Digitalisation and the new modalities of accumulation it enabled were accompanied by the fragmentation and emasculation of organised labour. First-generation digital technologies allowed capital to create globally integrated production and finance sectors with flexibility as their signature management technique. Flexible management methods (e.g. subcontracting, outsourcing and the general disintegration of vertical production) called for flexible terms of employment. Flexible employment did not necessarily dispense with contracts of employment. However, it subverted the measure

6 Nancy Fraser, 'Expropriation and Exploitation in Racialised Capitalism: A Reply to Michael Dawson' (2016) 3(1) *Critical Historical Studies* 163; see also George Yancy, *On Race: 34 Conversations in a Time of Crisis* (OUP 2017) 155–66.

7 Fraser (n 6) 166, 168.

of protection and empowerment which they had offered and which had set Fraser's exploited apart from the expropriated. The exploited, having been reduced to the status of precariat labouring casually, part-time, piecemeal and on-call pursuant to zero hours contracts, were transformed into the super exploited, 'a subcontracted component rather than a fixture internal to employer organisations'.[8] They are consumers-in-the-making of the predatory loans by which capital has commodified their poverty and transformed it into a new zone of accumulation.

If first-generation digital technologies brought the exploited and expropriated closer together, second-generation digital technologies promise to conflate them. Nike Corporation summed it up as 'engineering labour out of the Product'.[9] Even precarious jobs are being swept away by cheaper automated tools, robots of growing sophistication, artificial intelligence and the internet of things. From construction and agricultural workers to those labouring in medicine, education and the law, all are at risk of tumbling into the ranks of the expropriated. They may even become 'surplus humanity'. Following Liza Elliott's dystopian book *Everything Is Known*,[10] Robinson defines surplus humanity as the discarded people, the cast-off who survive on the unsellable excesses of opulence. They are the millions who have been expelled from formal employment to congregate in the informal economy. There, some work in marginal, insecure jobs. Others scrounge for scraps among the leftovers.[11] Hoogvelt calls this new social architecture peripheralisation. It signifies a transition from post-colonial politics of incorporation to the politics of exclusion. Those who lack the requisite specialised knowledge and technology are ejected. Saskia Sassen similarly observes a social design of expulsions. Ever greater segments of the world population are being expelled from the process of capitalist globalisation.[12] Expulsions take on diverse forms and are represented by a range of processes and conditions. Yet, they all share a single feature: they are acute, particularly when measured by the scale of displacement they produce.[13] They form part of a downwards trajectory in which multifaceted forms of taking – dispossession, appropriation, exploitation and expropriation – elide North-South distinction. As in the case of German and English enclosures, criminalisation and a mushrooming penal system operate as a method of social control.[14]

8 William I. Robinson, *The Global Police State* (Pluto Press 2020) 43; see also Guy Standing, *The Precariat: A New Dangerous Class* (Bloomsbury Academic 2014). Unlike Standing, Robinson argues that the precariat forms part of the working class rather than a new, separate class.

9 Robinson (n 8) 60.

10 Liza Elliott, *Everything Is Known: The Straight Shooter of the World* (Liza Elliott/E. Elliott Studio 2018).

11 Ibid 1.

12 Ankie Hoogvelt, *Globalization and the Postcolonial World: The New Political Economy of Development* (2nd edn, Palgrave Macmillan 2001) 67, 128–31; Saskia Sassen, *Expulsions: Brutality and Complexity in the Global Economy* (The Belknap Press of HUP 2014).

13 Sassen (n 12) 3–4.

14 Robinson (n 8) 48–8, 50, 68–9.

In post-colonial theory, the term appropriation denotes the acts by which post-colonial societies take over concepts of imperial culture, including its ways of thinking.[15] The usurped concepts are then adapted and used to articulate the appropriators' own cultural and social identity. Once adapted, they are redeployed to challenge the dominant imperial discourse and resist control. Robert Nichols counts among them the concepts of dispossession, expropriation and *eminent domain*. These three terms – commonly understood as acts involving forcible taking of private property by a state or its agents – boast rich and varied history. As juridical categories they featured prominently in Roman law. As tools of social criticism, they were used to challenge feudal land tenure and landed aristocracy in Europe of the 18th and 19th centuries. They were also to be found in the debates between Marx and anarchists about the intrinsic nature of property. More recently, they resurfaced in theorisations such as the one by Nancy Fraser discussed earlier.[16] However, argues Nichols, their force as tools of social criticism is undermined by the fact that dispossession and expropriation are at heart conservative concepts. They derive their meaning and moral force from a recognition that first, a generally accepted model of proprietary relations actually exists, and second, this model has been violated. Consequently, even radical examinations tend 'to reinforce the very proprietary models of social relations that these critical traditions generally seek to undermine'.[17] Nichols draws on the reworking of the concepts of dispossession and expropriation by indigenous scholars and activists – particularly in Anglophone settler societies – to re-conceptualise dispossession as a historical process. It is associated with colonialism and refers to the spread of liberal/capitalist models of private property to non-European societies. This process preceded rather than presupposed the existence of property. Further and uniquely, it actively produced property. The dispossessed became the original owners only retrospectively, when viewed backwards so to speak. The 'term therefore names not only the forcible *transfer* of property but *transformation* into property' and its actualisation 'under structural conditions which require its simultaneous negation'.[18] The concept of 'simultaneous negation' brings together the juridical and social aspects of the dispossessive process. Property rights were being negated by the surrounding social environment. In the societal sphere on the other side of the legal boundary, the savage 'other' was constructed as incapable of forming a proprietary relationship

15 Bill Ashcroft, Gareth Griffiths, and Helen Tiffin, *Post-Colonial Studies: The Key Concepts* (2nd edn, Routledge 2007) 15.

16 See for example Etienne Balibar, 'The Reversal of Possessive Individualism' in Etienne Balibar (ed), *Equaliberty: Political Essays* (Duke University Press 2014) 67–98; Judith Butler and Athena Athanasiou, *Dispossession: The Performative in the Political* (Polity 2013); David Harvey, *The New Imperialism* (OUP 2003); Edward Said, *The Politics of Dispossession: The Struggle for Palestinian Self-Determination 1969–1994* (Random House 1994); G. A. Cohen, *Self-Ownership, Freedom and Equality* (CUP 1995).

17 Robert Nichols, 'Theft Is Property! The Recursive Logic of Dispossession' (2018) 1(46) *Political Theory* at p. 9.

18 Nichols (n 17) 5, 14.

with that which she possessed and used. It is this which rendered colonial taking 'a unique species of theft for which we do not always have adequate language'.[19]

Arnulf Becker Lorca observes a dynamic of intertwined appropriation and indigenisation in the spread of international law (IL). Non-European jurists who came to the continent during the second half of the 19th century accepted its legally prescribed standard of civilisation as a minimum requirement for joining the family of nations. Yet, they also adapted the appropriated legal principles to articulate their own national needs, cultural heritage and the specificities of their juridical regimes. By the end of the century, this dual process also produced the occasional challenge.[20] Sophia Sabrow points to a contemporary reiteration of this dynamic among post-colonial peripheral states. This time the pull is conceptualised as between adaptation and differentiation. Against the backdrop of power inequality, a potentially harmonious process of mutual enrichment has become a self-contradictory 'dilemma of the marginalised'. Peripheral states find themselves needing to navigate a path between two competing narratives. One dictates that international/transnational norms must be mimicked if the legitimacy which goes with compliance is to be attained. Implementation, though, may prove problematic when strategies for the imposition of an alien 'standard of civilisation' fail to overcome or encounter resistance from extant local structures. In turn, failure to implement perpetuates inequality. Conversely, peripheral states may react to their inequality by challenging the purported universalism of Western standards and, instead, reinforce their own particularities. However, rejection of the compulsion to appropriate the identity of others equally reduces legitimacy. In addition, it has tangible repercussions, such as deprivation of access to international aid.[21]

Moving on to extractivism, the term refers to the act of taking associated with international trade and investment and narrated from the perspective of Global South ancillary economies. Alberto Acosta, Ecuadorian economist and former minister of energy and mines, defined it as a mode of accumulation and incorporation into globalised circuits of capital that is centred on the extraction of natural resources.[22] Large quantities of unprocessed or partially processed resources are

19 Ibid 14; for a view of the colonies as a site in which the imposition of property law on population with no pre-existing notions of ownership of land informed the development of modern property law in England and its racialised nature see Brenna Bhandar, 'Title by Registration: Instituting Modern Property Law and Creating Racial Value in the Settler Colony' (2015) 2(42) *Journal of Law and Society* 253.

20 Arnulf Becker Lorca, 'Universal International Law: Nineteenth Century Histories of Imposition, Appropriation and Circulation' (2010) 51 *Harvard International Law Journal* 475.

21 Sophia Sabrow, 'Peripheral States and Conformity to International Norms: The Dilemma of the Marginalised' (2020) 41(2) *Third World Quarterly* 187.

22 The term 'circuits of capital accumulation' refers to 'the process by which the production of a good or a service is first planned and financed (by capitalists), followed by attaining and then mixing together the component parts (labour, land, raw materials, buildings and machinery, etc.) in production sequences, and then by the marketing of the final product. At the end of this process the capitalist recovers his initial capital outlay as well as profit and has thus "accumulated" capital'. Robinson (n 8) 10.

removed from poor, peripheral regions of the world where they are found and transported for consumption in centres of wealth. As Acosta puts it: 'The former export Nature, the latter import it'.[23] This export-import process necessitates collaboration between multinational enterprises ('MNEs') and the state. Alternatively, the state is captured by MNEs. Extractivism produces poverty, particularly in economies which depend on the extraction and exportation of primary commodities. Countries rich in resources are mostly poor in every other economic way. This perverse state of affairs is known 'in the specialist literature as "the paradox of plenty" or "the resource curse"'.[24] The words are nevertheless misleading. There is nothing natural, unavoidable or mystical about the proximity between natural wealth and human poverty. It is entirely man-made, the outcome of excessive extraction and seizing of the wealth created through it. It is both political and systemic.

Extractivism as a political and systemic phenomenon is situated on a continuum of colonial and imperial structures of 'appropriation and plunder' which extend to both nature and the communities which inhabit it.[25] As to nature, because the rate of extraction exceeds the rate of regeneration, renewable resources such as forests and the soil are transformed into non-renewable ones.[26] As to human communities, extractivism in its contemporary form is associated with state violence, dispossession, societal dislocation, distortion of local economies, recurrent economic crises and rent-seeking. Acosta observes its more recent evolvement into what he terms 'neoextractivism'. Progressive governments in South America have made important changes to the extractivist model through the imposition of greater state control. A larger proportion of the surplus value created was taken and used to finance large and significant social programs. However, the extractivist model remained at the core of the country's developmental model. Ownership has become public, but there was little change to the rules and methodologies of the productive processes. In this Acosta appears to side with Wood. At least in South America, transfer of ownership to the state did not alter the essentially capitalist nature of the extractivist model. Competitiveness and profit maximisation remained the rules of the game. Contemporary neoextractivism, in line with its colonial and imperialist heritage, continues to maintain the subordinate position of the site of extraction in worldwide, now globalised, supply chains.[27]

The term 'neoextractivism' is also used to denote an era in which technological advances necessitate intensification of mining. Transnational capital's mode of accumulation 'is based on the overexploitation of natural resources' and the

23 Alberto Acosta, 'Extractivism and Neoextractivism: Two Sides of the Same Curse' in M. Lang and D. Mokrani (eds), *Beyond Development: Alternative Visions from Latin America; Permanent Working Group on Alternatives to Development* (Foundation Rosa Luxemburg, Transnational Institute 2013) 62 <https://www.tni.org/files/download/beyonddevelopment_extractivism.pdf> accessed 21 March 2022.

24 Ibid 61.

25 Ibid 63.

26 Ibid 62.

27 Ibid 72.

expansion of the 'frontiers of extractivism' into new territories. According to the United Nations Economic Commission for Latin America and the Caribbean (UNECLAC), exportation of minerals from this region went up from 289m tons in 2002 to 443m tons in 2008 to 600m tons in 2017.[28] So-called clean energy is expected to accelerate this expansion. The International Energy Agency (IEA) estimates that an offshore wind plant requires around 12 times more minerals than an equivalent gas plant. Supply of lithium, nickel, cobalt, silicone and other key minerals will need to quadruple over the next two decades if the Paris Agreement's warming target of below 2°C is to be achieved. It will have to expand six-fold to reach net-zero carbon emissions globally by 2050 and is likely to necessitate mining of the oceans' seabed.[29] Supply of cobalt alone is expected to increase by 44%. In the Republic of Congo where some 80% of the world supply of cobalt is mined, men, children and women slave in perilous conditions with stunted development and foetus deformities among the effects of labour in a quarry. Paradoxically, therefore, the technology-based response to the climate emergency exacerbates exploitation and extractivism. Once again, the Global South is made to pay the cost of (environmental) improvement in the Global North (or the pretence thereof). Marx conceptualised this manner of exploitation as the expropriation of nature to be distinguished from its appropriation. Whereas the free appropriation of nature is the starting point of production and therefore of property and human societies, expropriation is specific to capitalism. Capitalist taking from nature is expropriatory because it is undertaken without exchange or reciprocity and without the opportunity for recovery and renewal.[30]

For Ye, Shanin et al. extractivism's main methodology and principal actors are unequal exchanges and imperial networks (MNEs) respectively. 'Drainage' is its essential feature. Drainage refers to the appropriation and transfer of value that is either in a dormant form – e.g. in the subsoil – or has already been produced by others. In other words, no truly new value is created. Rather, the world is scanned 'for already existing, but still "hidden" wealth' which is then exploited until it is no more.[31] The presence of 'hidden' value and its drainage via worldwide, monopolised supply chains feature also in Donald Clelland's concept of 'dark value'. Dark value refers to the expropriated surplus value created by invisible energy. It comprises and is measured by concealed costs such as the unrecorded true cost of cheap labour and ecological externalities. It is carried by 'hidden un(der) costed' flows which journey from places of extraction to places of accumulation. In the course

28 Aldo Orellana López, 'Neoextractivism and State Violence: Defending the Defenders in Latin America' in *State of Power 2021: Coercive World* (Transnational Institute) <https://www.tni.org/en/publication/state-of-power-2021> accessed 28 May 2021.

29 IEA, 'The Role of Critical Minerals in Clean Energy Transitions' May 2021 <https://iea.blob.core.windows.net/assets/24d5dfbb-a77a-4647-abcc-667867207f74/TheRoleofCriticalMineralsinCleanEnergyTransitions.pdf> accessed 28 May 2021.

30 John Bellamy Foster, 'Marx, Value and Nature' (*Monthly Review*, July 2018) <https://monthlyreview.org/2018/07/01/marx-value-and-nature/> accessed 22 Sep 2018.

31 Ye, Shanin et al., (n 24) 6.

of this journey, they pass through and are captured at the many nodes of unequal exchanges and degrees of monopoly which make up the globalised supply chains of commodities. The direction of their travel is from the submerged and unseen part of the capitalist iceberg to its above-the-surface structure. There, having been monetised as profit, dark value turns bright and visible.[32]

With the rise and spread of the so-called knowledge or intelligence economy, extractivism is also used to describe the digital mining of the human mind by tech oligopolies on a quest for data. Data extractivism engages Acosta's focus on the appropriation of primary resources in order to extract the value hidden therein. It renders existing but yet to be commodified information 'just as invaluable a resource as land for the creation of goods and services'.[33] This resource, however, is to be found wherever humanity is located, highlighting the trajectory observed by Fraser, Sassen and others towards globally homogenised sites and types of taking. Data extractivism also encompasses Ye, Shanin et al.'s concept of drainage whereby existing but as yet dormant value is being captured by MNEs in their role as extractivism's main protagonists. Gurumurthy and Chami view the extraction of data from social exchanges as a platform-based iteration of Marx's original accumulation.[34] In an instance of contemporary enclosure, people are being dispossessed of the information they produced through their interactions in the digital commons. Information is then turned into data-capital owned by the corporate expropriator. From that moment on, the now dispossessed producer of this data is disenfranchised. She has no claim to the profits she was instrumental in creating or a say in the way her information is accumulated, managed and exploited. She is deemed to have consented to this bargain by accepting non-negotiable terms and conditions.

Finally, with regard to taxation, its understanding as a coercive act of taking, tantamount to the deprivation of freedom, may be traced to the 17th century. John Locke's innovation of property rights as embedded in the proprietary relationship with one's own body has facilitated their recasting as integral to the concept of individual liberty. Property-as-liberty must be guarded against restrictions and external interference such as taxation. Montesquieu, a lawyer and an Enlightenment political philosopher, likened the taxing of property to despotism.[35] Among contemporary philosophers, Nozick's entitlement theory posits that the imposition of taxes gravely takes away liberty. Such act of taking may be justified only insofar as it is undertaken for the protection of personal and property rights. Distribution that is not founded on consent represents coercion. In a departure from the classical

32 Donald A. Clelland, 'The Core of the Apple: Degrees of Monopoly and Dark Value in Global Commodities Chains' (2014) 20(1) *Journal of World-Systems Research* 82.

33 Anita Gurumurthy and Nandini Chami, 'The Intelligent Corporation: Data and the Digital Economy' in Nick Buxton (ed), *State of Power 2020: The Corporation* (Transnational Institution 2020) 15. Commodification refers to the process of transforming people, that which they make and Nature into privately owned, monetised and alienable things.

34 Ibid 14.

35 Domenico Losurdo, *Hegel and the Freedom of Moderns* (Duke University Press 2004) 80.

liberals' notion of self-ownership, it ignores the 'separateness of persons', violates their absolute rights to their body and infringes their liberty.[36] Taxing income, says Nozick, 'is on a par with forced labour. Taxation makes other people part owners of you'.[37] For Friedrich Hayek, theorist of neoliberalism, the recognition of private property is an essential condition for the prevention of coercion. Given that people of independent means play an 'indispensable role in civilized society', attacking private property (e.g. by taxing it) is tantamount to attacking civilization itself.[38] Moreover, progressive taxation only serves to perpetuate existing inequality since it takes newly-made fortunes out of private hands, thereby making their acquisition less possible. The less possible the acquisition of new fortune becomes, 'the more must the existing fortunes appear as privileges for which there is no justification'.[39]

In the 20th and 21st centuries, the shielding of capitalist civilisation from acts of taking which interfere with its hallmark of private property rights may be said to have found its strongest expression in the foreign investment protection regime and its investor-state dispute settlement mechanism (ISDS), to which I now turn my attention.

Taking as a legal concept: conflation and expansion

The contours of protection

The foundation on which the juridical regime of investors' protection rests is the IL doctrine of state responsibility. Rules of state responsibility prescribe international standards for the treatment of aliens and create state liability for the injurious consequences which flow from a breach of an international obligation. Largely derived from US practice in the context of its relations with Latin America, the doctrine purports to universalise Western principles of civility said to constitute an international minimum standard (IMS). The effect is to marginalise municipal laws insofar as they depart from the IMS when applied to aliens. Rules of state responsibility and their outgrowth in the form of an investment protection conjure up colonial extraterritoriality adapted to the realities of a post-colonial, globalised 'empire of capital'.[40] In the empire of capital, military coercion – formally outlawed under Article 2(4) of the UN charter 1945 – has become subsidiary to the more covert and cheaper to administer ecopolitical and juridical penetration, as well as outright economic wars.[41]

36 Jonathan Wolfe, *Robert Nozick: Property, Justice and the Minimal State* (Polity Press 1996) 7–8, 11–12, 88–92; for an examination of Nozick's theory on taxation see, for example, G. A. Cohen, *Self-Ownership Freedom and Equality* (CUP 1995) 53–55, 216–21.

37 Ibid 91.

38 F. A. Hayek, *The Constitution of Liberty* (Routledge 1960) 109; for Hayek's discussion.

39 Ibid 278–79; for more about taxation see 268–81.

40 For 'empire of capital' see Ellen Meiksins Wood, *Empire of Capital* (Verso 2003).

41 See for example David Chandler, *Empire in Denial: The Politics of State-Building* (Pluto Press 2006).

Formally, IIAs are entered into pursuant to sovereign consent freely and autonomously exercised. In reality, once the surrounding circumstances and the different ways in which power is exercised are factored in, freedom, autonomy and independent decision-making become at best equivocal. One example of such surrounding circumstances is the discourse which predicates development on a promised land of economic growth. It posits the opening up of a country to flows of transnational capital as this land's sole, inevitable and inescapable point of entry. Notwithstanding the formal prohibition under the UN charter, in the face of resistance, discourse may be aided by the use of force or a threat thereof. Further, the negotiations and conclusion of IIAs may mirror interstate power hierarchies. All too often, peripheral states are compelled to sign core states' model bilateral investment treaties (BITs). In addition, transnational governance organisations such as the World Bank Group may make finance and political risk insurance conditional on the state entering into an investment treaty. Customary IL is unclear about what constitutes economic duress and, by extension, whether such conditionalities are capable of invalidating a treaty.[42] Despite Global South states' opposition, non-military coercion as a ground for voiding a treaty has been excluded from the express wording of Article 52 of the Vienna Convention on the Law of Treaties 1969 (VCLT). Corten argues that, nevertheless, Article 52 on its broader interpretation does extend to economic and political compulsions.[43] Antonios Tzanakopoulos disagrees. He concludes that the internationally protected sphere of states' sovereign freedom contains no positive, objectively definable and irreducible right to be free from economic coercion.[44]

Either way, the rooting of foreign investment protection in principles of state responsibility injects into this matrix of discourse, governance and power structures the justificatory force of customary IL. In turn, in ebb and flow of expansion, the protection regime widens the scope of impugned state conduct. It inflates the range of situations capable of giving rise to a cause of action and the mouth-watering pecuniary remedies which go with it. Expansion is facilitated by vague drafting and adjudicative discretion. It is further aided by the lack of clarity as to how treaty law and the general norms of customary IL interface. Consequently and paradoxically, 'excessive emphasis on treaty law as a *lex specialis* may be subtly eroding the room for customary law investment regulation and, thereby, the legitimate expression of sovereignty'.[45] In other words, on the one hand customary IL

42 On the lack of clarity see for example Barry E. Carter, 'Economic Duress' in Max Planck (ed), *Encyclopedia of International Law* (MPEPIL 2009) <https://opil.ouplaw.com/view/10.1093/law:epil/9780199231690/law-9780199231690-e1518> accessed 12 March 2021; Charles E. Partridge, 'Political and Economic Coercion: Within the Ambit of Article 52 of the Vienna Convention on the Law of Treaties?' (1971) 5(4) *The International Lawyer* 755.

43 Olivier Corten, 'Article 52–1969 Vienna Convention' in Olivier Corten and Pierre Klein (eds), *The Vienna Convention on the Law of Treaties – A Commentary* (OUP 2011) 1201, 1205–11.

44 Antonios Tzanakopoulos, 'The Right to Be Free from Economic Coercion' (2015) 4 *Cambridge Journal of International and Comparative Law* 616.

45 Jorge E. Viñuales, 'Customary Law in Investment Regulation' (2014) 23(1) *Italian Yearbook of International Law* 23 at 26.

is brought in to legitimise and aid in the task of institutionalising protection. On the other hand, its rules are flouted. Excessive emphasis on treaty-based exceptions and arbitral practice inhibits customary IL's function as regulator of interstate interactions.

Originally, state responsibility was directed at injuries to the person and the physical property of aliens who entered the host state's territory. However, it was property which was to become the backbone of international investment protection. US Secretary of State Cordell Hull articulated this ring-fencing of private property for special treatment in his famous diplomatic exchanges with the Mexican government. The exchanges came about in response to Mexico's agrarian reforms in the first half of the 20th century which, *inter alia*, impacted US citizens' properties. 'Under every rule of law and equity, Hull declared, 'no government is entitled to expropriate private property, *for whatever reason*, without provision for prompt, adequate and effective payment thereof' [emphasis added].[46] The expression 'for whatever reason' is highlighted because it repudiates the customary IL's police powers doctrine. The doctrine provides that state conduct which champions certain collective well-being objectives is legitimate and non-compensable.[47] Hull then went on to characterise 'the principle of just compensation' as a 'rule of the law of nations'.[48] Mexico's and other Global South countries' contestations did not win the day. By means of incorporation into IIAs, Hull's construction of IL and the measure of compensation he advocated came to dominate the protection regime. As shall be seen further later, this shift has significant implications for the interface between property and the protected spheres of sovereign freedom and public interest.

With the proliferation of IIAs as the means by which cross-border capital flows are to be governed, property was conceptualised as 'investment' to become a threshold for tribunals' subject-matter jurisdiction.[49] 'Investment' proved a capacious conception. Its contours are kept hazy and fluid by the absence of definition in the ICSID Convention 1966, the breadth of treaty definitions and the non-exhaustive lists of qualifying assets which habitually accompany them. These lists now also include intangible and purely financial assets such as shares, bonds and debt instruments. Some IIAs expressly incorporate portfolio investment. The concept of portfolio investment refers to instruments which are either directly or indirectly connected with the investment vehicle (e.g. non-primary shares and bonds respectively), are used to raise capital and are freely circulated through stock exchanges

46 Andreas F. Lowenfeld, *International Economic Law* (2nd edn, OUP 2008) 478.

47 The word 'police' originates from the Greek and 15th-century medieval Latin word *politia* meaning 'government, citizenship'. It is to be distinguished from the current sense of the word 'police' which dates back to the 19th century. The concept of 'police powers' refers to a state's inherent competence to exercise public policy and, within constitutional limits, to curb personal freedom and private property in the interest of public safety, health, morals and general well-being.

48 Lowenfeld (n 46) 478.

49 Subject-matter jurisdiction refers to tribunals' power to adjudicate the dispute.

or other markets.[50] As a matter of customary IL, portfolio investment engages ordinary commercial rather than political risk. Thus, but for this treaty exception, it would have fallen outside the protection available to direct foreign investment (FDI) pursuant to principles of diplomatic protection and state responsibility.

The extension of treaty protection to purely financial assets/portfolio investment had jurisprudential and jurisdictional implications. Portfolio investment enlarges the scope of state responsibility since the category of protected investors now also includes those whose identity the state is unable to ascertain and which identity may easily and instantaneously alter. At the same time, the objective test devised by tribunals for enquiring into the existence of 'investment' was narrowed down in an important respect. It used to contain a requirement that there be substantial commitment and significant contribution to the host state's economy. In the case of purely financial assets, satisfaction of this requirement is likely to prove elusive. Portfolio investment, in particular, may leave the country rapidly having made no discernible difference and, potentially, with devastating consequences. In due course, in the context of, for instance, disputes involving shares and a two-year hedging contract, the significant-contribution-to-economic-development requirement was marginalised, if not dispensed with altogether.[51] This is notwithstanding that this requirement was at the heart of the narrative which kick-started the contemporary protection regime. This narrative, with its heyday in the oil arbitrations of the 70s, elevated state contracts to a status akin to a treaty. An important justification for this elevation was their role as instruments of long-term contribution to a country's economic development. As instruments akin to a treaty they were to be governed by IL irrespective of the parties' choice of the applicable law.[52] In other words, the now discarded narrative of significant contribution to development was the means by which the protection of property from taking and, to this end, the privileging of foreign investors was justified and institutionalised in the first place.

An example of jurisdictional implications concerns the territorial requirement found in the majority of IIAs. It limits a tribunal's subject-matter jurisdiction to

50 M. Sornarajah, *The International Law on Foreign Investment* (3rd edn, CUP 2010) 12–13, 232–33. See for example *Fedax N.V. v Republic of Venezuela* (ICSID Case No. ARB/96/3) and *Deutsche Bank AG v Democratic Socialist Republic of Sri Lanka* (ICSID Case No. ARB/09/2) in which debt instruments and a hedging contract respectively qualified as investments.

51 For the objective test of investment which includes the substantive contribution requirement see *Salini Construttori SpA and Italstrade SpA v the Kingdom of Morocco* (ICSID Case No. ARB/00/4); see also *Joy Mining Machinery Ltd v Arab Republic of Egypt* (ICSID Case No ARB/03/11); for an interpretation of the *Salini* test see *Biwater Gauff (Tanzania) Ltd v United Republic of Tanzania* (ICSID Case No. ARB/05/22); for cases where the requirement of substantial contribution was dispensed with see for example *Phoenix v Czech Republic* (ICSID Case No. ARB/06/5) *Saba Fakes v the Republic of Turkey* (ICSID Case No. ARB/07/20) and *Deutsche Bank v Sri Lanka*. In *Phoenix* the tribunal devised a six-pronged test with, arguably, lower threshold for risk and duration and with the contribution requirement dispensed with altogether. The *Phoenix* test comprised a contribution in money or other assets, a certain duration, an element of risk, an economic activity, assets invested in compliance with the host state's law and good faith.

52 *Texaco Overseas Petroleum Co. v Libya* (1978) 17.I.L.M.

investments located within the territory of a host state.[53] This nexus between jurisdiction and territoriality is foundational because IIAs' *raison d'être* is the protection from and mitigation of risks associated with states' enforcement jurisdiction. A state may enforce its rules and regulations only against property situated within its territorial borders. Insofar as the property is located outside these borders, it is beyond the state's jurisdiction and the limits of its responsibility. Simply put, property located outside the state's geographical borders is not exposed to the risk posed by its sovereignty. However, application of the territorial requirement is problematic when it comes to purely financial property, since financial assets are impossible to locate as an observation of fact. In three claims brought by Argentinian bondholders in response to government attempts at debt restructuring, the tribunals resorted to a so-called benefit test.[54] The tribunal in *Abaclat v Argentina* held that the criteria relevant to establishing the location of purely financial investments cannot be the same as those applying to physical ones. Instead, they should be 'where and/or for the benefit of whom the funds are ultimately used, and not the place where the funds were paid out or transferred'.[55] The benefit was identified as the continuous availability of credit to finance economic development.[56] In this way the *Abaclat* tribunal circumvented the fact that the place where the funds had been deposited – determinative of the location of securities as a matter of private international law – was evidently not Argentina. They were thus not governed by Argentine's Emergency Law and, ordinarily, should not have engaged Argentine state responsibility. Moreover, arguably, the bondholders could not be said to have been foreign investors since they never entered the territory of Argentina. The tribunal in *Deutsche Bank* sided with the *Abaclat* tribunal when it accepted Deutsche Bank's submission that '[t]he nature of any territoriality requirement must depend on the nature of the investment at issue'.[57] It did not address Sri Lanka's argument that financial products emanating from Deutsche Bank London – a separate legal entity – could not be said to have been located within its territory for the purpose

53 The territorial requirement is found mostly in IIAs' definition of an investment and/or as a characteristic of a covered investment. But see the EU-Canada Comprehensive Economic and Trade Agreement (CETA) 2017 which makes no reference to the territoriality requirement <https://www.international.gc.ca/trade-commerce/trade-agreements-accords-commerciaux/agr-acc/ceta-aecg/text-texte/toc-tdm.aspx?lang=eng> accessed 15 August 202.

54 See *Abaclat and others v Argentine Republic* (ICSID Case No. ARB/07/5) Decision on Jurisdiction and Admissibility (2011); *Ambiente Ufficio SpA v Argentine Republic* (ICSID Case No. ARB/08/9) in which the Abaclat tribunal's statement was endorsed and applied; *Giovanni Alemanni and others v Argentine Republic* (ICSID Case No. ARB/07/8) Decision on Jurisdiction and Admissibility (2015). This case was discontinued.

55 *Abaclat* (n 54) 374.

56 This interpretive approach to the territoriality requirement echoed a line of reasoning introduced in *Fadex v Venezuela.* It rested on a factual assumption that the issuance of bonds on the primary market and the selling of securities entitlements on the secondary market form a single operation and make sense only when looked at together for the purpose of establishing where the investment was made. FEDAX N. V. v Republic of Venezuela (ICSID Case No. ARB/96/3) Decision on Objections to Jurisdiction 1997 para 41; *Abaclat* (n 54) para 377; see also *Ambiente Ufficio* (n 54) para 429.

57 *Deutsche Bank v Sri Lanka* (n 51) para 143.

of the BIT.[58] Thus, the 'benefit test' enlarged investors' protection from taking through broad interpretation which played on the elasticity of the jurisdictional threshold of investment. Zachary Douglas opines that the 'benefit test' stretches the jurisdictional threshold to the point of absurdity.[59] The territoriality requirement was emptied of physical connection and transformed from an objective criterion of locality to a subjective one of attributable benefit. An established principle of IL was derogated from and, contrary to the foundational rationale which underpins and legitimises the protection regime, rendered tenuous the connection between the investment and the host state.[60]

The link between the investment and the host state is further weakened by the inclusion of contractual rights in the non-exhaustive list of qualifying assets which habitually forms part of the definition of investment. As in the case of financial instruments, a contract's territorial connection is not readily ascertained by observation. It thus gives rise to the 'location' issues discussed in the preceding paragraph. The bonds issued by Argentina are a case in point since they involved purely contractual relationships. Further, contractual rights may arise in connection with an investment, but are not proprietary *per se*. In and of themselves, they are personal to the parties or their representatives. In the context of a jurisdictional regime which derives its legitimacy from the protection of property, their inclusion may be said to cross the outer limits of this regime and render it potentially open-ended.

The extension of tribunals' subject-matter jurisdiction to include contractual rights dramatically shifts the contours of the concept of an internationally wrongful act. It is a long-standing principle of customary IL that, in and of itself, a simple breach of contract which is free of illegality does not offend IL and does not constitute an international wrong capable of engaging state liability. In many BITs, the bringing of contractual breaches under the treaty's protective umbrella is mediated by the aptly named umbrella clause. Umbrella clauses come in different formulations. The controversies which surround their scope and meaning are underpinned by inconsistent arbitral practice.[61] However, the principle that they cover contractual rights is now deemed settled. A typical umbrella clause requires each party to the IIA to observe obligations entered into with regard to the other party's investors or investments. The words 'entered into' indicate 'specific commitments', which is why an umbrella clause 'would be very much an empty base unless understood as

58 Ibid para 224.

59 Zachary Douglas, 'Property, Investment and the Scope of Investment Protection Obligations' in Zachary Douglas, Joost Pauwelyn et al., (eds), *The Foundations of International Investment Law: Brining Theory into Practice* (OUP 2014) 28.

60 For a critique of the 'benefit test' and suggested solutions see Caroline Kleiner and Francesco Costamagna, 'Territoriality in Investment Arbitration: The Case of Financial Instruments' (2018) 9 *Journal of Internal Dispute Settlement* 315.

61 See for example Yuval Shany, 'Contract Claims v. Treaty Claims: Mapping Conflicts between ICSID: Decisions in Multi-Sourced Investment Claims' (2005) 99 *American Journal of International Law* 835.

referring to contracts'.[62] Contractual breaches are thereby elevated to the status of internationally enforceable treaty violations.

Zachary Douglas advances a preferred view according to which umbrella clauses are limited to contractual rights associated with investment-as-property.[63] However, whilst in some treaties the scope of these clauses has been narrowed down, in others, in an instance of expansion within expansion, it has been enlarged. They include undertakings given to third parties in a different BIT, commitment to put in place and maintain a legal system in which contractual rights are respected and, generally, protection against any interference with contractual rights 'whether it results from a mere breach of contract or a legislative or administrative act, and independently of whether or not such interference amounts to expropriation'.[64]

Finally and briefly, ISDS in and of itself is another example of the ease with which juridical principles are sidestepped and their derogated form retrospectively legitimised. Arbitration is a private, consensual arrangement whereby disputes are to be adjudicated by a tribunal of choice rather than a national court and its state-appointed judges. In line with contractual principles, the tribunal's jurisdiction is founded on the parties' agreement. On the whole, pursuant to the common law rule of privity, a tribunal has no jurisdiction over a non-party to the arbitration agreement. A complication arises where the ISDS provision forms part of a treaty since the agreement to resort to arbitration is concluded between the sovereign signatories alone. The foreign investor as the future claimant is not a party to it. Moreover, where the agreement to arbitrate is contained in a contract between the investor and an entity the acts of which may be attributable to the state, the state may find itself a respondent in proceedings arising out of an arbitration clause of which it had no knowledge. This is compounded by ambiguity in the application of customary IL rules of attribution. The case of independent state entities is one example. These entities are constituted as separate legal personalities but are controlled by the state structurally, functionally or through equity relationship. Consequently, attribution of their conduct to the state is not straightforward.[65] The need to explain these

62 Douglas (n 59) 388.

63 Ibid.

64 F.A. Mann, 'British Treaties for the Promotion and Protection of Investments' (1981) 52(1) *British Year Book of International Law* 241 at 246 cited in Mavluda Sattorova, 'Investment Treaty Breach as Internationally Proscribed Conduct: Shifting Scope, Evolving Objectives, Recalibrated Remedies?' (2012) 4(2) *Trade Law and Development* 315 at 345.

65 The IL rules of attribution prescribe the circumstances in which a breach of an international obligation may be attributable to and deemed wrongful conduct on the part of the state; see the ILC Draft Articles on Responsibility of States for Internationally Wrongful Acts 2001 Art. 4(1) <https://legal.un.org/ilc/texts/instruments/english/commentaries/9_6_2001.pdf> accessed 19 June 2021; see also ICSID Convention Regulations and Rules 2016 Art 25 <https://icsid.worldbank.org/sites/default/files/ICSID%20Convention%20English.pdf> accessed 19 June 2021; for a discussion of the problematics of the attribution rules when applied to independent state entities see for example Asser M. Harb, 'The Wrongful Acts of Independent State Entities and Attribution to States in International Investment Disputes' (2006) 3(5) *Transnational Dispute Management* <https://www.transnational-dispute-management.com/article.asp?key=902> accessed 19 June 2021.

anomalies gave rise to much debate among scholars and jurists about the existence and nature of consent to ISDS as a matter of both contract law and IL.[66] As shall be seen later, this rush to create treaty-based exceptions to established legal principles goes all the way to the doctrine of corporate veil, corporate law's most foundational doctrine.

Expropriation

Sornarajah makes the point that taking as a legal category in international economic law used to comprise three distinct acts. They were confiscation, expropriation and nationalisation. Confiscation captured the elements of capriciousness and personal gain. Both nationalisation and expropriation, on the other hand, engaged economic considerations and public interest. Over time, differences have become blurred. Early law on taking was forged in the 1970s and 80s, a time when nationalisations were common, particularly in Asia and Africa. By contrast, in contemporary globalism, confiscations are rare. Nationalisations are sporadic and vulnerable to reversal. Against this backdrop, the law on taking, argues Sornarajah, is best described as the law on expropriation.[67] It has developed in a manner which does not distinguish between the different types of state conduct and the discreet compensatory regime each should properly attract. The term 'wealth deprivation' advanced by Weston[68] serves to clarify that at issue is the free and uninterrupted accumulation of wealth, irrespective of purpose, rationale or the possibility that the accumulators themselves are takers.

That the three types of taking are often conflated may be explained by what they have in common. Their singular preoccupation with wealth deprivation translates into the following shared features: first, the taker is the state and its organs. At issue are sovereign measures, acts or omissions which intervene in the liberty of the person to create, accumulate and hold property. Second, the taking is that of private property – a juridical formation of European origins centred on a concept of ownership that is defined primarily by the formalities of titling and the expectation of security. Over time, it was made to migrate from Europe to other regions of the world where it is being reproduced to replace divergent local formations. Third, the deprived party is a foreign investor, a vexed term which relies for its juridical interpretation on definitions in legal instruments, such as IIAs and their construction in arbitral awards.

66 The debate ranges from reliance on contractual principles (the host state's consent represents an offer to arbitrate accepted by the foreign investor when commencing arbitration) and the doctrine of estoppel (the host state's is estopped from revoking the offer) to conceptualising the ISDS provision in a treaty as an irrevocable international obligation. For a well-known analysis see Jan Paulsson, 'Arbitration Without Privity' (1995) 2(10) *ICSID Foreign Investment Law Journal* 232.

67 Sornarajah (n 50) 433–4.

68 Burns Weston ' "Constructive Takings" under International Law: A Modest Foray into the Problem of Creeping Expropriation' (1975) 16 *Virginia Journal of International Law* 103 at 112.

The differences subsumed under these shared features are nevertheless significant. Nationalisation refers to the assertion of state ownership over the national economy or sectors therein. It follows on from a juridical reorganisation affecting the population as a whole. At issue is a large-scale taking which is based on an executive or legislative act, and which involves 'fundamental changes in the political system and economic structure of the state'.[69] The intention is to achieve 'industrial reform or redistribute income'.[70] Expropriation, on the other hand, applies to *ad hoc* measures targeted at individuals. It signifies episodic government interference with proprietary rights and the original contract which created them.

The distinction between nationalisation and expropriation raises the question of whether they are or should be equally compensable. This question engages a broader debate about the nature of property. Does property have a social function or is it an entirely private affair? The debate was brought to the forefront by the revolutionary events of the 20th century and the New International Economic Order (NIEO) advocated by the new states upon decolonisation.[71] Property was to have a social function and nationalisation was to be a sovereign right exercised outside a rigid, market-based compensatory regime. The 1962 GA resolution on the rights of people and nations to Permanent Sovereignty over Natural Resources and Article 2(c) of the Charter of Economic Rights and Duties of States 1974 advanced the concept of 'appropriate' compensation. The measure of compensation was to include the surrounding circumstances such as duration of the investment, profit already made and the state's ability to pay. As to nationalisation, the proposition that it attracts a different measure of compensation was not new to IL. The 1937 edition of Lauterpacht qualified a state's obligation to respect the property of aliens by reference to cases involving 'fundamental changes in the political system and economic structure of the state'. In such cases, '[i]t is probable that, consistently with legal principle, such solution must be sought in the granting of partial compensation'.[72] Franck suggests that nationalisation may be seen as analogous to general taxation 'for which contemporary remedies are not provided by international law'.[73] The network of IIAs settled this debate in the opposite direction. On the whole, nationalisation and expropriation were conflated and the concept of appropriate compensation gave way to a market-based compensatory regime as the dominant norm. Many IIAs, in particular the older ones, do not carve tax policies out of the scope of the protection on offer. Insofar as general taxation policies are not compensable under customary IL, a carve-out should not be necessary.

69 L. (Lassa) Oppenheim, *International Law* (9th edn, Jennings and Watt 1992) 407.

70 Thomas M. Franck, *Fairness in International Law and Institutions* (OUP 2002) 462.

71 For the exchanges between US Secretary of State Cordell Hull and the Mexican government on these questions see Andreas F. Lowenfeld, *International Economic Law* (2nd edn, OUP 2008) 477–81.

72 L. Oppenheim, *International Law* (9th edn, Jennings and Watt 1992) 407.

73 Franck (n 70) 462; see also Derek William Bowett, 'State Contracts with Aliens: Contemporary Developments on Compensation for Termination or Breach' (1988) 59(1) *British Yearbook of International Law* 49.

Nevertheless, UNCTAD points out that in the absence of exclusion, 'a wide range of tax-related measures, whether of general or specific application' are covered by IIAs.[74]

Indirect expropriation

With events of nationalisation and direct expropriation on a downward trajectory, investors turned to indirect expropriation as a route to a cause of action. The word 'indirect' denotes the incidental diminution in property rights by means of a broad spectrum of regulatory or legislative acts, omissions and other forms of state conduct where such conduct deprives the rights holder of much of the value of assets or the benefit they yield.[75] Terms such as '*de facto*', 'regulatory', 'creeping', 'tantamount to', 'constructive' and 'disguised' expropriation are also used to capture indirect expropriation's potential to be incremental, unintended and covert. Neither the transfer of title nor the seizure of physical assets need necessarily take place. Rather, the title and the assets have lost their utility and were rendered worthless. In the words of the tribunal in *Middle East Cement Shipping and Handling v Egypt*, at issue are

> measures taken by a state the effect of which is to deprive the investor of the use and benefit of his investment even though he may retain nominal ownership of the respective rights being the investment. . . . As a matter of fact, the investor is deprived by such measures of parts of the value of his investment.[76]

In *Suez v Argentina*, in the context of measures enacted in response to an economic crisis, the tribunal described indirect expropriation as a reduction in 'the benefits investors derive from their investments but without actually changing or cancelling investors' legal title to their assets or diminishing their control over them'.[77]

The expansion of the scope of protection to intangible and financial assets was observed earlier. The addition of a cause of action which 'lacks the usual physical manifestations that come with depriving an investor of title and control' adds another layer of abstraction.[78] The question arises whether value and profit expectations are assets in and of themselves; if not, whether interference with a proprietary

74 UNCTAD, 'International Investment Agreements and Their implications for Tax Measures: What Tax Policymakers Need to Know' (2021) 3 <https://unctad.org/system/files/official-document/diaepcbinf2021d3_en.pdf> accessed 17 November 2021.

75 Sornarajah (n 50) 363–4; see also Gus Van Harten, *Investment Treaty Arbitration and Public Law* (OUP 2007) 90–1; Anne K. Hoffman, 'Indirect Expropriation' in August Reinisch (ed), *Standards of Investment Protection* (OUP 2008) 152.

76 *Middle East Cement Shipping and Handling Co. S.A. v Arab Republic of Egypt* ICSID Case No. ARB/99/6 para 107.

77 *Suez et al. v Argentine Republic* ICSID Case No. ARB/03/09 Decision on liability para 121.

78 *Suez V Argentine* para 121.

right is a prerequisite for the establishment of an indirect expropriation claim. The uncertainty surrounding these questions is illustrated by the two tribunals cited previously. The earlier *Middle East Cement* tribunal did include deprivation of the proprietary right of 'use' in its definition of indirect expropriation. The later, *Suez* tribunal dispensed with the need to show loss of the proprietary right of 'control'. Zachary Douglas questions the coherence of this approach. He points out that 'not anything of value . . . can be the object of expropriation'. Just because the state measure has rendered the investment worthless 'does not transform value into a right that can be expropriated'.[79] The diminution in the worth of the investment may have a probative value for the purpose of establishing that taking has taken place as a matter of fact. It may also assist in quantifying the loss occasioned in consequence. However, of all the rights connected to the investment only proprietary ones are separable from the person and capable of being alienated. Therefore, they alone are capable of being expropriated. By contrast, personal rights cannot be taken and given to someone else. The centrality of proprietary rights to the design of what Douglas terms ISDS's 'investment-as-property' jurisdictional architecture is for a reason.[80] At issue is legal certainty. Tests for what constitutes property and the rights attached to it are readily available as a matter of national laws. Location is easily ascertained. Further, proprietary rights are good against the whole world. By virtue of title registration, the state as a non-owner duty-bearer is deemed to be on constructive notice of these rights. Against this backdrop, in the absence of interference in the underlying proprietary rights, such as deprivation of use, control or possession, argues Douglas, loss of value may go to the quantum of damages, but, in and of itself, is incapable of establishing that expropriation has taken place or meet the tribunal's jurisdictional threshold.

Yet, as in *Suez*, in search of a desired outcome, tribunals may and do incorporate 'investment-as-value' into the investment-as-property jurisdictional architecture.[81] Right to market access and market share, for example, were held capable of supporting a claim for indirect expropriation.[82] Both rights, argues Zachary, lack the two hallmarks of proprietorship. They are neither exclusionary nor can they be alienated. Thus, contrary to the tribunal's reasoning in *Pope & Talbot Inc. v Canada*, the fact that Pope's right to market access was valuable did not convert it into

79 Douglas (n 59) 375.

80 Ibid and generally; an investment arbitration tribunal's subject-matter jurisdiction is grounded in legal disputes arising out of foreign investment. Since the recourse available under a treaty is contingent on the existence of investment, it is this rather than property *per se* which IIAs seek to define. Nonetheless, the two come together in the definitions of investment. Treaty definitions of investment habitually refer to assets, a catch-all phrase which is then followed by a non-exhaustive list of their qualifying forms (supplemented by certain economic requirements to be ascertained as questions of fact).

81 Douglas (n 59) 377 and generally.

82 *Pope & Talbot v Canada*, Interim Award ICC 192 (2000); *S.D. Myers, Inc v The Government of Canada* (1976) UNCITRAL; *Methanex Corporation v United States of America* (1976) UNCITRAL; *CME Czech Republic B.V. Czech Republic* (2003) UNCITRAL.

a proprietary right.[83] In justifying a finding of expropriation, the tribunal in *CME v Czech Republic* overlooked the fact that there was no deprivation of or even interference with CME's proprietary rights. It focused instead on the diminution in the value of CME's shares.[84] Investment-as-value, argues Douglas, 'cannot be relied upon to establish a covered investment'. It cannot satisfy the tests of certainty and should be distinguished in the context of an investment-as-property jurisdictional regime.[85]

Indirect expropriation and sovereignty

Property abstracted as value opens up new routes to pecuniary rewards and enlarges the range of proscribed state conduct. The loss may amount to no more than a side effect of an otherwise lawful and even socially desirable state practice. Nonetheless, sovereign powers may be deemed to have been wrongfully exercised. The protection regime thus lends itself to being weaponised as a tool of deregulation.[86] It may inhibit the state from putting its legislative competence at the service of its population.[87] Capital, having won its war on nationalisation, has devised an even more versatile method for further restraining the state and gaining access to the collective wealth it holds in its coffers.

IIAs offer little guidance on where wealth protection ends and legitimate exercise of sovereign competences begins. As to arbitral practice, the *Feldman* tribunal observed, 'it is much less clear when governmental action that interferes with broadly-defined property rights . . . crosses the line from valid regulation to a compensable taking, and it is fair to say that no one has come up with a fully satisfactory means of drawing this line'.[88] A prime example of inconsistency in the drawing of this line is the cases of *CME v Czech Republic* and *Lauder v Czech Republic* brought under the US-Czech Republic and the Netherlands-Czech Republic BITs respectively ("TV Nova cases").[89] The two arbitrations were based on virtually identical facts. In both, the state and the conduct attributed to it were the same, as were the investment and relief sought. Nevertheless, the conclusions reached by the two tribunals in a matter of a few days apart were diametrically opposed. The *Lauder* tribunal identified three elements which had to be present

83 *Pope & Talbot v Canada* (n 82) para 96.

84 *CME Czech Republic B.V. Czech Republic* Partial Award on the Merits (2001) IIC 61.

85 Douglas (n 59) 374.

86 *Suez V Argentine* para 121.

87 The concept of a regulatory chill is defined as a situation in which 'a state actor will fail to enact or enforce a bone fide regulatory measure because of a perceived or actual threat of investment arbitration'. Christian Tietje, 'The Impact of Investor-State-Dispute Settlement (ISDS) in the Transatlantic Trade and Investment Partnership' (2014) study prepared for Minister for Foreign trade and Development Cooperation Ministry of Foreign Affairs, the Netherlands MINBUZA-2014.78850 at pp. 7, 20.

88 *Marvin Roy Feldman Karpa v The Mexican States* ICSID Case No. ARB(AF)/99/1 Award para 100.

89 *Ronald S. Lauder v Czech Republic* UNCITRAL (2001) IIC 205; *CME Czech Republic B.V. Czech Republic* (2003) UNCITRAL, (2006) 9 ICSID Rep 264.

for a claim of indirect expropriation to be established. There had to be (i) an action or a measure; (ii) taken by the State for its own benefit; and (iii) which seriously interfered with the investor's property rights. The tribunal concluded that the facts of the case did not support a finding of indirect expropriation. The *CME* tribunal applied the same principle of serious interference but enlarged its scope by dispensing with the requirement of benefit to the State. Adopting a broader construction of the same facts and relying on textual interpretation of the scope of expropriation in the applicable BIT, it held that CME was coerced into giving up its contractual protection and legal certainty. This, the tribunal said, amounted to a 'substantial devaluation of the Claimant's investment'.[90] The Czech Republic was ordered to pay over US$300m in compensation. In *Biwater v Tanzania* the tribunal set a particularly low threshold for a finding of indirect expropriation. It held that the state expropriated 'rights to termination of the contract in accordance with the contractually specified procedures'.[91] The investor's termination rights constituted only a small part of its bundle of contractual rights, and it is difficult to see how they can be said to have met the essential requirement of deprivation of the investment's use and benefit.

Treaty practice, arbitral awards and academic literature all acknowledge the existence of a category of taking for which no compensation is payable.[92] Pursuant to the police powers doctrine, a state possesses an inherent right to regulate for protection of the public. Restraint of personal freedom and property rights does not constitute an international wrong as long as the regulatory measure is *bone fide*, non-discriminatory, proportionate and accords with due process. Regulatory measures fairly enacted in areas essential to the state's efficient functioning, such as taxation, health, antitrust, consumer protection, the environment, securities, morals, planning and land use should not constitute indirect expropriation and should not give rise to an obligation to compensate.

The concept of non-compensable regulatory taking is consistent with the general rule that a state's engagement with law-making carries a presumption of validity

90 *CME v Czech Republic*, UNCITRAL 599. The CME tribunal noted that the Netherlands-Czech Republic BIT did not even use the word 'expropriation'. UNCITRAL 149.

91 *Biwater Gauff (Tanzania) ltd v United Republic of Tanzania* (n 51) para 487.

92 The distinction between lawful and unlawful taking was first made by the Permanent Court of Arbitration in the case of *Factory at Chorzow* (1928) PCIJ Series A No 17; each of lawful and unlawful taking attracts a different remedy. Whereas the remedy for lawful taking is in damages, in the case of unlawful taking, it is restitution alternatively, an expansive measure of damages including, arguably, an element of loss of future profits. Franck (n 70) 465–72. The tribunal in *Methanex Corporation v USA* UNCITRAL (1976) formulated the lawful, non-compensatory category of taking as follows: 'A non-discriminatory regulation for a public purpose, which is enacted in accordance with due process, and which affects, *inter alios*, a foreign investor or investment, is not deemed expropriatory and compensable unless specific commitments had been given by the regulating government to refrain from such regulation'; see also *Chemtura Corporation v Government of Canada* UNCITRAL (1976); *Marvin Roy Feldman Karpa v United Mexican States* ICSID Case No. ARB(AF)/99/1; *Suez v The Argentine Republic* ICSID Case No. ARB/03/17; see also Franck (n 70) 465–72.

and lawfulness associated with its permanent sovereignty over the economy. Recognition that the police powers doctrine forms part of customary IL began to gain traction in the second half of the 20th century. In 2006, the *Saluka* tribunal held that a state does not expropriate and is not obliged to compensate when it adopts regulations commonly accepted as within its police powers.[93] The doctrine was also invoked in later cases such as *Chemtura*, *AWG* and *Philip Morris*.[94] That said, recognition is by no means across the board.[95] Further, in the words of the *Saluka* tribunal, 'international law is yet to identify in a comprehensive and definite fashion what regulations are considered "permissible" and "commonly accepted" as falling within the police or regulatory power of States and, thus, non-compensable'.[96] In the context of investment protection, uncertainty is enhanced by the fact that the powers conferred on the state by the doctrine are not open-ended, whereas the standards for the treatment of foreign investors are. On the whole, IIAs do not set out the circumstances in which investors' rights may be restricted. Mostly, they do not usefully address the tension between private property and public interest. Consequently, the scope of the state's powers and the basis on which they may be exercised lend themselves to unpredictability and controversies. There is the additional concern about the effect which full implementation of the police powers doctrine will have on the system's ability to deliver the protection for which it was devised. The *Pope & Talbot* tribunal expressed this sentiment when it said, 'a blanket exception for regulatory measures would create a gaping loophole in international protections against expropriation'.[97] Strict application of the police powers doctrine now competes with a restricted approach comprising a balance of interests test. The Hull Formula discussed previously, the sole effect doctrine and a proportionality analysis present alternative methodologies.[98] They cast a shadow

93 *Saluka Investments BV v Czech Republic* UNCITRAL Partial Award March 2006 para 262.

94 *Chemtura Corporation v The Government of Canada*, UNCITRAL, Award 2 August 2010; *AWG Group Ltd v The Argentine Republic* (ICSID Case No ARB/03/19); *Philip Morris v Uruguay* ICSID Case No. ARB/10/7.

95 See for example *Compañía de Aguas del Aconquija S.A. and Vivendi Universal S.A. v Argentina* (ICSID Case No. ARB/97/3) Award 20 August 2007; *Metalclad Corporation v Mexico* (ICSID Case No ARB/97/1) Award 30 August 2000.

96 *Saluka*, para 263.

97 *Pope & Talbot* (n 82) para 99; See also *Santa Eelna v Costa Rica* in which the tribunal stated that no matter how laudable and beneficial to society environmental measures may be, where property is expropriated the state's obligation to compensate remains.

98 Pursuant to the sole effect doctrine, the decisive test of whether a measure is expropriatory and compensable is its effect, not its purpose or the intent behind it. For examples see *Compania de Desarrollo de Santa Elena S.A. v Republic of Costa Rica* (ICSID Case No. ARB/96/1) Final Award February 2000 para 72; *Metalclad*, para 103; proportionality analysis is a methodology of legal interpretation and decision which distinguishes between conflicting principles 'on the basis that they do not work in an "all-or-nothing" fashion'. Benedict Kingsbury and Stephan W. Schill, 'Public Law Concepts to Balance Investor's Rights with State Regulatory Actions in the Public Interest – The Concept of Proportionality' in Stephan W. Schill (ed), *International Investment Law and Comparative Public Law* (OUP 2010) 75 at p. 79 and generally; see for example *Azurix Corp. v Argentina* (ICSID Case No ARB/1/12) Award July 2006 paras 311–12.

of uncertainty over the place the police powers doctrine occupies in IL and provide rationales for a softer approach.[99] Claimants continue to challenge and seek compensation in relation to a wide range of public policy areas, including the environment,[100] public health,[101] labour relations[102] and taxation. By 2016 over 24 states were sued for policies such as withdrawal of tax breaks or the introduction of a windfall tax. Claims were brought in defiance of taxation carve-out clauses in the relevant treaty.[103] Catharine Titi observes a tendency in both ISDS and recent treaty practice to decouple indirect expropriation from the exercise of a state's police powers.[104]

In *Philip Morris v Uruguay*, the claimant sought to challenge regulations aimed at curbing the ill effects of smoking. *Inter alia*, Philip Morris argued that the measures infringed its intellectual property rights. This, in turn, reduced the value of its investment. The tribunal, by majority, dismissed all of Philip Morris's claims. In determining whether the measures adopted by Uruguay were expropriatory, it followed the two-stage reasoning adopted also in *Chemtura* and *AWG*. First, it applied the sole effect doctrine to hold that the measures did not constitute indirect expropriation since they did not have the requisite major adverse impact on Philip Morris's investment and did not cause a substantial deprivation of its value. The tribunal then went on to affirm the police powers doctrine. The measures in question, it held, were shown to be a *bone fide*, reasonable attempt to address a public health concern. This sufficed for them to qualify as regulatory. However, arbitral awards do not have the force of precedents. It is questionable whether such an outcome would be replicated in relation to the environment or where there is no strong scientific consensus supported by an international legal framework such as the World Health Organisation Framework Convention on Tobacco Control.

99 Catharine Titi, 'Police Powers Doctrine and International Law' in Filippo Fontanelli, Andrea Gattini et al., (eds), *General Principles of Law and International Andiarbitration* (Brill 2018) 323.

100 For example *Vattenfall v Germany* ICSID Case No. ARB/12/12; *Pacific Rim v El Salvador* ICSID Case No. ARB/09/12; *Rockhopper exploration Plc Rockhopper Italis S.p.A and Rockhopper Mediterranean Ltd v Italian Republic* (ICSID Case No ARB/17/14) in which Rockhopper is claiming that Italy's decision not to grant it a production concession for the Ombrina Mare field following reintroduction of a general ban on oil and gas exploration and production within a 12-mile limit of the coastline is in breach of the Energy Charter Treaty (ECT); in 2020 Ascent Resources issued proceedings against Slovenia on the ground that Slovenia breached the ECT and the UK-Slovenia BIT when it required Ascent Resources to conduct an environmental impact assessment before fracking near a water source.

101 See for example *Philip Morris V Uruguay*.

102 See for example *Veolia Properté v Arab Republic of Egypt* ICSID Case No. ARB/12/15.

103 Global Justice Now and Transnational Institute, 'Taxes on Trial: How Trade Deals Threaten Tax Justice' (February 2016); for a list of ISDS cases see pp. 3–4 including for example *Vodafone International Holdings BV v Government of India* PCA Case No. 2016–35; Perenco Ecuador Ltd v Republic of Ecuador ICSID Case No ARB/08/6.

104 Titi, at 334.

Reforms

Expansion proved a double-edge sword. On the one hand, it facilitated, normalised and legitimised a larger concept of taking and the greater availability of pecuniary remedies. On the other hand, it triggered a backlash. Transparency deficit, inconsistent awards, absence of appeal mechanism, arbitrators' impartiality, the regulatory chill imposed on states, the cost of proceedings and their structural bias all came up for criticism. The rhetoric of mutually beneficial protection risked being unravelled as a stealthy process of state-capital power restructuring and transfer of public money into private pockets taking place in the twilight zone of secretive negotiations and confidential arbitrations. Global South countries such as Ecuador, South Africa and Indonesia moved to terminate the BITs they had entered into. Pakistan, having been exposed to ten ISDS claims and the prospect of having to pay billions of dollars in compensation, announced in August 2021 that it would be terminating 23 of its BITs. In addition, it would not ratify 16 other BITs it had signed. Bolivia denounced ICSID in 2007 followed by Ecuador in 2009 and Venezuela in 2012. This threat to legitimacy was compounded by changes to the pattern of foreign investment. A handful of Global South states such as China, Brazil and India came of age as exporters of capital. They became the unintended beneficiaries of a system constructed with the interests of the Global North in mind. Consequently, the Global North found itself at risk of being at the receiving end of a system it had installed at a time when FDI was its exclusive domain. In the Global South, awareness was growing of the need to develop a 'more balanced, more responsive and more accountable' South-South treaty practice, one which would take account of countries' level of development, regulate investors' conduct and incorporate the concept of sustainable development.[105]

Reforms focused on rebalancing the interface between wealth protection and states' regulatory authority.[106] They are found in treaties rebranded 'new-generation BITs' and range from outright 'right to regulate' provisions to general exceptions clauses, clauses which limit the scope of covered assets and those which limit or clarify the host state's obligations.[107] The Netherlands model Investment Agreement 2019 preserves the overall framework of investment protection and promotion. Yet, it also places greater emphasis on states' right to regulate investors' activities for legitimate policy objectives. Article 2 expressly provides that the mere fact that a regulation or a legal modification negatively impact an investor and its expectations, including the expectation to make profit, is not in itself a

105 See for example Cai Congyan, 'Change of the Structure of International Investment and the Development of Developing Countries BIT Practice – Toward a Third Way of BIT Practice' (2007) 8(6) *The Journal of World Investment & Trade* 830 and generally.

106 UNCTAD, 'Taking Stock of IIAs Reforms: Recent Developments' (June 2019) 3 *IIA Issue Note* 3 p. 2 and generally <https://unctad.org/en/PublicationsLibrary/diaepcbinf2019d5_en.pdf> accessed 15 February 2022.

107 Ibid 2.

breach of an obligation.[108] The 2016 Indian Model BIT pursues a similar double act. In an attempt to stem the flow of ISDS claims which followed on from *White Industries v India,* it employs a host of exceptions and carve-out provisions to put limits on protection. It reasserts sovereignty and conserves the country's regulatory autonomy.[109] *Inter alia,* it affirms in its preamble the signatory states' right to regulate 'in accordance with their laws and policy objectives'. It seeks to clarify and reframe the definition of investment and standards of treatment so as to curb the wide interpretive discretion associated with textual vagueness. It tightens the ISDS provision by upholding the important IL principle of exhaustion of local remedies. The controversial most favoured nation (MFN) standard is discarded altogether as is the umbrella clause.[110] Also of potential significance is the model BIT's new title. The words 'promotion and protection of investments' which appeared in the 2003 version were abandoned in favour of a simple 'bilateral investment treaty'. The treaty program initiated by Brazil goes even further in its objective to replace the investment protection paradigm with one of cooperation and facilitation. The open-ended nature of the Agreements on Investment Cooperation and Facilitation (AICFs) which make up this program shields the state's regulatory/legislative space from treaty commitments and allows space for changes in developmental needs. AICFs featured in multilateral discussions such as the G20 and the World Trade Organisation (WTO) with open support from China. Since 2015, some 12 AIFCs have been signed with other Global South countries.[111]

Reforms have rendered BITs less homogenous.[112] Their greater diversity detracts from the force of calls to upgrade them from *lex specialis* to general customary IL. Such calls are founded on the density of this network of treaties coupled with similarities in the provisions they contain. BITs, it is argued, have become customary IL because they represent state practice created with the intention of enshrining it

108 Netherlands model Investment Agreement 2019 <https://investmentpolicy.unctad.org/international-investment-agreements/treaty-files/5832/download> accessed 25 February 2020; see also Art 8.9 of the European Union-Canada Comprehensive Economic and Trade Agreement (CETA) <https://ec.europa.eu/trade/policy/in-focus/ceta/ceta-chapter-by-chapter/index_en.htm> accessed 12 March 2020.

109 The case involved alleged judicial delays which left the claimant unable to enforce for nine years an ICC arbitration award against Coal India, a state-owned mining entity. The case was particularly worrying for India because the claimant successfully imported into the Australia-India provisions from a third party BIT (India-Kuwait) by using the MFN clause. Subsequently, India faced the greatest number of claim among Asian countries. *White Industries Australia Ltd v The Republic of India* UNCITRAL 2011 Final Award <https://www.italaw.com/sites/default/files/case-documents/ita0906.pdf> accessed 12 March 2020.

110 Model Text for the Indian Bilateral Investment Treaty <https://dea.gov.in/sites/default/files/ModelBIT_Annex_0.pdf> accessed 15 February 2022.

111 Fabio Morosini, 'Making the Right to Regulate in Investment Law and Policy Work for Development: Reflections from the South African and Brazilian Experiences' (2018) International Institute for Sustainable Development Investment Treaty News <https://www.iisd.org/itn/en/2018/07/30/making-the-right-to-regulate-in-investment-law-and-policy-work-for-development-reflections-from-the-south-african-and-brazilian-experiences-fabio-morosini/> accessed 15 February 2022.

112 UNCTAD (n 106) 2.

in law. Upgrading BITs to the status of customary IL would render at least some of their aspects binding on non-signatory states.[113] Seen from this perspective, greater diversity is significant since the claim of a unitary state practice becomes more difficult to sustain.

Moreover, on some views, the so-called new generation BITs have the potential to launch a new custom.[114] India followed the adoption of its 2016 Model BIT with notices to 58 countries advising them of the termination of existing BITs.[115] Pakistan is expected to terminate or renegotiate all of its 53 BITs. The Netherlands, traditionally a leader in the development of IL, is second only to the US in its popularity as investors' home country of choice. It is moving to renegotiate its 78 treaties with non-EU members. The aim is to align them with the country's new model BIT.[116] In the wake of the European Court of Justice (ECJ) decision in *Slovak Republic v Achemea*, the Netherlands is also among the 23 EU member states which in May 2020 agreed to terminate their intra-EU BITs.[117] All of which presents potential opportunities for its new model BIT to be put into practice and play a role in redressing the status quo of investors bias. The same may be said about the Indian Model BIT 2016. Both its proponents and critics share the view that it represents a significant structural and philosophical transition towards a different treaty practice. Rajput goes as far as to say, 'The 2015 Model BIT represents the priority of the host state in conserving its regulatory space and relegates the objective of protection of foreign investors to a subsidiary level'.[118]

113 See for example Andreas F. Lowenfeld, 'Investment Agreements and International Law' (2003) 42 *Columbia Journal of Transnational Law* 123; Stephen M. Schwebel, 'The Influence of Bilateral Investment Treaties on Customary International Law' (2004) 98 *American Society of International Law (Proceedings of the Annual Meeting)* 27; Stephen W. Schill, *The Multilateralization of International Investment Law* (CUP 2009). For a counter argument see for example Jose Enrique Alvarez, 'A BIT on Custom' (2009) 42 *NYU Journal International Law & Politics* 17 <https://nyujilp.org/wp-content/uploads/2013/02/42.1-Alvarez.pdf> accessed 15 February 2022.

114 Statute of the International Court of Justice Art 38(1) <https://www.icj-cij.org/en/statute> accessed 15 January 2022.

115 Ondrej Svoboda, 'EU-India Negotiations and Their Prospects in Era of Backlash and Reform' (2018) 15 *Transnational Dispute Management* 2 <https://papers.ssrn.com/sol3/papers.cfm?abstract_id=3416452> accessed 15 February 2022.

116 The Netherlands is party to only 3% of all investment treaties. Yet, according to a recent report compiled by the Center for Research on Multinational Corporations (SOMO), 12% of all known investments arbitration claims were filed by investors who claimed the Netherlands was their home country. <https://www.somo.nl/nl/50-jaar-isds-een-mondiaal-machtmiddel-voor-multinationals/> accessed 25 February 2020.

117 *Slovak Republic v Achemea BV* (2018) Case C-284/16 <http://curia.europa.eu/juris/document/document.jsf?docid=199968&doclang=EN> accessed 15 February 2022. The ECJ held that the ISDS clause in the Netherlands-Slovakia BIT 1991 was incompatible with EU law.

118 Aniruddha Rajput, 'India's Shifting Treaty Practice: A Comparative Analysis of the 2003 and 2015 Model BITs' (2016) 7(2) *Jindal Global Law Review* 201 at 203; for an argument that the Indian Model BIT tilts the balance in favour of the state's regulatory space see also Prabhash Ranjan and Pushkar Anand, 'The 2016 Model Indian Bilateral Investment Treaty: A Critical Deconstruction' (2017) 38(1) *Northwestern Journal of International Law & Business* 1.

Constancy and continuity

Reforms open a path to changes. Yet, whether these changes will prove transformative remains at best uncertain. By asserting the state's right to legislate, new-generation BITs such as the Dutch and the Indian model BITs simply state the obvious. A state's competence to regulate and legislate within its territorial boundaries inheres in the IL foundational principle of sovereignty and precedes any treaty provision. The fact that this competence has to be affirmed at all underscores the extent to which investment protection jurisprudence has derogated from established legal principles. Further, the language of rights derogates from what is in effect a duty intrinsic to the concept of the state as an institution charged with the well-being of an entire population. The duty of the state to protect the public interest 'is its very raison être'.[119] Seen from this perspective, expropriation should properly be an exception carved out of this duty rather than the other way round as formulated by the *Saluka* tribunal and echoed in the defensive language of a 'right to regulate'.

The state's regulatory role, having been downgraded from a duty to a right, is then further constrained. The Dutch model BIT requires that the policy objectives behind the measure be legitimate. In the India model BIT, the regulatory nature of a measure is contingent on whether it accords with policy objectives. Who will decide? As things stand, it will fall to privately appointed arbitrators to pronounce on issues of domestic policies and public interest. This is in circumstances where they sit at a geographical, cultural and political distance from these policies and, arguably, are vulnerable to bias attendant on the pursuit of reappointments. Moreover, when pronouncing on the legitimacy of the state's regulatory acts, investment arbitration tribunals assume a constitutional role. Yet, they do so in the absence of the range of constitutional values, principles and past interpretations available to national courts. The treaty is their guiding document and international law – originated to regulate interstate relationship – is their point of reference. This near-vacuum is compounded by the problematics of drafting. Ranjan and Anand question the success of the Indian Model BIT's endeavour to qualify indirect expropriation. They point to the contradiction between its Article 5.3(a)(ii) and Article 5.3(b)(i–iv). Article 5.3(a)(ii) introduces the sole effect test which is concerned merely with the severity of the measure's impact on the investment and does not require looking at its purpose. By contrast, Art. 5.3(b)(i–iv) introduces the proportionality analysis which requires consideration of both the effect and purpose of the measure.[120] The jurisdiction to resolve this mixture remains vested in tribunals whose decision 'would either result in foreign investment protection trumping over the host state's regulatory power or vice versa based on the subjective determination of the tribunal'.[121] Thus, the spectre of private individuals indulging in law-making by pronouncing on the force and validity of state measures remains only lightly touched.

119 Sornarajah (n 50).
120 Ranjan and Anand (n 115) 33–5.
121 Ibid 35.

Further, the extent to which model BITs may translate into actual treaties is uncertain. India tops the list with only 34 (out of some 84) treaties based on its 2003 Model BITs. The number of old-generation treaties is ten times greater than that of new generation ones.[122] Similarly uncertain is the impact of model BITs on the investment chapter in the growing number of regional agreements. As to the AIFCs, none bar the Brazil-Angola one are in force. Further, they are vulnerable to shifts in political power. When Jair Bolsonaro's government came to power in Brazil, the search for an alternative to mainstream foreign investment protection jurisprudence is said to have been put on hold and the policies reflected in the AICFs program risked losing ground.

In the main, the asymmetry in the allocation of entitlements and obligations persists. The host state continues to bear the bulk, if not all, of the obligations as a matter of both the customary IL doctrine of state responsibility and investment treaty jurisprudence. On the whole, a host state's commitment to the prescribed standards of treatment comes with no strings attached. A consequence of this asymmetry is to deprive the host state of the possibility of a cause of action, confining it to the position of a perennial respondent. Absence of obligations eliminates the possibility of a breach. The imposition of duties on investors in the 'balanced' treaties, such as the Netherlands model Investment Agreement and a handful of new generation South-South IIAs may be seen as constituting exceptions to this asymmetry and as pointing to a transformative potential.[123] However, the rationale underpinning IIAs – treaty arbitration's constitutional instruments – is the protection of investors from taking by the state. It is therefore not surprising that investors' obligations are typically weak and lack an effective enforcement mechanism. In most instances, dispute resolution clauses are drafted too restrictively to allow a state to assert a claim and seek a remedy. In some treaties, investors' exposure to a claim is further evaded by attributing responsibility for their transgressions to the signatory state.[124]

The aforementioned weaknesses are in addition to the problematics which inhere in treaty-based consent to ISDS. In and of itself, states' consent to international claims being brought against them by individuals is not new.[125] However, the consent to those arbitrations was retrospective and confined to disputes arising out of specific past events, period and/or subject matter. By contrast, in line with commercial arbitration, in the case of IIAs, the consent is general, comprehensive

122 UNCTAD (n 106) 1.

123 For example the 2012 South-African Development Community Model BIT, the 2016 draft Pan-African Investment Code, the 2016 Morocco-Nigeria BIT and the 2017 Intra-MERCOSUR Investment Cooperation and Facilitation Protocol 2017; see for example Arts 14 (2), 17 (2) (3), 18, 19 and 20 of the Morocco-Nigeria BIT <https://investmentpolicy.unctad.org/international-investment-agreements/treaty-files/5409/download> accessed 18 December 2019; see also Part 3 of the South African Development Community Model BIT, in particular Art 15 (1) which specifically impose on investors human rights obligation <https://www.iisd.org/itn/wp-content/uploads/2012/10/sadc-model-bit-template-final.pdf> accessed 18 December 2019.

124 See for example Cariforum States-EU EPA Art 72.

125 For example the Iran-US Claims Commission established following the Islamic revolution in Iran and the UN Compensation Commission established after the 1990–91 Gulf War.

and relating to future events. In this, it resembles 'a blank cheque' which 'may be cashed for an unknown amount at an unknown future date'.[126]

Moreover, as discussed earlier, consent to treaty ISDS challenges one of arbitration's most fundamental rules. The foreign investor as the future claimant is not party to it. The contractual analysis of this exceptional arrangement is that when the state enters into the IIA, it makes an open and irrevocable offer to an indeterminate group of investors. The offer is accepted by an investor when it files a notice of arbitration. Clearly, this analysis does not envision a host state as a claimant. On some views, it also confines the scope of the investor's consent to its own claim only, thereby precluding the host state from asserting a counterclaim.[127] Such a restrictive view is not without challenge. One argument is that as long as the counterclaim is within the tribunal's jurisdiction pursuant to the applicable IIA and arbitration rules, the investor cannot unilaterally contract out of it.[128] Yet, even on this construction, dispute resolution clauses are often drafted too restrictively to allow for the assertion of a counterclaim.[129] The jurisdictional entry point is then further narrowed down by the need to overcome the hurdle of showing that the counterclaim arose directly out of the subject matter of the claim.[130] This is in circumstances where the subject matter of the claim is most likely to be grounded in a breach of a treaty whereas a state counterclaim may arise out of a contractual breach or regulatory non-compliance. Difficulties are exacerbated by investors' obligations clauses that are drafted so broadly as to be vulnerable to arguments over their substantive content. Finally, since a counterclaim is the only recourse available to the host state (if at all), it would have to wait for and be dependent on being sued first before it can contemplate pursuing a remedy.

To conclude, reforms diffuse the clouds of delegitimisation currently darkening the sky of protection with the aim of ensuring overall survival. Second, as the flows of foreign investment change course, reforms shield Global North states from exposure to the harsh edges of a legal regime originally designed to counter

126 Nigel Blackaby, Constantine Partasides QC et al., *Redfern and Hunter on International Arbitration* (6th edn, OUP 2015) 19; Van Harten (n 75) 99–101.

127 Christoph Schreuer, Loretta Malintoppi et al., (eds), *The ICSID Convention: Commentary* (OUP 2009) 756.

128 See for example Pierre Lalive and Laura Halonen, 'On the Availability of Counterclaims in Investment Treaty Arbitration' (2011) 2 *Czech Book of International Law* 141; Alessandra Asteriti, 'Environmental Law in Investment Arbitration: Procedural Means of Incorporation' (2015) 16 *The Journal of World Investment and Trade* 248 at 256–60. For an example of rules which confer on the tribunal jurisdiction to hear a host state's counterclaim see Art 46 of the ICSID Convention, Regulation and Rules (2006) <https://icsid.worldbank.org/en/Documents/resources/2006%20CRR_English-final.pdf> accessed 16 April 2020.

129 *Spyridon Roussalis v Romania,* ICSID Case NO ARB/06/1 where the tribunal declined jurisdiction over Romania's counterclaims on the ground that the arbitration clause in the Greece-Romania BIT limited claims to breaches of the BIT so as to exclude counterclaims from a tribunal's subject-matter jurisdiction.

130 ICSID Convention Art 46.

the adverse effects which decolonialisation would have had on access to Global South resources. Third, reforms also divert calls to interrogate the logic and fundamentals of a system in which states have been enlisted to the task of protecting capital against themselves. Protection has been weaponised to restrict their sovereign competences. In line with Hayek's conception of a true order, the state installed a juridical structure dedicated to the regulation of deregulation.

In the main, the interests and needs of capital remain writ large on the aim, substance and structure of IIAs. Taking as a legal concept continues to be moulded by a propensity for expansive adaptations and interpretive flexibility. At times, such propensity does not shy away from sidestepping the constraints of juridical principles, producing an exceptional and anomalous legal regime. Its architecture has remained strikingly constant and narrow in its essential principles and design. On the whole, protection has endured as its primary purpose. Foreign investors and their investments continue to be its foremost subjects. This is despite the fact that such foreign investors are by now powerful transnational networks with a seat at the negotiation table and possessing a myriad of nationalities and resources which may top those of states.

New-generation BITs do little to change the essentials of a governing arrangement arching over a world of make-believe. The state and the investor face each other as if both are private commercial entities. The state, however, is neither a private nor a commercial body. It has greater duties. It is responsible for an entire population whereas the investor answers to a group of shareholders. Yet, the space allocated to the state for the performance of its duties diminishes whereas the space allocated to preservation of investors' superior entitlements correspondingly expands. New-generation BITs remain located at the intersections between the commons and the private sphere with the boundary dividing the two kept porous by design. Private capital can continue to cross over and penetrate the commons, site of humanity's shared wealth, raising the question of who in reality is the true expropriator.

Taking, populations and the commons

Critics point to the fact that when the state consents to elevate capital's complaints to the international sphere, when it permits a selected group of persons to exit its jurisdiction in what are in effect internal disputes, correspondingly it also reins in the jurisdiction it enjoys within its own territorial boundaries. Its obligations to the rest of the population within its borders lose their primacy. Populations may be deprived of policies from which they would have otherwise benefited. Public initiatives may be ruled out for fear of an ISDS claim. Prior to the introduction of ISDS, 'for most of the twentieth century, international courts and tribunals rarely had jurisdiction concerning state regulation of foreign nationals'.[131] Aliens, including

131 Van Harten (n 75) 9.

foreign investors, had to rely on their own state to take up their dispute with the host state through the mechanism of diplomatic protection. [132] Foreign investors had no direct cause of action against the host state. Within this framework, disputes were habitually resolved by interstate negotiations rather than adjudication. This arrangement was grounded in 'the elemental principle of international society . . . that the state is the legal representative of the population of its territory'.[133] ISDS is an exception to this elemental principle. Insofar as most host states are formerly colonised territories, this exception may be seen as a renovated and legitimised form of imperialist penetration. The post-colonial state may have been allowed entry into the international society. Yet, it is denied the status of a representative of its people vis-à-vis other states and the opportunity to meet its Global North counterparty as equal participant in interstate diplomatic protection negotiations.

In the country's economic and political interior, protection of capital from taking entails enclosure. A legal space is carved out of the commons and enclosed to become the protected habitat of foreign wealth accumulation. Within this enclosure, risk is distanced from property and its proprietors and dispersed in the direction of host populations and their habitat. Collective wealth is then channelled in the opposite direction: from the commons to foreign private pockets. As in 18th-century Germany, the transgressor is to be reformed through the improvement of the percentage of profit devolving to the property owner. To this end, the penalised host state is compelled to expropriate its own population, or using Weston's formulation, deprive it of the wealth produced by its labour. Protection of MNEs necessitates taking from the commons. For instance, measures adopted by Argentina in 2001 in response to a severe economic crisis gave rise to some 46 treaty claims. Their value exceeded the country's financial reserves.[134] In 2019, mining companies claiming against Pakistan were awarded US$6 billion. Exactly the same amount had been given to Pakistan only two months earlier as part of an IMF bailout of the country's economy.[135] All Pakistan was to be left with is the debt.

The narrative constructed by way of justification conjures up a vision of the prosperity to be ushered by foreign investment and related incorporation into globalised circuits of capital. In this narrative, the nurturing of private interest is aligned with the public interest. A bargain is struck pursuant to which the host

132 Diplomatic protection is a rule of customary IL and part of the law of state responsibility, whereby a state may espouse a claim by its own nationals against another state. The International Law Commission defined it as consisting of 'the invocation by a State, through diplomatic action or other means of peaceful settlement, of the responsibility of another State for an injury caused by an internationally wrongful act of that state to a natural or legal person that is a national of the former state with a view to the implementation of such responsibility'. Draft Articles on Diplomatic Protection 2006.

133 Van Harten (n 75) 9.

134 Charles H. Brower, 'Obstacles and Pathways to Consideration of the Public Interest in Investment Treaty Disputes' in Karl P. Sauvant (ed), *Yearbook on International Investment & Policy 2008–2009* (OUP 2009) 350.

135 Guy Standing, *The Corruption of Capitalism: Why Rentiers Thrive and Work Does Not Pay* (3rd edn, Biteback Publishing 2021) xli.

state's undertaking to restrain its sovereign powers is exchanged for the possibility of increased capital flows. The premise of this bargain is that curtailing political action will incentivise FDI and will produce win-win outcomes. Populations will benefit from imported technology, employment and the opportunity to acquire new skills. Any dispossession and regulatory deprivation associated with the entry and establishment of FDI will be no more than a transitory side effect soon to transmute into benefits.

This narrative, however, is flawed both empirically and substantively. Substantively, in circumstances where most BITs are power instruments with one party a capital-exporting home state and the other a capital-importing host state, the allocation of risk is unequal. Whilst the host state's promise of reduced sovereignty is legally fixed, the prospective home state is under no fixed obligation to generate investment. The purported benefit is no more than a future prospect which may or may not materialise and may or may not correspond to national needs if and when it does. By the time the investment arrives, economic conditions and policies may have changed. However, the host state is bound by its treaty commitments and its hand are tied. Empirically, the existence of positive correlation between BITs and increase in investment flows is at best inconclusive. Brazil is often advanced as an example of a state hosting a large volume of foreign investment, notwithstanding that only one out of the 27 BITs it signed between 1994 and 2020 is in force.[136] The US and China have been major sources of foreign investment for each other despite the absence of an investment protection arrangement.

Similarly questionable is the proposition that foreign investment ushers prosperity, or that such prosperity (however defined) benefits populations at large rather than narrow, collaborative and transnationalised local elites. Indeed, it seems that the prospect of widely distributed prosperity may well act as a deterrent. In a 2021 commentary published by the *Wall Street Journal*, billionaire George Soros criticised the US company Blackrock for deciding to launch mutual funds and other investment products in China. Soros put the blame on the country's policy of 'common prosperity', *inter alia,* aimed at reducing inequality. Reduction in inequality, Soros opined, would entail 'distributing the wealth of the rich to the general population. That does not augur well for foreign investors'. [137] Further, the entry and establishment of FDI in the Global South may involve the state in debt bondage and may produce a net economic deficit. For example, the state may have to expend foreign exchange on constructing the infrastructure necessary to attract foreign investors. Other factors include investors' repatriation of profits (a provision common to most if not all IIAs), a myriad of interest payments, fees, tax breaks and subsidies, environmental harm, distorted economic development, dependency and

136 Brazil-Angola BIT 2015; UNCTAD, 'International Investment Agreement Navigator' <https://investmentpolicy.unctad.org/international-investment-agreements/countries/27/brazil> accessed 31 May 2020.

137 George Soros, 'Blackrocks China Blunder: Pouring Billions into the Country Now Is a Bad Investment and Imperils US National Security' (*Wall Street Journal*, 6 September 2021).

social fracturing. In addition, vast amounts of local elites' illicit money are deposited in Western banks and offshore secrecy havens, a problem acknowledged even by the IFIs and the Organisation for Economic Co-operation and Development (OECD). Once the price of satisfying hefty ISDS awards and the costs of truncated sovereignty are added into the mix, even the minimal baseline of net benefit to the least advantaged participants is likely to become difficult to sustain.[138] In Itan Sunwandi's research into what she terms 'the new economic imperialism', she speaks of the presence of Clelland's 'dark value' in globalised labour-value chains as 'the means to extract surplus value through the exploitation of workers in the Global South'.[139] On this view, foreign investment is more intimately associated with taking in its sociopolitical sense rather than prosperity. It produces poverty through extractivist drainage, including the demise of local industries and the dispossession of producers located outside of globalised capitalist circuits of capital. State resources are being extracted out of national coffers and diverted from the commons to the private pockets of corporations and their shareholders.

In the face of growing worldwide poverty and inequality, there is little with which to substantiate this narrative of mutual enrichment. Nevertheless, it remains a powerful discursive tool in the contest over popular consciousness. Its longevity is aided by strategies of concealment. Whilst MNEs participate in the drafting and negotiations of IIAs and are allowed to cast a watchful eye over their terms, populations are kept at arm's length. For them, IIAs are typically secretive arrangements, entered into away from the public gaze and free from its scrutiny. The design of investment protection is in principle foreclosed to the public.[140] Moreover, secrecy (aka confidentiality) is a foundational principle of commercial-cum-treaty arbitration. The ICSID Convention does not create a general duty of transparency so that cases are not made public unless with the agreement of the parties.[141] Agreement may be found in the terms of consent to arbitration contained in a treaty, contract or national law. Where there is no agreement, the parties may request the tribunal to decide.[142] In *Giovanna a Beccara*, the tribunal overrode the claimants' request for a broad confidentiality order. Instead, it analysed the types of information involved in the proceedings and ordered varying degrees of confidentiality/transparency in relation to each.[143] The 2022 amendments to ICSID arbitration rules are said to represent an attempt at greater transparency. Yet, the request that publication of the

138 Johannes Kniess, 'Must We Protect Foreign Investors?' (2018) 5(2) *Moral Philosophy and Politics* 205 at 2013.

139 Itan Sunwandi, *Value Chains: The New Economic Imperialism* (Monthly Review Press 2019) 18–19.

140 Examples of successful resistance are the OECD 1995–98 Multilateral Investment Agreement initiative (MIA) and the proposed EU-US Transatlantic Trade and Investment Partnership (TTIP).

141 ICSID Convention Article 48(5).

142 ICSID, 'Confidentiality and transparency – ICSID Convention Arbitration' <https://icsid.worldbank.org/services/arbitration/convention/process/confidentiality-transparency> accessed 23 October 2021.

143 *Giovanna a Beccara & ors v The Argentine Republic* (ICSID Case No ARB/07/05).

award be made mandatory was rejected. Rule 62 provides for publication only in default of objection. The same applies to third-party observation of the proceedings and the publication of the submissions and supporting documents. These may be redacted by agreement.[144] The absence of a higher standard of transparency is particularly glaring considering the nature and implications of ISDS proceedings. They raise issues which involve public policy, affect entire populations and result in monetary compensation with significant impact on national budgets and public spending.

Occasionally, references to the welfare of populations may be found in a treaty's preamble.[145] This is not without significance. Preambular texts have limited interpretative impact. However, they inform the general object and purpose of the treaty. Tribunals use it as aid to the construction of substantive provisions. In addition, investors and home states' obligations to comply with the host state's human rights, labour rights and environmental commitments contained in new-generation BITs may be said to have brought host populations under the treaty's protective umbrella.[146] However, enforcement deficit means that their actual impact on the imbalance between the treatment of capital and that of populations is at best uncertain. In particular, populations have no recourse to a cause of action whether directly or indirectly through the state. They cannot access ISDS in pursuit of compensation for investors' injurious conduct and the harmful effects or side effects of their operations. Thus, the protective wall which encircles investors and their investments remains on the whole legally impervious to the dispossessive processes they may trigger in the world beyond it.

Proponents of the investment protection regime contend that the extent to which IIAs foreclose regulatory initiatives is overstated. Vandevelde, for example, argues that most host states retain considerable discretion to regulate foreign investment. They can narrow down the scope of a BIT, limit free access provisions and adjust standards of treatment. Further, he posits, once investment is admitted, enactments

144 ICSID Rules and Regulations Amendment, Rules 62–5. The amendments are to be entered into force or apply to arbitrations commenced on or after 1 July 2022 <https://icsid.worldbank.org/resources/rules-amendments> accessed 22 May 2022.

145 For an example see the EU-Viet Nam Investment Protection Agreement (2019). The Preamble refers to the 'objective of sustainable development, in its economic, social and environmental dimensions' and reaffirms the parties commitment to promoting investment to the end of raising standards of living, creating employment opportunities and improving general welfare; see also the EU-CARIFORUM 2008 and UK-CARIFORUM 2019 Economic Partnership Agreements. <https://investmentpolicy.unctad.org/international-investment-agreements/treaties/treaties-with-investment-provisions/3616/eu-viet-nam-investment-protection-agreement-2019> accessed 3 October 2021. To date, the Agreement has been signed but as yet is not in force.

146 See for example Art 14 of the IISD Model International Agreement on Investment for Sustainable Development 2005 revised in 2006 imposes on investors the duty not to breach human rights or cause them to be breached, abide by the International Labour Organisation's (ILO) core standards and not circumvent the host state's international obligations relating to human rights, the environment and labour. <https://www.iisd.org/sites/default/files/publications/investment_model_int_handbook.pdf> accessed 3 October 2021.

and regulatory measures are permitted, provided they relate to legitimate regulatory objectives, are non-discriminatory and are consistent with prior commitments to the investor.[147] Yet, even on this argument's own terms, the restrictions imposed on national policymaking are patently significant. They limit the host state's ability to change course and/or adjust to evolving developmental needs. The state may wish to adopt policies vulnerable to a charge of discrimination because they aim to protect local industries and livelihoods from destabilising competition. In particular, the catch-all requirement of consistency with prior commitments to investors may mean that there is little the state can do in any event in response to changing needs and popular demands. All of which is aggravated by the fact that adjudication of these restrictions is in the hands of an arbitral cohort sitting at a geographical, cultural and economic distance. Given the uncertainty which surrounds the scope of the police powers doctrine and its status as part of customary IL, the fate of policies and legislation remains excessively dependent on the way arbitrators elect to exercise their adjudicative discretion.

It is said that the legal regime of protection, in addition to being a carrier of prosperity, also plays an important role in remedying host states' institutional deficiencies and invigorating their adherence to the rule of law. In this regard, Vandevelde posits that promotion of the rule of law is a BIT's primary function. BITs, he argues, catalyse the establishment of the institutional framework necessary for a modern developed economy and enable host states to benefit from globalisation.[148] The process is said to go like this: in the beginning BITs prevent host countries from acting in an arbitrary manner towards foreign investors only. However, over time, this experience leads them to avoid arbitrariness in the treatment of their own nationals. Institutional improvement and respect for the rule of law follow.[149] Putting aside for now this narrative's undertones of an imperialist civilising mission, there is little evidence that such dynamic takes place in practice. According to Tom Ginsburg's 2006 research, under some circumstances BITs may impact negatively on local institutions. The ability of powerful actors to exit the jurisdiction may hinder progress.[150] Kniess observes that countries with weak institutions do not attract significant additional flows of foreign investment, whilst 'in those with strong institutions, the causal effect of investment treaties is unclear'.[151]

147 Kenneth J. Vandevelde, *Bilateral Investment Treaties: History, Policy and Interpretation* (OUP 2010) 9–11.

148 Vandevelde (n 147) 3.

149 Jeswald W. Salacuse, 'The Treatification of International Investment Law' (2007) 1(13) *Law & Business Review America* 155 at 161.

150 Tom Ginsburg, 'International Substitutes for Domestic Institutions: Bilateral Investment Treaties and Governance' (October 2006) Series Working Paper No. LEO-027 Illinois Law and Economics Working Papers 28–9 <http://papers.ssrn.com/sol3/papers.cfm?abstract_id=916351> accessed 3 October 2021.

151 Kniess (n 138) 2012 following Mary Hallward-Driemeier, 'Do Bilateral Investment Treaties Attract Foreign Investment? Only a Bit and They Could Bite' (2003 last modified 2021) World Bank Policy Research Working Papers 3121; Jason Yackee, 'Bilateral Investment Treaties, Credible Commitment and the Rule of (International) Law: Do BITs Promote Foreign Investment?' (2008) 42(4) *Law and Society Review* 805.

Either way, for the rule of law to be truly embedded, the society as a whole must first reconcile to it, identify with it and internalise it in a process that is lengthy and difficult, yet indispensable. When it is completed, a political idea transmutes into a shared cultural belief that the law is a worthy ruler.[152] A legal regime which partitions the population along lines of entitlements is inconsistent with this process. The singling out of one group by according it privileges denied to others, and the asymmetry in access to the law produced in consequence, run contrary to the essential principles of reciprocity and fairness which together form the 'golden rule' of liberal law.[153] Asymmetry in access to the law also means that, in reality, the legal regime of protection from taking does not lend itself to the reasonableness, security, non-discrimination and due process which, according to Vandevelde, form the essential elements common to both BITs and the rule of law.[154]

Access to ISDS is also said to promote public interest by virtue of the fact that it engages the ability of individuals to scrutinise the government and the availability of a juridical framework within which they can do so, a core constitutional principle of the rule of law. Accordingly, ISDS should properly be understood as a 'governance mechanism to serve public interest without jeopardising private rights'. On this view, the legal regime of protection is a form of private-public partnership rather than a 'battle between the binaries of private contract or public governance'.[155] It is not the state alone which represents the public interest, but also the individual challengers who, empowered by the rule of law, brings it to heel. Even if one is to accept this view, its application in the context of investment protection is fraught with difficulties. Particularly problematic is the fact that the individuals in question are mostly MNEs whose standing to confront the government is contingent on them being foreign nationals.

With regard to the equation of MNEs with individuals, it is premised on the legal fiction that corporations are persons whom the law creates and on whom it confers competences aligned with those enjoyed by humans. On the whole, the individuals about whom Bjorklund, Petrochilos et al. speak are not natural persons. They are man-made, juridical make-believe abstractions sanctioned by state legislation. The interests of these two groups do not necessarily coincide. Where they collide, such rights as real people may possess to confront the state may well be diminished by their extension to a small elite of fictitious ones. MNEs' standing to challenge the state may well operate to discipline and restrict natural persons' ability to do the same.

152 Brian Tamanaha, 'A Concise Guide to the Rule of Law' in Gianluigi Palombella and Neil Walker (eds), *Relocating the Rule of Law* (Hart Publishing 2009) 11.

153 David Beatty, 'Law's Golden Rule' in Palombella and Walker (n 149) 101. Beatty posits that reciprocity and fairness are the two elements of the 'golden rule' of proportionality.

154 Vandevelde (n 147) 2.

155 Andrea K. Bjorklund, Georgios Petrochilos et al., 'Investment Law at the Crossroads of Public and Private International Law' in Christina Binder, August Reinisch et al., (eds), *International Law and: Select Proceedings of the European Society of International Law* (Vol. V, Hart Publishing 2016) 151.

An example is the full protection and security (FPS) standard of treatment, contained in the majority of IIAs. It imposes on the state the obligation to protect foreign investors and their investments from harm occasioned by its acts or omissions as well as by the acts of non-state actors. The FPS has remained relatively dormant until the 2020s. More recently, it seems to have been given a new lease of life, with some commentators and arbitrators availing themselves of the standard's broad treaty formulation to expand its scope beyond its mooring in customary IL.[156] The customary FPS standard is limited to physical security. It requires the state to abstain from employing its monopoly over the use of force to threaten or impair the physical integrity of foreign investors and their assets. This negative duty to abstain is supplemented by a positive duty to secure the investment and protect it from physical violence by third parties, where such violence can be reasonably anticipated.[157] To this end, the customary standard engages not only host states' police forces, but also their judicial or administrative systems. At issue is 'the availability of the judicial and administrative system to protect the interests of the investor'.[158] Whilst construction of the FPS standard may vary in line with its treaty formulation, more recently, tribunals attempted to introduce into it a wider and more abstract notion of stable environment. The tribunal in *Biwater v Tanzania*, for example, implied into the FPS 'a state's guarantee of stability in a secure environment – physical, commercial and legal'.[159] The tribunal in *Siemens v Argentina* reasoned the expansion of the standard beyond physical force by reference to the fact that the treaty's definition of investment included intangible assets. It concluded that Siemens's legal security was affected by the state's initiative to reduce costs through renegotiations.[160]

New-generation BITs expressly specify that the FPS is limited to protection from physical violence only.[161] However, either way, insofar as the standard extends to non-state actors and to the administration of law, it has the potential to make natural

156 The FPS featured prominently in the first ever treaty arbitration: *Asian Agricultural Products Ltd (APPL) v Republic of Sri Lanka* ICSID Case No ARB/87/3; for commentary on its expansion beyond physical security see for example Thomas W. Walde, 'Energy Charter Treaty-based Investment Arbitration: Controversial Issues' (2004) 5 *Journal of World Trade & Investment* 373 at 390.

157 Sornarajah (n 50) 242; for cases where the FPS standard was held to be limited to physical security see also *Saluka v the Czech Republic*, paras 483–4; *BG Group Plc v The Republic of Argentina* UNCITRAL (2007) para 327; for the state's obligation with regard to third parties see for example *Wena Hotels Ltd v Arab Republic of Egypt* ICSID Case No. ARB/98/4 para 84; *Eastern Sugar B.V. v Czech Republic* SCC Case No. 088/2004 para 203.

158 Giuditta Cordero Moss, 'Full Protection and Security' in Reinisch (n 75) 144; see also 131, 143 and generally; see also *Frontier Petroleum Services Ltd v The Czech Republic* (2010) UNCITRAL para 273; Dolzer and Schreuer classify the state's sanctioned behaviour according to three stages of historical development: riots, the police and the military and finally regulatory acts. Rudolf Dolzer Christoph Schreuer, *Principles of International Investment Law* (2nd edn, OUP 2012) 161.

159 *Biwater Gauff (Tanzania) Ltd v United Republic of Tanzania* (n 51) at para 729.

160 *Siemens A.G. v The Argentine Republic* ICSID Case No. ARB/02/08 Award (2007).

161 See for example the Indian Model BIT 2015 which provides at Clause 3.2: 'For greater certainty, "full protection and security" only refers to a party's obligations relating to physical security of

persons the object of violence – legal or otherwise – necessitated by obligations to juridical ones. Security for corporations' assets may well mean less security for people. This is exacerbated by power differentials. The MNE is likely to be a powerful protagonist with vast resources at its disposal. It may hold sway over the state, the policies it enacts and the legislation it promulgates. It is also able to exit the state's authority to access an additional layer of protection at the international level.[162] There, it acquires sovereign-like status. As an exception to the customary IL rule that only states have standing to sue other states, and with IL at its disposal, it is able to confront the state as if it was its equal.

Also at the international level, it falls to a privately appointed tribunal to determine whether direct actions in the form of protests, demonstrations, sit-ins and occupations are the legitimate exercise of a democratic right immune to suppression. The surrounding circumstances may or may not be considered when determining the reasonableness of the state's vigilance and performance of its due diligence obligation. The requirement of good faith is irrelevant as is the absence of malice or negligence on the part of the state.[163] The *Tecmed* tribunal's finding of insufficient evidence of breach of the FPS followed on from consideration of whether the Mexican authorities had reacted reasonably, 'in accordance with the parameters inherent in a democratic state', to the 'direct action movements conducted by those who were against the Landfill'. It also appraised the judicial system's adequacy, *inter alia*, 'in relation to efforts to take action against the community's opposing demonstrators'.[164] In so doing, the tribunal assumed a '"proto-constitutional"

investors and to investments made by the investors of the other Party and not to any other obligation whatsoever'.

162 MNEs' entitlement to exit the host state's authority is mostly automatic. As such it constitutes an exception to the well-established rule of customary IL known as 'exhaustion of local remedies'. Pursuant to this rule, subject to constraints such as unavailability, domestic courts applying domestic law are the first port of call for the resolution of disputes. Local remedies must be exhausted before a claim may be espoused under IL. In a testament to the importance of this principle, in *ELSI*, the International Court of Justice (ICJ) did not accept that the rule can be dispensed with tacitly and in the absence of words making clear the intention to do so. Case Concerning *Elettronica Sicula S.p.A (ELSI)* (United states of America v Italy) Judgement (1989) ICJ Reports 15 para 50. Most main stream IIAs dispense with this rule.

163 Moss (n 158) 139–40. In *APPL v Sri Lanka* the tribunal rejected APPL's argument that the FPS due diligence obligation is result-based and therefore attracts strict liability. However, the decision in *AMT* is equivocal on this point. *American Manufacturing & Trading v Zaire* ICSID Case No. ARB/93/1 Award (1997) para 6.05. The exact meaning of the obligation of good faith in both contract and IL is context sensitive. Contractual definitions include honesty in performance, loyalty to the bargain struck and consistency with its purpose as well as with the parties 'reasonable expectations. In IL, the good faith obligation also has different manifestation including equity, honesty, estoppel and no abuse of rights. Central to it in the context of treaty law is the principle of *pacta sunt servanda* (agreements must be kept).

164 *Technicas Medioambientales Tecmed S.A. v The United Mexican States* ICSID Case No ARB (AF)/0002 para 177; see also *Noble Ventures Inc. v Romania* ICSID Case No ARB/01/11 para 166.

power of judicial review'. It carried out a 'de facto review on the exercise of sovereign powers' as they pertain to people's rights to challenge the state.[165]

The gravity of this *de facto* judicial review is difficult to overstate. Its scope may extend to the executive and legislative branches of government and to the judiciary. It potentially impacts on foundational legitimacy issues, such as the rule of law and the sanctity of civil society as a sphere of resistance. In the case of ISDS, these *de facto* judicial reviews are put in the hands of privately appointed outsiders. As observed earlier, unlike state-appointed judges, arbitrators operate in a relative legal vacuum. The only constitutional document available to them is an investment treaty. Whereas national courts assess and balance a whole array of values and interests under the guidance of a large body of laws, precedents, interpretations and interpretive rules as well as written or unwritten constitutional principles, ISDS arbitrators are guided by a single document which promotes a single value – foreign investment protection. Past awards lack the force of precedents, so they are not binding on subsequent tribunals. Arbitrators may be unfamiliar with the applicable national law and may find customary IL of limited usefulness given that its rules were developed to regulate interstate relationships.[166] Thus, the task of evaluating the state's response may appear near impossible to complete. Despite this, and to top it all, the arbitral process and its resulting awards are either partially or, as in the case of ICSID arbitration, entirely autonomous of any appellant or supervisory body. Moreover, constitutional courts are a legitimate part of sovereign power. The judicial review they undertake is directed at the validity of norms pursued by the state and the reasonableness of its conduct. The remedy is typically declaratory. By contrast, the remedy pursued in ISDS is pecuniary. The state, to satisfy the damages awarded to foreign investors, is compelled to raid the public purse to the detriment of its own nationals.

Turning to the nationality requirement, Article 25 of the ICSID Convention provides that for the tribunal to have personal jurisdiction over the parties to the dispute, the claimant investor must be a national of a contracting state other than the respondent state. This reflects the IL principle that nationals cannot claim against their own state internationally. The smooth operation of this jurisdictional architecture is hindered by the legal fiction of separate legal personality known as the corporate veil. The veil fragments the group into legally autonomous units, each with its own rights and obligations and, in the case of MNEs, its own nationality. The nationality of each of the units is determined by reference to its place of incorporation, alternatively, the place where its central administration is located. The corporate veil constitutes a foundational doctrine of corporate law. It exist across jurisdictions and is affirmed by IL.[167] The veil provides the MNEs with a powerful

165 Ivan Pupolizio, 'The Right to an Unchanging World: Indirect Expropriation in International Investment Agreements and State Sovereignty' (2015) <https://papers.ssrn.com/sol3/papers.cfm?abstract_id=2676166> accessed 31 December 2021 at pp. 1, 5.

166 Pupolizio (n 165).

167 For the determination of corporate nationality in IL see *Barcelona Traction, Light and Power Company, Limited (Belgium v Spain)* Judgement [1970] ICJ Reports 3.

tool for the management of risk. Internally, risk may be distributed among the various legally autonomous units in line with strategic objectives. Externally, it may be distanced from the group and dispersed in the direction of creditors, voluntary and involuntary (i.e. populations and nature). Corporations may be unveiled only in extremely limited circumstances.

For all the innumerable benefits conferred on MNEs by the corporate veil, in the context of the jurisdictional requisite of foreign nationality, it presents a problem. Foreign investment, in compliance with a legal requirement or pursuant to a commercial consideration, habitually enters the host state's territory through a locally incorporated subsidiary. Applying the corporate veil, the nationality of the subsidiary through which the investment is channelled would be that of the host state. Accordingly, it would not qualify as an investor for the purpose of establishing an ICSID tribunal's jurisdiction, rendering ISDS a rarely used dispute resolution mechanism. To prevent this, Article 25(2)b of the ICSID Convention provides that a local corporation may be treated as possessing the nationality of another contracting state where, because of foreign control, the parties have so agreed. Article 25(2) b opens the door for the subsidiary's nationality to be subsumed by that of the parent. The veil, ordinarily so robust as to be immovable even in the face of an unjust outcome, is lifted as the two nationalities merge into one.[168]

This specially devised rule of nationality is not the only instance where the law acknowledges the commercial reality of control and influence which tie together the different units of the MNE and transform them into an organisation. Acknowledgement is found, for instance, in the concept of a 'single undertaking' in EU anti-trust law. The presence of control may also be argued in transnational tort litigation.[169] However, in all these instances, the enquiry into the MNE's commercial reality does not challenge the legal separateness of its corporate units. For example, proving the existence of a duty of care owed by the parent to third parties injured by the acts of its overseas subsidiary is premised on the existence of two separate entities. Consideration of whether the parent is a proper and necessary party to the proceedings for the purpose of establishing the court's jurisdiction does not disturb the proposition that at issue are two persons, each with its own nationality.

168 *Adams v Cape Industries* [1990] CH 433 where the UK court of appeal said that a court is not free to disregard the company' separate legal personality (The rule in *Salomon v A Salomon Co Ltd* [1896] UKHL 1) merely because justice so requires. But see the 14 February 2014 judgement of the Provincial Court of Justice of Sucumbios, Ecuador, in *Aguinda v Chevron*. At p. 26, the president reasoned in relation to Texaco's liability for the acts of its Ecuadorian subsidiary, Texaco Petroleum Company (Texpet), 'failing to lift the corporate veil would imply a manifest injustice'. Ejolt, 'The Texaco-Chevron Case in Ecuador' (2 August 2015) at 6 <http://www.ejolt.org/wordpress/wp-content/uploads/2015/08/FS-42.pdf> accessed 27 November 2021.

169 The concept of foreign direct liability refers to legal actions brought by foreign nationals in the courts of the parent company's home state for loss and damage caused by a foreign subsidiary. For UK cases where the question of control and influence was considered in the context of permission to serve out of the jurisdiction see for example *Vedanta Resources & another v Lungowe & Others* [2019] UKSC 20 and *Okpabi and Others v Royal Dutch Shell Plc and Another* [2021] UKSC 3.

By contrast, pursuant to Article 25(2)b, the investor's nationality is subsumed by that of its controlling entity.[170]

The anomaly of attributing foreign nationality to an entity created in accordance with the laws of the host state, in addition to being an exception to Article 25, also departs from the important rule that the control test cannot be used to determine corporate nationality.[171] Moreover, it is inconsistent with the *Barcelona Traction* rule which distinguished the company's nationality from that of its shareholders. Broche explains this inconsistency by suggesting that the *Barcelona Traction* rule is restricted to the field of diplomatic protection.[172] By contrast, in the context of ISDS, he argued, tribunals are directed to give effect to the parties' agreement by adopting a broad approach which looks at the economic reality of control.[173] Nonetheless, the magnitude of the anomaly is such that Article 25(2)b was agreed against strong opposition and only by a small minority.[174] In his commentaries on *Holiday Inns v Morocco*, Professor Lalive considered it a major exception, one which constitutes 'in itself a relatively bold departure from the traditional principle of international law, according to which a state cannot be sued internationally by its own nationals'.[175]

Article 25(2)b leaves unanswered questions such as what should happen where the local investing company is controlled by a number of entities, each with its different nationality, or what should happen where the control is several layers of corporate units removed. It also means that whilst Article 25 demarcates the ICSID Convention's outer limits, within these limits, much room is left for the exercise of parties' autonomy and their freedom to agree. Similarly, much room is left for tribunals' discretion. For MNEs, it means greater versatility in the management of disputes. In a class action brought in the US by Ecuadorian and Peruvian indigenous communities for severe environmental damage and personal injury occasioned by oil exploration and waste disposal practices in the Ecuadorian Amazon, Texaco Petroleum Company invoked the corporate veil to distinguish itself from

170 Shareholding is viewed by ISDS tribunals as an indicator of control. In most cases the controlling entity is a parent holding shares in the local company. However, control was found to exist even in the absence of an equity link. See *S D Myers Inc. v Government of Canada* (1976) UNCITRAL.

171 Christoph H. Schreuer, *The ICSID Convention: A Commentary* (CUP 2001) 278.

172 This is notwithstanding that diplomatic protection is not entirely excluded from the ICSID Convention. See Article 27.

173 Aron Broche, 'The Convention on the Settlement of Investment Disputes between States and Nationals of Other States' 1972 *Hague Academy Collected Courses Online series Recueil des cours* 331 at 361.

174 Article 25(2)b was admitted by the Legal Committee by 24 votes to 20 with three abstentions. *ICSID, History of the ICSID Convention: Documents Concerning the Origin and the Formulation of the Convention on the Settlement of Disputes between States and Nationals of Other States* (ICSID Publications 2006 Vol II-2 at 871) <https://icsid.worldbank.org/sites/default/files/publications/History%20of%20the%20ICSID%20Convention/History%20of%20ICSID%20Convention%20-%20VOLUME%20II-2.pdf> accessed 28 November 2021.

175 Pierre Lalive, 'The First "World Bank" Arbitration (*Holiday Inns v Morocco*) – Some Legal Problems' (1980) 51(1) *British Yearly Book of International Law* 123 at 140.

its Ecuadorian subsidiary. The opposite position was adopted in a subsequent ISDS proceedings against Ecuador.[176]

Moreover, lifting of the veil opened the gates for another anomaly. A corollary of the fragmentation of groups into separate juridical persons is that their rights are correspondingly fragmented. Claims by a shareholder (the parents company) against third parties in respect of the subsidiary's rights is inadmissible as a matter of both municipal law and IL.[177] In *Barcelona Traction*, the ICJ had this to say about the 'firm' distinction between the parent's personality and that of its subsidiary and the corollary of a distinction between their respective rights: 'So long as the company is in existence the shareholder has no right to the corporate assets. . . . For although two separate entities may have suffered from the same wrong, it is only one entity whose rights have been infringed'.[178] According to Schreuer, the Convention drafters rejected the suggestion that controlling entities are to be granted direct access to ICSID facilities based on the rights of the local company.[179] The Traveaux Preparatoires record that actions by shareholders based on the rights of the company in which they hold shares are incompatible with the ICSID Convention. Article 25(2)b was adopted in substitution and as an outer limits exception. Nevertheless, tribunals habitually allow claims by foreign shareholders arising out of state measures which have affected the locally incorporated entity.[180]

A foreign parent's ability to be a party to the proceedings means also access to any compensation awarded. The money may not go to the local subsidiary, potentially leaving populations harmed by its operations without recourse to assets against which to enforce any judgement. If so, they may wish to claim against the foreign parent. However, no concessions are available to them in the face of the jurisdictional hurdles presented by the operation of the corporate veil. The Morocco-Nigeria South-South new-generation BIT seeks to redress this imbalance by providing that investors shall be subject to civil judicial processes in their home states for causing significant damage, personal injuries or loss of life in the host

176 *Aguinda v Texaco Inc.* [2002] 303 F.3d 470; *Chevron Corporation (USA) and Texaco Petroleum Company (USA) v The Republic of Ecuador* UNCITRAL PCA Case No. 34877 Final Award August 2011; for an analysis of these cases and an argument that the investment protection regime's answer to the corporate veil challenge could be transported to the proposed business and human rights treaty see Anil Ilmaz Vastradis and Rachel Chambers, 'Overcoming the Corporate Veil Challenge: Could Investment Law Inspire the Proposed Business and Human Rights Treaty?' (2018) 67(2) *International and Comparative Law Quarterly* 389.

177 UK law, for example, upholds the rule against recovery of reflective loss. That is, claims by a parent against a third party for loss which is reflective of the damage to the company are admissible. The rule is also known as the Rule in Prudential after *Prudential Assurance v Newman Industries* (No 2) [1982] 1 Ch 204; for a later landmark ruling see *Marex Financial Ltd v Sevilleja* [2020] UKSC 31.

178 Barcelona Traction (n167), paras 41–44.

179 Schreuer (n 171) 291.

180 For a fuller discussion see Gabriel Bottini, 'Indirect Claims under the ICSID Convention' (2008) 29(3) *University of Pennsylvania* 563.

state.[181] However, this type of provision remains exceptional. As yet, the Morocco-Nigeria BIT is not in force.

Conclusion

The legal regime of investment protection has no conception of investors or their home states as expropriators. Only taking effected by a host state and directed at foreign investors and their investments amount to a mischievous transgression capable of invoking the right to claim compensation internationally. A legal boundary has been drawn which demarcates acts of taking according to the taker's and the dispossessed respective identity and the nature of that which is being taken. On the inside of this boundary, expropriation of private property deemed unlawful is punished by way of lawful expropriation of populations. Excluded are the dispossessive processes which accompany the plenary roaming of capital. This is notwithstanding that the impact of these dispossessive processes goes beyond loss of profit and may include devastation of human and other species' access to the means of reproduction and survival. In particular, the indirect expropriation standard of treatment ensures that the value to be extracted by foreign investors must not diminish and may even be augmented by the extension of compensation to loss of future profits. The abstraction of property as anything which has exchange value in conjunction with the abstraction of expropriation as regulatory conduct shackle host states' sovereignty and may confer on foreign capital what Ivan Pupolizio terms a 'property right to unchanging world'.[182] The world may be frozen by an expansive conception of property operating in tandem with an expansive conception of taking. These mutations and the 'right to unchanging world' they may breed are then further protected from contestations by a move to enlarge the FPS standard of treatment.

In the premises, it is difficult to avert one's eyes from the political aspect of the law as producer of legal forms and techniques through which interstate and social relations are managed and ordered. This political dimension formed part of modern property rights' from inception. In what follows, we locate such inception in the English countryside. As the system of enclosure swept through it, 'the world was being enclosed, life was being closed off, people shut in'.[183] Thus, the taking of land and associated 'expropriation of the agricultural producer, of the peasant, from the soil', signalled the onset of a political/juridical process pursuant to which access to the means of survival was removed from the commons and put in private hands.[184] The English countryside was to be the nursery where the seeds of modern property law germinated to become 'a crucial mechanism for the colonial accumulation of

181 Reciprocal Investment Promotion and Protection Agreement between the Government of Morocco and the Government of the Federal Government of Nigeria 2016 Art 20.

182 Pupolizio (n 165) generally.

183 Linebaugh (n 1) 80.

184 Ibid 68.

capital'.[185] The taking of land proved indispensable to this process of germination, enabling it, defining its contours and grooming it for the role it was to play in Western expansion and domination.

Thus, property, now so vigilantly protected against taking, was itself born out of taking. Throughout, ruling elites used the state apparatus to secure their class interests. Expropriation was carried out with the aid of sovereign monopoly over violence and the power and domination integral to law-making and law-preservation. In due course, the outcomes of law-making were to be made lawful and permanent. In the colonies, land was taken by the sovereign and distributed among its colonial agents. There was to be no compensation for those who formerly had possessed and used it. Only the legal boundary was adjusted to make subsequent dispossession of the appropriators unlawful. As the neoliberal of the Geneva School understood so well, it was never a question of no state intervention but rather what kind of intervention.

185 Brenna Bhandar, *Colonial Lives of Property: Law, Land and Racial Regimes of Ownership* (Duke University Press 2018) 2, 3.

4 Taking by improvement

Enclosures and settlement

Introduction

It began with land – a commonly held wilderness to be tamed; empty spaces to be filled with the paraphernalia of civilisation. It is no coincidence that an emergent capitalist system should make land its first object of taking. Land is central to survival and reproduction. Without it, there is no possibility of life. It is the source of food, a prerequisite for shelter and, in the context of industrial society, the place where natural resources are to be found and where production can take place. If people were to be reinvented as labour, it was necessary that they should first lose direct access to land. Its appropriation, privatisation and commodification was paramount if the abstraction of social relations as exchange of value was to take hold. As long as access to land was uninhibited, people were shielded from unmitigated dependency on the market as a mediator of their continuing existence.

Commodification, however, is not straightforward where land is concerned. As pointed out by Polanyi, land intrinsically is not a commodity. It is not an object produced for sale on the market.[1] Indeed, it is not produced at all. It is never-ending, yet quantitatively fixed. The words attributed to Mark Twain sum this up: 'Buy land – they're not making it anymore'.[2] Its commodification is thus 'entirely fictitious'.[3] Fictitiousness, the fact that no act of production needs take place, may enable landlords and rentiers to 'grow richer as it were in their sleep'.[4] Nonetheless, something else had to be brought into the equation in order to construct land as a fungible commodity capable of being taken, owned, measured and priced for alienation. That other thing was labour and associated notion of improvement. It was improvement and labour combined which served to reason out the transformation of land from producer of life to producer of value. In due course, as in

1 Karl Polanyi, *The Great Transformation: The Political and Economic Origins of Our Time* (Beacon Press Boston 1944) 75.

2 Josh Ryan-Collins, *Toby Lloyd and Laurie Macfarlane with the New Economics Foundation, Rethinking the Economics of Land and Housing* (Zed books 2017) 3–4.

3 Polanyi (n 1) 76.

4 John Stuart Mill, *Principles of Political Economy with Some of Their Applications to Social Philosophy* (7th edn, Book V Longmans Green and Co 1909) 28.

DOI: 10.4324/9781315386782-6

the surveying techniques developed by William Petty, 17th-century surveyor and progenitor of modern political economy, land and labour would be lumped together as factors in the mathematical calculation of value and national wealth. Yet, labour too is one of Polanyi's fictitious commodities. It is but 'another name for a human activity which goes with life itself, which in its turn is not produced for sale but for entirely different reasons', nor can it be 'detached from the rest of life, be stored or mobilized'.[5] Thus, capitalism as a system of commodification began with a fiction.

Tania Murray Li suggests two other characteristics which impede land's intrinsic usefulness as producer of value, problematise its conversion into a resource and render its complete commodification near impossible. First, 'land is not like a mat. You cannot roll it up and take it away. It has presence and location'.[6] Land cannot be physically removed. Second, 'its usefulness to humans depends on exclusion: two people cannot occupy the same spot'.[7] Thus, turning land into productive use 'requires regimes of exclusion that distinguish legitimate from illegitimate use and users and the inscribing of boundaries', material, legal, regulatory and discursive. [8] These boundaries are drawn using a multitude of techniques such as survey, titling, registration, leasing, rent and classification. In this way, land is reordered and distanced from its material form to become what Li terms 'an assemblage of materialities, relations, technologies and discourses that have to be pulled together and made to align'.[9] Land abstracted as an assemblage is more investable. Yet, it is also more vulnerable to disorder, challenges and contestations. Relations change and 'legitimacy can wax and wane, as people who concede to their exclusion at one point in time may change their position'.[10] As we shall see, of particular longevity in the contest between lawful and unlawful taking is the discourse of 'frontiers' and the classification of uncommodified land as empty, waste or degraded.

England: enclosures of improvement

The countryside, the state and property relations

Ellen Meiksins Wood locates the birth of capitalism in rural England and the enclosure movement which swept through it.[11] Outwardly, enclosures merely changed

5 Polanyi (n 1) 76.

6 Tania Murray Li, 'What Is Land? Assembling a Resource for Global Investment' (14 July 2014) *Plenary Lecture, Transactions of the Institute of British Geographers* 589 <file:///Users/yonitpercival/Documents/publications%20and%20articles/property%20rights/What%20is%20land%3F%20%20Tania%20Li%20-%20Academia.edu.webarchive> accessed 11 October 2017.

7 Ibid 589.

8 Ibid.

9 Ibid.

10 Ibid 591.

11 For a summary and a critique of this and other views on the transition to capitalism see for example Alexander Anievas and Kerem Nisancioglu, *How the West Came to Rule* (Pluto Press 2015) 13–42.

the physical appearance of the countryside. Fences were erected and hedges were planted to parcelise common land and order the ejection of its occupants. However, the significance of these changes went much deeper. According to the economic historian Richard Henry Tawny, the enclosure movement marked the transition from 'the medieval conception of land as the basis for political functions and obligations to the modern view of it as an income-yielding investment'.[12] Wood called it 'the most famous redefinition of property rights'. It brought about 'the extinction of common and customary use rights on which many people depended for their livelihood'.[13]

Why England? Wood points to the early emergence in England of a centralised state formation. By the 16th century, at a time when Europe was still a place of monarchies reigning over a landscape of post-feudal military powers, corporate privileges and fragmented legal systems, the English state was already unitary. It had at its disposal networks of infrastructure, a national legal and judicial system and a functioning administration.[14] As part of the centralisation of political functions the English aristocracy became part of the state. In the bargain struck between the two, extra-economic powers employed to extract value from direct producers were traded off for state protection of property. The landed aristocracy submitted to the common law in exchange for a private and exclusive form of property that was free of feudal obligations and 'was more forcibly implanted and rigorously enforced'.[15] Thus, what members of the aristocracy lost 'in "extra-economic" powers of surplus extraction they more than made up for with increasing "economic" powers'.[16]

This state-aristocracy bargain was enabled by the equally early rise of freehold/tenancy property formation. Whilst in Europe land was still being cultivated by 'peasants/proprietors', in England, it was already heavily concentrated in freeholdings cultivated by tenured farmers.[17] This engendered property relations in which competition was not over sales in the market but over access to land as determined by the market. Once customary limits on rent were removed, farmers' ability to secure tenancy became dependent on being productive, efficient and able to pay market rent. Wood illustrates the difference between English and French property relations in the late 16th and early 17th centuries by looking at surveyors' reports of that time. Whilst the French surveyor was still studying records for the purpose of reviving or creating feudal lords' rights and peasant obligations,

12 Richard Henry Tawney, *The Agrarian Problem in the Sixteenth Century* (Longman 1912) 189 cited in Ellen Meiksins Wood, *Empire of Capital* (Verso 2003) 77.

13 Ellen Meiksins Wood, *The Origin of Capitalism: A Longer View* (Verso 2002) 108.

14 Ibid 99; Ellen Meiksins Wood, *Citizens to Lords: A Social History of Western Political Thought from Antiquity to the Late Middle Ages* (Verso 2006) 174–5.

15 Wood (n 14) 175–6.

16 Ibid 99.

17 The word farmer originally denoted a bailiff or a steward who farmed the land on the owner's behalf, or a tenant.

the English surveyor was already preoccupied with establishing market value and rental yield.[18]

From there it was only a short step to enclosure. Freeholders erected fences and privatised for their exclusive use land previously common and available to tenants for their life necessities. Once the land was enclosed and taken, it could be made more profitable by the grazing of sheep for the wool industry and the felling of forests for the timber industry. In the words of Thomas More who both observed and participated in the enclosure movement, in the name of the ideology of improvement (about which more later) sheep have 'become so great and so wylde, that they eate up and swallow downe the very men them selfes. They consume, destroye, and devoure whole fields, howses and cities'.[19] The waves of enclosures which swept through the English countryside included transfers by Henry VIII of huge expanses of land as royal favours. In the 17th century, Cromwell continued in the same vein when he handed over public land to his followers. The result was 'an extraordinary degree of concentration of land ownership that persists till today'. According to an 1873 survey, less than 5% of the population owned the entirety of the land whilst the rest owned nothing at all. Common land now occupies a mere 5% of the land in England compared with roughly 50% in the Middle Ages.[20]

In the name of improvement: enclosures and the law

This time of intense transformations was also a time of law-making. To begin with, the exercise of violence and the assertion of domination could be justified by the just ends (improvement) attributed to the act of taking and without the need for the cover of legitimacy. Taking unfolded outside and in defiance of not only customary but also state-made law. Both were disregarded as gatekeepers of access to land. Such was the fate of the Charter of the Forest 1225.

If the enclosures were in performance of a state-aristocracy bargain, the Charter of the Forest gave voice to the demands of common people. Much like the ruling elite, commoners also looked to the state to secure their class interests. This required that their customary rights and the protection of their environment from overexploitation be given statutory force. The Charter of the Forest was extracted from the Magna Carta to affirm free people's eternal rights to work for subsistence on the commons 'without danger'. It included their entitlement to pick fruit, gather wood, dig and use clay for utensils and housing, pasture animals, fish and take peat for fuel, as well as the right to water and even honey.[21] It was a class statement, a

18 Wood (n 13) 104; for a critique of Wood's argument that original accumulation was a purely domestic process, see for example Anievas and Nisancioglu (n 11) 148–52 and generally.

19 Cited in Guy Standing, *Plunder of the Commons: A Manifesto for Sharing Public Wealth* (Pelican Books 2019) 11.

20 Ibid 11, 13–14.

21 The National Archive, 'Charter of the Forest, 1225' <http://www.nationalarchives.gov.uk/education/resources/magna-carta/charter-forest-1225-westminster/> accessed 4 January 2022. The Charter was repealed in 1971 by a Tory government.

'manifesto for the property-less'.[22] The Charter protected commoners against deprivation and homelessness, as well as against outside surveillance and control. It provided for reparations to those who were deprived of their common rights. It introduced the concept of stewardship of the forest and, in what became in effect a system of local governance, devolved authority from the state to the people. It was among the first ever environmental laws and an inspiration to social movements. Importantly, the word 'forest' in its 13th-century sense was not confined to wooded areas. It applied to all and any land appropriated by the monarch to the exclusion of common people, including fields, farms and villages. The Charter was to become the longest piece of legislation on the English statute book until its repeal by the Thatcher government in 1971.[23]

Yet, calls for enforcement of the Charter in the face of unlawful enclosures carried with them the risk of death. In the Newton battle, the culmination of the Midland Revolt of 1607 and one of many protests and riots which broke out throughout the land, the tinker John Reynolds and his one thousand dispossessed fellow rebels, known as Diggers and Levellers, dug out and flattened the erected hedges and fences. They also petitioned the king to enforce his own laws, which the enclosing landed aristocracy was breaking. This peaceful resistance was met with deadly violence. Forty to 50 levellers were massacred by landowner-backed militias. Charged with sedition, the rebels' leaders were hung, drawn and quartered by the king whose laws they sought to protect.

With 'agrarian disturbance' and 'class insubordination' rocking society, and with the aristocracy's victory already secured by facts on the grounds, it was time for disorder to be halted and for Benjamin's 'peace ceremony' to take place.[24] An assemblage of state-made laws legitimised what hitherto was expropriation by brute force. Between 1860 and 1870, a landowner-dominated Parliament passed over 5,000 acts, resulting in the enclosure of seven million acres of common land. Pursuant to the General Inclosure Act 1845, newly appointed enclosure commissioners were given the power to enclose without the need for prior parliamentary approval.[25] Thus, unlawful appropriation – described by Marx as the most brazen violation of the sacred rights of property – was legitimised and given permanence.[26]

Conversely, hitherto lawful acts, including the exercise of rights under the Charter of the Forest, were criminalised. Thus, an orderly façade was manufactured by, on the one hand, legalising unlawful acts by the aristocracy and, on the other hand, criminalising all manners of newly invented petty infringements by commoners.

22 Standing (n 19) 5, 9.

23 Ibid 3 and generally 3–9.

24 E. P. Thompson, *Whigs & Hunters: The Origin of the Black Act* (Breviary Stuff Publications 2013) 192.

25 Guy Standing, 'Why You Haven't Heard of a Charter That's as Important as the Magna Carta' (2017) Open Democracy UK<https://www.opendemocracy.net/uk/guy-standing/why-youve-never-heard-of-charter-thats-as-important-as-magna-carta> accessed 5 January 2022; Standing (n 19) 12–13.

26 Domenico Losurdo, *Liberalism: A Counter-History* (Verso 2011) 121.

In May 1723 the Black Act was enacted in a matter of four weeks and without debate or division.[27] It introduced 50 new capital offences. Vague drafting in the hands of a judiciary guided by a 'sense of natural justice' meant that the number of offences expanded in the course of enforcement.[28] In some cases no formal process was required for the hangman to be summoned.[29] Hundreds, if not thousands, of 'Necessitous Wretches', wrote the liberal philosopher Mandeville, were hanged 'for Trifles'.[30] Thompson observed that the case law which arose out of the Black Act did not support the 'greatest of all legal fictions'. That is, the liberal fiction that the law evolves 'by its own impartial logic' and 'true only to its own integrity'. He concluded his narration of the battle between poachers and keepers in Enfield Chase and Richmond Park thus:

> as between petty predators, such as horse thieves and deer traders on the one side, and great predators who occupied the realm of 'interest' and enjoyed Court favour, money and power on the other . . . at the point where the petty seriously inconvenienced the great, then the entire apparatus of power and law could be brought to the side of the latter. The Black Act put unprecedented legal power in the hands of men who had . . . a direct and personal interest in the conviction of men who were a nuisance to them . . . It was power which made nonsense of a whole costly historical paraphernalia whose proclaimed object was to safeguard the liberty of the subject.[31]

The 'historical paraphernalia' of liberty had to be adapted if it was to avoid irremediably being made nonsense of. As 'non-monetary use-rights were being reified into capitalist property rights by the mediation of the courts of law', 'free men' were recast as free labourers.[32] Their 'eternal rights' were extinguished in the name of aristocratic liberty to take their land. In exchange, they were given the liberty to sell their labour in the market. They were to be free to leave their rural habitat, – now designated zones of idleness, debauchery and subversion – to embark on a search for access to the market.[33]

Yet another route to legitimisation was the evergreen discourse of public interest. Mandeville accepted that the reason theft took place was because 'what they can get Honestly is not sufficient to keep them'. He similarly acknowledged that it was terrible when innocent people were put to death. Nevertheless, he also called on judges not to let their conscience and compassion override the interests

27 Thompson (n 24) 1.
28 Ibid 198.
29 Losurdo (n 26) 85; one of the issues that taxed the minds of lord justices was whether the statue extended to aiders and abettors. Thompson (n 24) 195–8.
30 Bernard de Mandeville, *The Fable of the Bees* (Vol. 1, Liberty Classics Frederick B. Kay 1988) 273 cited in Losurdo (n 26) 85.
31 Thompson (n 24) 146.
32 Ibid 191.
33 Standing (n 19) 15.

of 'Peace of the Society' and the 'advantage to a Nation'.[34] How did the erasing of entire villages, exile, urban slums and workhouses, mass vagabonding and the extinction of life transform into a national advantage? By what sleight of hand were private gain and corresponding dispossession metamorphosed into a public good? To contemporary ears accustomed to the discourses of development, modernisation and the miracles of technology the answer would sound familiar: it was improvement. By the 17th century the word became firmly embedded in the language, literature, judiciary decisions and work of the Royal Society, home to some of England's leading scientists, as well as members of its ruling class. Among them was John Locke, theorist of capitalist property rights and his patron, the encloser Earl of Shaftesbury.[35]

In its original sense, as used in the 16th century, the word 'improve' meant to make a profit, increase the value of things.[36] Viewed through this perspective, the fact that customary use-rights lacked monetary value meant they were wasteful and an obstacle. They stood in the way of a more efficient, productive and profitable use of the land and, by extension, the public benefit to be derived from progress. In what may be seen as an earlier version of modern 'trickle down' economics, improvement was posited as ultimately in the interest of all and for the benefit of the economy as a whole.[37] This was notwithstanding the immiseration and killing of some. And so, when customary and private rights collided in the courts of law, judges recognised 'improvement' as capable of displacing centuries-old, guaranteed 'eternal rights'.[38] During the 18th century, repeated court decisions 'signalled that the lawyers had been converted to the notions of absolute property rights . . . and the law abhorred messy complexities of coincident use-right. . . . capitalist modes transmuted offices, rights and perquisites into round monetary sums'.[39] Within the legislative arm of the state, between 1709 and 1710, for example, a House of Lords bill authorised the enclosure of Ropley common on authority to 'improve' Farnham Old Deer. Customary tenants' efforts to petition the House of Commons both before and after the passing of the bill proved in vain.[40]

In conclusion, as political functions were being centralised in the hands of the state, in parallel, *dominion*, the world of property, was being privatised and liberated from social functions. At the material level, the land was carved up and its stewards ejected to be replaced with grazing sheep. The forest was being emptied

34 Mandeville (n 30) 87, 272–3 cited in Losurdo (n 26) 85.

35 Wood (n 14) 106–7.

36 This sense was later enlarged to mean 'make greater in amount or degree'. The word could now be applied to scientific innovations in agricultural techniques, new technologies and a new concept of property relations. Finally, it reached the general sense of being better.

37 'Trickle down' economics or theory postulates that wealth and benefits for the wealthy in forms such as tax cuts, capital gains and dividends trickle down to everyone else. The assumption is that corporations and shareholders are the drivers of growth.

38 Wood (n 14) 108–9.

39 Thompson (n 24) 188.

40 Thompson (n 24) 90.

of 'free men' to be filled with the cacophony of improvement. At the superstructure, state-made law provided the 'traffic lights' which were to manage the circulation of agrarian capitalism's strategies of accumulation. In the name of national advantage and the benefit of all, a legal boundary was drawn and a regime of exclusion was constructed: it was 'green' for taking by some and a deadly 'red' for taking by others. This juridification of class power and domination unmasked the narrative of an autonomous law possessing its own impartial logic as the 'greatest of all legal fictions'.

In due course, agrarian capitalism's strategies of accumulation were transported from the English countryside and the Scottish Highlands, via colonised Ireland, to the 'New World' and the Anglophone empire of agriculture and commerce. The 'New World' provided a new frontier, a carefully constructed fiction of *tabula rasa* where property could be further abstracted and strategies of accumulation practiced and developed with greater ease. The racialised nature of the civilised–savage dichotomy in colonial narratives facilitated the construction of the exclusion regime necessary for the transformation of land into property. It also smoothed the way for the cultural and physical erasure of native populations and the taking of their land. Physically, native populations were made to disappear through the deliberate spread of rum, infectious disease, deportations and finally reservations. Culturally they were made to disappear through the European translation of their kingship systems 'into the terms of property'.[41] All of which made for a season of easy living as dispossession translated into methods of distribution.

Empire of improvement: taking by settlement

Settlement

Agrarian capitalism was not without its own challenges. One such challenge was presented by the many dispossessed and those excluded by new technologies from sharing in the proceeds of improvement. Exclusion by new technologies brings to mind contemporary financialised capitalism. However, in the earlier version of agrarian capitalism, a solution could be found in the colonies. Most colonies were initially seen as an outlet for 'waste population'.[42] Pursuant to the Beggars Act 1597 and a 1652 act which empowered magistrates to ship vagrants and beggars to the colonies, vast numbers of the English poor were being sent there to enhance settlement and supplement the native labour force. With the intensification of evictions which accompanied the Cromwellian conquest of Ireland in the 17th century, the Irish are said to have made up much of the white migration to the West Indies.[43] In the Scottish Highlands too, by the 19th century, expulsions, primarily to Canada

41 Losurdo (n 26) 18, 169 referring to Benjamin Franklin's autobiographic record of the annihilation of whole tribes in the seacoast and Alexis de Tocqueville's description of the 'frightful sufferings' inflicted on the native populations of Africa and America.

42 Hugh Trevor-Roper, *The Rise of Christian Europe* (Thames and Hudson 1966) 17.

43 Wood (n 14) 155.

but also to Australia, came to replace forced domestic resettlement. The cleansing of England of its surplus population, Francis Bacon advised King James I, proffered the double benefit of 'the avoidance of people here, and . . . making use of them there'.[44] The availability of this colonial vent, argue Anievas and Nisancioglu, enabled English capitalism to survive the limits of domestic production by which it otherwise would have been constrained.[45] Once in the colonies – whether as an act of resistance or in a bid to recapture lost communal access to subsistence– the newcomers joined indigenous communities. Alternatively, they established new settlements, thereby joining in the act of taking.[46] Some Irish settlers then engaged in bringing indentured servants from Ireland to work on their plantations.[47]

Settlement signalled the 'death agony' of entire populations and their divergent forms of relationship with the land they inhabited. Losurdo observes that, in the colonies, it was not the liberation from church control but the 'death agony' of divergence which injected the 'more potent existence' into colonists' property.[48] The unfolding of this project of annihilation, mused Bartolome de Las Casas, would be improbable to future generations. As Columbus and his followers settled on the island of Hispaniola, in a matter of 14 years (1494–1508), recorded de Las Casas, 'over three million people had perished from war, slavery and in the mines'.[49] By 1650, the 90-million strong population of the Americas was reduced to a mere 10 million.[50] The English colonial project in North America, aimed as it was at clearing the land for settlers, proved even more intentionally genocidal.[51] It was, says Losurdo, a 'gigantic' and tidal process of privatisation that extended to the birds who flew over the land and the animals whose habitat it was'.[52]

Thus, expropriation as a political moment of 'capital positing' violence was the means by which assets were confiscated and one order was made to replace another. The colonies became spaces for 'imagining and experimenting with new ways of organising social production for profit'.[53] By the 17th century, the discourse of 'improvement' migrated to the 'New World' where it was to become a feature of the language of settlers as they eyed ever greater stretches of what Locke called the vacant place of America. The dismantling of social structures (and related property regimes) in England and in the colonies, commented Polanyi,

44 Anievas and Nisancioglu (n 11) 151; see also Wood (n 14) 152–6.
45 Anievas and Nisancioglu (n 11) 152.
46 Ibid 153.
47 Wood (n 14) 155.
48 Losurdo (n 26) 320.
49 Jason Hickel, *The Divide: A Brief Guide to Global Inequality and Its Solutions* (Penguin Random House 2018) 70.
50 Anievas and Nisancioglu (n 11) 152.
51 Ellen Meiksins Wood, *Liberty & Property: A Social History of Western Political Thought from Renaissance to Enlightenment* (Verso 2012) 90.
52 Losurdo (n 26) 78, 320.
53 Onur Ulas Ince, 'Primitive Accumulation, New Enclosures, and Global Land Grab: A Theoretical Intervention' (2014) 79(1) *Rural Sociology* 104 at 112.

represented analogous processes, so that by the early years of the 19th century, the condition of some African tribes resembled that of the English labouring classes.[54]

Rationale of empire

At the ideological level, a repertoire of explanations and justifications was constructed to shore up colonial settlement. It was anchored in facts on the ground but mutated over time and across purposes. Anievas and Nisancioglu argue that, at least to begin with, the Americas were vast and lacking in central authority. In the absence of a strong state capable of coercion and enforcement, the theorisation of property rights was of lesser value to imperial agents.[55] Benton and Straumann observe the adoption of practices aimed at establishing title by combining ceremonies and rituals of possession with the exercise of legal authority. The rationale of enforcement communicated through trials and the meting out of punishment was used as a 'creative shorthand' for the assertion of sovereignty.[56] Particularly in the context of French and English expansion, legitimisation also relied on legal techniques such as purchases and treaties.

The repertoire of apologia also mirrored variations in imperialist formations and their discontents. Spain's imperial rivals, for instance, contested the legitimacy of discovery, conquest and papal grants as bases for claims to title. In the colonies, the violence which permeated the Spaniards' relationships with local polities infringed the terms of at least the first two papal bulls. The threat of a rising colonial aristocracy with feudal ambitions and assertions of property rights had to be balanced against the need to allow colonist landholders sufficient autonomy to extract the gold and silver on which Spain's wealth and power depended.[57] Overall though, argues Wood, it is hard to avoid the conclusion that colonial structures 'depended on social property relations at home and the particular economic processes set in motion by them'.[58] Wood made this statement in the context of her controversial intervention in the debate about the origins of capitalism and the distinction she drew between commercial and capitalist empire building. The Spanish empire, she argued, engaged a feudal-type state-private partnership modelled on past medieval conquests. England, by contrast, was driven by the logic of its homemade agrarian capitalism and its imperatives of clearing land for exploitation.[59] If Vitoria's preoccupation was with the legitimisation of Spanish title to territory and the right to a share in its natural wealth, Locke's interest lay in the theorisation of the origin and

54 Polanyi (n 1) 165, 172.

55 Anievas and Nisancioglu (n 11) 153.

56 Lauren Benton and Benjamin Straumann, 'Acquiring Empire by Law: From Roman Doctrine to Early Modern European Practice' (2010) 28(1) *Law and History Review (American Society for Legal History)* 1 at pp. 34–5.

57 Anthony Pagden, *Lords of All the World: Ideologies of Empire in Spain, Britain and France c.1500–c.1800* (Yale University Press 1995) chap 2; Wood (n 51) 87–8.

58 Wood (n 14) 149.

59 Ibid 147–56; for a more detailed analysis of the different types of empire see Wood (n 12) 26–88.

nature of private property rights with the logic of 'improvement' and value creation at its core.

The search for a rationale gave rise to debates which engaged both the metropolis and its imperial peripheries. They revolved around the interface between conquest, occupation, possession and use on the one hand and the greater rights of private ownership and sovereignty on the other. Assertions of Roman law principles such as *res nullius* (things without owners), its derivative by analogy *terra nullius* (land without owners), prescription (the Roman principle that rights are created by continuous occupation and the passage of time) and *jus gentium* (law of nations) shared space with colonists' deadly biblical pathos about taking possession of the promised land of America, the Christians' Palestine.[60]

The prevalence of Roman legal concepts in the colonial repertoire testifies to the significant role which the Roman model of empire played in these debates. In some ways, Rome was 'the first "colonial" empire, as we have come to understand the word'. It embodied 'the criterion . . . of European imperialism'.[61] This criterion was property, specifically land. In the Chinese empire, for example, the criterion for power and wealth was the holding of office within the framework of a strong, centralised and bureaucratic state apparatus. By contrast, the Roman republic was ruled by an oligarchy congregated around land ownership. This bred an appetite for territorial expansion. The empire which this appetite produced mimicked the republic in that it too was structured around the nurturing of propertied elites. It was governed by a purposefully created network of local landed aristocracies acting in collaboration with colonial settlers and administration.[62] Thus, the Roman governance model of strong private property adjacent to an imperial state translated into an empire similarly administered by a state-property alliance.

Roman law managed this state-property alliance by drawing a boundary which transformed the pair into two distinct spheres – *imperium* and *dominium*. *Dominium* represented the world of private ownership (as opposed, for example, to the loose conception of possession characteristic of ancient Greece). *Imperium* represented the notion of sovereignty as a public right of command vested in magistrates and then the emperor (as opposed to the Greek conception of the *polis* as a community of citizens).[63] The problem this division posed for theorists of empire was that the feudal conception of conditional and politically constituted property

60 For a survey of scholarly interpretations of the ways in which the Roman principle of *res nullius* was applied see for example Benton and Straumann (n 56) 1–12; for a critical survey of the *Vacuum domicilium* (vacancy) as a precept of Roman origins and justification for settlement by reference to Locke's theorisation of property see Paul Corcoran, 'John Locke on the Possession of Land: Native Title v the Principle of *Vacuum domicilium*' Proceedings, Australian Political Studies Association Annual Conference Melbourne 2007 <https://digital.library.adelaide.edu.au/dspace/bitstream/2440/44958/1/hdl_44958.pdf> accessed 12 January 2022.

61 Wood (n 12) 27; Benton and Straumann (n 56).

62 Wood (n 12) 28–31.

63 Larry Patriquin (ed), *The Ellen Meiksins Wood Reader* (Historical Materialism Book Series Vol. 40, Brill 2012) 66 <https://cominsitu.files.wordpress.com/2016/01/the-ellen-meiksins-wood-reader-2012.pdf> accessed 20 October 2022.

did not lend itself to this type of partition. Where claims to sovereign title were at stake, the unison between private property and public power which characterised feudal lordship injected uncertainty into the coherence of the division under Roman law. In consequence, theorists of empire found themselves revisiting medieval jurists' ruminations about the nature of property – e.g. is it a natural right or a social convention?[64] This delving afresh into old questions prompted legal innovations of enduring significance for Western legal theory.

Rationale of taking: Vitoria and Locke

Two innovators who made an enduring contribution to the development of Western jurisprudence were the 16th-century theologian and jurist Francisco de Vitoria and the 17th-century physician and enlightenment philosopher John Locke. As Anghie and others point out, Vitoria's 1539 addresses on the relationship between the Spaniards and the Indians (*Relectio de Indis*) are regarded as founding texts of IL. His analysis of the colonial encounter in these addresses had long-lasting influence over Grotius, the main progenitor of IL, the law of war and the discipline in general.[65] Vitoria's reasoning also reverberates in the language, premise and provisions of modern IIAs. Both dress up a reality of power differentials with the language of reciprocity, equality and righteousness. His theorisation of the 'discovered' other as simultaneously equal and unequal may be one reason why opinions differ on the question of whether Vitoria was a critic or advocate of empire.[66] As for Locke, Macpherson accredits him with being the first to have made the case for unlimited property.[67] Wood describes his use of the concept of 'improvement' as 'emblematic' of the tide of agrarian capitalist property relations.[68]

Vitoria's main concern was with the public domain of sovereign title, whereas Locke's prime interest lay in the private domain of property rights. Pursuant to the Roman model, the two are said to occupy two distinct realms of activities. Paul Corcoran, for instance, warns against the tendency among legal theorists to gloss over or ignore 'the significant difference between a theory of the origins of private property and a theory of political sovereignty'.[69] Yet, the investment protection regime discussed earlier is a reminder that the legal boundary between sovereignty and property is not hermetic. On the contrary, the public and the private are co-constitutive and interdependent in their mutual engagement. Examples of nodes of linkages are found in European legal systems which tended to be more acceptable of the idea that private property represents a governmental concession and has a

64 For a discussion of medieval debates see Wood (n 14) 182–6.

65 Anthony Anghie, *Imperialism, Sovereignty and the Making of International Law* (Cambridge Studies in International and Comparative Law, CUP 2004) 14.

66 See for example, Wood (n 51) 85–9 arguing that Vitoria's stand in relation to empire was ambivalent.

67 C. B. Macpherson (ed), *Property: Mainstream and Critical Positions* (University of Toronto Press 1999) 17.

68 Wood (n 14) 110, 157.

69 Corcoran (n 60) 3.

social function.[70] Even in Rome – home to the original sovereignty–property distinction – some types of property could be excluded from the private sphere and, by extension, from legal transactions by virtue of their social function. Roads, constantly flowing water, ports and squares, among others, were deemed communal and freely available to all people.[71] Medieval debates about the nature of property went hand in hand with enquiries into the scope of the pope's jurisdiction.[72] By the early 16th century, Domingo de Soto, a pupil of Vitoria, followed in his master's footsteps when he critiqued 13th-century canon lawyers' assertions that the pope's jurisdiction extended also to private property and included the exclusive rights to distribute it. De Soto considered this 'a prescription for tyranny'.[73] In the context of European expansion – be it the Spanish empire of conquest or the English empire of commerce and agriculture – the Roman private law concept of *res nullius* was applied to both property and sovereignty.[74] Its application to sovereignty enabled European kings and/or the pope to treat the colonies as their private property. In the British Columbia province of Canada in the 19th century, the blanket assertion of sovereignty was a precondition for and the means by which an economy of private property could be established. Settlement was contingent and followed on from sovereignty. Once sovereign title was established, the settlers could then arrive to survey, divide, appropriate and make the land their own.[75] In other words, the questions of who or what category of people can hold and alienate private property and the terms on which this can be done are not freestanding. They interface with the sovereign competence to define, assert, accord or extinguish property rights. Property rights are integral to the matrix of state formation, production structures, class relations and power. From this perspective, in their different ways, Vitoria and Locke provided nested layers of reasoning within a single rationale of empire.

Vitoria's dissection of the workings of colonial relations in *Relectio de Indis* was framed by the specificities of the Spanish experience. As well as rivals' contestations over the legitimacy of the Spanish title, there was the additional challenge posed by the sophistication of the conquered polities. According to the legal doctrines of the day, these were polities of heathen lacking the legitimacy which only religious authority could confer. As communities of unbelievers they were to have no rights, including rights to property. Yet, the high level of their civilisation was

70 M. Sornarajah, *The International Law on Foreign Investment* (3rd edn, CUP 2010) 371 giving as an example Article 14 of the German post-war constitution. For a discussion of different perspectives of property rights see also Janet Dine, *Companies, International Trade and Human Rights* (Cambridge Studies in Corporate Law CUP 2005) 250–7.

71 Baha Yigit Sayin et al., 'Land Law and Limits on the Right to Property: Historical, Comparative and International Analysis' (2017) 6(1) *European Property Law Journal* 4 <https://papers.ssrn.com/sol3/papers.cfm?abstract_id=2972489> accessed 13 January 2022.

72 For a fuller discussion of medieval debates see Wood (n 14) 182–6.

73 Pagden (n 57) 51.

74 Benton and Straumann (n 56) 18.

75 Brenna Bhandar, 'Status as Property: Identity, Land and the Dispossession of First Nations Women in Canada' (2016) at p. 5 SOAS Research Online <https://eprints.soas.ac.uk/22445/> accessed 2 May 2018.

impossible to deny. Vitoria responded to these challenges by creating a new jurisprudence from which divine law as the basis for civil authority had been removed. He divested the pope of his temporal authority, confined it to the spiritual dimension of the Christian world and grounded both public and private ownership in natural law and its man-made derivative, the law of nations. With property now detached from religion, the path was clear for the Indians to be eligible for ownership notwithstanding their status as non-believers. They could possess 'true dominion, both in private and public affairs'.[76] As to conquest, the pope no longer had the prerogative to ordain it. As to the fruits of discovery, pursuant to the law of nations, there could be no title to things already owned. Since ownership by the Indians preceded the Spaniard's arrival, there could be no title in discovery *per se*.[77] Out of this natural law-based secular universalism, the Indians emerged as possessing 'the facility of reason and hence a means of ascertaining *jus gentium*'.[78] Therefore, they qualified to hold title and rights over their land and could partake in the universal realm of commerce. They were equal fellow humans with their own coherent institutions and the capacity to engage in reciprocal commercial exchanges.[79]

Yet, egalitarianism and reciprocity then took a reductive turn on two grounds. First, there was the problem of the Indian personality. On the one hand, the Indian was capable of reason. Therefore, he could access the law of nations and was equally bound by it. On the other hand, his customs and practices were at variance with the universal norms represented by Spanish customs and practices. The ontological Indian was thus the same and equal. The 'particular' one, however, was different and inferior. His equality was contingent on 'the adoption or the imposition of the universally applicable practices of the Spanish'.[80] Until such time, Spanish rule was justified, including the right to demand submission to the law and the right to intervene on behalf of those seen as victims of Indian rituals.[81]

Second, there was *res nullius* – the land and its resources deemed vacant, unowned and available for taking. Title to *res nullius* was to be established through 'natural partnership and communication'.[82] The meaning of 'natural partnership', however, was to be prescribed by the Spaniards. First, there was to be no discriminatory conduct. The Spaniards could not be excluded from sharing in property already shared with others.[83] Second, as a matter of natural law, title could not be denied to the first taker and occupier: 'if gold in the ground and pearls in the sea or anything else in the rivers has not been appropriated, they will belong by the

76 Anthony Pagden and Jeremy Lawrence (eds), *Vitoria Political Writing* (Cambridge Texts in the History of Political Thought CUP 2010) 251.
77 Benton and Straumann (n 56) 21.
78 Anghie (n 65) 20, 22.
79 Pagden and Lawrence (n 76) 251; Anghie (n 65) 17–19.
80 Anghie (n 65) 22.
81 Ibid 22.
82 Pagden and Lawrence (n 76) 278.
83 Benton and Straumann (n 56) 21–2.

law of nations to the first taker, just like the little fishes in the sea'.[84] Finally, there were to be no restrictions on the Spaniards' freedom to travel and trade in Indian territories, again as a matter of the law of nations.[85] In the event of Indian contestations, the system was to be protected by a right to a 'just war'. Just war, much like contemporary humanitarian intervention, 'might be necessary to defend the "innocent" or, more broadly, to promote the values of "civilized" life' . . . or on behalf of a universal 'human republic' whose peace, order and free commerce have come under threat.[86]

Theoretically, *res nullius* was to bind both Spaniards and Indians equally. Yet, the reality of this purported equality was airbrushed out of this narrative. In reality, it was the Spaniards who were present in the Indies. The Indians were not present in Spain, nor did they intend to go there. At issue was only the Spaniards' right to the Indians' gold, pearls and everything else. Thus, the narrative of equality before the law legitimised inequality in practice and underscored the Spaniards' entitlement to a share in Indian wealth. Simultaneously, it delegitimised and silenced the Indian's sovereign right to oppose such entitlement. In a double act of reasoning, taking was first negated but then reaffirmed through the language of equality and reciprocity. Conquest and settlement as originators of title were replaced with free travel and entitlement to reside. Together, they operated to justify Spanish intrusions into Indian society. The use of force was then brought full circle to regain its utility, now dressed up as a right of the civilised to defend their civilisation in the face of contestation by the uncivilised.

Vitoria's explanation of colonial relations leaves unanswered questions such as how and on whose terms owned and unowned were to be understood. What constitutes vacancy? Enter John Locke and his enquiry into the origin of property. Green identifies two queries as central to it. The first is 'how men have come to appropriate'. The second is 'how the idea of right has come to be associated with their appropriation'.[87]

By the late 17th century, agrarian capitalism was already well rooted in the English countryside. Outside of England, a 'New World' had been 'discovered'. These transformations provided the backdrop to the two pillars on which rested Locke's enquiry into the origin of property relations. One was the concept of improvement and the other was the theory of labour. The idea that the expenditure of labour may create a proprietary right is not new in and of itself. It is found in Roman as well as Islamic jurisprudence. Similarly, Locke's starting point that the earth was gifted by God for humanity to hold in common is present in medieval and 17th-century puritan theory. It also featured in Vitoria's writings. Locke, however, innovated these ideas by injecting them with his defence of appropriation, the

84 Pagden and Lawrence (n 76) 280 cited in Benton and Straumann (n 56) 22.
85 Benton and Straumann (n 56) 22, 23.
86 Wood (n 51) 91–2; see also Anghie (n 65) 23–8.
87 Thomas Hill Green, 'The Right of the State in Regard to Property' in Macpherson (n 67) 103.

meaning he gave to 'cultivation' and his abstraction of improvement as exchange value. This singled him out as a pioneer of the logic of capitalist relations and the rationale of an empire of commerce and agriculture. Four aspects of his theorisation of the origin of property are examined next.

The first is Locke's understanding of the individual as self-proprietary and self-governing. People's right to their body and therefore to their labour is natural, inherent and inalienable. All other rights flow from it. Private ownership emerges out of the womb of common ownership not through divine reward or even general consent but 'as an extension of a man's person and his labour, in which he has an exclusive right by nature'.[88] Thus, property needs no societal or governmental grant since it is imprinted in the essence of a person. It is inescapably intrinsic to a person's humanity and her liberty to live through it. Property forms an indispensable part of a person's 'primal individuality'.[89] It is 'individuality itself'.[90] Therefore, the defence of property is tantamount to the defence of the individual and the enforcement of natural law.[91] From this understanding of the individual as tied to her body by the bond of property flows the narrative of a commercial society with which we have come to be so familiar. That is the account of history as a struggle towards freedom from the fetters of beliefs, ideologies, morals and the vagaries of politics which tether humanity's yearnings to pursue its natural and rational inclination. That is, the inclination 'to maximize profit through acts of exchange' and to improve 'the organization and instruments of work in order to enhance the productivity of labour'.[92]

Second is the notion of money and commerce as an answer to the limits of production imposed by the divine injunction against spoilage. Locke solves the problem of limits to accumulation by abstracting improvement as value, which is then attached to 'durable movables' such as gold and silver.[93] Macpherson raises the following question: given that the Lockean subject is a rational being in both moral and utilitarian respects, 'why would anyone want to appropriate more than he could make use of for the support and conveniency of life?'[94] Moreover, why would she want to do so, as Locke suggests, after but not before the introduction of money? Locke's answer, argues Macpherson, is to treat money not merely as means of exchange, but as capital. Both money and land are 'to be laid out in

88 Wood (n 51) 267.

89 Asad (n 48, chapter 2) 168; Eric Cheyfitz, 'Savage Law: The Plot Against American Indians in Johnson and Graham Lessee v M'Intosh and the Pioneers' in Amy Kaplan and Donald E. Pease (eds), *Cultures of United States Imperialism* (New Americanists series Duke University Press 1993) 110.

90 Étienne Balibar, 'The Reversal of Possessive Individualism: From Locke to Derrida' (2002) 9 *Constellation* 299 at p. 302 cited in Bhandar (n 75) 17.

91 Wood (n 51) 272; C. B. Macpherson, *The Political Theory of Possessive Individualism: Hobbes to Locke* (OUP Canada 2011) 218–19; Corcoran (n 60) 17.

92 Wood (n 14) 5–6.

93 Macpherson (n 91) 204.

94 Ibid.

trading stock or materials and wages, the land to be used to produce commodities for trade'.[95] This benefits not only the individual improver but also humanity as a whole. As value augments, so does humanity's common stock. Via the mediums of money and commerce, excess value is not wasted but is there for others to enjoy. Both the property owner and the propertyless are enriched.[96] The act of taking transforms into an act of giving so that a person 'who accumulates and improves large holdings, far from violating the rights of others, actually enhances their well-being'. [97] It is true that inequality is produced in consequence. However, since the fusion of value, money and commerce is consensual, so is inequality. 'Hence, an individual is justified in appropriating land even when it does not leave enough and as good for others'.[98] The consequential inequality is inevitable, part of 'the necessity of affairs and the constitution of human society'.[99]

Third, improvement is understood in its original meaning of making a profit, increasing the value of a thing. In other words, labour in and of itself does not suffice. It is only through its expenditure in a manner which produces value that communal ownership dissipates and private ownership materialises. Importantly, the value contemplated is not use but exchange value. An acre of land in England and an equally fertile acre in unimproved America have the same natural, intrinsic value. Yet, 'the Benefit Mankind receives from the one, in a Year, is worth 5l and from the other possibly not worth a Penny, if all the Profit an *Indian* received from it were it valued and sold here; at least, I may truly say, 1/1000'.[100] The figure of 1/1000 is significant because therein lies the answer to the following question: if property originates from an act of improvement and improvement equates added value, why is it that the improver is entitled to the whole thing rather than only to that portion which represents the added value? This is because the thing in its original, uncultivated state has no value. 'Thus it would be petty to insist that one should receive only the increment in value produced, and not the entire object'.[101] The earth has no intrinsic value. Where it is worked in a manner which stops at use, it is not being cultivated. It is waste. It belongs to everyone, meaning that it belongs to no one and is available for appropriation. Moreover, since uncultivated land is of no value, its appropriation attracts no compensation. There is nothing to compensate for. On the contrary, there is every reason for the dispossessed Indian and English commoner to be grateful for the improvement bestowed on them. From this flows an account of 'European history' as a march towards progress. It comprises 'continuously productive actions defining as well as defined by law'

95 Ibid 205.
96 Wood (n 51) 267–8.
97 Ibid 268.
98 Macpherson (n 91) 211.
99 Ibid 207.
100 Matthew Clayton and Andres Williams, 'John Locke: Of Property' in *Social Justice* (Blackwell Publishing 2004) 28.
101 Jonathan Wolfe, *Robert Nozick: Property, Justice and the Minimal State* (Polity Press 1996) 104 following Karl Olivercrona, 'Locke's Theory of Appropriation' (1974) 24 *Philosophical Quarterly* 24.

and is 'narrated in terms of improvement and accumulation'.[102] The description of uncultivated/unimproved land as 'waste' continues to feature not only in the narratives surrounding contemporary land grabs, but also in the context of the purported regeneration and gentrification of poor urban areas.

Fourth, the transformation from being 'unowned' to being 'owned' is mediated by the fusion of labour with the land. The mere fact of the *res/terra* being *nullius* does not suffice. An additional act of 'mixing' is required. Robert Nozick questions why it is that the mixing of that which is private with that which is common results in privatisation rather than the other way round. If I spill a can of tomato juice into the sea where it evenly mingles with the water, he asks, do I thereby come to own the sea?[103] Locke makes the same point in paragraph 40: 'Nor is it so strange, as perhaps before consideration it may appear, that the *Property of labour* should be able to over-balance the Community of Land'.[104] The answer lies in the distinctiveness of labour as a creator of value. 'For 'tis *Labour* indeed that *puts the difference of value* on everything'.[105] This gives rise to another question, one which Morris Cohen poses in his discussion of the tension between the theory of labour and the way society works in reality. In real life, goods are rarely, if ever, produced by a single person and without the aid of others. How then is value creation and associated ownership to be divided among the various participants?[106] 'It turns out', says Wood, 'that there is no direct correspondence between labour and property' after all. This is 'because one man can appropriate the labour of another'.[107] The act of mixing is not exclusive to one's own body but may entail the appropriation or purchase of another's. Given that one's natural right to one's own body is of a proprietary nature, it follows that it can also be sold and exchanged. From the buyer's perspective, the purchase of labour amounts to the purchase of a proprietary right including the value created through it.[108] Thus the question of 'division among the participants' does not arise: whether the landlord uses her own body or the body of others, it is invariably she who is the improver. This understanding shapes contemporary discourses. When we talk about producers we normally refer to the capitalists and/or the corporate form through which they operate. The worker labours to produce, but it is the capitalist who is accredited with the act 'production'.[109] Therefore, it is the capitalist, not the worker, who is entitled to the entirety of that which was produced including its surplus value. Thus, when foreign capital enters a country in the exercise of the Vitorian right to free movement, trade and now also investment, proprietary rights and rewards attach to it rather than to the working

102 Talal Asad, *Formations of the Secular: Christianity, Islam, Modernity* (Stanford University Press 2003) 168.
103 Wolfe (n 101) 103.
104 Clayton and Williams (n 100) 27.
105 Ibid 27.
106 Morris Cohen, 'Property and Sovereignty' in Macpherson (n 67) 163.
107 Wood (n 14) 111.
108 Macpherson (n 91) 214–15.
109 Wood (n 14) 112.

population. The manner of the attachment is such that the entirety of the investment is subsumed and nothing is owed to society for it.

In summary, in the Lockean world appropriation is constitutive of property. It is twin to the divine injunction to curb waste, improve and make profitable God's original grant of commonly held yet worthless earth.[110] 'So that God, by commanding to subdue gave Authority so far to *appropriate*'.[111] The power to appropriate, says Balibar, is the Lockean subject's point of origin. Its exercise is central to her being.[112] There is no property in anything which has not been appropriated in some manner or at some point in time.[113]

In their different ways, both Vitoria and Locke ended up having to explain inequality. Locke's version centred on improvement. Improvement through labour as the centrepiece of the natural history of autonomous property ran in parallel with self-improvement, education and industry in the natural history of the autonomous individual. From this flowed a belief in the inevitability of economic inequality and the literate master's domination over the illiterate 'servant' or the wild Indian who roamed the land, oblivious to labour, value and money.[114] Both the servant and the Indian were at once equal and inferior. Ontological equality was simultaneously also contingent and differentiated insofar as it concerned abilities, customs, habits and property relations.

Also in the Lockean world, the social functions attached to property were discounted and public ownership as a possible route to improvement was not considered.[115] As articulated by Nozick, enhancing the social product is not private ownership's purpose or rationale. The social product grows because the means of production are in the hands of those best equipped to make efficient use of them. The benefit to others is merely incidental to the improving owner's success.[116] Thus, having been liberated from church and state control, property was placed in the hands of private owners said to be best placed to manage its circulation in the market.[117]

Appropriation as the handmaiden of property is also at the heart of the transition from a state of nature to the superior state of a civilisation. A civilisation–property nexus was constructed in which property acquired an enlarged meaning. It was no longer merely the essence of the individual. It was also the foundation of civilised society. In the words of James Madison, 19th-century political theorist and fourth president of the US, property is a 'broad and majestic term', one that 'embraces everything which may have a value to which man may attach a right'.[118] Similarly,

110 Clayton and Williams (n 100) 21–2; Macpherson (n 91) 200; Wood (n 14) 110.
111 Clayton and Williams (n 100) 24.
112 Balibar (n 90) 302–3.
113 Green (n 87) 104.
114 Wood (n 51) 257–8; Losurdo (n 26) 24.
115 Cohen (n 106) 164; Macpherson (n 91) 221.
116 Wolfe (n 101) 109.
117 Asad (n 102) 192.
118 Cited in Pagden (n 57) 78.

for Emerich de Vattel, the 18th-century Swiss philosopher and jurist accredited with the development of some of IL's foundational principles, the cultivation of land, the realisation of nature's potential is an obligation imposed on man by nature. It forms a fundamental part of what it means to be human. And so, as the colonial project shifted from 'the cultivation of souls to the cultivation of land', religious conversion was being supplemented with production as the path to civilisation. Property was pivotal to this transition. For instance, the 1887 Dawes Act which terminated treaties as the means of negotiating with the Indians was justified by the intention to 'civilise' them 'by turning them into American property holders'.[119] This private property–civilisation nexus is still with us. The right to property is a key human right and adherence to human rights is a mark of civilisation. For Hayek, attacking private property is tantamount to attacking civilisation itself. In turn, civilisation is to be underpinned by what Wallerstein identifies as the gift of universalism – the process by which the powerful bestows on the powerless the opportunity to join in.[120] In the words of Chief Justice Marshall in *Johnson and Graham's Lessee v M'intosh* (1823) 21 US 543: 'The potentates of the old world found no difficulty in convincing themselves that they made ample compensation to the inhabitants of the new, by bestowing on them civilization and Christianity'.[121] Thus, the opportunity to be brought in from the cold is in and of itself a sufficient reward. Nothing of value was taken in comparison with that which was given. When Britain abolished slavery in 1834, it paid its slave owners £20m (equivalent to $30 billion today) by way of compensation for the loss of their property. The slaves received the opportunity to participate in a civilised way of life as ostensibly free and equal people. This reasoning which transformed the act of private taking into an act of public giving was shared by both Vitoria and Locke. It is possibly the part most evocative of the contemporary discourse of development.

Locke, like Vitoria before him, dismissed conquest as originator of title. However, for him, the constraint imposed on conquest emanated from the sacredness of property rights and their higher ranking compared with the right to life. Title-by-conquest, he said, was achieved by despotic force and violated the inheritance right of the descendants who had no part in the miscarriages committed by their fathers. Therefore, it was unjust and unlawful even where the war itself was just and lawful. The conqueror, said Locke, has absolute power over those who have put themselves in a state of war, but 'he has not thereby a right and title to their possession'. '[H]e that, by conquest has a right over a man's person to destroy him if he pleases, has not thereby a right over his estate to possess and enjoy it'.[122] Locke then pioneered an alternative route to title. For Vitoria it was the right to own unowned things and the 'reciprocal' right to reside, travel and trade founded

119 Cheyfitz (n 89).

120 Immanuel Wallerstein, *Historical Capitalism* (Verso 1983) 85.

121 At 572.

122 John Locke, *Second Treatise of Government* (The Project Gutenberg EBook 2012) paras 180, 182. <https://english.hku.hk/staff/kjohnson/PDF/LockeJohnSECONDTREATISE1690.pdf> accessed 22 January 2022.

on a universal law of nature. For Locke it was the right to settlement. The right to settlement was in turn rooted in his theory about the origin of property. Whether or not conquest had intervened, and whether or not Indian lands were occupied and used, insofar as they were not improved, they remained on the other side of the boundary which demarcated protected private property from the rest.[123] Historically speaking, 'use that would justify an ownership right was defined by cultivation, and cultivation was understood within the relatively narrow parameters of English agrarian capitalism'.[124] Thus, title went to the settlers who, by their labour and the labour of others, performed the divine injunction to appropriate and cultivate. Dispossession replaced conquest as the route to ownership. For 19th-century anarchist philosopher Pierre-Joseph Proudhon, all property was theft and a form of homicide. Theft, however, did not materialise through the occasional individual act. It was systemic and organised. For Nichols, drawing on the works of indigenous scholars and activists, it was in the Anglophone colonies that this system of theft generated a system of property.[125]

Practices of taking by settlement

How was this mode of generating property to be implemented, and did it necessarily exclude recognition of the Indians' right to their land? Settlers' growing ambitions and rapidly changing conditions dictated adaptability. The practice of settlement combined with speculative rush necessitated speed, flexibility and commercial expediency. The rule of law administered in conjunction with extra-legal violence mutated as the initial weakness or absence of a central authority alluded to by Anievas and Nisancioglu was being replaced with strategies of centralisation and state-building. The specificities of local settings and the geographical distance which separated England from its colonies meant that actual modes of property production were not at all times in step with theories developed in the metropolis.[126] Nonetheless, broadly, they were shaped by a shift from conquest and religion towards what Montesquieu referred to as the more refined view of the Americas as an object of commerce. The first step was settlement among the Indian population for which the Indian's consent was not required. Thereafter, the rights of

123 See for example, James Tully, 'Rediscovering America: The Two Treatises and Aboriginal Rights' in G. A. J. Rogers (ed), *Locke's Philosophy: Content and Context* (Clarendon Press 1994) 143; see also John Douglas Bishop, 'Locke's Theory of Original Appropriation and the Right of Settlement in Iroquois Territory' (1997) 27(3) *Canadian Journal of Philosophy* 311 interrogating the coherence of Locke's case that the Amerindian use of their land did not create property rights and whether their proprietary rights can be justified on Locke's own principles; for an argument that Locke did not deny the Amerindians' title to the lands see Corcoran (n 60).

124 Brenna Bhandar, *Colonial Lives of Property: Law, Land and Racial Regimes of Ownership* (Duke University Press 2018) 35.

125 Robert Nichols, 'Theft is Property! The Recursive Logic of Dispossession' (2018) 1(46) *Political Theory* 19, 20.

126 Stuart Banner, *How the Indians Lost Their Land: Law and Power on the Frontier* (HUP 2005) 47–8.

occupation and possession thereby created could be enlarged into the greater right of ownership upon improvement.[127]

Corcoran points to the importance which colonists and colonial governments attached to consensus. Consensus was enacted through treaties and sale contracts.[128] Contractual arrangements were governed and regulated by both colonial and indigenous laws. Titles to purchased land 'were certified by colonial governing councils and disputes adjudicated by colonial courts. No colonist or colonial government was under any illusion about lands being unused and unoccupied'.[129] By the time Locke completed his *Second Treatise*, writes Corcoran, these practices had been long-standing and standardised. He must have known about them given his various public positions, private interests and extensive scholarship. Therefore, he could not have regarded the Americas as 'vacant'.

According to Pagden, the practice of sales contracts or treaties was adopted where the Indian inhabitants proved difficult to displace.[130] Thus, contractual arrangements were a contingency against resistance. They operated in conjunction with 'partial recognition and selective affirmation' of Indian rights.[131] Colonial agent Jeremiah Dummer accepted in 1721 that, undervalued as Indian land was, purchase was the only means by which a just and fair right could be acquired.[132] In the metropolis too, the jurist and diplomat Georg Friedrich von Marten, among others, asserted the existence of natives' property rights irrespective of race or religion. 'The law of property being the same for everybody, independently of their religion or habits', he said, 'natural law does not authorise Christian peoples to appropriate areas that are already occupied by savages against their wish'.[133] However, he went on, 'such a well-entrenched right of property did not . . . position native communities as equal to European states'.[134] Here we meet again the Vitorian Indian subject who is ontologically equal as a matter of law of nature and an inferior savage in reality. Acknowledgement that the land was occupied and the constraint this imposed on taking did not mean the Indians attracted the full bundle of rights which go with ownership. Moreover, it did not entail recognition of their sovereign competence to adopt, reject or redefine the meaning, scope and application of this right, including the manner of its disposal. On Corcoran's own account, titles were certified by colonial councils, not by the Indians. Disputes were heard in colonial, not Indian courts.[135] This was notwithstanding that it was Indian land which was being taken.

127 Pagden (n 57) 73, 77.
128 Corcoran (n 60) 7.
129 Ibid 5.
130 Pagden (n 57) 83.
131 Nichols (n 125) 14.
132 Pagden (n 57) 82–3.
133 Cited in in Martti Koskenniemi, The *Gentle Civilizer of Nations: The Rise and Fall of International Law 1870–1960* (Hersch Lauterpacht Memorial Lectures CUP 2002) 113.
134 Koskenniemi (n 133) 113–14.
135 Cheyfitz (n 89) 109.

In other words, the organisations tasked with defining and giving effect to Indian rights were in the hands of the settlers. It follows that contractual arrangements exercised 'by lawful enterprises of constituted authority' did not necessarily speak to consensus and a contractual meeting of the minds.[136] As in the case of the enclosures and contemporary IIAs discussed earlier, Thompson's legal fiction of impartial logic was unravelled by power differentials, racial hierarchies and class interests. It cloaked partiality and overt violence with the purported neutrality and the covert violence of an imposed legal reasoning. The political moment of expropriation was to be stabilised by the legal technologies of a prescribed new order. Colonial officials, when encountering Indians' complaints about colonists' fraudulent and speculative purchases of their land, felt compelled to offer no more than sympathy.[137]

Moreover, the law was one method by which the savage 'other' could be made to disappear in an instance of 'death agony' that was as effective as it was silent. The Proclamation Act 1763 obliterated the Indian communal form of landholding by requiring that their land be partitioned into individual plots as a precondition to citizenship. The 18th-century Supreme Court decision in *Johnson* translated 'Indian notions of native peoples' relation to their lands into the language of Anglo-American property law'. This was not, says Cheyfitz, in order to empower the Indians, but 'so that ultimate power over their lands, the historical inalienability of which constituted their cultures, could be "legally" transferred to the federal government'.[138] In *Johnson,* the court was guided by the assumption that the Indians held their territories in common and that a tribal chief's consent to the transaction could be taken as consent by the entire tribe. These assumptions articulated a Western understanding of common ownership and political representation. At the centre of this understanding is the individual as a self-contained and separate entity, exclusive of all others. Accordingly, communal ownership refers to the coming together of disparate individuals whose consent to their momentary togetherness is given via an individually elected representative. By contrast in Indian culture, 'identity is conceived of as exclusively mutual rather than, as in the West, mutually exclusive'.[139] Thus, the law was located in what Anghie conceptualised as a 'dynamic of difference'. That is to say, the process of creating a cultural gap between a civilised and non-civilised society and the development of techniques to normalise the latter in accordance with the former's norms.[140]

From the settlers' perspective, sales contracts evidenced consensus. From the Indians perspective, sale contracts demarcated the limits of their humanity and established a truncated form of proprietorship. When the white man discovered that the Indian tribes still owned valuable land, wrote the Lakota philosopher and

136 Corcoran (n 60) 18.
137 Banner (n 126) 87.
138 Cheyfitz (n 89) 110.
139 Ibid 111–12.
140 Anghie (n 65) 4.

Standing Rock Sioux activist Vine Deloria Jr, 'it took no time at all to discover that Indians were really people and should have the right to sell their lands . . . Discovery took away their title to their land and gave them the right only to sell'.[141] The same applied to treaties. Treaties were often fraudulent and must have been incomprehensible to most Indians who had no analogous concept of land ownership. In Indian society – as also in other first-nation societies – property relations were underpinned by cultural and spiritual beliefs. These dictated that land could be occupied and used but not exclusively owned. Nevertheless, in European eyes, treaties represented due process of law and the basis on which legal relations crystallised. It appears that the Indians had the capacity to sign treaties even though their sovereignty was at best debatable and, in any event, differentiated and capable of being appropriated.[142]

As to Locke's contribution, his theory was 'repeated . . . in nearly every discussion of potential rights over 'unoccupied' land'.[143] The Reverend John Bulkeley of Colchester, Connecticut, pointed out in 1725 that the Indians had right or title only to such land as they had subdued or improved. Given the paucity of such land, the proposition of a native right to all land was an absurdity.[144] The Native Americans, said Thomas Pownall, Governor of Massachusetts (1757–1760), were 'not landowners, but hunters, not settlers but wanderers, with no idea of property in land, of that property which arises from a man's mixing his labour with it'.[145] The Lockean narrative clearly applied to Indian hunting grounds deemed *terra nullius*. However, it could also apply to Indian agricultural communities. In the absence of improvement, mere use and occupation did not convert the original communal right into the superior right of private ownership. As pointed out by Arneil with whom Corcoran takes issue, occupation was subsumed by the additional requirement of value creation. [146] Even if occupation and use of the land was not entirely so subsumed by the compulsion of value creation, even if consent had to be manufactured and a contract entered into, the contractual price could not but be low. Indian land was unimproved and therefore of low value. Unimproved land of low value signified life of low value. It was Petty who first fused land and human lives together when, in colonised Ireland, he included labour productivity and level of consumption in his calculations of the market value of land.[147] Since the Indians were neither labour nor consumers, the market value of both their life and their unimproved lands did not amount to much.

141 Vine Deloria Jr, *Custer Died for Your Sins: An Indian Manifesto* (University of Oklahoma Press Norman [1969] 1988) 7, 30 cited in Nichols (n 125) 15.

142 Anghie (n 65) 5–6 and generally.

143 Pagden (n 57) 83.

144 Ibid.

145 Cited in Pagden (n 57) 77.

146 Corcoran (n 60) 18; for an enlarged discussion of the concept of 'use' and 'improvement' see for example Bhandar (n 124) 33–76, 115–48.

147 For a discussion of Petty's work see Bhandar (n 124) 39–47.

Moreover, Locke's theory was easy to absorb for being familiar. From Thomas More's *Utopia* to Gentili to Grotius, endorsement of the injunction against waste and the associated notion 'that uncultivated land was unoccupied and may be simply appropriated' formed part of the development of natural law in European juridical and political scholarship.[148] In More's words, opposition to possession of land otherwise left idle by 'others who by the rule of nature ought to be maintained by it' amounts to 'a most just cause for war'.[149] Locke built on this tradition by redefining vacancy through the redefinition of waste.[150] Land was vacant and waste not merely when it was uncultivated, but when cultivation was unproductive. The 'first producer' was not necessarily the first cultivator. The first producer was the improving landlord who, like Locke's patron, Lord Shaftesbury, benefited society by industriously making his lands profitable and engaging in colonial trade for the purpose of further investing the profits of such trade.[151] Locke's theory of value also served other purposes, such as highlighting self-made colonists' independence from their mother country.[152] Thus, it was integral to the norms and power structures of settler colonialism whether or not the rights of the Indians were recognised sometimes and in some form. Indeed, the use of the word 'rights' in and of itself testifies to that which is being negated. It demonstrates that the language, concepts and terminology used to assess the fate of the Indians are not theirs. Whether or not Locke recognised the Indians' right to occupy their lands, such recognition was not on their terms. Either way they were going to be annihilated whether through the 'death agony' of physical extinction or the 'death agony' of divergence or both. Locke's theory of the origin of property served to erase from memory the horrors of this 'death agony' and replace it with a tale of progress – a narrative of peaceful and publicly beneficial exploitation of agriculture and commerce.[153] The obliteration of non-capitalist structures became a civilising mission that was concerned less with the spread of Christianity and more with integration into capitalist logic, subjugation to its imperatives and the production of capitalist subjectivities.

Those who survived morphed into a separate juridical category. Bhandar locates it on her 'identity-property' nexus. In Canada of the mid-19th century, she observes, two distinct juridical identities were created, each occupying its own economy. One economy was a market place where the settler, a Lockean self-proprietary subject, exercised her right to appropriate and barter. The other was the economy of the reservation, a space of domination where the non-proprietorial,

148 Richard Tuck, *The Rights of Peace and War: Political Thought and the International Order from Grotius to Kant* (OUP 1999) 50, 123–5.

149 Thomas More, Edward Surtz and J. H. Hexter (eds), *Utopia* (Yale University Press 1965) 137 cited in Pagden (n 57).

150 Wood (n 14) 163.

151 Wood (n 51) 275.

152 Anthony Pagden, 'The Struggle for Legitimacy and the Image of the Empire in the Atlantic c.1700' in Nicholas Canny (ed), *The Oxford History of the British Empire: Vol 1: The Origins of Empire* (OUP 1988) 53.

153 Pagden (n 152) 36.

non-appropriating Indian lived.[154] '[A]s aboriginal people were to be assimilated into the nonaboriginal population, the "Indian" was confined to the economy of the reservation where the colonial government attempted to control and regulate every aspect of Indian life'[155] As part of the Canadian economy of reservations, tens of thousands of aborigine children were kidnapped and placed in residential schools where, in the course of their conversion into whiteness, they were abused physically, emotionally and sexually. Thousands died. The last residential school was closed as late as 1997. Bhandar's focus is on Canada. However, the practice of kidnapping reservation children and their assimilation into white civilisation was to be found also in Australia until the 1990s. The US system of reservations transformed the Indians into a differentiated minority in their own land. In *Cherokee Nation v Georgia*, the court described US–Indian relations as those between a ward and its guardian.[156] It was to prove a guardianship of questionable credentials. Carried out between 1951 and 1992 were 928 nuclear tests in the lands of the Shoshone first-nation in violation of the 1863 Treaty of the Ruby Valley. The tests and the 620 kilotons of nuclear fallout they left behind, writes Ian Zabarte, made the Shoshone the most bombed nation on earth.[157]

This chapter looked at the origin of capitalist property and its birth out of the act of taking in both England and the colonies. In the following chapter the historical narrative is paused to examine the concept of property, the rights attached to it and the relationship it gives rise to. The examination is unavoidably brief and incomplete given the vast literature and polemics surrounding the concepts of both 'property' and 'rights'. The hope is that, nevertheless, it will provide some insight in advance of returning to the historical account, particularly the 19th century, when contemporary protection of invested property began to take shape against a redesigned act of taking.

154 Bhandar (n 75) 1; for an account of the legislative process in Canada see pp. 2–3.

155 Bhandar (n 75) 2.

156 (1831) 30 US (5 Pet) 1

157 Ian Zabarte, 'A Message from the Most Bombed Nation on Earth' (*Aljazeera*, 29 August 2020) <https://www.aljazeera.com/opinions/2020/8/29/a-message-from-the-most-bombed-nation-on-earth> accessed 30 January 2022.

5 Property

Property as abstraction

There is nothing new about property or the rights attached to it. Sayin et al., having traced the different representations of property rights in Islamic, Jewish, Hindu and Roman jurisprudential traditions, conclude that they are probably 'the oldest real right, much before concepts such as "right" or "real" (as opposed to "personal") were outlined'.[1] This statement speaks to the proposition that there is no society without some form of property whether or not expressed in terms familiar to the modern mind. Marxists would judge such proposition circular since, according to Marx, property presupposes the existence of production and therefore of social organisation. The three are co-dependent and co-constitutive. There is no property if there is no society and there is no society if there is no production.

For Marx, all property is social relations. The nature of these relations is determined by the forces and mode of production at a given historical moment. Since the forces and modes of production are historically contingent, so is property. Thus, an enquiry into property relations is an enquiry into a specific form of production and therefore a specific form of the society through which the appropriation of nature is mediated and possession of the object is recognised (or not) as a relation of belonging. Engaged in this mediation is the matrix of state formation, class relations and power structures. Marx defined the specificity of capitalist property by its detachment from social embellishments and its 'final and most complete expression of the system of producing and appropriating products, that is based on class antagonism, on the exploitation of the many by the few.' It is founded 'on the antagonism between capital and wage labour'.[2]

Things take on a commodity form when they satisfy needs (have use value) and are exchanged for something else (have an exchange value). In capitalist societies, commodities replace concrete goods as the elementary unit of wealth. They are

1 Baha Yigit Sayin et al., 'Land Law and Limits on the Right to Property: Historical, Comparative and International Analysis' (2017) 6(1) *European Property Law Journal* 4 <https://papers.ssrn.com/sol3/papers.cfm?abstract_id=2972489> accessed 13 January 2022.

2 Karl Marx and Fredrick Engels, *The Communist Manifesto (1848)* (Pathfinder Press 2008) 48, 49.

DOI: 10.4324/9781315386782-7

produced privately and distributed by means of market exchange. That is, impersonally and without direct social organisation. This manner of exchange is one of the defining features of capitalist social relation as opposed to, for instance, earlier societies where exchange was governed by custom or religion. The effect of this mechanism of exchange is to abstract the product's specific and concrete use value into an equalised exchange value. Two different use values in a relationship of exchange are abstracted as exchange value; so much of one commodity equals so much of another. Two commodities may differ concretely but may be of equal value. Consequently, value no longer reflects some natural property of the object but assumes a social form. The physical particularities of products – their material attributes – are spirited away to be subsumed by their value. In parallel, since the only thing which different commodities have in common is the fact that their value is the product of human labour, when their material particularities are made to disappear, so do those of labour. Together with commodities, human labour also becomes human labour in the abstract. It is no longer viewed through the concrete attributes which distinguish the baker from the blacksmith. All are lumped together regardless of what each does in particular.

> With the disappearance of the useful character of the products of labour, the useful character of the kinds of labour embodied in them also disappears . . . They can no longer be distinguished, but are all together reduced to the same kind of labour, human labour in the abstract.[3]

Thus, abstraction is not an idea. It is not a product of the human mind. Rather, it is a social process shaped by the manner of social organisation in which it is situated. Bhandar, following Evgeny Pashukanis, makes the point that in capitalist societies the legal forms which abstractions assume mask and render invisible the many different ways in which people relate to each other and produce and reproduce their existence.[4] They operate to cover the human topography of variegated histories, memories and concrete practices with an ever-denser blanket of impersonal, market-based exchange.

The concept of exchange value featured in the earlier discussion about Locke's theory of property. John Commons, in his seminal book, *Legal Foundations of Capitalism*, chartered US law's adaptation to this process of abstraction. The legal meaning of property was reversed 'from the use-value to the exchange value of things, and therefore from the producing power that increases use-values to the bargaining power that increases exchange values'.[5] The definition of property

3 Karl Marx, *Capital: Critique of Political Theory* (Vol. 1, Penguin Books 1976) 128 cited in Beverly Best, *Marx and the Dynamic of the Capital Formation: An Aesthetics of Political Economy* (Palgrave Macmillan 2010) 12.

4 Brenna Bhandar, 'Title by Registration: Institution Modern Property Law and Creating Racial Value in the Settler Colony' (2015) 42(2) *Journal of Law and Society* 253 at 265.

5 John R. Commons, *Legal Foundation of Capitalism* (The Lawbook Exchange, Ltd 2012) 21.

advanced by the minority in the 1872 *Slaughter House* judgement as 'everything which has exchangeable value' gradually gained traction. By 1890, in the *Minnesota Rate* case, the Supreme Court itself changed the definition of property from a physical thing which has only use value to anything which has an exchange value.[6] Property's transition from visibility to 'the most ethereal invisibility' was confirmed in 1902 when the lower court declared that it 'is not, in its modern sense confined to that which may be touched by the hand, or seen by the eye'.[7]

As understood by Marx, exchange value refers to the value which may be obtained upon sale/exchange of the product in the market. Marx also echoes in Commons's comment about the centrality of this enlargement-by-abstraction to capitalism as a worldwide system. Under conditions of plenary capitalism no production, even that of the farmer, is undertaken for one's own use. Production is invariably for use by others.[8] Morton Horwitz locates this doctrinal transition in the US transition from agrarian to industrial capitalism. Whereas at the stage of agrarian capitalism, protection had to be directed at landowners and their physical property in the form of land, industrialisation brought about a reversal into 'a dazzling variety of abstract and intangible property claims . . . developed out of an increasingly commercial society'.[9] Following this reversal, wrote Commons, 'Assets' have transformed into intangible property since from now on they were to represent the expected exchange-value of anything which yields income in the course of transacting modern business'.[10] Correspondingly, the right to free access to the market became essential since in its absence no exchange value is possible.[11]

This departure from old principles of common law was criticised for its circularity and 'theoretical absurdity'.[12] For example, the level of rates charged by a utility company determines their expected returns and therefore their market value. It follows that for a court to decide on the level of rates based on their fair value, it would need to fix them first.[13] American courts were also criticised on the ground that, by converting profit expectations into property, they 'came as close as they

6 *Slaughter House* (1872) 16 Wall. 36; *Chicago, M &St. P.RY. Co. Minnesota* (1890) 134 US 418; both cases and others are discussed in Commons (n 5) 11–16.

7 *National Telegraph News Co. V Western Union Tel. Co* (1902) 119 Fed. 204, 294 discussed in Commons (n 5) 18.

8 Commons (n 5) 21.

9 Morton J. Horwitz, *The Transformation of American Law 1870–1960: The Crisis of Legal Orthodoxy* (OUP 1992) cited in Ivan Pupolizio, 'The Right to an Unchanging World: Indirect Expropriation in International Investment Agreements and State Sovereignty' (2015) 2 <https://papers.ssrn.com/sol3/papers.cfm?abstract_id=2676166> accessed 31 December 2021.

10 Commons (n 5) 19.

11 Ibid 17.

12 Gerard C. Henderson, 'Railways Valuation and the Courts' (1920) 33(8) *The Harvard Law Review* 1031 <https://www.jstor.org/stable/pdf/1327629.pdf> accessed 20 February 2022.

13 The US Supreme Court was asked to fix the reasonable rates to be charged by private companies for the provision of public services in *Allgeyer v Louisiana* (1891) 165 US (*the Rates Cases*) discussed in Commons (n 5) 17; On the point of circularity see Henderson (n 12) 1031–2, 1033–6.

ever had to saying that one had a property right to unchanging world'.[14] The US Supreme Court later abandoned this reversal of the meaning of property and, by extension, the proprietary right to an unchanging world it created. However, it has been revived on a global scale as part of the investment protection regime, specifically in the context of the indirect expropriation standard of treatment. The same circularity applies. A decision on the occurrence of indirect expropriation engages questions of value and profit expectations. Yet, legal protection and the availability of ISDS in particular are in themselves constituents of market value and profit expectations. ISDS claims have become assets capable of being securitised and financialised. Financial speculators increasingly purchase companies in possession of an ISDS claim deemed winnable, at times using shell companies to do so. With compensation payable out of the public purse proving lucrative, third party funding (TPF) of ISDS claims by hedge and equity funds has expanded significantly in recent decades.[15] Rule 14 of the 2022 Amendments to the ICSID Arbitration Rules requires a party to the proceedings to disclose the name and address of 'any non-party from which the party, directly or indirectly, has received funds for the pursuit or defense of the proceeding through a donation or grant, or in return for remuneration dependent on the outcome of the proceeding'. The main aim of this amendment is to circumvent potential conflicts between funders and arbitrators. Accordingly, a demand that the terms of funding be disclosed was successfully resisted on ground of irrelevancy. The provision includes TPF for the defence of ISDS claims. However, the best outcome a respondent state can hope for is not having to pay out. Therefore, it is not as attractive to TPF providers and its participation in the proceedings is likely to be financed using public funds.

The definition of 'ethereally invisible' assets as investment and the undetermined nature of indirect expropriation in vaguely drafted IIAs mean that ISDS tribunals are well positioned to re-create a world in which property stands in the way of change. Zachary Douglas's critique in this regard and his insistence on the essential nature of proprietary relations seeks to impose limits on the propensity to abstract property as value. Douglas questions the extent to which value fits in with a jurisdictional regime of investment-as-property. Access to market, valuable as it may be, lacks the hallmarks of proprietary relations since it is neither exclusionary nor alienable. Loss of value may have a probative function and may go to the question of quantum. However, in and of itself, it may not be relied upon for the purpose of identifying covered investment. Yet, legislation and regulatory change which affect investors' profit expectations remain at risk of tumbling into the status of a compensable transgression, casting doubt over the justificatory force of the promise of progress and institutional improvement.

14 Horwitz (n 9) 151 cited in Pupolizio (n 9) 3.

15 On third party funding see for example Brooke Guven, Lise Johnson, 'The Policy Implications of Third-Party Funding in Investor State Arbitration (2019) Columbia Center on Sustainable Investment <https://scholarship.law.columbia.edu/cgi/viewcontent.cgi?article=1007&context=sustainable_investment_staffpubs> accessed 21 February 2022.

Brenna Bhandar advances the Torrens system of title by registration as another example of the logic of abstraction which inheres in capitalist commodification.[16] Title by registration was introduced in the UK through the Law of Property 1925 and the subsequent Land Registration Rules 1930. It signified a reversal from ownership derived from concrete and individualised practices of possession, use and alienation. Concrete ownership was replaced with a fictitious concept constructed around an expectation of security and codified in impersonal administrative procedures. The Land Registration Rules encouraged postal rather than personal searches of the register so that practitioners were no longer assessing the quality of the title. Instead, they were transferring a pre-processed one.[17] 'Property ownership came to be defined by these abstract qualities and required different legal forms and techniques, such as title by registration, to structure and realize newly configured relations of exchange and modes of alienation'.[18]

Title by registration arrived at UK shores following a period of gestation and experimentation in the colonies. The colonies were a suitable laboratory because they were free from the landed aristocracy and the leftovers of feudalism which continued to blemish the English proprietary landscape and presented obstacles to change. Moreover, the colonies offered a clean canvass on which new designs could be drawn. Obstacles to the distancing of ownership from possession and use could be overcome with relative ease by the removal of native populations. In the forests of England and Germany troublesome dispossessed were disciplined through their abstraction as criminals. In the colonies they were made to disappear altogether through their abstraction as savages. Their existence was negated by reason of their savagery. In turn, '[t]he racial abstraction embodied in the figure of the Savage or Native . . . enabled English settlers to impose the Torrens system of registration first in South Australia, and then elsewhere'.[19] Nichols termed this demarcation between the white world of property and the dark world of the savage 'simultaneous negation'. Proprietary rights were being negated by the surrounding social environment. Settlement represented the capacity to own, 'savagery' represented a right to sell.[20] Construction of the savage 'other' as incapable of forming a proprietary relationship (other than the right to sell) was integral to the colonial process of transformation into property. Property could then be abstracted through taking that was grounded in a racialised taxonomy.

16 Bhandar (n 4) 253.

17 Alain Pottage, 'The Originality of Registration' (1995) 15(3) *Oxford Journal of Legal Studies* 371 at 372, 383.

18 Bhandar (n 4) 255.

19 Ibid 256; see also 257, 275–9.

20 On whiteness as property see Cheryl Harris, 'Whiteness as Property' (1993) 106 *Harvard Law Review* 1709.

Property as social relations

Liberal theorists are divided along two main, competing conceptions of property. On one view it is a bundle of rights realisable by people against each other. This view follows on from Wesley Hohfeld's analysis of legal regulations as sets of correlatives and opposites involving four entitlements (claim-rights, liberties, power-rights and immunities) and four dis-entitlements (duties, no-rights, liabilities and disabilities). The rival view is that of property as a person's right to a thing to which secondary rules of social practices and enforcement are attached. It stems from a distinction which originated in ancient Rome, developed in medieval times and resurfaced in the 18th century. That is, the distinction drawn between personal (*in personam*) rights and those that are 'real' or in *rem*. The Latin concept of *in rem* denotes in and against the thing (*res*), propping up an understanding of property as relations with a thing. Timothy Earle, for example, defines it as 'the complex relationship between people and their land, animals, slaves, facilities and moveable goods'.[21] Hohfeld considered this distinction crude and fallacious.[22] In John Austin's famous words: 'The phrase *in rem* denotes the *compass*, and not the *subject* of the right. It denotes that the right in question avails against persons generally; *and not* that the right in question is a right over a *thing*'.[23] The comment touches on the main criticism levelled against the 'bundle of rights' theory. It is said to be reductive of the essential distinction between proprietary and personal rights because of its focus on 'the number of persons who owe a duty and the number of persons to whom a duty is owed'.[24] It fails to capture the absolute nature of property in the sense that the rights it gives rise to are good against the whole world. The effect is to 'emasculate the special role that the institution of property rights plays in complex societies'.[25] Another criticism of the 'bundle of rights' theory is that it confuses the primary relations between the person and the subject of property – the *res* – with the secondary rules which regulate interventions by others in these relations.

The distinctive feature of the 'right to a thing' view of property is its exclusivity. The proprietor's right to exclude has 'sometimes been described as the defining characteristic of property in Anglo-American jurisprudence'.[26] It follows that,

21 Timothy Earle, 'Property in Prehistory' in Michele Graziadei and Lionel Smith (eds), *Comparative Property Law: Global Perspectives* (Research Handbooks in Comparative Law Edward Elgar Publishing 2017) 3.

22 Wesley Newcomb Hohfeld, 'Fundamental Legal Conceptions as Applied in Legal Reasoning' (1917) 26(8) *The Yale Law Journal* 710.

23 John Austin, *Lectures on Jurisprudence or the Philosophy of Positive Law*, Vol. 1 Lecture XIII (5th edn, Revised and edited by Robert Campbell The Lawbook Exchange 2005) 380.

24 J. E. Penner, 'The "Bundle of Rights" Picture of Property' (1995–1996) 43 *UCLA Law Review* 711 at 731 cited in Zachary Douglas, 'Property, Investment and the Scope of Investment Protection Obligations' in Zachary Douglas, Joost Pauwelyn et al., (eds), *The Foundations of International Investment Law: Brining Theory into Practice* (OUP 2014) 370.

25 Douglas (n 24) 370.

26 Ibid 371; Nicholas Blomley, 'Law, Property, and Geography of Violence: The Frontier, the Survey, and the Grid' (2003) 93(1) *The Annals of the Association of American Geographers* 130.

whichever liberal view one sides with, in the final analysis they both underscore the Marxist understanding of property as inherently relational. Whether property binds together a person and a thing or a person and other people, it comprises entitlements which guide social interactions. Correlative to these entitlements (and any state-imposed limits to which they may be subjected) are duties that bind all non-owners. Unlike duties in *personam*, non-owner duties are typically negative, notably the obligation not to do anything which conflicts or interfere with the incidence of ownership. In other words, the exclusivity and inviolability of capitalist property rights is grounded not only in positive rights such as possession, use and transfer, but is further enhanced by negative duties imposed on an indeterminate group of excluded non-owners. At its core, the incidence of ownership entails legitimated expulsion.[27] The benefits enjoyed by one may be foreclosed to everyone else unless with the owner's permission, such as the grant of a licence or, in the absence of permission, against compensation.

The relational nature of property is further underscored by the possibility that ownership may be enjoyed in different ways and by more than one person. Again, there is nothing new in this proposition. The possibility of multiple ownerships is found, for example, in Hindu jurisprudence. Even in Roman jurisprudence the existence of multiple types of ownership was recognised at different times based on the level of power or authority vested in the rights holder.[28] Singer challenges the 'classical view' and its premise that most, if not all of the rights which come with ownership, are vested in a single owner.[29] In reality, matters are rarely as clear cut as this, unearthing an underbelly of complex and uncertain relationships involving owners' identity, transferred entitlements as well as conflicts among equally legitimate titleholders. According to Singer, 'most property rights are divided or shared among several persons' and their rights disaggregated.[30] In English law, things may be owned by more than one person as joint tenants. A thing may be owned legally by one person and beneficially by another. The complexities involved in the extraction and exploitation of natural resources often mean that rights over them are carved up among several owners. Legitimate use by one titleholder may interfere with legitimate use by titleholders of neighbouring land, requiring a balancing act that blows a hole in the notion of ownership as comprising open-ended privileges.

Property rights, argues Dine, 'are made up of a web of rights and responsibilities operating interpersonally'.[31] She summarises: 'The concept of ownership

27 Blomley (n 26) 130.

28 Sayin et al., (n 1) 16–17.

29 Joseph William Singer, 'Property and Social Relations: From Title to Entitlement' in Charles Geisler and Gail Daneker (eds), *Property and Values: Alternatives to Public and Private Ownership* (Island Press 2000) 69; also. <http://scholar.harvard.edu/files/jsinger/files/property_and_social_relations.pdf> accessed 2 February 2022.

30 Singer (n 29) 6, 8.

31 Janet Dine, *Companies, International Trade and Human Rights* (Cambridge Studies in Corporate Law CUP 2005) 254.

is . . . firmly rooted in social expectations which have come to be embedded in legal rules'.[32] For Jeremy Bentham, philosopher and jurist of late 18th–early 19th century, property in and of itself is an 'expectation' contingent on the security provided by the law.[33] Security is the reason why law is indispensable. It is the law's *raison d'être*.[34] Property cannot be exploited and enjoyed where rights to exclude and prevent intervention by outsiders are absent or indeterminate. Since property is indivisible from security and since civilisation is indivisible from property, civilisation is also indivisible from security. Insecurity, 'the fear of losing one's property arguably functions as a fear of losing civilization altogether'.[35]

Secure expectations make for power. In the words of John Adams, late 18th-century US president, 'The balance of power in a society accompanies the balance of property and land'.[36] Singer defines property rights as those that 'regulate relations among people by distributing powers to control valued resources'.[37] Powers to control resources, particularly when they are distributed in conjunction with the right to exclude, inevitably produce hierarchies and lend themselves to the creation of a continuum of possession and dispossession. Thus, property rights reveal a landscape strewn with acts of taking and their social justice implications; the more expansive, absolutist and sacrosanct they are, the more marginalised are those against whom they lie.[38] The stronger, denser and more concentrated the right to exclude, the greater the number of the excluded. All of which raises the spectre of the anomie which the institution of property was meant to prevent. This spectre is removed by the formation of a state-property alliance. Ultimately it is not property in and of itself but the state which, in the exercise of its regulatory and legislative monopoly, dispose of the threat of anomie. Since property underpins the edifice of capitalist civilisation as gatekeeper of access to the means of survival and since the state is the medium through which access to the means of survival is translated into practical experiences, the state becomes centre stage for Marx's class struggle and the antagonism between Locke's and Hayek's winners and losers. As the neoliberal globalists of the Geneva school understood, at issue is not the size of the state, but what kind of a state.

Property as politics

It follows from the previous section that insofar as property is productive of contestable social relations, it cannot be confined to a discreet individual sphere. Contrary

32 Dine (n 31) 251–3 referring to Jim Harris, *Property and Justice* (OUP 1996).

33 Jeremy Bentham, 'Security and Equality of Property' in C. B. Macpherson (ed), *Property: Mainstream and Critical Positions* (University of Toronto Press 1999) 52.

34 Bhandar (n 4) 266.

35 Ibid 266.

36 Charles Francis Adams (ed), *The Works of John Adams, Second President of the United State* (Vol. 9, Books for Libraries Press 1969) 367 cited in Blomley (n 26) 122.

37 Singer (n 29) 3.

38 Dine (n 31) 283.

to a dominant narrative of separation between the economic and the political, property brings the two together. It originated in a political moment and remains rooted in it.

Wood described that originating moment as a 'political *devolution*, the assumption by private proprietors of functions originally invested in a public or communal authority'.[39] When communal land was taken and placed in private hands, the appropriators cum proprietors assumed control over the land and, through it, over the means of production and access to survival. The political nature of this process of privatisation was buried under discursive structures which severed the political from the economic and civil spheres, using notions of freedom to contract, to exchange and to labour. *Dominium* was separated from *imperium* and placed firmly in the individual sphere.[40] In this way, says Wood, the moment of coercion was cut off from the moment of appropriation.[41] Polanyi named this process of partition 'disembedding'. It denotes a methodology for the creation of a market society (to be distinguished from a society in which there are markets). Through the destruction of 'pre-modern' communal structures, the economy (and therefore property) is detached from society and made autonomous of it. In turn, society becomes an adjunct to the economy, a subordinate of so-called self-regulating markets.[42]

Thus, if feudalism augmented the authority of property by integrating it with political authority, capitalism did the opposite. It augmented the authority of property by partitioning it from the realms of the political. Feudalist integration was enacted by making property conditional on the lord also acting as a particle of the state. Capitalist detachment was enacted by ostensibly removing this and all other conditionalities. In this way, the representation of property as private, autonomous and absolute was perfected.[43] To quote Marx, property received its 'purely economic form by discarding all its former political and social embellishments and associations'.[44] The purported disposal of political embellishments enabled property to become the bedrock of what Macpherson terms 'possessive market society' to be distinguished from a society of independent producers. In both, production and distribution are regulated by the market. The difference turns on the treatment of labour as property. In a possessive market society people's labour is their own. It is a possession to be put at the disposal of others for a price.[45]

39 Larry Patriquin (ed), *The Ellen Meiksins Wood Reader* (Historical Materialism Book Series Vol. 40, Brill 2012) 23 <https://cominsitu.files.wordpress.com/2016/01/the-ellen-meiksins-wood-reader-2012.pdf> accessed 20 October 2022.

40 Ibid 66, 117.

41 Ibid 19.

42 Fred Block, 'Introduction' in Karl Polanyi (ed), *The Great Transformation: The Political and Economic Origins of Our Time* (Beacon Press Boston 1944) xxiii–xxix.

43 Patriquin (n 40) 25.

44 Karl Marx, *Capital Vol III* (Progress Publishers 1971) 618 cited in Patriquin (n 39) 18.

45 C. B. Macpherson, *The Political Theory of Possessive Individualism: Hobbes to Locke* (OUP Canada 2011) 48; Wood, argues that in the context of capitalist social relations, without direct access to the means of survival, freedom to negotiate one's labour in the market transforms into a compulsion. Wood (n 13) 6–8.

Fragmentation of the political and economic spheres meant that the law had to step in as mediator. In the words of Bentham, property and law 'are born together and die together. Before laws were made there was no property; take away laws, and property ceases'.[46] David Hume wrote in a similar vein, 'our property is nothing but those goods whose constant possession is establish'd by the laws of society; that is, by the laws of justice'.[47] The very creation, continuance and expansion of property, argues Blomley, rely on it being demarcated from the domain of non-property.[48] On one side of the divide lie secure ownership and tenure; on its other side lie 'uncertain and undeveloped entitlements' and 'communal claims'.[49] The upkeep of this boundary is shouldered by the state and its legislative and regulatory authority. It is the state which mobilises 'bodies, technologies and things' to produce 'organised and disciplined practices' through which the ownership side of the divide is institutionalised and guaranteed.[50]

Thus, in reality, the economic rests upon the political; the economic looks to the political to order, establish legal boundaries and prevent a return to what was conceptualised in liberal ideology as the disorder, 'fears and continual dangers' of an anomic world before property.[51] It is the state which, using its sovereign competence to legislate and enter into treaties, delimits individual authority, imposes or dispenses with restrictions and generally manages the social interactions in which the institution of property is embedded. The introduction of title registration in the UK, argues Pottage, constituted a political programme involving political judgements and campaigns. The issues at the core of the debates which accompanied the formulation and implementation of the policy of registration were political. 'Conceptual issues were mobilized and coloured by political rhetoric'.[52] As part of the undertaking of reform, not only economic, but also 'political influences were absorbed into the conceptual fabric of the land transfer process'.[53] Similarly, in Macpherson's possessive market society, it is the state which regulates the overall framework within which persons may alienate or withdraw their labour-as-property. It does so using assemblages of law, ideology and coercion. It is also the state which confers or retracts privileges and manages the balancing act called upon when rights collide and compete. This applies both in the interior of the institution of property as well as in its interface with other bundles of rights, such as human rights and rights of Nature. IIAs take this interface a step further. The state

46 Bentham (n 33) 52.

47 David Hume, in L. A. Selby-Bigge and P. H. Nidditch (eds), *A Treatise of Human Nature* (Clarendon Press Oxford 1978/1739) cited in Johannes Kniess, 'Must We Protect Foreign Investors?' (2018) 5(2) *Moral Philosophy and Politics* 216.

48 Blomley (n 26) at 124.

49 Ibid 124.

50 Ibid 122, 124.

51 John Locke, *Second Treatise on Government* (Hackett Publishing 1980) 124 cited in Blomley (n 26) 124.

52 Pottage (n 17) 371.

53 Ibid 372.

resolves to restrict its sovereign competences insofar as they relate to the taking of or intervention in the sanctity of property. To this end, it confers on foreign investors privileges productive of a hierarchy of legal entitlements and obligations, including the right to challenge its regulatory authority. In so doing, the state consents to corporations in effect partaking in the exercise of sovereign powers.

This legal hierarchy underscores the proposition that the purported boundary drawn between *dominium* and *imperium* is interspersed with gateways through which property can make forays into sovereignty whilst retaining its liberation from feudal-type conditionalities and political and social associations. It bring to mind what Philip Stern conceptualised as a company-state. Stern coined this term in the context of his enquiry into the East-India Royal Charter Company and his view of it 'as an experiment in the notion that . . . corporations . . . 'often act as political communities in their own rights'.[54] A company-state is a proprietor and a government all at once, adjoining sovereign competences with commercial ones. In the case of the East India Royal Charter Company, its exclusive access to and control over designated colonised territories meant that it operated as both a merchant and a government. The scope of its authority extended to legislation, adjudication, coining money and declaring war and peace. English subjects who attempted to rebel by bypassing or evading this hybrid state-company jurisdiction were deemed interlopers acting outside of the law. When Thomas Sandys fitted a ship with the intention of making an unauthorised voyage to the East Indies, the East India Company had the ship stopped in the Thames and in 1682 brought proceedings in the Court of Chancery for confiscation of Sandys's goods. The legal battle which ensued became a leading case and a precedent on a range of contested issues of the day. It was 'a watershed moment in the history of political economy'. *Inter alia*, Sandys's lawyers argued that the royal charter amounted to an unlawful monopoly. In response, the company's lawyers turned to the ever handy concept of improvement as public good. They argued that the trade with the colonies would not have come into existence but for the improvement the company brought about by its efforts and investments. A public good, they contended, cannot amount to a monopoly.[55] Nonetheless, ultimately, the East India Company was a creature of the state. As we shall see, by the 19th century, the governing role conferred on it would be terminated to be replaced by direct imperial rule. Arguably, the investment protection regime represents a culmination of MNEs' incremental attempts to recapture their former self as a semi-sovereign, provider of public good, a private entity fulfilling public functions and now with the standing to face the state as its equal in the halls of arbitration. All of which makes for a complex relationship of opaque power structures. Competition and collaboration co-mingle with the balance struck between them reflecting differences in state formations and periodic adjustments.

54 Philip J. Stern, *The Company-State: Corporate Sovereignty & the Early Modern Foundations of the British Empire in India* (OUP 2011) viii.

55 Stern (n 54) 41–60 and generally.

In sum, property is located at the juncture where the private intersects with the commons. This is true in a variety of social settings and belief systems. In Islamic jurisprudence, for instance, property rights are subject to the purpose of contribution to greater national wealth, communal benefit and charitable acts.[56] In Jewish law they are moderated by environmental and social justice considerations as well as the concept of *midat sdom*, roughly analogous to the doctrine of abuse of rights.[57] Even in Roman times, in practice, *dominium* and *emporium* operated in tandem to produce a state-property regime pursuant to which things in the nature of public utilities were excluded by a sovereign act from alienability. The social territory of this state-property alliance is alive with perennial struggles, interruptions and the threat of instability. They call for state intervention if order is to be restored. It is no coincidence that Leon Duguit (1859–1928), credited with being the first to have dispensed with the language of rights in order to highlight the public function of property, was not only a jurist, but also a theorist of the modern state and its relationship with the law.

Philosophers such as Bentham and Hume focused on property's relationship with the law. They saw property as a juridical formation created and managed by the law and interwoven with political beliefs about security and justice. It follows that the rights it gives rise to are neither natural nor pre-political. Rather, they 'only exist through the arrangements that recognise them'.[58] At first blush this view stands in contradiction to the understanding of property as a natural right. However, as Kniess points out, even if property rights are to be understood as natural and pre-political, it cannot follow that 'their precise content or value is independent of politics'.[59] Such a claim would mean that any attempt to regulate foreign investment, for instance, amounts to a violation. Property and the rights attached to it are intensely relational. Therefore, they cannot be insulated from the social and political context in which they are situated. Their context may differ since different societies make different choices and construct different systems. They may even occur spontaneously, as a survival-driven response to material mutations. However, even on the neoliberal's own case, a point comes when it is necessary for the state to step in. The question is not whether there is intervention *per se* but, rather, its substantive content and structural implications. Neoliberals would say intervention is legitimate and desired only when it protects private property and the liberty to contract said to go with it. Social democrats may favour a somewhat more restrictive approach to the protection of private property. Socialists would emphasise its public function and, therefore, the prerogative of re-embedding it in society. Either way, even if property rights are understood as natural, they are also intertwined with what for Hayek was the legislator's designed order. Even if they are pre-political, they are necessarily also political.

56 Sayin et al., (n 1) 5.

57 Ibid 8.

58 Kniess (n 47) 216.

59 Ibid 219.

Property and the body

In 2022, the Canadian government declared a state of emergency and moved to disperse protestations against mandatory COVID-19 vaccination. The protests, led by Canadian truck drivers, swiftly swept across geographical and cultural distances and were replicated in some form or another in the US and Europe. A central theme of these protests was opposition to the state's compulsory intervention with the body, articulated in terms of state coercion and loss of liberty. That a proposed state intervention in the human body should invoke such associations and incite such strong feelings attests to the enduring memory of the narrative about the proprietary relationship which binds the autonomous subject to her body and thereby renders it indivisible from her liberty.

The thesis of self-ownership is found not only in the work of Locke but also in various forms in those of Hobbes, Kant, Mill and contemporary Nozick and Hayek. It lies at the heart of the liberal conception of property.[60] Hobbes's not to be voluntarily ceded 'right to govern one's body' and Locke's 'every Man has a *Property* in his own *Person*' instigated property rights in their modern incarnation as private and autonomous.[61] The conception of the individual as a self-possessing subject also lays the foundation on which a market society of ownership and a property-liberty-life hierarchy could be constructed. In Macpherson's words, once the individual was understood 'as essentially the proprietor of his own person or capacities, owing nothing to society for them', ownership has become 'the critically important relation determining . . . actual freedom and actual prospect of realizing . . . full potentialities'.[62]

The brief and much simplified discussion of religious laws which follows illustrates the turn taken by modern property rights and the way such turn is tied to understanding ownership as, in the first instance, vested in and radiating from the human body. In religious laws, property is embedded in theological assumptions which bring together a view of the world and its origin with ethical rules that govern humanity's place in it.[63] In both Islamic and Jewish jurisprudence, ownership resides in God as the Creator. Ownership's passage into human hands is by way of a gift bestowed on the faithful and the observant and is contingent on proper conduct. Within the *Hanafi* school of Islamic jurisprudence, dominant in the Ottoman legal system, private property is grounded in an agreement entered into between God and the faithful. Pursuant to this agreement, the rights vested in the faithful are subject to the fulfilment of divine commands. Property rights therefore do not exist naturally. They assume life upon the acceptance and discharge of duties to be

60 Jonathan Wolfe, *Robert Nozick: Property, Justice and the Minimal State* (Polity Press 1996) 7–8.

61 Eleanor Curran, 'Hobbes Theory of Rights: *A New Application*' in S. A. Lloyd (ed), *Hobbes Today: Insights for the 21st Century* (CUP 2013) 27; John Locke, 'On Property' in Matthew Clayton and Andres Williams (eds), *Social Justice* (Blackwell Publishing 2004) 22.

62 Macpherson (n 45) 3.

63 Sayin et al., (n 1) 5.

undertaken conjointly with the enjoyment of rewards.[64] Land occupies a central place in Jewish law and rights over it are contingent.[65] Similarly, medieval jurists conceptualised property rights in a state of nature in terms of 'claims' to denote a relationship of reciprocity between them and divinely ordained obligations.[66]

It is this relationship of conditionality and reciprocity which in feudalist Europe took on a political form but was dispensed with altogether in late medieval age. It was replaced with articulation of the human individual as sovereign, independent owner of his body, possessor and disposer of rights held against others, originator of moral and economic decisions and the bearer of their consequences.[67] Thus, property is unconditional and absolute not only in the sense that the rights attached to it are good against the world. It is also unconditional and absolute in the sense that it is no longer subordinated to an external, higher authority, be it God, communal custom or society at large. As observed by Polanyi, in the Great Transformation the economy (and therefore property) was detached from society. In a similar vein, Macpherson observed that the self-proprietary individual owes nothing to society (let alone God) for it. Adam Muller, the German political economist of the late 18th–early 19th centuries noted that 'unconditional private property' and the 'one-sidedness of ownership' entailed the nullification of 'reciprocal obligations'.[68] Following Richard Tuck's classification of rights, Talal Asad suggests that, with the introduction of personal sovereignty, modern property rights transformed from passive to active rights. Passive rights are contingent on a matrix of obligations whilst active ones follow Polanyi's route of disembedment: they become inherent in the individual irrespective of their social context.[69]

The impact of this transition from passive to active rights is illustrated by the way it transformed owner–slave relationship. In Spain, in the second half of the 13th century, the institution of slavery was subject to both church and state supervision. This meant that owners had to guarantee slaves' ability to live in conformity with Christian principles and respect the honour of female members of a slave's family for fear of being brought to the attention of the inquisition. In addition, the state kept a disciplinary eye on punishment meted out to slaves. Slaves were rewarded for engaging in nationally beneficial deeds. They were emancipated and their owner compensated for the intervention in her property. With the freeing of property rights from state and religious intervention, once the state was stripped of its role as an arbiter, owners could treat slaves with impunity. Pursuant to a law in force in Virginia in the 17th century, killing a slave could not qualify as murder

64 Ibid 6.

65 Ibid 7.

66 Talal Asad, *Formations of the Secular: Christianity, Islam, Modernity* (Stanford University Press 2003) 130.

67 Asad (n 66) 130–1.

68 Cited in Domenico Losurdo, *Hegel and the Freedom of Moderns* (Duke University Press 2004) 173.

69 Richard Tuck, *Natural Rights Theories: Their Origin and Development* (CUP 1979) discussed in Asad (n 66) 130.

because a person could not be presumed to intentionally 'destroy his own estate'.[70] Thus, the life of the enslaved was now governed exclusively by the will of their owners.

Ownership of one's body meant ownership of one's labour. This was the premise at the root of Locke's justification of appropriation. The *Labour* of his Body, and the Work of his Hands', he said, 'we may say, are properly his'.[71] It is the expenditure of this labour-as-property which overrides the state of nature in which 'the Earth and all inferior Creatures be common to all Men' and puts in place the conditions for the coming into being of private property.[72]

Yet, labour constitutes a truncated form of property since its owner is entitled to a mere fraction of the proceeds of its sale. That which the labour of her body produces belongs to 'those who have the capital and land' and can therefore 'by employing the labour of others, get a net transfer of some of the powers of others (or some of the product of those powers) to themselves'.[73] Macpherson posits that this entitlement to only a fraction of the proceeds of sale represents the price of access to the market. As in the case of the colonised subject whose 'uncultivated' land and therefore her body is of little value, in the absence of access to the market, labour and the body it inhabits are similarly of little value. Macpherson analyses the interface between labour, market access and price as follows: where the ownership of one's labour is divested of free access to the means through which it may be activated, a person's powers 'are reduced by the price he has to pay for access, and that price measures the amount of his power that is transferred to another'. Where there is no access at all, a person's powers 'are reduced to zero, and in a competitive society he ceases to exist'.[74] He may become one of Fraser's expropriated, eking out a living at the margins of society where surplus humanity congregates. There, he may continue to participate in market exchanges by drawing, lawfully or otherwise, on his only property – his body. A womb may be rented out to the babies industry, a kidney may be sold to the organs trade or, in what one interviewee in Pierre Monnard's documentary *Blood Business* called 'new cannibalism', the blood of his body may be alienated in the plasma market. Alternatively, the unemployed may become self-employed thereby becoming the purchaser and employer of his own labour. His self is thereby detached from the labour of his body. The self and the body are then reunited in an impersonal commercial relationship.

In a fully developed capitalism, argues Wood, direct producers are propertyless. Their deprivation of direct access to survival makes for a historically unique relations of market-mediated dependency.[75] Marx called this the 'silent compulsion of economic relations'. It has put the 'seal on the domination of the capitalist over

70 Losurdo (n 25, chapter 4) 38–9.
71 Locke (n 61) 22.
72 Ibid.
73 Macpherson (n 45) 56.
74 Ibid.
75 Wood (n 13) 96, 99.

the worker'.[76] This seal of domination meant that the path which started in self-ownership led ultimately to exclusion from the realm of property. To cite Marx and Engels, 'But does wage labour create any property for the labourer? Not a bit. It creates capital'.[77] The conversion of the fruits of waged labour into capital and its appropriation by the owners of the means of production went hand in hand with the downgrading of self-owning subjects into Benjamin Constant's 'the eternally dependent'. Edmund Burke saw them as 'speaking tools'. For Emmanuel Sieyes they were 'human instruments of production' or 'two footed machines'.[78] In the context of colonial regimes, since the savage 'other' was deemed incapable of ownership, he was also deemed incapable of self-ownership. Therefore, he lacked the capacity to negotiate the sale of his labour. Negotiation was substituted for manufactured indebtedness as one way by which colonised people could be compelled to enter the labour market. The East India Company and later the imperial state 'instituted debt peonage as their primary means of creating products for sales abroad'.[79] Taxation facilitated debt-induced taking of land in 19th-century South Africa. In the 20th and 21st centuries, in both the Global North and South, indebtedness is generated by, for example, the compulsion to plant patented GMO seeds at unaffordable cost. In consequence, as Indian peasants and farmers lose their land and face the prospect of becoming inhabitants of the land of 'silent compulsion', the rate of suicides spikes.

In the context of the fourth industrial revolution, as Nike has put it, the aim is to engineer labour out of the product altogether. Marxists would consider this an impossibility since, for Marx, the only labour is human labour. The value it creates merely passes through the machines which it produced in the first place. For instance, the world of artificial intelligence does not come into being in a moment of magic. The raw materials necessary for the production of robots are extracted by human labour, often that of the Global South poor and their children. Robots are similarly built by human labour. Their artificial intelligence is trained to recognise commands by a globalised army of invisible precariat labouring online, at the rear end of what then appears and is sold as the wizardry of progress.

Property, liberty and life

The innovation of property as embedded in the body brought it into close proximity to life and liberty. Proximity created the potential for tension and contradictions. For instance, the liberty of the property owner may need to be balanced against deprivation of the non-owner's liberty. The expansion of the sphere of self-determination through the abolition of slavery was said by opponents to derogate

76 Marx, *Capital Vol 1* 899 cited in Onur Ulas Ince, 'Between Equal Rights: Primitive Accumulation and Capital's Violence' (2018) 14(16) *Political Theory* 18.

77 Marx and Engels (n 2) 48.

78 Domenico Losurdo, *Hegel and the Freedom of Moderns* (Duke University Press 2004) 80, 273.

79 Graeber, *Debt: The First 5,000 Years* (Melville House Publishing 2011) 351.

from the property rights and the liberty of other members of society.[80] Risk to property may necessitate consideration of the comparative value of life. Hegel, among others, dismissed the possibility of equivalence between life and property as absurd given the qualitative difference between them. Damage to property is external to the body. In contrast, injury to the person is immediate and actual. Therefore, damage to property is not punishable by death.[81] It was not so in the English countryside as it was being enclosed. 'While attempted homicide was regarded as a petty crime until 1803', crimes such as 'theft of a shilling or handkerchief, or the illegal clipping of an ornamental bush could entail hanging' even when committed by a child.[82] For Locke, this system of killing had a just cause. Property's close connection with liberty elevated it above the right to life so that damage to it justified the death penalty. This is because crimes against property offended not only property, but also liberty.[83] It was lawful to kill a thief because what appeared on the face of it a petty crime amounted in reality to the greater crime of deprivation – brief as it may be – of the right to liberty. Threat to the property of another was a moment of enslavement. Since enslavement carried with it power over life and death, the possibility of homicide could not be overlooked.[84] Losurdo calls this sanctioning of one type of violence while castigating another 'terrorist legislation in defence of property'.

How did the slave fit into this hierarchical order? The view of the individual as morally and economically sovereign, argues Talal Asad, could in and of itself deliver defence of slavery. This is because the proposition that awareness of the obligations and punishment attendant on natural rights as a mark of humanity may easily lead to the conclusion that only those who have rights are human.[85] According to David Davis, Locke, an advocate of liberty, was also 'the last major philosopher to seek a justification for absolute and perpetual slavery'.[86] Malouet, a French slave-owning aristocrat, liberal publicist and politician, derived his inspiration from Locke's writings when he declared that slavery did not offend natural rights when applied to barbarous people.[87]

The justificatory link which ties property to liberty (and its absence) animate the pronouncements made by German political economist Adam Muller and German jurist Gustav Hugo. For Muller (1779–1829), the refusal to furnish poor individuals with survival necessities was intrinsic to the absolute status of private property.[88] If

80 Hillel Steiner, 'Slavery, Socialism, and Private Property' (1980) 22 *Nomos* 222 at 245 <https://www.jstor.org/stable/24219429> accessed 9 May 2022.

81 Losurdo (n 25, chapter 4) 79; Losurdo (n 79) 161.

82 Losurdo (n 25, chapter 4) 77.

83 Ibid 78.

84 Ibid 78.

85 Asad (n 66) 131.

86 David B. Davis, *The Problem of Slavery in the Age of Revolutions 1770–1823* (Cornell University Press 1975) 45.

87 Losurdo (n 25, chapter 4) 139.

88 Losurdo (n 78) 173.

survival of the poor came second to the absolute status of property, it is easy to see why Gustav Hugo (1764–1844) would justify slavery on the ground that slaves at least had the security of being able to eat. Slaves, he said, enjoyed the guarantee of being fed by their master while the free poor had no access to the means of survival where such means belonged to another.[89] In 16th-century Portugal, a centre of the Atlantic slave trade at the time, Spanish theologian Luis de Molina went as far as equating liberty with property meaning that it could be owned, alienated and traded.[90] For Thomas Hobbes human life itself was a tradable commodity. 'The *Value*, or worth of a man', he said 'is as of all other things, his Price'.[91]

The view of liberty as grounded in exchange value made its way to the US by the 19th century. The 1868 Fourteenth Amendment of the US Constitution prohibits a state from depriving any person of life, liberty or property without due process of law. In the 1872 *Slaughter House* case the majority construed 'liberty' as freedom from slavery or personal servitude. The minority sought to extend the meaning of slavery to include also economic coercion. If labour is property and property is exchange value, it follows that liberty extends to 'the right to realize that exchange value in the labor market'.[92] This definition of liberty as going beyond physical restraint of the person was finally confirmed in the 1897 *Allgeyer* case.[93] The liberty guaranteed by the Fourteenth Amendment was held to embrace the right 'to pursue any livelihood or avocation, and for that purpose to enter into all contracts which may be proper, necessary, and essential'. Thus, following in the footsteps of property's abstraction as exchange value, liberty was also abstracted as the 'expected activity in acquiring, using and disposing of things'.[94]

It is tempting to explain away the proximity between property and legalised violence as of its time. Indeed, in some respects, much has changed. On the whole, the law does differentiate between capital crimes against life and non-capital crimes against property. Nevertheless, the treatment of life, liberty and estate as a unitary triad persists in the works of contemporary philosophers such as Nozick and Hayek. It has found constitutional expression not only in the U.S. but also in the European Convention of Human Rights (ECHR). Article 1.1 of Protocol No. 1 of the ECHR establishes a human right to property.[95] If anything, aggregation of the absolute moment property with liberty and life has acquired renewed vigour in the course of capitalism's neoliberal restructuring. Locke-type reasoning continues to

89 Ibid 175.
90 Asad (n 66) 130–1.
91 W. G. Pogson Smith, *Hobbes's Leviathan* (Oxford 1929) 67.
92 Commons (n 5) 13.
93 *Allgeyer v Louisiana* (1897) 165 US 578.
94 Cited in Commons (n 5) 14, 17, 21–2.
95 European Convention of Human Rights 1953 <https://www.echr.coe.int/documents/convention_eng.pdf> accessed 27 February 2022; for a guide on Art. 1 of Protocol No. 1 see European Court of Human Rights, 'Guide to Article 1 of Protocol No. 1: Protection of Property' (last updated 31 December 2021) <https://www.echr.coe.int/Documents/Guide_Art_1_Protocol_1_ENG.pdf> accessed 27 February 2022.

animate questions such as whether killing a thief is a legitimate act of self-defence, whether and the extent to which labour should be free to organise, as well as the view of poverty as morally reprehensible, a state of idleness and profiteering from the public purse that is in need of discipline. Crimes against property may carry long imprisonment, and squatting by the homeless has been criminalised. Arguably, the proposition that property ranks above life now faces its greatest challenge as humanity looks to manage its survival against a backdrop of accelerating climate change and the destruction of the ecosystems on which its survival depends.

Conclusion

From self-ownership to slavery and 'speaking machines', the road to what Polanyi termed 'machine civilization' was littered with 'stunning contradictions'.[96] Welding these contradictions into a 'scheme of philosophy and theology' was no small feat given that 'stubborn facts' and 'the brute laws' that abolished freedom 'had in one way or another to be reconciled with freedom'.[97] Locke's pathos of liberty had to be aligned with his support for slavery and the brutality meted out to the dispossessed.[98]

Yet another, no lesser paradox concerns Wood's observation of a 'political devolution'. The de-socialisation and de-politicisation of property was in and of itself intensely political. It implicated class privileges and state restructuring. In England, the Glorious Revolution of 1688 marked the consolidation of the aristocracy's domination over the legislative organ of the state. The resistance that haunted the enclosures movement in the 16th and 17th centuries (including some opposition from a monarchy anxious about the threat to social order) was brought to an end by transforming a campaign of seizures into 'parliamentary enclosures'.[99] Now, 'the extinction of troublesome property rights' could be put into practice through legislative acts.[100] It turns out that not all property rights were sacred. Those held in common were not. Those held privately were. Taking of the former was lauded as improvement. Taking of the latter was punishable by death. Marx called it 'a parliamentary coup d'état'. In this new structure of domination, social duties vested in the state were separated from freely entered into contracts. Property was to become a pure matter of commerce. Through this separation, formerly overt coercion could turn covert.[101] Overtly, dispossessed peasants morphed into emancipated labourers, at liberty to choose their path to survival. With the relaxation of restrictions on movement, they were free to disperse in search of work. Put in modern political

96 Karl Polanyi, *The Great Transformation: The Political and Economic Origins of Our Time* (Beacon Press Boston 1944) 85, 88.
97 Polanyi (n 1) 88.
98 Losurdo (n 25, chapter 4) 319.
99 Wood (n 13) 108.
100 Ibid.
101 Patriquin (n 39) 18–19.

parlance, they could 'get on their bikes'.[102] Covertly, whatever the appropriators cum proprietors lost in direct political power, they gained indirectly via ownership and control over production. Ensuring indirect political power necessitated 'a rich political life'.[103] Araghi captured the nature of this interdependency when he said that the invisible hand of the market is 'rooted in political power, and its power is to make its politics invisible'.[104] In what Polanyi described as 'the wholesale destruction of the traditional fabric of society',[105] the two-faced Janus, goddess of beginnings and transitions, presided over the sanctification of property in one direction, and, simultaneously and inextricably, over 'the most shameless violation of the "sacred rights of property"' and 'the forcible expropriation of the people' in another.[106] 'Formerly unlawful appropriations were upheld and formerly lawful entitlements were criminalised'.[107]

There is another contradiction to be observed concerning the detachment of property from society, its designation to the exclusivity of the private sphere and the equation of such designation with liberty. It controverts the collective underpinnings of production. Economic production through which property comes into being is unlikely to be an individual affair. It forms an essential constituent and a core purpose of social organisation. As Cohen pointed out, in real life, goods are rarely, if ever, produced by a single person and without the aid of others. It is this collective effort which creates the material conditions in which individual freedom may be entertained. In real life, individual freedom to develop desires and aspirations is contingent on the presence of a material, scientific and moral infrastructure capable of securing the elementary needs of survival. Only then, consciousness of personal wants has the space in which to develop. This infrastructure comes into being through social collaboration. In its absence, liberty, the freedom to become aware of and follow one's own will, is nothing but a hue at the end of a rainbow. Spaces where individual will may be actualised are carved out of material conditions. When these deteriorate, when the battle for pure physical survival intensifies, these spaces shrink. The call of the sirens of self-awareness are drowned by the complaints of empty stomachs. Social discipline and collaboration create collective property creates individual liberty. In the words of the poet Christopher Caudwell, 'all the "constraints", "obligations", "inhibitions" and "duties" of society are the very means by which freedom is obtained by men'.[108]

102 Paul Waugh, 'Tory MP Tells Jobless to Find Work on Farms So They Can Meet 'Loads of Gorgeous EU Women' (*Huffpost UK*, 2 February 2017) <http://www.huffingtonpost.co.uk/entry/tory-mp-craig-mackinlay-jobless-get-on-bike-farms-gorgeous-eu-women-dawn-butler-offensive_uk_59d259dce4b06791bb1208f2> (accessed 4 December 2017).

103 Losurdo (n 25, chapter 4) 105.

104 Farshad Araghi, 'The Invisible Hand and the Visible Foot: Peasants, Dispossession and Globalization' in A. Haroon Akram-Lodhi and Cristobal Kay (eds), *Peasants and Globalization: Political Economy, Rural Transformation and the Agrarian Question* (Routledge 2010) 111.

105 Polanyi (n 1) 81.

106 Karl Marx, *Capital: Volume One* (Penguin 1976) 889, 891 cited in Losurdo (n 25, chapter 4) 121.

107 Losurdo (n 25, chapter 4) 78.

108 Christopher Caudwell, 'A Study in Bourgeois Illusion' in David Margolis (ed), *Culture as Politics: Selected Writings of Christopher Caudwell* (Pluto Press 2018) 44.

The project of taking by colonial settlers is said to have come to an end with decolonialisation. Indeed, much has changed as the nation-states system expanded through the grant of sovereignty to formerly colonised territories. Yet, much has also remained unchanged, producing what Hoogvelt calls 'continuity in change'. It is to this that we now turn our attention.

6 Taking by transfer

A time of giving

We are about to take a leap from colonial times to the 20th and 21st centuries. In the intervening years, the act of taking assumed the form of wealth transfer practiced through trade, foreign investment and debt repayments within a framework of integration into globalised circuits of capital. Momentous events punctuated this passage of time, culminating in the current clash between different economic systems led by China on the one hand and the U.S. on the other. Sanctions-based economic wars of attrition declared by the U.S. on China, Russia and Iran among others have driven these countries into an alliance engaged in looking for an alternative to the U.S.-designed international financial order. For the last five years or so, says economist Michael Hudson, these countries have been discussing how to counter U.S. control by de-dollarising their economy and holding instead gold and each other's currency. This strategy is but one manifestation of a larger question. 'At issue is what kind of economy is the world going to have' now that the unipolar moment of the U.S.-designed order has given way to multipolarity. Resistance is growing to a system devised by the U.S. under its own terms and in its own interest. The conflict is between neoliberalism, a financialised world order of privatised infrastructure and monopoly rents as against a world of a productive economy in which infrastructure is located in the commons, is subsidised and made available at minimum cost. It is a clash between a neoliberal order centrally planned in Wall Street and an order centrally planned by governments.[1]

Rejection of external control signifies resistance to what Kwame Nkrumah, Ghana's first prime minister and president, termed 'neo-colonialism'. 'The essence of neo-colonialism', he wrote, 'is that the State which is subject to it . . . has all the outward trappings of international sovereignty. In reality its economic system and thus its political policy is directed from outside'.[2] Neo-colonialism followed on from an earlier though no less momentous 20th-century event involving the

1 Michael Hudson, 'Changes in Superimperialism: The Position of the US and China in our Global Economic System' (23 January 2021) Presentation to the Oxford Economics Society <https://www.youtube.com/watch?v=PtHX23Trvy4> accessed 11 August 2022.

2 Kwame Nkrumah, *Neo-colonialism: The Last Stage of Imperialism* (Panaf Books 1970) ix.

DOI: 10.4324/9781315386782-8

restructuring of the interstate system. Statehood was disseminated to formerly colonised nations. In at least one important way, this represented a point of no return. Once a territory was declared independent, said Nkrumah, its independence is irreversible. It may be nominal but it cannot be taken away. A handful of formal colonies may still linger on, but no new ones will be created.[3] Independence also meant the potential to negotiate, legislate and choose sides or stay neutral in periods of clash such as the one currently gripping the world. Further, the IL principles of self-determination and non-intervention furnished this new, non-European sovereignty with at least a layer of legal protection. In the words of the ICJ in the *Nicaragua* case: 'The Court cannot contemplate the creation of a new rule opening up a right of intervention by one state against another on the ground that the latter has opted for some particular ideology or political system'.[4]

At first blush, it was a time of giving, a moment when the past was uncoupled from a new and qualitatively different historical episode. Colonised people won their struggle to become masters of their own lands and were gifted equalised entry into the international community from which hitherto they had been excluded. Advocates of modernity and neoliberal theories would say that if this gifting did not produce benefits, the reason was the new states' own mismanagement. Their inability to undertake the self-reform necessary for progress, resolve Sabrow's 'dilemma of the marginalised' and maintain legitimacy through mimicking all contributed to modernisation failure. Internal factors such as shortcomings in good governance and institutions-building lie at the root of developmental deficiencies.[5] Progress could not but stall in the absence of the moral, intellectual and institutional underpinnings of democracy, transparency, accountability, rule of law and free markets. As against this, dependency theorists would draw attention to the structural inequality which persists in the global order and the colonial and imperial legacies which continue to inform it. They would point to core states' ongoing domination over formerly colonised territories as evidence of a change more in form than substance, a transition from colonialism to neo-colonialism.[6]

3 Nkrumah (n 2) ix.

4 *Military and Paramilitary Activities in and against Nicaragua* (*Nicaragua v United States*) [1986] ICJ reports para 14 at p133; for GA resolutions see for example Declaration on the Granting of Independence to Colonial Countries and Peoples, GA Resolution 1514 (XV); General Assembly Resolution defining the three options for self-determination, GA Resolution 1541 (XV) <http://www.un.org/en/decolonization/ga_resolutions.shtml>; 2131(XX) Declaration on the Inadmissibility of Intervention in the Domestic Affairs of States and the Protection of their Independence and Sovereignty <http://www.un-documents.net/a20r2131.htm> accessed 30 June 2021.

5 For a general summary of modernisation theories see Ankie Hoogvelt, *Globalization and the Postcolonial World: The New Political Economy of Development* (2nd edn, Palgrave Macmillan 2001) 35–7.

6 for dependency theorists see Paul Baran, *The Political Economy of Growth* (Monthly Review Press 1968); Andre Gunter Frank, *Capitalism and Underdevelopment in Latin America* (Monthly Review Press 1967); Samir Amin, *Accumulation on a World Scale: Critique of the Theory of Underdevelopment (Marxist Theory and Contemporary Capitalism)* (Branch Line 1978); for a helpful summary of the theory see Hoogvelt (n 5) 37–43.

The charge levelled at neo-colonialism is that under the surface of giving, taking continued unabated. The grant of sovereignty to colonised people constructed as a historical interruption was in reality no more than adapted continuity. Adapted continuity was by design. According to Hoogvelt, colonialism was a time when the stage was set for the next historical episode. It was a period of 'preparatory construction, of laying the foundations of future wealth creation and surplus extraction'.[7] This preparatory construction took the form of an administrative and legal project during the Mandate period, a time when non-European independence looked increasingly inevitable. According to Anghie, the Mandate system was devised in the aftermath of the First World War (WWI) to commandeer independence and pre-empt the nationalist policies about to accompany it. The European tutelage aimed at preparing the embryonic new states for self-governance and self-reform centred on 'well-being and development'. These were understood primarily in economic and legal terms. Article 22 of the Covenant of the League of Nations provided that colonised people's 'well-being and development' formed 'a sacred trust of civilization'.[8] Thus, the civilising mission, the white man's burden of the past was adapted and reimagined as the burden of developing the native and presiding over a sacred trust dedicated to her welfare. Much like in settler colonialism, local people died in performance of this trust. This time the 'death agony' was that of labourers, including forced labour, engaged in the construction of the infrastructure projects with which imperial states sought to make their colonies more accessible to foreign corporate interests. Nevertheless, in the mind of Mandate theorists, this was to be the beginning of a new, enlightened colonialism in which European taking of resources, markets and cheap labour would benefit all.[9] Taking by the North from the South was to become an act of giving by the North to the South. By 1949, Truman, in search of an exciting theme for the inaugural speech of his second term, grabbed the public imagination with his talk about First World nations' good-will commitment to the development of the Third World. The narrative of development, says Hickel, 'began as a public relations gimmick'.[10]

Appropriation and European awakening

Yet, it was a gimmick laden with historical legacies. They were embedded in European consciousness and memories which pre-dated the Mandate system's discourse of enlightened colonialism. The concept of development resurrected that of 'improvement' as a route to progress and public good. The commitment to

7 Hoogvelt (n 5) 26.

8 The Covenant of the League of Nations 1924 <https://avalon.law.yale.edu/20th_century/leagcov.asp> accessed 13 March 2022.

9 Anthony Anghie, *Imperialism, Sovereignty and the Making of International Law* (Cambridge Studies in International and Comparative Law, CUP 2004) 119–94 for a discussion of the Mandate system.

10 Jason Hickel, *The Divide: A Brief Guide to Global Inequality and Its Solutions* (Penguin Random House 2018) 7.

developing the 'other' was also associated with European awakening, which historian Hugh Trevor-Roper traced back to the 18th century. It was then, following a 'long and uneven chain of events' and in the wake of an Age of Enlightenment, that 'the European relics of the deceased Roman Empire were re-animated to become the heart of the modern world'.[11] Up to that time, posits Trevor-Roper, European civilisation was neither wholly original nor did it aspire to be so.[12] Awakening was founded on appropriation. This time it was the appropriation of Eastern technologies, ideas and institutions. Leading European enlightenment thinkers such as Leibniz, Voltaire and Quesnay, among others 'looked to China for moral instruction, guidance in institutional development, and supporting evidence for their advocacy of causes such as benevolent absolutism, meritocracy, and an agriculturally based national economy'.[13] The efficiency of the Ottoman administrative system was similarly admired by European diplomats and visitors. As early as the 16th century, jurists and philosophers such as Bodin, Bacon and Montaigne sang the praises of Ottoman military discipline and administrative competence. King Henry VIII sent a mission to Türkiye to study Suleiman II's legal code.[14] Talal Asad, following Trevor-Roper, makes the point that most European ideas and techniques were imported, taken up and then creatively reworked. Gunpowder, printing and the compass, three inventions which according to Francis Bacon changed the state of the world, came from China. The escape mechanism pivotal to all clockwork originated in Byzantium.[15] Asad calls these acts of taking and reworking a civilisation of 'productive elaboration'.[16] Its theoretical support, he argues, is to be found in the Lockean principle of appropriation of property which is then transformed by industry and reason from that which is common to that which is one's own. 'Applied to whole people, property was "European" to the extent that Europeans appropriated, cultivated, and then lawfully passed it on to generations of Europeans as their own inheritance'.[17]

Integral to this change of course towards originality was the elevation of the market from a mere venue of exchanges to a container of power and authority, a boundless enclosure into which life in all its forms is compelled to enter. It was in the 18th century, says Foucault, that the market was conceptualised not only as natural, but as a site of truth – a standard for a new governmental practice, a benchmark enshrined in law and applied to differentiate right from wrong, veracity from

11 Hugh Trevor-Roper, *The Rise of Christian Europe* (Thames and Hudson 1966) 25.

12 Trevor-Roper (n 11) 22.

13 Li Xing, 'Introduction: The Rise of China and the Capitalism World Order: The "Four-China" Nexus' in Li Xing (ed), *The Rise of China and the Capitalist Order* (Ashgate 2010) 3 citing from Michael Adas, *Machines as Measure of Men: Science, Technology and Ideologies of Western Dominance* (Cornell University Press 1989) 79; see also Giovanni Arrighi, *Adam Smith in Beijing: Lineages of The Twenty-First Century* (Verso 2007) 3–4.

14 Alexander Anievas and Kerem Nisancioglu, *How the West Came to Rule* (Pluto Press 2015) 95.

15 Trevor-Roper (n 11) 23–4.

16 Asad (n 67, chapter 5) 167.

17 Ibid 168.

falsehood.[18] The 18th century was also the first time that Europe 'has the entire planet for its horizon'. For the first time, Europe saw the world as its own economic domain, a space of competitive production and exchange, of a global market to be internationally organised and juridified, integral to the continent's uninterrupted enrichment and an underwriter of its perpetual peace.[19] This was to be the new state of nature: 'Nature intended the entire world, the whole of its surface, to be given to economic activity of production and exchange'.[20] Yet, production and exchange were also to be regulated and buttressed by, *inter alia*, juridically ordered property.[21] By the 18th century, says Alden Wily, in most of Europe and the Americas, dealings in land had to be registered if they were to have legal effect. As we saw, the practice of registration progressively matured to become the yardstick of ownership.[22] The land of the non-registered customary occupier thus became formally unowned and outside legal protection. These legal formalities were to play an important role in the way development was to be practiced.

Informality of control

From a European perspective, the decolonialisation moment of giving was also a moment of risk. By the end of the 19th century, management of the colonial enterprise was taken from royal charter trading corporations, such as the British and Dutch East India Companies, and put in the hands of states. It was 'the imperial European state, with its formidable powers and massive military and economic resources, that systematically set about the task of making profit out of the colonies'.[23] Independence and sovereignty thus threatened to intervene in the commercial well-being of the European sate by restraining or even blocking its free access to markets and resources. It also cast a shadow over 'awakened' Europe's vision of the world as its dominion. The sense of anxiety over these potential losses comes through in a 1966 paper written by Vince Cable, later to become the UK trade secretary. As part of his outline of 'a new agenda for trade', Cable pointed to 'economic autarky' as one of the factors which operated to damage the 19th-century economic order.[24] That is, the economic order which Hoogvelt defines as formal colonialism and theorists of the Mandate system sought to differentiate as a departure from intense exploitation.[25] The borderless world, which mobile

18 Foucault (n 7) 32.
19 Ibid 56–7, referring to Kant's 1795 writing on perpetual peace, specifically to his chapter 'On the Guarantee of Perpetual Peace'.
20 Foucault (n 7) 57.
21 Ibid 57.
22 Lily Alden Wily, 'Customary Tenure: Remaking Property for the 21st Century' in Michele Graziadei and Lionel Smith (eds), *Comparative Property Law: Global Perspectives* (Research Handbooks in Comparative Law Series Edward Elgar 2017) 458.
23 Anghie (n 9) 141.
24 T. J. Cole, *Britain's Secret Wars: HOW and WHY the United Kingdom Sponsors Conflicts Around the World* (Clairview Books 2016) 3–4.
25 Anghie (n 9) 157.

capital required if it was to nurture European well-being, was incompatible with a world of greater sovereignty. There was tension between the world of expanded national self-determination and its adjacent world of property.

The answers developed to address this tension encompassed a range of discursive, structural and institutional adaptations. Discursively, the narrative of 'development' became the contemporary face of 'improvement'. The 'uncivilized' were transformed into the 'economically backward' as racial and cultural concepts of savagery were substituted, at least formally, for economic categories of absence of development and incompetence similarly posited as objective, natural and universal.[26]

Structurally, one way of dealing with the threat of 'economic autarky' was to carve the economy out of sovereignty and single it out for grooming. Approaches differed. According to Slobodian, the Chicago and Virginia schools of neoliberalism assumed that America was a 'working model' for a globalised world economic order irrespective of national specificities. By contrast, central European neoliberal globalists, having themselves experienced US hegemony and conscious of the US advantage in the form of a vast domestic market, looked to solutions in trade-based dependency. 'The early end of empire in Central Europe after the First World War . . . required them to contemplate strategies for balancing state power with economic inter-dependence'.[27] The difficulty was that, in reality, *imperium* and *dominion*, property and statecraft are intimately intertwined so that one could not be shaped without intervention in the other. In consequence, as pointed out by Nkrumah, momentous as the grant of sovereignty was, its potential to transform the relationship between the young states and their former masters was curtailed not only economically but also politically and juridically. In a manner reminiscent of the Vitorian colonial subject, the new states were to be equal but also differentiated. Their sovereignty was to be free and protected, yet also fragmented, truncated and receptive to external prescriptions. Wood's 'empire of capital' became also David Chandler's 'empire in denial'. Imperial designs persist but they are informal, indirect and covert. They fashion the way subordinated sovereignties are exercised. They do so through the back door of invasive structural adjustments, so-called capacity or state-building programs and manufactured regime changes, as well as free trade commitments, IIAs and debt obligations.[28]

This strategy too had deeper historical roots. John Gallagher and Ronald Robinson, in their 1953 path-breaking article, traced it back to 19th-century British imperialism of free trade. The outflow of goods and capital operated in tandem with the home state's intervention in support of its economic interests.[29] The degree to which imperialism was 'formal' or 'informal' was determined by the fluctuations

26 Ibid 189.

27 Quinn Slobodian, *Globalists: The End of Empire and the Birth of Neoliberalism* (HUP 2018) 9.

28 David Chandler, *Empire in Denial: The Politics of State-Building* (Pluto 2006) generally.

29 John Gallagher and Ronald Robinson, 'The Imperialism of Free Trade' Second Series VI (1953) 1 *The Economic History Review* <https://moodle2.units.it/pluginfile.php/101074/mod_resource/content/2/Gallagher-Robinson_Imperialism_of_Free_Trade_EHR_1953.pdf> accessed 28 June 2018.

between the two. Informality was not to be confused with a retreat in imperial activity. Rather, when it was necessary for formality to take a back seat, economic dependency stepped in to keep the colonies bound to Britain and enable their use as agents for further expansion.[30] Once the target market had been prized open, stable governments, those which did not require ongoing overt coercion, were preferable. They were deemed to lessen investment risks.[31]

In the 20th century, as the empire itself was about to lose its formal existence, management of economic sovereignty was entrusted to multilateral and regional organisations. The League of Nations was but the first international body installed to fulfil this function of constructing the non-European, post-colonial state. The league was pivoted by the Permanent Mandate Commission (PMC) charged with implementing Article 22 of its charter and relevant Mandate Agreements. The Bank of International Settlements (BIS), a bank of central banks and the first international financial institution (IFI) was established pursuant to the Hague Agreement 1930. To start with, it was charged with managing the collection, administration and distribution of German Treaty of Versailles reparations, including the loans issued to finance them. In the aftermath of the WWII, as the US further established itself as the new hegemon, the organisations set up to manage *Pax Americana* on a plenary scale included the UN and the Bretton Woods IFIs. The Bretton Woods order comprised the International Bank of Reconstruction and Development, later to become part of the World Bank Group, and the International Monetary Fund (IMF). The role of the BIS changed to, *inter alia*, supporting the Bretton Woods order, as well as supplementing the IMF as a funder of last resort. Negotiations for the establishment of an International Trade Organisation (ITO) stalled and it was not until 1995 that the World Trade Organisation (WTO) was established. By 1952 the mandate of the World Bank was extended from lending for the reconstruction of Europe to lending for infrastructure projects in Global South 'less developed' countries. By the late 60s, its then president, Robert McNamara, renounced Article IV Section 10 of the Bank's charter which prohibited the exertion of political pressure on member states to change their social institutions. The World Bank thus joined the IMF in making lending subject to conditionalities by way of austerity policies and structural adjustments. Economies were told to liberalise, privatise, de-unionise, borrow and restructure. The WTO was charged with opening up economies to free trade and monitor their compliance with the terms of their membership through a dispute resolution mechanism.[32] All of which rendered purchase of the bonds which the World Bank issued to raise finance in private capital markets a particularly secure investment.

30 Gallagher and Robinson (n 29) 3.

31 Ibid 6.

32 Michael Hudson, *Super Imperialism: The Economic Strategy of American Empire* (3rd edn ISLET-Verlag 2021) 207–99; see also Dine (n 32, chapter 5) 97–166; Joseph Stiglitz, *Globalization and Its Discontents* (Penguin 2003) generally; Joseph Stiglitz, *Globalization and Its Discontents Revisited: Anti-Globalization in the Era of Trump* (W.W. Norton & Company 2017) generally.

IL provided another answer to the dilemma of sovereign constraints on access to markets and resources. Colonial territories, previously excluded from the realm of IL, were to become incorporated sovereign states. As part of this transition, argues Anghie, IL had to be revisited. The aim was to distance it from the project of validating the exploitation of non-European people. It was to act instead as a legal framework for a world system propagated as humanist and developmentalist. To this end, the League of Nations revisited Vitoria's previously discarded concepts of 'wardship' and 'trusteeship' through which the Indian 'other' was to be cared for. Thus, 'The circle was complete: in seeking to end colonialism international law returned to the origins of the colonial encounter'.[33] With regard to the protection of property, 'General principles of law recognised by civilised nations' as a source of IL were to include doctrines such as acquired rights, state succession, the international minimum standard, state responsibility and its derivative in the form of IIAs. They served to put former colonial entitlements on a legal footing, protect them from sovereign intervention and prescribe parameters for national legislation.[34] The PMC sought to fuse the rigidity of legal standards with the flexibility of administrative guidelines but saw its function primarily in legal terms. It seems the project of development as a whole was 'essentially a legal enterprise'.[35] Subsequent IFIs, though lacking the standing to legislate, were to act as gatekeepers of access to international finance. This gave them a say in the way state monopoly over legislation and treaty-making was to be exercised. For instance, the Multilateral Investment Guarantee Agency (MIGA), part of the World Bank Group tasked with insuring political risk, as part of the World Bank Group may require that host states enter into a BIT as a condition for extending insurance to foreign investors. ICSID operates to discipline states through the threat of international arbitration and the spectre of hefty compensation. 'BIT partners', wrote Jose Alvarez, 'turn to the US BIT with the equivalent of an IMF gun pointed at their heads . . . For many, a BIT relationship is hardly a voluntary, uncoerced transaction'.[36] Against this backdrop, Anghie concludes that Global South participation in the post-colonial world was on essentially unchanged terms. Its engagement with IL was as a colonial subject

33 Anghie (n 9) 145 and more generally about the Mandate system and IL at 144–6.

34 Broadly, acquired rights refers to the principle of customary IL pursuant to which a range of property rights acquired by or vested in an alien are protected under IL from state interference, including where sovereignty is transferred; the 1978 Vienna Convention on Succession of States in Respect of Treaties defines state succession in Article 2(1)(b) as 'the replacement of one state by another in the responsibility for the international relations of territory'. Examples are decolonialisation, unification and cecession.

35 Anghie (n 9) 150–1.

36 Jose E. Alvarez, 'The Development and Expansion of Bilateral Investment Treaties: Remarks' (1992) 86 *American Society of International Law* 532; but see M. Sornarajah, *The International Law on Foreign Investment* (3rd edn, CUP 2010) 23–4 attributing the spread of BITs to factors such as pragmatic attitudes among Global South countries, subsequent willingness to compromise upon the dismantling of socialist alternatives, competition and the rise of neoliberalism spread.

whose subordination and dispossession continued as before, except that now, these could take place in a manner which appeared 'legally coherent'.[37]

This combination of organisational and legal structures ensured that formerly colonised territories, now integrated new states, 'continued to serve their traditional purpose in the larger global economic order' albeit in an adapted form.[38] Global North states and corporations reunited to form a globalised state-property alliance in which MNEs were supported by back-door statecraft strategies, centralised management of the transnational space, legal innovations, enforcement mechanisms and, where necessary, regime change and wars. These structures functioned to break through states' territorial and legislative boundaries and enable the smooth passage of capital.

In sum, the 19th century set the scene for a framework founded on formal integration combined with informal transfer of benefits. Within this framework, adapted 19th-century technologies of taking migrated to the 20th and 21st centuries. Discursively, a narrative of humanism and the distinction made by colonial administrators between economic development and economic exploitation replaced previous debates about the rationale of empire. The renovated discourse made for a 'friendlier theory of imperialism'.[39] Yet, more than anything else, it reflected a shift in former colonial powers' conception of their interests and the way by which these are to be secured in response to changing circumstances. In the mind of the Mandate administrators, exploitation 'would exhaust the colony'. By contrast, the purpose of development was 'ongoing benefits to the metropolis'.[40] The emphasis was no longer on unrestraint and localised taking, but on organised transfer of surplus value from Global South host states to Global North home states. Its flows 'darkened' and lost visibility as they became increasingly juridified and institutionalised. By the end of the 20th century, informal transfer became a 'highly monopolized form of corporate capitalism under the leadership of finance capital'.[41]

The rest of this section will examine the mechanisms by which taking by transfer is realised. They make for a neo-colonial order in which relations of uneven and combined development are produced and reproduced through unequal exchanges, transfer's key dynamic.[42] The promise is one of 'catching up' with the West. Yet,

37 Anghie (n 9) 242.

38 Ibid 156.

39 Sam Moyo et al., 'Imperialism and Primitive Accumulation: Notes on the New Scramble for Africa' 1 (2012) 2 *Agrarian South: Journal of Political Economy* 188.

40 Anghie (n 9) 143.

41 Moyo et al., (n 39) 181 at 191.

42 The concept of 'uneven and combined development' was developed by Leon Trotsky in his study of Russia's industrialisation and integration into the world economy primarily by means of foreign finance and investment. The 'combined' aspect of the concept supplements the theory of uneven development, which holds that societies develop at a different pace at different points in time. Trotsky argued that capitalism's unique expansionary motion leads it to penetrate pre-capitalist societies and turn them into hybrid societies in which the world's most advanced and most backward features exist in combination. Leon Trotsky (tr), *History of the Russian Revolution (1932)* Penguin Classics 2017).

catching up rarely materialised. Poverty and uneven development in countries of the Global South remain the norm. In turn, this locks these countries even further into relations of unequal exchange. Tropes such as 'the paradox of plenty' or 'the resource curse' conceal more than they reveal. The terms 'paradox' and 'curse' seem to gloss over the fact that poverty, just like wealth, is manufactured. It is neither a curse of unknown origins nor a paradox of nature. Rather, it is the other face of accumulation by means of unequal exchanges.

Unequal exchanges of free trade are treated here as including also foreign investment and the debt bondage by which 'backward' spaces are integrated into the post-colonial globalist project. Each is different. However, together, they form what the Egyptian economist Samir Amin conceptualised as imperialist rent, a theoretical home to variegated forms of unequal exchanges in the post-1945 order of monopoly capitalism. The section concludes with a brief examination of the cultural and racialised forms of imperialist rent.

Unequal exchanges of free trade

The rise and rise of free trade

Free trade's core tenet is that unrestricted cross-border exchanges of commodities is the optimal system for the creation of equalised prosperity.[43] Prosperity is optimised by reliance on a country's own endowments, such as soil fertility, the cost of labour, productivity and natural resources to the exclusion of the political dimension of economic relations. The doctrine is traced back to 19th-century Manchester, at that time the centre of Britain's manufacturing exports. Manchester's textile industry was dependent on access to markets in Europe, North America and the Empire. Removal of restrictions was therefore aligned with its commercial interests, including the sourcing of cotton picked by slaves.

The moment at which the rhetoric and informal practices of free trade congealed into a formal, legally articulated doctrine is said to be 1846, when the Corn Laws and the protectionist tariffs they imposed on its importation were repealed.[44] According to Marx, repeal of the Corn Laws was achieved by a political alliance between manufacturers and the working class. The alliance resulted in a victory for both. The working class saw the promulgation of the 1844 Factory Act designed to control women's working hours and impose stricter restrictions on the use of child labour.[45] As to Manchester's manufacturers, the repeal of the Corn Laws two years later was followed by 68 years of British commitment to zero tariffs. The

43 Dine distinguishes between this understanding of free trade and its understanding by some economists as freedom from regulation and obligations. The two, she argues, often get confused. Dine (n 32, chapter 5) 132.

44 For a discussion of free trade debates of that period as a debates about tariffs, see Michael Hudson, *Trade Development and Foreign Trade: How Trade and Development Concentrate Economic Power in the Hands of Dominant Nations* (Islet 2009) 93–117.

45 Hugh Collins, *Marxism and the Law* (Marxist Introductions OUP 1982) 46–7.

Anti-Corn Law League (ACLL) thus became one of the most successful social movements in the last two hundred years.[46] Since then, free trade theory has been assigned the force of 'a truth-like status' and enjoys the ubiquity of 'a scientific fact as indisputable as gravity'.[47] Free trade emerged out of its history of uneven implementation as a key narrative of a US-made world order and a standard for assessing the way in which sovereignty is exercised.

The rise and rise of free trade despite uneven implementation and allegations of 'rigging of the rules' attests to the force of the narrative by which it was legitimised.[48] Rooted in Lockean liberalism, it articulates a vision of self-interest and public good harmoniously co-existing in a Kantian state of perpetual peace. Much like the narrative of enclosures, it harnesses the combined allure of liberty and common benefit to depict a world in which differences are opportunities for value creation. The physical gain derived by humanity from free trade, pronounced Cobden, a textile capitalist and leader of the ACLL, will be small compared with the moral one. The principle of free trade, he said in his 1846 'Free Trade for all Nations' speech, 'shall act on the moral world as the principle of gravitation in the universe, drawing men together, thrusting aside the antagonism of race and creed and language, and uniting us in the bonds of eternal peace'.[49]

Cobden's prophetic words were of their time. They echoed European concepts of linear progression towards secularised, private property and science-based material prosperity and the moral force of de-politicised markets, growth and value creation. By the beginning of the 20th century, free trade came to be associated with social legislation, national independence, the progress of British civilisation compared to the backwardness of tariffs imposition and the freedom to buy abroad as a political right.[50] Renato Ruggiero, the first director-general of the WTO, pledged a historically unique prosperity when he asserted that free trade, multilaterally organised and juridified on a plenary scale, had 'the potential for eradicating global poverty in the early part of the next [21st – our comment] century'. This, he said, was 'a Utopian notion even a few decades ago, but [is] a real possibility today'.[51] In the

46 Eric Sheppard, 'Constructing Free Trade: From Manchester Boosterism to Global Management' 30 (2005) 2 *Transactions of the Institute of British Geographers* 151 <https://geog.ucla.edu/sites/default/files/users/esheppard/514.pdf> accessed 8 March 2022.

47 Sheppard (n 46) 151 accessed 29 June 2018.

48 For a study of rigging of trade rules in the sugar industry see for example Dine (n 32, chapter 5) 134–7; see also Yash Tandon, *Trade is War: The West's War against the World* (Or Books 2018).

49 Cited in Sheppard (n 46) 158.

50 Sheppard (n 46) 163–4.

51 Ha-Joon Chang, *Bad Samaritans: The Guilty Secrets of Rich Nations & The Threat to Global Prosperity* (Random House Business Books 2007) 23 citing from R. Ruggiero, 'Whither the Trade System Next?' in J. Bhagwati and M. Hirsch (eds), *The Uruguay Round and Beyond – Essays in Honour of Arthur Dunkel* (University of Michigan Press 1998) 130; Shaikh argues that, in reality, the WTO is not about poverty reduction but about enabling countries to negotiate market access. Anwar Shaikh, 'Globalization and the Myths of Free Trade' Paper for the Conference on Globalization and the Myths of Free Trade (April 2003) 13 <https://www.researchgate.net/publication/238541036_Globalization_and_the_Myth_of_Free_Trade> accessed 19 March 2022.

event that this pledge fails to materialise (as indeed it did), a disciplinary warning that there is no alternative (TINA) is at hand to warn off heretics.

Ruggiero's pledge lies at the heart of contemporary promotion of globalised free trade. As in the case of investment, the promise is that of an end to poverty. Neoliberals' pet expression of 'win-win' solutions has now been adopted by relative newcomers to globalised circuits of capital, such as China. The phrase acts as a discursive shorthand to convey the country's commitment to the fair management of globalised free trade and the harmonious world of common prosperity this will produce. Low-income countries can grow at 8% or more a year for several decades, promised Lin Yifu, a Chinese economist and former vice president and chief economist of the World Bank. All they need do is nurture the private sector and advance on the basis of each country's comparative advantages. 'Upon success, the global crisis can be turned into an opportunity for achieving a win-win outcome for developing countries and developed countries alike, for today and tomorrow'.[52]

Lin's vision of countries achieving prosperity by focusing on their comparative advantages speaks to standard free trade theory. Pursuant to David Ricardo's 19th-century tenet of comparative cost advantage, for trade to be beneficial, each nation should specialise in exporting the commodities it produces more efficiently compared to other nations. Conversely, it should import those commodities which are produced comparatively more efficiently by others. The assumption that cost structures and productivity rates are 'inherent and presumably permeant' makes for 'static' economic models.[53] Thus, international trade rests on specialisation and comparative advantage as its two static yet interactive pillars. Specialisation enables countries to practice a more efficient allocation of resources. Differences in efficiency mean that it is advantageous for them to depend on each other for the commodities each can produce at the greatest relative cost advantage. The invisible hand of the market operates to ensure that specialisation and comparative advantage correlate so that exports are exchanged for the equivalent amount of imports and the resulting trade is balanced. Together, the two lead to greater output, so that all trading partners end up being better off. Further, the same dynamic applies to all countries regardless of their stage of development. Since everyone has something to offer, even economically weak countries would benefit and need not fear competition. Their resources would be better utilised, rendering free trade a universal good available to all.

Free trade? Yes, maybe, not for me

According to Hudson, when America designed its post-World War II world order of free trade, it focused less on universal good and more on domination. Despite internal debates about the specifics of the order to be designed, '[l]ocal interests and national politicians were in agreement that in principle, free trade policy was

52 Justin Yifu Lin, *Against the Consensus* (CUP 3013) 100.

53 Hudson (n 44) 94, 95.

an essential lever in maintaining U.S. dominance in the world – at least for foreign countries to adopt with regard to American exports'.[54] Hudson is not the first to suggest that the true intent behind free trade evangelism is the pursuit of dominance and the creation and/or preservation of national advantages. Chang, following 19th-century German economist Friedrich List, makes the point that, while still at the stage of industrial development, core countries did not follow the 'good practices' now preached to peripheral ones.[55] Rather, their manufacturing success was achieved on the back of protectionist policies of tariffs and export subsidies. List is said to have been moved to develop his 'infant industry' theory by his concern about the detrimental effect which competition with the more advanced British industries had on Germany's ability to develop its own manufacturing capabilities. He argued that in circumstances of unequal international competition, strong political steering is needed to dissociate the weaker economy from its powerful rivals and thereby create the political and economic space necessary to counteract their debilitating effects. The British narrative of free trade as a practice of universal application, he contended in his 1842 book, *The National System of Political Economy*, masked a narrow nationalist interest. The aim was to avoid competition by depriving others of the non-free trade policies practiced by Britain on its path to dominance. Britain has 'kicked away the ladder by which he has climbed up, in order to deprive others of climbing after him'. 'Any nation', wrote List,

> which by means of protective duties and restrictions on navigation has raised her manufacturing power and her navigation to such a degree of development that no other nation can sustain free competition with her, can do nothing wiser than to throw away the ladder of its greatness, to preach to other nations the benefits of free trade.[56]

The Navigations Acts referred to by List were a series of laws dating in the main to the British mercantilist policies of the 17th and 18th centuries. Their aim was to build up England's naval power, protect its slave trade and disable Dutch competition. Until its repeal in the 19th century, the legislation variously stipulated that goods brought to England from Asian, African or American colonies could only be transported on English ships. Fish imports and exports were to be the reserve of English shipping as was the English coastal trade. Between 1660 and 1739, as part of a system of 'enumerating', certain colonial products such as sugar, tobacco, indigo and molasses could be shipped directly only to England, Ireland or another British colony. In the Atlantic, measures such as low import

54 Ibid 283.

55 Ha-Joon Chang, *Kicking Away the Ladder: Development Strategy in Historical Perspective* (Anthem Press 2003) 1–3. In economics, the term 'infant industry' refers to industries which, being at the early stage of their development, are incapable of competing against mature, foreign rivals and should be protected.

56 Friedrich List (tr), *The National System of Political Economy* (Longman Green and Company 1885) cited in Chang (n 55) 4–5.

tariffs for British exports, as well as the 1764 tightening of the Navigation Acts, are said to have at least contributed to the American colonies' rebellion.[57] Following their independence, for a while, attitudes were split between the North and the South. The North wished to pursue protectionism which would facilitate the construction of its industrial base. The South, by contrast, favoured free trade in support of its slave labour-based economy of cotton exportation. When the North prevailed in the Civil War and, thereafter, from the 1860s to the 1930s, the US became the 'mother country' of protectionism with its economy the most shielded in the world.[58] In Europe, ruling elites' initial predilection for free trade produced a flurry of agreements that criss-crossed the continent. However, the doctrine soon lost its appeal. By 1860 France reduced tariffs pursuant to the Cobden-Chevalier trade treaty it had signed with Britain, only to raise them again 15 years later. Other countries followed suit with the Netherlands the only exception.[59] France's second elected president, Adolphe Thiers (1871–1873), is said to have described British free trade campaigning as 'a siren beckoning less developed Europe to its destruction' and a strategy pursued as part of a 'quest for world domination'.[60] By 1913, in the face of stiff competition from Germany and the US, Britain introduced some import tariffs. In 1932, in response to the Great Depression and in line with John Maynard Keynes's economic theory which called for interventionist and protectionist policies in such exceptional circumstances, it operated a *de facto* imperial preference system.[61] This system was abandoned in the 40s with the rise of the US empire.

The US, its industry having hitherto prospered behind a wall of protectionism, now moved to establish the Bretton Woods economic order as part of its shift towards free trade. The rationale behind this shift, says Sheppard, was to break up the non-US preference systems and, more recently, to promote the spread of neoliberalism. It was nevertheless to be a 'regulated free trade'. In what Hudson refers to as a built-in double standard, the US retained the right to determine its trade policy at the national level. By so doing, it preserved the flexibility to respond to changing circumstances. Whereas all other participants in the post-war American order were to be bound by fixed rules modifiable only through international agreements, the

57 Hickel (n 10) 184–6.

58 Sheppard (n 46) 165; Hickel (n 10) 186.

59 Sheppard (n 46) 163–4 providing analysis of the background to the fluctuations in European attitude to free trade.

60 T. J. Coles, *Britain's Secret Wars: HOW and WHY the United Kingdom Sponsors Conflict Around the World* (Clairview 2016) 4.

61 The imperial preference system was a commercial arrangement practiced in the first half of the 20th century by most countries with dependent territories. Of these, the British one was the most important. Pursuant to this policy, implemented by means of bilateral agreements, constituents of the empire were to grant each other tariff rates below the official ones. It also included other types of preferences, such as positive discrimination in the grant of public contracts, indirect shipping subsidies and preferential access to capital markets. The principle underpinning the policy – home producers first, imperial producers second and foreign producer last – was established in the 1932 Ottawa Imperial Economic Conference.

US Congress retained its authority to pass trade rules and to unilaterally abrogate international agreements. The Trading Agreement Act was passed in 1945 and, thereafter, renewed periodically. 'Each renewal afforded wider opportunities for domestic industries and corporations to claim injury from imports'. One consequence was the 1963 trade war with the EU. The EU imposed tariffs on imported American poultry in retaliation for the US imposing tariffs, principally on imported Belgian glass.[62]

Currency revaluation proffers an additional, indirect technique for protecting American foreign trade. In 1971, for instance, the US called for major trading currencies to be revalued upward. 'Properly interpreted, this amounted to a 10 per cent tariff on German imports to the United States, a 12 to 15 per cent tariff on Japanese imports, and so on, while simultaneously granting an equivalent subsidy for U.S. exports'.[63] In 2018, American president Donald Trump, as part of his election promise to put America first, imposed tariffs on imports of steel and aluminium from the EU, China and Mexico. The Mexican and EU's complaints to the WTO were resolved by mutual agreement and the cases were withdrawn in 2019 and 2022 respectively. Resolution of the complaint by China, a major trading rival, is ongoing.[64] China's refusal to comply with US demands for the Renminbi to be revalued was met with a flurry of tariff impositions. The 'double standard' which the US introduced into the ITO negotiations continued into the General Agreement on Tariffs and Trade (GATT).[65] It meant, says Hudson, that whereas 'the conduct of other nations was to be a constant, that of the United States was to be a variable'. Once the GATT no longer served American interests, it too was effectively destroyed, leaving its legal status a mere pretence.[66]

The aforementioned is but a brief outline of trade theory's chequered history and the interests and quest for power which propelled it one way or the other. However, it illustrates the gulf between the discourse of freedom and the practice of protectionism, between the narrative of free markets and states' *de facto* regulatory intervention. We are reminded by Dine that, earlier on, this gulf extended to the slave trade. One of the arguments used by proponents of slavery was that its abolition would inhibit free trade. In reality, though, slavery was 'protected by a network of laws, including company, contract and insurance law, as well as . . . the Navigation

62 Hudson (n 32) 285. The 1963 trade war is known in the US as the Chicken War. In the EU the war is known as the Glass War.

63 Hudson (n 32) 297.

64 WTO Dispute Settlement DS548, 'United States – Certain Measures on Steel and Aluminium Products' <https://www.wto.org/english/tratop_e/dispu_e/cases_e/ds548_e.htm> accessed 13 March 2022; WTO Dispute Settlement DS551, 'United States – Certain Measures on Steel and Aluminium Products <https://www.wto.org/english/tratop_e/dispu_e/cases_e/ds551_e.htm> accessed 16 March 2022; WTO Dispute Settlement DS543, United States – Tariff Measures on Certain Goods from China' <https://www.wto.org/english/tratop_e/dispu_e/cases_e/ds543_e.htm> accessed 16 March 2022.

65 The GATT was in effect from 1948 and, subject to modifications in 1994, is still in effect under the framework of the WTO.

66 Hudson (n 32) 290, 297 and generally 281–98.

Acts'.[67] Monopoly over the trade in slaves was secured under both national company law (the 1672 incorporation of the Royal Charter African Company) and IL (the 1713 Utrecht treaty which conceded to Britain trade in black people destined to the Spanish colonies).[68]

State-property alliance takes free trade also into the realms of foreign policy and national security. The most important heads of the World Bank were former secretaries of defence, such as McNamara and John McCloy. 'In truth', wrote Martin and Garnett in a 1997 Chatham House book, 'security interests and economic interests enjoy a symbiotic relationship'.[69] 'We cannot simply take a narrow, territorial-based view of our security', states a 2010 UK Ministry of Defence (MOD) green paper. 'Our economy is exceptionally open to trade with many parts of the world and relies on the free passage of goods, services and information'. It follows that a 'stable international order is essential if those interests are to prosper'.[70] Another 2010 MOD paper predicts that by 2029 the UK will be 'critically dependent upon energy imports and securing them will be non-discretionary'.[71] The conclusion which flows from this prediction can be found in the Chatham House 1997 publication. The issue, declare the authors, 'is not "what does justice and the law require?" but "how much we can get away with?" '[72]

Free trade: a critical perspective

For critics, free trade is one way by which 'how much we can get away with' is practiced. It is argued that the doctrine is flawed on its own terms, wrapping the reality of how free trade actually works in an illusion of how it should work.[73] Comparative cost advantage, posits Samir Amin, 'makes it possible to justify the international order and the insertion of new states into this order'.[74] It does so by perniciously omitting from its narrative facts such as the protectionism practiced by those with the capacity to do so, the so-called 'paradox of plenty' and related power differentials whereby 'small jurisdictions have always been at the mercy of the rules governing international trade and . . . in this respect, little has changed'.[75]

67 Dine (n 32, chapter 5) 134.

68 Ibid 137–42.

69 Laurence Martin and John Garnet, *British Foreign Policy: Challenges and Choices for the 21st Century* (Chatham House Papers) (Royal Institute of Foreign Affairs, Pinter 1997) 64.

70 Ministry of Defence, 'Adaptability and Partnership: Issues for the Strategic Defence Review' (2010) <https://assets.publishing.service.gov.uk/government/uploads/system/uploads/attachment_data/file/35927/defence_green_paper_cm7794.pdf> accessed 17 March 2022 cited in Coles (n 60) 11.

71 Ministry of Defence (n 70) cited in Coles (n 60) 11.

72 Martin and Garnet (n 69) 80.

73 See for example Shaikh (n 51) generally.

74 Samir Amin, *Imperialism and Unequal Development: Essays by Samir Amin* (Monthly Review Press 1977) 184.

75 Dine (n 32, chapter 5) 134.

Citing Gunnar Myrdal, Hudson refers to 'the unrealistic assumptions which are required if this theory is to hold'. Broadly, the assumptions are unrealistic because they are static and 'sidestepped the world economy's most dynamic changes and self-transformation'.[76] Hudson describes Ricardo's assignment to wine-producing Portugal the gains derived from its trade with textile-producing England as a 'travesty of reality'.[77] When analysing free trade, argues Anwar Shaikh, it is necessary to refer to competitive rather than comparative advantage. Echoing List and Chang, he says, 'There are no magic mechanisms that will automatically make all regions (nations) . . . equal.' Rather, free trade 'exposes the weak to the competition of the strong. And as in most such cases, the latter devours the former'.[78]

Left out of free trade standard theory is the difference which the nature of the specialisation makes. The emphasis is not on the substance of reciprocity, but reciprocity as a process of *quid pro quo*. Primary and hi-tech goods are treated as having the potential to be equally profitable. In practice, trade in manufactured goods is more gainful than trade in primary commodities. The Prebisch-Singer hypothesis of the late 1940s and into the 60s challenged free trade theory on precisely this ground.[79] Where pricing is left to market forces, it was argued, trading agricultural for industrial commodities destines low-income countries to decline and permanent poverty. This is because, in the long run, the price of primary goods goes down relative to that of manufactured ones, locking primary exporters into worsening trade terms. They would thus be better off adopting import substitution policies with focus on industrialisation. Critics of the Prebisch-Singer hypothesis argue that it has been overtaken by a reality of technological advances and the ability of mobile capital to scan the world for cheap labour. This produced a downwards trajectory of wages also in the Global North. Consequently, the price of manufactured goods has gone down relative to the cost of primary goods. The wrinkle in this critique is its failure to account for the impact of that which takes place in the space between the supply chain's starting point – the peripheral producer in receipt of a small fraction of the ultimate price – and its end point, the price paid by consumers. Clelland's 'dark value' gets inflated on its travels through nodes of unequal exchanges. The price charged at the centre of consumption includes the profits of middlemen, the costs of product development, advertising etc. It also reflects price manipulations scattered along supply chains. Price manipulations are present, for instance, in trading undertaken in the interior of MNEs between its different corporate units and pursuant to contractual arrangements of fictitious arm's

76 Hudson (n 44) 99, 114 citing at p. 99 from Gunnar Myrdal, *The Political Element in the Development of Economic Theory* (Routledge 1953) 62.

77 Hudson (n 32) 281; for an analysis of Ricardo's Portugal-Britain trade example see Hudson (n 44) 104–7, 298–301.

78 Shaikh (51) 8.

79 Raul Prebisch was an Argentinian economist who headed the UN Economic Commission for Latin America established in 1948 in Chile. Hans Singer was a German British economist associated with heterodox economics also active in the UN. Their hypothesis formed the basis for the dependency theory.

length nature. Notwithstanding fluctuations in the world wholesale prices, prices to the consumer invariably go up, and in any event, never seem to fall.[80] Coffee is but one of many such examples. The cost expended on coffee growers in the Global South is on average less than 10 cents on every coffee dollar earned in sites of consumption.[81] It may be even less. In August 2018, dozens of workers filed a complaint with the Organisation for Economic Co-operation and Development (OECD) accusing McDonald's, Dunkin' Donuts and Nestle of violating the organisation's Human Rights and Sustainability Guidelines. The complaint was based in part on evidence of the use of slave labour on Brazilian farms.[82]

Unequal exchanges of free trade

The rise in capital's mobility referred to by critics of the Prebisch-Singer hypothesis takes centre stage in the concept of unequal exchanges. First coined in 1972 by the Marxist economist Arghiri Emmanuel, it marked an important development in the theory of international trade and beyond as a 'theory of unequal relations of domination/dependence between the center and the periphery of the world capitalist system'.[83] Unequal exchanges refer to the practice of transferring to wealthier nations the profit created in poorer ones. Inequality is intrinsic to these transfers because of the difference between the modality of capital and that of labour. Whilst capital has turned mobile, labour has remained more or less immobile and determined by specific national and historical conditions. Whereas contemporary capital flows throughout a unitary globalised capitalist system in which the tendency is towards equalised value, the price paid for labour is determined within territorial boundaries and has remained variable. In other words, commodities, wherever produced, are all destined for a single worldwide market where their profit rates are equalised. By contrast, they were produced by labour the value of which is not equalised. Put simply, Asian and African labour creates the same international value (translated into international prices) as the Western one. However, Asian and African labour is cheaper. Consequently, the production price of the commodities made in these countries is lower than the production price of Western commodities. It follows that the rate of the surplus value or profit (the increase in labour's productivity exceeding the price paid for it) being transferred from Asia and India is higher. 'It is this primary

80 Amin (n 74) 220. Amin makes this point in the context of the price to consumers in core countries. However, the same applies to consumers in the Global South.

81 Kelly F. Austin, 'Brewing Unequal Exchanges in Coffee: A Qualitative Investigation into the Java Trade in Rural Uganda' (2017) 2(23) *Journal of World-Systems Research* 326 at 327.

82 Marina Lopes, 'The hidden suffering behind the Brazilian coffee that jump-starts American mornings'(*The Washington Post*, 31 August 2018) <https://www.washingtonpost.com/world/the_americas/the-hidden-suffering-behind-the-brazilian-coffee-that-jump-starts-american-mornings/2018/08/30/e5e5a59a-8ad4-11e8-9d59-dccc2c0cabcf_story.html?utm_term=.5faa33053b8f> accessed 22 March 2018.

83 Amin (n 74) 83; Arghiri Emmanuel, *Unequal Exchanges: A Study of the Imperialism of Trade* (Monthly Press Review 1972).

problem of transfer which Emmanuel calls unequal exchanges'.[84] Moreover, since profit is an important source of growth, 'the transfer of profits out of the underdeveloped regions is at the same time a reduction in their rate of growth relative to what it could have been in the absence of the intrusion of foreign capitals'.[85]

The conception of unequal exchanges informs Amin's broader concept of imperialist rent. Imperialist rent provides a theoretical umbrella under which congregate 'a whole series of cases of "unequal exchanges" which go beyond the unequal reward for labour'.[86] Imperial rent refers to the above average or extra profits realised through a higher rate of exploitation. Higher rate of exploitation and associated superprofits are in turn attendant on the shift from competitive to monopolistic capitalism with multinational oligopolies at its core.[87] It is said that superprofits are justified because corporations, extractive ones in particular, operate in high-risk countries and in volatile markets. Superprofits in boom times thus balance out shrinking profits in leaner ones. As against this, following Amin, Higginbottom points to the fact that superprofits or 'extra-surplus values' are not limited to boom times. Rather, 'they are typical of sectors of British and other imperial capitals for the last century or more. They are part of what makes capitalism imperialist in a structural way'.[88] Three main mechanisms are in operation separately or in combination: exploitation and exhaustion of labour through low wages, depletion of resources through excessive extraction and private monopoly over technology.[89] Additionally, the free movement of capital, the fact that it can pick and choose its destinations, produces uneven development, be it sectoral, technological or regional. By contrast, the social and environmental costs amassed on the way and externalised are borne by Global South societies as a whole.[90]

Awareness of the costs of unequal exchanges has led to the broadening of the concept to include also its social, distributive and ecological dimensions. The term 'social/ecological unequal exchanges' refers to the negative impact they have on the well-being, health and education of so-called less developed populations, the disruption to their local markets, their labour and land ownership structures

84 Anwar Shaikh, 'Foreign Trade and the Law of Value Part I' (1979) 3(43) *Science and Society* 281 at 299 where Shaikh also critiques Emmanuel's analysis. <https://www.jstor.org/stable/40402184> accessed 21 March 2022.

85 Shaikh (n 84) 299.

86 Amin (n 74) 212.

87 For a quantitative metric of the surplus transferred through imperial rent see Samir Amin, 'The surplus in Monopoly Capitalism and the Imperialist Rent' (2012) 3(64) *Monthly Review* 78.

88 Andy Higginbottom, '"Imperialist Rent" in Practice and Theory' (2014) 11(1) *Globalizations* 23 at 25.

89 Higginbottom (n 88) generally.

90 Alberto Acosta, 'Extractivism and Neoextractivism: Two Sides of the Same Curse' in M. Lang and D. Mokrani (eds), *Beyond Development: Alternative Visions from Latin America; Permanent Working Group on Alternatives to Development* (Foundation Rosa Luxemburg, Transnational Institute 2013) 62 <https://www.tni.org/files/download/beyonddevelopment_extractivism.pdf> accessed 21 March 2022.

as well as the degradation of their environment.[91] For example, Kelly Austin's 2012 research linked unequal exchanges in the trading of coffee to greater hunger, higher rate of deforestation and lower rates of educational enrolments. Epidemiological research links ecological transformation attendant on expansive cultivation to the spread of infectious diseases such as malaria.[92] To this Alberto Acosta adds depletion of resources due to excessive rate of extraction, rent-seeking, recurrent economic crises, wealth concentration, oligopoly, regional and communal tensions, as well as practices of corruption and clientelism.[93] These costs are on the increase. Food prices go up in consequence of agricultural land being grabbed for speculation, agrofuel production and World Bank backed, colonial-type plantations. Extractive technologies become more expensive as they venture into ever more remote corners of the globe and ever greater depth of land and oceans in return for ever smaller rates of extraction. Underpinning these costs, says Lang, is the aim of maintaining Western concepts of success and happiness, an 'ideology of progress' that is grounded in quantitative rather than qualitative ideas about growth, accumulation and consumption.[94] While the increase in externalised costs impacts also on the global North, its consequences are most acute in the South. It is there that peasants whose land has been taken to be put to a more profitable use are pushed into destitution and suicide. It is there that rise in food prices translates into widespread hunger and climate change into thousands of deaths.[95]

Formal colonialism: practices and legacies of taking by transfer

Hoogvelt distinguishes between two different periods of colonial taking. To begin with, surplus was transferred through disorderly looting and plundering masquerading as trade (1500–1800). It was followed by a period of formal colonialism when surplus was transferred from the colonies to the metropolis through unequal terms of exchange (1800–1950).[96] In formal colonialism looting and plundering gave way to organised collaboration between home states and their local colonists in the development and implementation of methodologies of control and surplus extraction. The colonists administered production, focusing on the suppression of the cost of labour. The metropolis regulated the price of traded goods by means

91 Austin (n 81) 329; for an early research that attracted attention to the ecological impacts of unequal exchanges see Stephen Bunker, *Underdeveloping the Amazon: Extraction, Unequal Exchanges and the Failure of the Modern State* (University of Illinois Press 1985).

92 Austin (n 81) 329–30.

93 Acosta (n 90) 63–4, 71.

94 The concept of 'ideology of progress' is advanced by Eduardo Gudynas, 'Debates on Development and Its Alternatives in Latin America: A Brief Heterodox Guide' in Lang and Mokrani (n 90) 28–9.

95 Miriam Lang, 'Prologue: Crisis if Civilisation and Challenges for the Left' in Lang and Mokrani (n 90) 5.

96 Hoogvelt (n 5) 17 following Paul A. Baran, *The Political Economy of Growth* (Monthly Review Press 1968) 17.

of tariffs, dumping policies and, where necessary, gunboat diplomacy.[97] England's negative balance of trade with China, for example, was to be made positive through the illegal importation into the country of Indian opium. Chinese resistance triggered gunboat diplomacy in the form of two Opium Wars (1839 and 1856–60). Following defeat of the Chinese army, the two states entered into treaties which secured wide-ranging trade privileges to the colonial state and its colonists.

Africa, specifically the continent's interior, became the focus of interest in the last decade of the 19th century as a way out of the economic contraction which took hold of Europe. Imperial rivalry and a 'scramble for Africa' ensued, leading to the Berlin Conference and an increased European control of the continent and its resources from 10% in 1870 to 90% by 1914.[98] From mining to trading, shipping and banking, the scramble soon became a breeding ground for extra profits and vast fortunes. With the aid of 'legislation backed by military force', local wages were suppressed to the minimum necessary for survival of the workforce.[99] Nigerian coal miners earned one shilling per day for working underground and nine pence per day for jobs on the surface. In Tanganyika under German rule, in Portuguese colonies, French Equatorial Africa and French Sudan, for example, peasants were forced at gun and whip point to grow cash crops. The price paid in exchange was so low as to render the produce no more than a 'tribute from conquered people'.[100] This pursuit of superprofits through suppression of the cost of labour was supplemented by the formation of 'pools' of trading companies engaged in price fixing.

For local populations, these strategies meant variously the pauperisation of artisans and the peasantry, widespread drug addiction and holocausts of famine on historically unprecedented scale. Scarcity of food killed an estimated 29m and 30m people in free trade India and China respectively.[101] Colonised and semi-colonised countries such as China entered a downward spiral towards marginalisation and dependency. Taking India as an example, advocates of free trade argued that local protectionist duties had to be abolished if the supply of cheap cotton into Britain and enlargement of the market for its manufactured goods were to be secured. Accordingly, experimental cotton cultivation by local farmers and railways construction were deemed 'state interference'.[102] In a process that was repeated in Egypt, Ottoman Türkiye and Iran, narrates Mishra, the Moslem population of Northern India

97 Dumping refers to the practice of selling goods in the colonies at prices lower than those charged domestically in order to destroy local competition without affecting profitability at home. Coles (n 60) 6.

98 Hickel (n 10) 95.

99 Walter Rodney, *How Europe Underdeveloped Africa* (Pambazuka Press 1972) 149–50.

100 Ibid 158.

101 In China, loss of control over the rice market and over national strategies for ensuring supplies in times of drought led to the death from starvation of 30 million people. The same applied to India. In the Congo, 10 million people, half of the country's population, was exterminated under King Leopold's regime of rubber extraction. Hickel (n 10) 92, 96; for detailed account of the famines of the 19th century see Mike Davis, *Late Victorian Holocausts: El Nino Famines and the Making of the Third World* (Verso 2001).

102 Coles (n 60) 6.

helplessly watched as 'the British set up plantations, dug canals, and laid roads, and turned India into a supplier of raw materials, and exclusive market for British industries'. The British goods which flooded the bazaars impoverished the local population.[103] Consequently India was transformed from a place of self-sufficiency famous for its exports to 'the greatest captive market in world history'. Its 27% share of the world economy plummeted to just 3%. In the second half of the 19th century, income declined by 50% and average life expectancy fell by 20%.[104] China's share of the world economy collapsed from 35% before the Opium Wars of resistance to a mere 7% thereafter. The practices of transfer which underpinned this downwards trajectory meant that, at the same time, European share of global GDP increased from 20% to 60%.[105] This manufactured food insecurity coupled with dependency on Western exports continued into the neo-colonial periods, this time, *inter alia*, through World Bank lending policies. Loans were to be made in US dollars to finance the importation of American and later other countries' agricultural products, capital goods and engineering services. The loans were not to be made in local currency so that no money was available for the implementation of land reforms and the modernisation of agriculture.[106]

The integration of colonised territories into the world economy necessitated an ensemble of political, legal and economic/financial designs. Such designs laid the foundations for the hierarchical world order later to be guarded against the threats posed by independence. Designs varied. Broadly, however, they may be said to have been implemented through direct political control shored up by a local administration with the power to make and enforce laws. In this way, the stability, predictability and regularity of taking was assured. In South Arica in 1857, for example, labour migration to mines and plantations was prompted in the first instance by the imposition of taxation. With subsistence farming no longer sustainable as means of survival, peasants were forced to leave their land in search of work. This indirect method of creating wage labour was later formalised by means of legislation that spawned the African persona as a special judicial category to be confined to a reserve economy. There, wages could be suppressed with even greater ease. By 1913 the Native Land Act (followed by a series of 'pass laws' which prohibited settlement in white areas) operated to directly force Africans off their lands and into 'homelands' totalling some 7% of South African arable land.[107] The precise statistics of land redistribution in post-Apartheid South Africa are subject to intense debate and a variety of measurements. However, it is generally accepted that, despite commitment to land reforms in the country's 1996 constitution, to date, huge disparities along racial lines remain.[108]

103 Pankaj Mishra, *From the Ruins of Empire: The Revolt Against the West and the Remaking of Asia* (Penguin Books 2013) 35–6.

104 Hickel (n 10) 90, 93.

105 Ibid 92, 93.

106 Hudson (n 32) 213–26.

107 Hickel (n 10) 97–8.

108 'Constitution of the Republic of South Africa (1996) Art 25 <http://www.blackpast.org/constitution-republic-south-africa-1996> accessed 13 September 2018.

Bengali novelist Bankim Chandra Chatterji (1838–1894) described these practices of taking as an 'epidemic of stealing other people's wealth'. The technological appropriation which shored up the awakening of Europe was thus followed by economic appropriation which shored up its wealth accumulation. It was not Europe which developed the colonies, concludes Hickel. Rather, 'The colonies developed Europe'.[109] Frank makes a similar point when he observes that Europe's ascent from a backwater to the centre of the world system was achieved by climbing 'up the Asian shoulders'.[110] As well as resources and labour, colonised shoulders also included the use of Chinese markets to absorb the silver mined in the Americas. The West's economic 'take off', says Hobson, would have been inconceivable without the East.[111] Thus, the transition to formal colonialism foreshadowed the integration of peripheral regions into the world system as ancillary economies in an increasingly potent network of unequal exchanges.

Unequal exchanges: foreign investment

Methodologies of integration had to be adapted as conditions changed and capital's needs mutated. Bieler and Morton, following Amin, point to a shift from expanding production through original accumulation in pre-capitalist spaces to expanding production through the restructuring of the way in which peripheral spaces are incorporated into the global economy in post-1945 monopoly capitalism.[112] The 19th century may be seen as a point of inflection in the unfolding of this transition. Whereas integration through penetration into pre-capitalist spaces is broadly associated with European expansion of the 17th century onwards, it was in the mid-19th century that investable capital grew dramatically to become a main protagonist in the project of turning the planet into a European domain. The effect was to complete the shift from a sovereign-private collaborative taking as a lawful act denoting progress to an unlawful sovereign act denoting deprivation.

Whereas Amsterdam was the reigning economic centre of 17th and 18th centuries' merchant capitalism, by the 19th century it was replaced by the City of London. The City of London moved to finance private, large-scale industrial enterprises and infrastructure projects. With the growth of available finance and decline in the price of communications and transportation, foreign investment increased sharply. Corporations extended their operations abroad to become overseas producers. They were no longer the trading houses of old but relative newcomers in the shape of farmers, manufacturers, electricity producers and providers of services. They formed a prototype of the modern MNE displaying its characteristics

109 Hickel (n 10) 93.

110 Andrew Gunder Frank, *ReOrient: Global Economy in the Asian Age* (University of California Press 1998) 277–83.

111 John M. Hobson, *Eastern Origins of Western Civilization* (CUP 2004) 2–3.

112 Andreas Bieler and Adam David Morton, 'Uneven and Combined Development and Unequal Exchange: The Second Wind of Neoliberal "Free Trade"?' (2014) 11(1) *Globalizations* 35 at 38.

of extensive cross-border operations through elaborate networks of foreign subsidiaries held together by tight integration and centralised control.[113]

This transformation underscored the need for stability and protection against political risk. To this end, property had to shed off its characteristic as a socially and politically constituted national institution. Together with capital, it was to be internationalised. A regime of property protection which started as legal arrangements formulated by European states to facilitate commercial interactions among themselves became an international system for the provision of juridical back-up to Europe's overseas commercial penetration. 'It was the transformation from a regional system into an international investment law which fundamentally changed its character'.[114] This change of character came with strategies of imposition. Nineteenth-century property protection 'involved few reciprocal relations, considerably more coercion, and constrained bargaining among radically unequal states'. It produced a 'history of colonial annexation, capitulation treaties, treaty ports and ad hoc intervention, backed up by gunboats when necessary'.[115] This history goes a long way to contextualise and explain the regime's contemporary form. Specifically, the protection of investors and their investments was to be buttressed by the exclusivity of host state obligations denoting a peculiar understanding of reciprocity as essentially a one-sided arrangement.

Foreign investment penetration transformed the colonies' internal landscapes. Then as now, the aim was to loosen national control over the economy, open up markets and secure stability of possession. This applied both within each country and to the system as a whole. Within countries, internationalised property rights provided a legal mechanism for distancing risks posed by popular resistance, sovereign restrictions and loss of value pursuant to political, legal and regulatory changes. The enforceability of local laws insofar as they applied to aliens could be made subject to international standards and remedies. An internationally constituted property defined the parameters beyond which taking was unlawful and an arbitrary confiscation entitling the investor to its home country's diplomatic protection. From a systemic perspective, the internationalisation of property injected coherence into a multi-jurisdictional order. It introduced nodes of agreement and mutual recognition into a world of competing imperial powers and disparate legal systems.[116] Seen from this perspective, the 1959 Germany-Pakistan BIT, often referred to as signalling the launch of contemporary investment treaties, was not its

113 Charles Lipson, *Standing Guard: Protecting Foreign Capital in the Nineteenth and Twentieth Centuries* (University of California Press 1985) 5, 6; the ways in which modern MNEs organise their business operations and the legal forms they take have changed dramatically since then, culminating in the emergence of platform MNEs. For a discussion of these changes see Peter Muchlinski, *Multinational Enterprises and the Law* (3rd edn, CUP 2021) 42–79.

114 Kate Miles, *The Origins of International Investment Law: Empire, Environment and the Safeguarding of Capital* (CUP 2013) 2.

115 Lipson (n 113) 12.

116 Lauren Benton, *Legal Regimes in World History, 1400–1900* (CUP 2002) 10–11.

true starting point.[117] Rather, the contemporary regime of foreign investment protection represents another instance of continuity, a legacy of Europe's colonial past.

Investment protection's early beginnings were relatively innocent. Fifteenth-century capitulation treaties concluded with the Ottoman Empire did provide for the extraterritorial application of investors' home laws. However, they were freely entered into and enjoyed in-built reciprocity. Protections offered to resident aliens were similar to those extended to Moslem merchants abroad.[118] This changed by the mid-19th century. With the dramatic rise in foreign investment, the scope of protection afforded by these treaties was deemed deficient if the Levant was to 'become more accessible, secure and stable'. The 1838 Anglo-Turkish Convention injected the concept of 'capitulation' with a new meaning as a one-sided treaty divested of genuine reciprocity. 'The treaty prized open the now-feeble Ottoman empire to European manufacturers and investments'.[119] In addition to the extraterritorial application of investors' home laws, internal barriers were removed and concessions were granted for mining, railroad and port construction, coastal navigation, banking and public utilities'.[120] With Ottoman grip over the entry of foreign investment all but disappeared, by the 1850s European business came to dominate the domestic economy.[121]

This formula of economic concessions buttressed by extraterritoriality shaped also the capitulation of the Far East. This time, it did involve a military surrender and its aftermath in the form of a network of treaty ports, part of what came to be known as unequal treaties. The term 'unequal treaties' denotes the inequality of the rights and obligations contained therein. A quintessential example was the Treaty of Nanjing 1842 imposed on China following its defeat in the Opium Wars of resistance. It foreshadowed the 'treaty ports system', a term used to describe the privileges secured by the British in subsequent negotiations with the Qing dynasty. Other foreign powers followed suit with MFN clauses converting a privilege afforded to one to a privilege enjoyed by all. MFN clauses were supplemented by a Vitorian-type prohibition on treatment deemed discriminatory compared to the treatment accorded to Chinese nationals.

Treaty ports were essentially zones governed by the European. They were selected with care. The port to be opened and the concessions that went with it had to serve local economies, respond to the requirements of international trade and investment as well as be integrated into the rest of the network of treaty ports.

117 Treaty between the Federal Republic of Pakistan for the Promotion and Protection of Investments 1959 (entered into force in 1962). <https://edit.wti.org/document/show/b5da3ab9-31f4-4ded-b25a-82a7f4807035> accessed 23 March 2022. It was replaced by Germany-Pakistan BIT 2009.

118 Capitulation as a concept of IL refers to treaties pursuant to which a state granted another state extraterritorial jurisdiction over its own nationals residing within the territory of the granting state.

119 Lipson (n 113) 13.

120 Concession agreement, a key tool of foreign investment particularly in the extractive and public utilities industries, are state contracts with a natural or juridical person pursuant to which the state allows the person to engage in an activity previously the sole realm of the state.

121 Van Harten (n 75, chapter 3) 15.

Agreements for the transfer of land formed the foundation on which the legal edifice of this network was constructed. Negotiations took place locally, but mostly against the backdrop of military intervention or a threat thereof. Upon failure to secure diplomatic solutions, the Europeans could call in their home country's gunboats to deal with disorder. For Arrighi, it was these gunboats rather than Marx's artillery of cheap commodities that ultimately were the 'true "midwife" of the subordination of China to the imperatives of the "endless" accumulation of Western Capital'.[122] 'On what do the English capitalists rely for their security?' asked Richard Graves MacDonnell, British governor of the Gambia in 1849. He went on to answer his own question: 'Of course on the prestige of English power'. The persuasive power of British troops and guns also brought with it 'the more civilized and juster notions of the rights of property which the continued presence of Europeans and the spread of legitimate commerce is producing'.[123] IL brought force and law together. Gunboats could be called and the right of military intervention triggered as an act of diplomatic protection in response to the commission of an international wrong, such as uncompensated expropriation or failure to discharge debt obligations. Overall, property protection was heavily weighted in favour of foreign investors. The aim was to preserve their privileges in disregard for the colonised state's interests and circumstances, its ability to meet compensation claims and investors' own conduct.

This combination of law and force formed an essential part of the collaboration between investors and their home states alluded to earlier. Their relationship was characterised by a mixture of interdependency and shared functions and objectives. Investors lobbied politicians in the metropolis regarding the imperatives of having a foothold in China and the fusion of private and state interests. They also participated in the development of IL insofar as it was pertinent to their interests.[124] Their ability to be governed by the laws of their home state was one such interest. Thus, whilst the foundational jurisdictional rule of territoriality applied in Europe, in the colonies and semi-colonies, extraterritorial jurisdiction became the norm. Europeans who traded and sojourned in non-European countries were deemed to be carrying with them the superior law of their nationality. They enjoyed the privilege of immunity from municipal law and courts. This translated into a practice of creating consular areas over which investors and traders' home state exercised exclusive jurisdiction.[125] Outside of these areas, imperial agents had civil and criminal jurisdiction in matters involving foreign citizens, notably the protection of their property.[126] In this way, a landscape of unequal intersections was created whereby local legal regimes co-existed side by side with European jurisprudence that was

122 Arrighi (n 86) 751.
123 Cited in Lipson (n 113) 16.
124 Miles (n 114) 33.
125 Van Harten (n 75, chapter 3) 15; Mishra (103) 61–2.
126 Miles (n 114) 27.

simultaneously exclusive and invasive. In the semi-colony of China, extraterritoriality played a particularly prominent role in the structuring of foreign control. Imperial powers were content to forego direct control in favour of carving out 'spaces for their subjects in the form of extraterritorial privileges and establishing foreign settlements and concessions that were increasingly beyond the reach of the Qing laws and jurisdiction'.[127] In the Ottoman Empire in the 19th century, disputes were resolved in mixed courts presided by both Ottoman judges and consular delegates. The proceedings were deemed invalid unless approved by the foreigner's own consular representative. Consequently, 'international property rights were effectively guaranteed by the extraterritorial application of American and European laws'.[128]

Latin America was somewhat different. The region retained its reputation as a place of higher civilisation so that, unlike in Africa and Asia, the need for direct intervention was less pressing. Civilisation was measured by reference to European 'superior' notions of economic openness and property rights protection. The Latin American new states introduced protection of property rights into their basic laws. In Argentina, foreign investors were assured of equal treatment. Immigration to the country was permitted, as was the purchase of property by aliens. In Brazil, an emerging class of large landowners quickly adopted British ideas about the commercially progressive nature of property rights. Yet, conflicts and resistance to foreign dominance and privileges did arise, producing periods of unrest and legal innovations such as the Calvo Doctrine. Conflicts were countered by diplomatic intervention, use of force and the imposition of sanctions facilitated by the European 'stranglehold over credit'.[129]

This contest between colonial legacies blended with neo-colonial impositions and resistance persist. The 2009 Bolivian constitution, for example, invokes the impact which 'the terrible times of colonialism' had on the country and lists the struggles undertaken against it by the 'martyrs' in whose memory it was drafted. The constitution then goes on to declare the Bolivian people's commitment to equality and wealth distribution before outlining the state's duties as guarantor of social justice, decolonialisation that is free of exploitation and discrimination, national plurality and indigenous autonomy. The state also guarantees universal and inalienable social, economic, environmental, civil and political rights. These include access to water, food, health, habitat, dignified work, social security, education and healthy environment. Emphasis is placed on the diversity of property formations as well as its social function and impact. Article 56 I stipulates, 'Everyone has the right to private, individual or collective property, provided that it serves

127 Par Cassel, 'Extraterritoriality in China: What We Know and What We Don't Know' in Robert Bickers and Isabella Jackson (eds), *Treaty Ports in Modern China: Law, Land and Power* (Studies in the Modern History of Asia, Routledge 2016) 23.

128 Lipson (n 113) 14.

129 Ibid 17.

a social function'. Article 56 II adds, 'Private property is guaranteed provided that the use made of it is not harmful to the collective interests'.[130] Nations and rural native peoples have a right to 'collective ownership of the intellectual property in their knowledge, sciences and learning, as well as to its evaluation, use, promotion and development'.[131] In a 2011 interview with Lang, the scholar Bouaventura de Sousa Santos commented on the innovations introduced through these constitutional processes. They include not only diversity in the way property may be held, but also more generally a new concept of development which goes by the name of 'living well' (*buen vivir*). 'Living well', mostly credited to the work of indigenous organisations, articulates a departure from Western-led representations of development. It imagines a way of life that distances itself from industrial capitalism, consumerism and economic growth in favour of 'harmonious coexistence' with nature.[132] In April 2017, the tiny country of El Salvador made history. In response to grassroots and church activism, and in an attempt to protect its ecosystems, specifically its dwindling sources of clean water, it was the first country to have turned a decade-long moratorium into legislation banning all forms of metallic mining.[133]

On the other hand, colonial legacies and the uneven development characteristic of an enclave economy have survived distributive and rebalancing efforts by progressive governments. On the whole, the country has remained incorporated into the globalised monopoly capitalism of extraction and transfer, or what Araghi describes as political regimes of global value relations.[134] That is to say, political regimes of production and extraction of value that are constituted on a plenary scale around a single prescription of free markets, trade and investment. Attempts at divergence are not only hard to sustain, but also risky. They trigger both overt and covert, direct and indirect interventions.[135] Internally, there is 'the weighty inheritance of states that are profoundly colonial'.[136]

Finally and briefly, by the latter part of the 19th century, taking by transfer within the framework of incorporation took the form of protectorates. Mandate territories were placed under the protection of European states. Protection included also the right to assume control over the country's internal affairs. In effect, the protected became part of its protector.[137] As noted by legal scholar John Westlake,

130 'Bolivia (Plurinational State) Constitution of 2009' Arts 56 I, II <https://www.constituteproject.org/constitution/Bolivia_2009.pdf> accessed 26 March 2022.

131 Bolivia Constitution Art 30 ii 11.

132 Arturo Escobar, *Encountering Development: The Making and Unmaking of the Third World* (Princeton University Press 1995) xxv.

133 'El Salvador Makes History as First Nation to Impose Blanket Ban on Metal Mining' (*The Guardian*, 2017) <https://www.theguardian.com/global-development/2017/mar/30/el-salvador-makes-history-first-nation-to-impose-blanket-ban-on-metal-mining> accessed 26 March 2022.

134 Farshad Araghi, 'Food Regimes and the Production of Value: Some Methodological Issues' (2003) 30(2) *Journal of Peasant Studies* 41.

135 Coles (n 60) generally.

136 Lang (n 95) 6–7.

137 Anghie (n 9) 87–90.

'the institution of protectorates over uncivilized nations has given greater freedom to the initial steps towards their acquisition'.[138]

Debt

The Western club

A by-product of the detachment of economic power from direct political control is rule by economic means.[139] One method of rule by economic means is indebtedness. In particular, says Wood, indebtedness has become 'the principal instrument of the post WWII "new imperialism" '.[140] Hoogvelt traces the rise of 'debt peonage' to the second neo-colonial period which began in the 1970s.[141] Wood and Hoogvelt are not alone in looking to the 20th century as the time when debt became central to rule by economic means within an 'empire of capital'. Sassen, among others, points to the substantial increase in governments' debt burden since the establishment of the Bretton Woods order of lending organisations. By now, the volume of Global South external debt has reached historically unprecedented levels. In 2018, it stood at US$55 trillion representing 170% of global GDP. In 63 impoverished countries, average repayments grew from 5.5% of government revenue in 2011 to 12.4% in 2019.[142] During COVID-19, against the backdrop of soaring unemployment and disruptions to exports, low-income countries turned to expensive short-term borrowing from the IMF and private lenders. In 2020, UNCTAD estimated that Global South countries' expenditure on servicing their external debt will rise by between US$26 and US$34 trillion. Its average ratio was projected to go up by between 7% and 10% of GDP in 2021.[143] In early 2022, the figure for actual rise in debt repayments in the previous two years was estimated at 45%, with half of all low-income countries officially in debt distress or at a high risk of it.[144]

138 John Westlake, *Chapters on the Principles of International Law* (Classic Reprint) (Forgotten Books 2018) 184 cited in Anghie (n 9) 87–8.

139 Wood (n 12) 12.

140 Ibid 131. By 'new imperialism' Wood refers to post-WWII capitalism which is founded on a global system of multiply states in complex and contradictory relations with capital's expansive economic power. Capital's economic power is sustained by states' provision of extra-economic force employed to extend the 'laws' of the capitalist economy. Thus, the territorial state is subsidiary to capital but is nevertheless more relevant than ever. 5–6, 20.

141 Hoogvelt (n 5) 17. Hoogvelt refers to the pattern of transfer of value through the instrument of debt as 'new'. As seen earlier, indebtedness as a route to subservience was practiced also in the 19th century.

142 Sara Murawski, 'Time to Resolve Debt Issues in the Global South' (2020) *Transnational Institute* <https://www.tni.org/en/article/time-to-resolve-debt-issues-in-the-global-south> accessed 27 March 2022.

143 UNICEF, 'COVID-19 and the Looming Debt Crisis' (April 2021) 7 <https://www.unicef-irc.org/publications/pdf/Social-spending-series_COVID-19-and-the-looming-debt-crisis.pdf> accessed 10 May 2022.

144 Mark Malloch-Brown, 'The Global South's Looming Debt Crisis – and How to Stop It (*Foreign Policy*, March 22) <https://foreignpolicy.com/2022/03/16/global-south-sovereign-debt-crisis-covid-economy-imf-reform/> accessed 10 May 2022.

In the context of the Bretton Woods lending order, rule by economic means translates into dependency on US agricultural exports and the absence of food sovereignty, colonial-type plantations for the provision of agricultural products the US cannot grow, suppression of the cost of labour and the privatisation of infrastructure and public services as sources of foreign investors' rental income.[145] Presently, against a backdrop of inter-state confrontations and related fracturing of the globalist project, sanctions, military campaigns and food and energy shortages, debtor countries are predicted to have to choose between feeding their population and keeping factories going on the one hand and debt repayments on the other. Hudson reads statements made by Janet Yellen, US Secretary of the Treasury, as indicating that, in the face of a threat to the American unipolar world order, the country will use the IMF and its special drawing rights (SDRs) as a lever to preserve its hegemony.[146] The bulk of the SDRs will go to the US to support its military spending abroad. The rest will be on offer to debtor states facing foreclosure, on condition that they privatise, lower wages and pass anti-labour legislation. Privatisations will be largely under the control of American investors, banks and financiers.[147] Whether Yellen's vision of this new brave world will come to pass remains an open question. It may be curtailed by new alliances and a redrawn map of centres of power. In defiance of sanctions, an African Union delegation headed by the president of Senegal went to Russia to negotiate the ongoing exportation to Africa of Russian wheat and fertilisers. The commodities are to be paid in roubles rather than dollars.[148]

The increase in the burden of debt is not exclusive to the Global South. However, there, its weight and implications differ substantially. Hudson, in his seminal book *Super Imperialism*, analyses the U.S. post-1971 methodology of domination as a transition from one that was based on lending to one that is based on borrowing. In what he terms 'monetary imperialism', once the US withdrew from the gold standard, it became free to run up trillions of treasury IOUs. They were to be held as foreign exchange dollars in the coffers of central banks and, through them, be incorporated into the world's monetary base. Treasuries, he says, finance American budget deficit by means of essentially non-repayable debt. They constitute 'a free ride' which saw the US 'run more deeply into debt without foreign constraint, a debt not to be repaid'. They are effectively 'a tax imposed on foreign

145 Michael Hudson, 'Changes in Superimperialism' (23 January 2021) presentation to the Oxford Economics Society <https://www.youtube.com/watch?v=PtHX23Trvy4> accessed 29 March 2021.

146 SDRs are a form of international money created by the IMF and consisting of the ability to claim on freely usable currencies of IMF members. It is defined as weighted average of a basket of convertible currencies.

147 Naked Capitalism, 'Michael Hudson Talks with Katie Halper and Aaron Maté About the Broader Ramifications of the US/NATO Conflict with Russia' (*Podcast*, May 2022) <https://www.nakedcapitalism.com/2022/05/michael-hudson-talks-with-katie-halper-and-aaron-mate-about-the-broader-ramifications-of-the-us-nato-conflict-with-russia.html> accessed 13 July 2022.

148 Kester Ken Klomegah, 'African Union Delegation Plans to Visit Russia and Ukraine' (7 May 2022) <https://indepthnews.net/index.php/the-world/africa/5340-african-union-delegation-plans-to-visit-russia-and-ukraine> accessed 7 June 2022.

dollar holders'.[149] David Graeber conceptualised treasuries as tributes, military bases abstracted as financial instruments.[150] By contrast, in the Global South, '[g]overnments now pay more to their lenders than they invest in basic components of development'.[151] According to John Perkins writing in 2004, in Ecuador, out of every US$100 of crude oil extracted from the Amazonian rain forest, $75 went to the oil companies. Three quarters of the remaining $25 was spent on debt servicing. After military and other governmental expenditure, only $2.5 was left for health, education and support for the poor.[152] Moreover, when debt servicing becomes difficult, countries of the Global South find themselves facing a coherent body of lenders holding coordinated positions and dictating repayment schedules which take no account of the debtor's ability to shoulder them. The interlocking structure of credit means that where a country unilaterally suspends repayments, there is no other lender to turn to.[153]

As in the case of foreign investment protection, the contemporary face of wealth transfer by indebtedness is rooted in earlier structures of domination. 'Debt's origins come from colonialism's origins', said Thomas Sankara, murdered president of Burkina Faso, aka Africa's Che Guevara in his 1987 speech to the Organisation of African Unity. 'Those who lend us money are those who colonized us. . . . Debt is neo-colonialism, in which colonizers have transformed themselves into "technical assistants". We should rather say "technical assassins". It is "a skilfully managed reconquest of Africa"'.[154] This view of Global South indebtedness as rooted in colonialism and, thereafter, in neo-colonialism is habitually lost in justificatory narratives about modernisation, the foreign finance it necessitates and the act of taking as an act of giving. Yet, this discourse with its emphasis on the universal benefits of Western-led progress paints only a partial picture. It overlooks, or at least treats as provisional, the economic costs modernisation cum development entail, including the cost of borrowing at compound interest. When the City of London replaced Amsterdam as an economic centre in the 19th century, in addition to issuing bonds as a way of financing private capital, it also engaged in lending to states.[155] The Ottoman Empire could ill-afford its ambition to modernise its economy and Europeanise Istanbul. Following its 1838 free trade capitulation treaty and subsequent loosening of control over the economy, Europeans 'attracted by the possibility of easy money' poured into the capital. European banks mushroomed,

149 Hudson (n 32) ix and generally.

150 David Graeber, *Debt: The First 5,000 Years* (Melville House New York 2011) 6.

151 Saskia Sassen, *Expulsions: Brutality and Complexity in the Global Economy* (The Belknap Press of HUP 2014) 27.

152 John Perkins, *Confessions of an Economic Hitman: The Shocking Story of How America Really Took Over the World* (Ebury Press 2006) xx.

153 Lipson (n 113) 161, 107; see also Charles Lipson, 'The International Organization of Third World Debt' (1981) 35(4) *International Organization* 603.

154 Thomas Sankara (tr), 'A United Front Against Debt' (*Addis Ababa*, 29 July 1987) <https://www.marxists.org/archive/sankara/1987/july/29.htm> accessed 27 March 2022.

155 Lipson (n 113) 5.

offering loans at extortionate rates of interest. 'As the Ottomans steadily sank into debt, European power inexorably grew'.[156] Egypt also embarked on a modernisation program in the wake of Napoleon's 1798 invasion. Cheered on by Western banks, the modernisation extravaganza they engaged in came at inordinate cost of borrowing. Egyptian peasants were made to focus on the cultivation of cotton as cash crop for exportation with which, *inter alia*, to service the country's external debt. When cotton prices collapsed following the American civil war, Egypt's indebtedness deepened, and with it, its subordination to foreign financiers.[157] These practices of inducing states to borrow continued into 20th century's decolonisation. In what came to be known as 'go-go' banking, representatives of banks such as Citibank, Chase and Deutsche Bank feverishly pushed borrowing onto the new states.[158] In particular, following OPEC's embargo on the sale of oil to the US in the 1970s, the two countries agreed that OPEC would be free to determine the price of oil on condition that all oil would be sold in US dollars to be recycled in the US. American banks became awash with petrodollars. With limited outlets for profitable investment in the then stagnant Western economies, the Global South beckoned. Its governments were looking to raise capital with which to finance their then import substitution, welfare and land reform policies. The business of lending to states was booming in the belief that states are unlikely to default. 'Countries don't go bust', Walter Wriston, Citibank CEO, liked to say.[159] Consequently, lending became a matter of quantity over quality. Global South debt rocketed, generating enormous profits. By 1980 profits to lenders reached more than US$100 billion.[160] In the meantime, Global States' ability to service their debts was being constrained by higher oil prices and lower prices for primary commodities relative to the cost of manufactured goods. Then came the Volcker shock in 1981. Interest rates went up to 21% practically overnight and Global South countries fell into a debt crisis. In the 1987 summit, Sankara called for a united, openly declared policy of non-repayment. This did not materialise. Instead, the Global South was made the object of lending institutions' stabilisation programs in the form of austerity and structural adjustments. It is estimated that during the heydays of the IMF structural adjustment programs, within no more than six years (1984–1990), the Global South transferred some $178 billion to Western commercial banks.[161] The current hike in interest rates is, once again, fuelling a debt crisis in the Global South. Countries with dollars debts must pay more to service them. Scarcer and costlier finance coupled with inflation threaten to slow down economic progress.

Also lost in the narrative of modernisation is the role which protection of property rights and the compensation they attract have played historically in the creation of indebtedness. The case of Haiti and colonial invasions poignantly illustrate

156 Pankaj Mishra, *From the Ruins of Empire* (Penguin Book 2013) 61.
157 Ibid 73–6.
158 Hickel (n 10) 150.
159 Hickel (n 10) 150.
160 Ibid 152.
161 Ian Goodrum, 'Correcting the Record on China and Africa' (*China Daily*, 3 September 2018).

the way the lawful/unlawful boundary, the colour white of property and the exclusion of labour from its compensatory orbit have guided the construction of the debt regime. Sankara called it 'blood debt', one which the greatest wealth cannot repay.[162]

The Republic of Haiti was made to pay France 150 million gold francs in compensation for the loss of foreign investors' plantations and slaves and for the cost to France of its failed military expeditions. These were sent to suppress and reverse the plantation slaves' 1804 rebellion which brought about the establishment of the Republic of Haiti. The debt was ten times the country's annual revenue. With the US agreement, an embargo was imposed until such time as it was paid in full. Subsequently, the amount was reduced. Nevertheless, Haiti still paid to France 90 million francs equivalent to 17 billion euros in today's money. In 2004, the then president of Haiti, Jean-Bertrand Aristide, suggested that France should pay back US$21 billion in reparations for the imposition of this debt. He was toppled by a CIA-backed coup shortly afterwards. There was to be no compensation for the former slaves.

As to invasions, throughout history, the conclusion of wars was followed by mutual debt cancellation so as to clear the deck and start afresh.[163] It was different for colonised people. Not only was there no clearing of the deck, but the imposition of reparations was inverted. It was not the invaders but the conquered who had to pay. 'Third World debtor nations are almost exclusively countries that have at one time been attacked and conquered by European countries – often, the very countries to whom they now owe money'.[164] In the case of the Opium Wars fought over Britain's illegal importation of opium into its semi-colony, it was China which had to compensate for the losses occasioned by its resistance to British crimes. Pursuant to the Nanjing Treaty, it was obliged to pay $21m in reparations. When France invaded Madagascar in 1985, the local population was made to defray the cost of invasion through heavy taxation. In addition, they also had to defray the costs of the infrastructure and plantations which the French built and which the Malagasy neither asked for, nor wanted, nor were consulted about. Popular objections were met with a military response. Over half a million Malagasy were killed in one rebellion in 1947. The country has remained indebted to France until today.[165] A similarly inverted logic was applied in the case of Bolivia and the Philippines.[166]

162 Sankara (n 154).

163 This changed in the wake of WWI when Germany was made to pay reparations. Belief in the sanctity of debt translated into insistence that the country puts its economy in order to enable its servicing. This included austerity policies and the opening up of the German economy to the operations of and acquisitions by the victors' corporations, supplemented with borrowing from the BIS. At present, Iraq is still paying compensation for its invasion of Kuwait.

164 Graeber (n 150) 5.

165 Ibid 5.

166 Ibid 5.

There was nothing out of the ordinary in these policies of making the colonised pay for their own submission, exploitation and the conversion of their people into productive labour. 'India', said Jawaharlal Nehru, former prime minister of India, 'had to bear the cost of her own conquest'.[167] The Mandate territories financed the big infrastructure projects initiated by their self-appointed guardians. The aim was to open up the territories' interiors and make them more accessible to a growing number of foreign mining, trading and agricultural corporations. Post-independence, collaboration between Western finance capital and corrupt dictatorships and oligarchies means that borrowed money often disappears in the private pockets of political and economic elites.[168] 'In this sense', says Hickel, 'the dictatorships that the US government helped install . . . suddenly proved useful in a new way'.[169] According to Hudson, the reason why the US established a thick network of military dictatorships, bases and client oligarchies in Latin America was to ensure that countries do not become food independent. 'The Americans said explicitly that any foreign country wanting to grow its own food instead of depending on U.S. grain exports was counted as an act of war and would be overthrown'.[170]

Hudson narrates the tale of the first Third World bond fund which he helped set up in 1990. The interest paid at that time by Argentina and Brazil on dollar bonds was 45%, enabling holders to double their money within a couple of years. Targeted buyers of the bonds were the countries' wealthy. Argentina's and Brazil's foreign debt was owned almost in its entirety by the domestic oligarchy, itself a product of the US-backed campaign of torture and killings in Latin America. The bonds enabled holders to move their money out of the domestic currency into dollars and reap the benefit of a high interest rate authorised by them in the first instance. By 2001, the IMF once again extended loans to Argentina. This was despite its own analysts warning that the country was in no position to pay its foreign debt. 'It was', says Hudson, 'a huge subsidy for capital flight out of Argentina into dollar denominated Argentine debt to the IMF and other bondholders'.[171] A deep economic crisis ensued. Argentina was transformed from the world's most prosperous country in the 19th century to one of its poorest and most debt-ridden a century later. It now faced some 46 investment treaty claims. Their value exceeded the country's financial reserves.[172] Claimants were Global North MNEs, such as Enron and Azurix of the US, Vivendi and Suez of France, Siemens of Germany, Gas

167 Anghie (n 9) 172.
168 Dine (n 32, chapter 5) 68–70.
169 Hickel (n 10) 151.
170 Hudson (n 145).
171 The Hudson Report, 'How Argentina Got the Biggest Loan in the History of the IMF' (*Counterpunch*, 18 July 2018) <https://www.counterpunch.org/2018/07/18/how-argentina-got-the-biggest-loan-in-the-history-of-the-imf/> accessed 31 July 2018.
172 Charles H. Brower, 'Obstacles and Pathways to Consideration of the Public Interest in Investment Treaty Disputes' in Karl P Sauvant (ed), *Yearbook on International Investment & Policy 2008–2009* (OUP 2009) 350.

Natural of Spain and National Grid of the UK.[173] They included 60,000 holders of government bonds who had refused to participate in the government's offer of debt restructuring.[174] In considering its jurisdiction, the *Abaclat* tribunal determined, *inter alia*, that the claims did not arise merely from the failure to perform payment obligations under the bonds, but rather from Argentina's intervention and exercise of its sovereign competences to restructure its sovereign debt.[175] In July 2018, the IMF once again offered Argentina a loan, this time in the amount of US$50 billion, the biggest in its history. What does this mean for the Argentinian people? Hudson was asked. He answered, 'The same that it's done to the Greek people and the Puerto Rican people. Many will try to emigrate. Some will commit suicide. Lifespans will shorten'.[176] This policy of lending that is based not on risk assessment but as a means of gaining control, shaping and extracting wealth from the debtor's economy, also underpinned IMF lending to Greece and Ukraine. The question posed to Hudson may be formulated more generally: Whom does so-called modernisation really serve? Loans, writes former economic hit man (EHM) John Perkins, are Mafia-like favours, the means by which the EHM secures subservience to the global empire he is engaged in building. This is not withstanding that the money never leaves the US. It is simply transferred from the bank to the corporations which are to be engaged by the borrower pursuant to the terms of the loan. If the EHM is really successful, the country will default in due course, thereby opening up the opportunity for the imposition of conditions, such as voting with the US in the UN, allowing military bases on its soil or opening up its resources to foreign exploitation. 'Of course, the debtor still owes the money – and another country is added to our global empire'.[177]

The Chinese interloper

Notable among the processes which shaped the geopolitical landscape of the 20th and 21st centuries is the emergence of China as an international creditor. The country started its integration into the global economy as an importer of capital, but by the end of the 20th century it was also exporting it. Its footprints as a capital exporter are relatively recent. Nevertheless, they are significant, in particular since the 2013 launch of the Belt and Road Initiative (BRI), President Xi Jinping's Project of the Century.[178] Foreign investment poured into participating countries, and the volume of Chinese lending rose dramatically. Yet, the Western club of international creditors appears less than receptive to this new Global South actor. On the whole, China is met with hostility and is looked upon as a competitor and a rival,

173 Van Harten (n 75, chapter 3) 2.

174 *Abaclat and Others v Argentine Republic*, ICSID Case No. ARB/07/5.

175 The Hudson Report (n 171).

176 Ibid.

177 Perkins (n 152) xvii.

178 The BRI aims to replicate the ancient silk route by constructing land and maritime infrastructure networks which connect Asia to Europe and Africa.

an interloper in existing hegemonic arrangements, flush with capital and ambition but short on subservience.

One complaint concerns China's purported failure to participate in the globally coordinated responses to debt distress, in particular that of economic restructuring. For instance, Chinese loan agreements contain a clause which expressly commits the borrower to exclude the debt from restructuring in the Paris Club and from any comparable debt treatment ('no Paris Club' clause).[179] A much-used example of Chinese foreclosure is the important Sri Lankan port of Hambantota. The port, located on one the world's busiest maritime route which connects Asia to Europe, was constructed in 2011 with the aid of Chinese financing. In 2017, amidst a debt crisis, Sri Lanka granted China a 70% equity in this port. The 99-year lease for its operation came with 15,000 acres of surrounding land earmarked for development. The deal was met with protests and trade union opposition. Another complaint concerns the opaqueness and secrecy which allegedly surround the volume and terms of Chinese loan agreements. The country is accused of systematically under-reporting its lending to international bodies such as the World Bank. Debts are said to be kept off public balance sheets through the use of special purpose vehicles, subsidiary on-lending and similar methods.[180] With unreported lending estimated at US$200 billion, concerns have been raised about other lenders' ability to undertake proper risk assessment and the capacity to evaluate stability at the macrolevel.[181] A 2021 report by AIDDATA, a research lab located in Virginia, puts the figure of unreported BRI debt across 154 low and middle-income countries at US$385 billion. It is said to represent an excess of 10% of these countries' GDP.[182]

Still, the People's Republic's growing role as capital exporter and financier of its own investments is by now established. Indebtedness binds Ecuador to Chinese investment in the oil, gas and mining sectors, particularly in Ecuador's Amazon region. In 2017, the country owed China, at that time its greatest creditor, US$15.2 billion (38.7% of GDP). Most of the loans were by way of cash for oil.

179 The Paris Club is an informal club of officials from most Western creditor countries who come together to coordinate responses to debtor countries' repayment difficulties. A precondition to debt relief is a current IMF economic restructuring program. A case-by-case approach and conditionality are two of its principles. The Paris Club operates in an unofficial capacity.

180 Ammar A. Malik et al., 'Banking on the Belt and Road: Insights from a New Global Dataset of 13, 427 Chinese Development Projects'(*AIDDATA*, September 2021) 6, 7 <https://docs.aiddata.org/ad4/pdfs/Banking_on_the_Belt_and_Road__Insights_from_a_new_global_dataset_of_13427_Chinese_development_projects.pdf> accessed 3 April 2022.

181 Sebastian Horn et al., 'China's Overseas Lending' (National Bureau of Economic Research working paper 26050 July 2019 Revised 2020) <https://www.nber.org/system/files/working_papers/w26050/w26050.pdf> accessed 2 April 2022; see also Sebastian Horn et al., 'How Much Money Does the World Owe China?'(*Harvard Business Review*, 26 February 2020) <https://hbr.org/2020/02/how-much-money-does-the-world-owe-china> accessed 28 March 2022; for criticism of the research and its authors' response see Sebastian Horn et al., 'China's Overseas Lending: A Response to Our Critics' (*Center for Global Development*, 7 May 2020) <https://www.cgdev.org/sites/default/files/chinas-overseas-lending-response-our-critics.pdf> accessed 2 April 2022.

182 Malik et al., (n 180) 1, 56.

Cash for oil is seen as a major driver behind Ecuador's opening up of pristine Amazon rainforest to oil drilling.[183] According to a 2019 research paper, much of the BRI debt was raised on private capital markets, but it includes also direct borrowing from China. The volume of direct borrowing is put at some US$1.5 trillion and the number of recipients at some 150 nations. Between 2000 and 2017, debt obligations to the People's Republic rose from US$500 billion to US$5 trillion, representing some 6% of world economic output. This, it is claimed, makes China the world's biggest creditor of Global South countries, surpassing traditional official lenders such as the World Bank, the IMF or all OECD governments combined.[184]

In 2021, the Peterson Institute for International Economics, a Washington-based think tank, in collaboration with AIDDATA, the Kiel Institute for the World Economy, a German research institute and the Center for Global Development, a London-based non-profit organisation, undertook a comparative study of 100 Chinese loan contracts entered into between Chinese state-owned enterprises (SOEs) and 24 foreign governments in Africa, Asia, Eastern Europe, Latin America and Oceania. Three main 'insights' were highlighted: Chinese contracts contain unusual confidentiality clauses, Chinese lenders seek advantage over other creditors by using collateral arrangements which include, *inter alia*, a promise to keep the debt out of collective restructuring and Chinese contracts confer on the lender the potential to influence the debtor's internal and foreign policies through cancellation, acceleration and stabilisation clauses.[185]

As against this, according to *China Daily*, as recently as 2018 China was a relatively small international lender. Its $115 billion lending to Africa that year, for example, constituted less than 2% of the continent's US$6 trillion total indebtedness.[186] As for Sri Lanka, the 'China debt-trap' narrative and the attribution of the country's debt crisis and economic distress to Chinese expensive and unprofitable

183 Kevin Koening, 'Amazon Threatened by China-Ecuador Loans for Oil' (*China Dialogue*, 7 May 2017) <https://www.chinadialogue.net/article/show/single/en/9651-Amazon-threatened-by-China-Ecuador-loans-for-oil> accessed 3 April 2022; a different figure for Ecuadorian debt to China is $17.4 billion. Thea Riofrancos, 'Ecuador: Digging Free of Poverty' (*Upside Down World*, 27 September 2017) <http://upsidedownworld.org/archives/ecuador/ecuador-digging-free-poverty/> accessed 3 April 2022.

184 Sebastian Horn et al., (n 181).

185 Anna Gelpern, Sebastian Horn et al., '21–7 How China Lends: A Rare Look into 100 Debt Contracts with Foreign Governments' (Working Paper Peterson Institute for International Economics 2021) <https://www.piie.com/sites/default/files/documents/wp21-7.pdf> accessed 2 April 2022; a stabilisation clause is a protection provision often found in long-term contracts such as state and concession ones. Main examples are in the extractive industries and infrastructure projects. The purpose of stabilisation clauses is to insulate the contract from changes to the legal and fiscal environment in which the contract is performed. They take on different form; for example, clauses which freeze or fix the law governing the contract on the date in which the contract was entered into. Stability clauses raise enforceability issues as a matter of both national and international law. One main issues pertains to the question of whether a contractual provision may override the state's sovereign competence to legislate.

186 China Daily Editorial, 'West Bias Not Reflected in Reality of African Ties' (*China Daily*, 3 September 2018).

investment projects are no more than a defamation campaign. China is merely Sri Lanka's fourth largest creditor, ranking behind international capital markets, multilateral development banks and Japan. Chinese loans amount to less than 10% of the country's total property-loan portfolios.[187] As to the Hambantota port, the deal was a rescue package for a failing enterprise. Out of the 36,000 ships which passed annually between 2015 and 2017, only 44 have made it into this port. China committed US$1.2 billion to make the port viable and with its 70% stake is taking on the bulk of the risk of failure. As to Sri Lanka's loss of control over this important port, '30% of something good is better than 100% of something that is losing money as it has been for quite some time', says Einar Tangen, investment banker and advisor to the Chinese government on economic development issues.[188]

Huang Meibo and Niu Dongfang of the Shanghai University of International Business and Economics take issue with both the methodology and substance of the Peterson Institute's joint study. They argue that the source of the contracts sampled is unclear. Both the choice of samples and the comparison methodology used are flawed and biased. The assertion that the sampled contracts were obtained from open sources contradicts the researchers' own accusation of lack of transparency. Moreover, the researchers failed to distinguish between contracts by reference to the lender's identity. Comparing multilateral development banks' terms of lending with those of commercial banks, for example, is comparing apples with oranges. As to confidentiality clauses, these are common in international loan agreements as is the practice of not disclosing details of their terms. Criticism of the 'no Paris clauses', argue Huang and Niu, amounts to 'attempts to obstruct the efforts of emerging creditor countries to build a new scheme'. The Paris Club principles are those of Western countries. Emerging creditor countries do not recognise them and are not bound by them. The 'no Paris Club' criticism is therefore no more than another instance of Western arrogant assumption that their model is the best and a demonstration of 'lack of basic courtesy'. As to cancellation and acceleration clauses, these too represent common practice. Moreover, risk control is of particular importance to China because of the greater level of risk it is willing to assume. Western lenders tend to shy away from infrastructure projects because of the significant capital inputs they require and their longer payback periods. This resulted in a prolonged period of limited infrastructure development. China is responding to Global South needs. In so doing, it is assuming risks other lenders would not take on.[189]

Moreover, most Chinese lending is official in the sense that it is undertaken by the government and its entities. Yet, unlike Western official lending, China does

187 Huang Lanlan and Chen Runze, 'GT Investigates: Rumours Behind China's Debt Trap: How Western and Indian Conspiracies Smear China-Sri Lanka Cooperation' (*Global Times*, 27 January 2022) <https://www.globaltimes.cn/page/202201/1248065.shtml> accessed 3 April 2022.

188 Al Jazeera English, 'What Is Behind China's Purchase of a Port in Sri Lanka? – Inside Story' 29 July 2017 <https://www.youtube.com/watch?v=qecR0PEZK1w> accessed 3 April 2022.

189 Huang Meibo and Niu Dongfang, 'How China Lends: Truth and Reality' (*Global Times*, 25 July 2021) <https://www.globaltimes.cn/page/202107/1229605.shtml> accessed 3 April 2022.

not impose extra contractual conditionalities and structural adjustments as protection against risk. Conditionalities and structural adjustments reduce the impact and significance of a default by ensuring enhanced market access and the assumption of control over the debtor economy. The entirety of a country's assets are made available for foreclosure and privatisation upon inability to pay. As pointed out by Perkins, default may even be welcomed. It opens up opportunities not only for greater political dominance, but also for greater control over resources and the greater profits to be generated by liberalisation and reduced labour cost. By contrast, because Chinese loans come with no conditionalities, they are securitised only by the assets bought or created. 'China is not acting as a moneylender or as a financial investor', says Hudson. 'It is not financial imperialism. It is investing essentially as a stockholder'.[190] Whereas Western official lending is carried out in conjunction with private finance and its imperatives of profit maximisation, Chinese official lending is located within a broad and long-term policy of intergovernmental win-win relationship. Principles of mutual respect, non-intervention, peaceful cooperation and mutual benefit operate alongside commercial considerations and market-based risk assessment. In the context of BRI investments, the Chinese government is developing an alternative dispute resolution mechanism. International arbitration is abandoned in favour of the People's Supreme Court jurisdiction. BRI contracts do not contain an ISDS clause, now viewed by Beijing as a system devised and controlled by Western countries and their agencies. No ISDS and an emphasis on mutual respect and benefit are also expected in a forthcoming fourth-generation Chinese model BIT.

Wherever the truth in this debate lies, the blend of similarities and divergence which characterises the way Chinese credit is dispensed raises a broader question. Does Chinese credit signal participation in and amplification of imperialist taking by transfer? Is China a mere competitor or is it blazing a new trail? In this context, we are reminded of Lenin's understanding of the export of capital as a key feature of monopoly capitalism, part of imperialism as the highest stage of capitalism.[191] We are also reminded of China's revolutionary period when Global South economic welfare was seen not as a nation's individual endeavour but as a collaborative effort by all Third World countries. Investments were solidarity-driven rather than profit-based. The 1965 Tazara railway which connects the port of Dar es Salaam in Tanzania with Zambia was built by the Chinese as a 'friendship' project in which resonated the Maoist repertoire of comradeship and shared commitment to true national independence. Zhou Enlai, the People's Republic's first premier, during a 1963 state visit to Ghana announced the Chinese government's Eight Principles for Economic Aid and Economic Assistance to Other Countries. These include not only equality, respect for sovereignty and mutual benefit but also

190 Michael Hudson in conversation with Patrick Bond, 'Is China's Trade Predatory or for Mutual Benefit?' (*Transcript, the Analysis. News*, 28 March 2022) <https://theanalysis.news/is-chinas-trade-predatory-or-for-mutual-benefit-hudson-and-bond-pt-2-2/> accessed 4 April 2022.

191 V. I. Lenin, *Imperialism: The Highest Stage of Capitalism* (Penguin Books 2010) 74–80.

no conditions, no privileges in exchange for aid (including for Chinese experts working in the recipient country), assistance in achieving self-reliance, independent development and true and complete technological transfer. The Eight Principles still resonate in China's contemporary paradigm of harmonious world and common prosperity.[192] However, contrary to the current focus on capital-intensive infrastructure projects which lock nations into long-term indebtedness, they call for focus on less capital-intensive projects which produce quicker returns. This is to enable governments to increase their income and accumulate capital.

China's critics on the left view its foreign investment and associated lending as an instance of capitalist expansion and reorganisation in response to domestic over-production and reduction in the rate of profit. In the context of the BRI, it is argued, many of the projects constitute public-private partnerships, a financing method reputed to generate avoidably expensive governmental debt obligations. Profits, it is said, are likely to be privatised and losses will be socialised. 'All projects are mediated through the existing balance of class forces in the recipient country and hence local and political elites will of course struggle to turn projects in their favour' leaving the masses to shoulder the burden of failures.[193] Infrastructure which should by publicly owned is being privatised. Further, it is said, China has been assimilated into the multilateral organisations at the heart of US-led imperialism, specifically the IMF. The country is now the IMF's third most influential member and, but for US opposition, would have replaced Japan to rank second. Yet, it has failed to criticise the organisation's policies and has remained silent in the face of a string of appointments of heads of the IMF with corruption convictions to their name. Political economist Patrick Bond also points to the many instances of Chinese involvement with and support for corrupt governments and oligarchies. China, he argues, is not an imperialist power since the surplus value which the West extracts from the country outstrips the surplus value transferred to it. The rate of Chinese surplus value transfer currently stands at some 20% of its inwards transfer, 'meaning China is losing a vast amount of its surplus'. However, it is integrated into a layer of sub-imperialist countries which participate in and support imperialism and its multilateral financial oppression. In this way, China legitimises and amplifies the world order. Instead of benefitting the US by recycling its dollar-denominated surplus there, it should use it to defray the enormous climate debt it owes Africa. China, he argues, should follow the Cuban example of exiting the imperialist order altogether.[194]

This type of critique overlooks the enormity of the task China has set itself at both national and transnational levels, as well as the turnabouts, adaptations and

192 For a discussion of China's harmonious paradigm see Yonit Manor-Percival, 'The China Dream: Harmonious Dialectics and International Law' in David Margolis and Qing Cao (eds), *Utopia and Modernity in China: Contradictions in Transition* (Pluto Press 2022) 53–77.

193 Stephanie Olinga-Shannon et al., *The Belt and Road Initiative (BRI): An AEPF Framing Paper* (Asia Europe People Forum (AEPF) 2019) 8, 10 <https://aepf.info/wp-content/uploads/2017/08/BRI_Framing_WEB_Final.pdf> accessed 2 April 2022.

194 Michael Hudson, in conversation with Bond (n 190).

Western hostility which pepper its path towards achieving it. Undoubtedly, at least from a left perspective, there is force in the argument that the People's Republic should have never incorporated itself into global capitalism in the first place. With its past as a semi-colony and study of Marxism, it should have known that, one way or another, incorporation into the dollar-denominated globalised circuits of capital exports cannot but be founded on extraction. However, the country, having deemed incorporation necessary, can no longer extricate itself without careful planning and a great deal of caution. The Chinese, says Hudson, explain their speeches in praise of liberalisation as a defensive policy dictated by concerns about the possibility of US-provoked military attack. Moreover, China is now locked into the dollar-based system. It is gradually increasing the volume of its trade undertaken in local currencies. It is also gradually replacing its US treasuries with gold. However, here too, the country is restricted by the risk of pushing up the RMB exchange value, thereby making its exports more expensive. Graeber introduced a historical perspective to shed light on China's apparently inexplicable subordination to the siphoning off of wealth by way of tribute-like treasury bonds. Acquisitions of these bonds, he said, are the contemporary face of the imperial court's strategy of consolidating the empire by dispensing gifts the value of which exceeded those of tributes. 'There is every reason to believe that, from China's point of view, this is a first step in a very long process of reducing the United States to something like a traditional client state'.[195]

Honest governments and true development, says Hudson, can only be achieved outside the dollar area. 'The Shanghai Co-operation Organisation is the only group that has the critical mass . . . to be able to create an alternative to dollarized neoliberal imperialism'.[196] In Sam Moyo's view, 'China is the clearest counterforce to the West. It is consistently exercising full strategic autonomy despite its economic dependence'.[197] In the meantime, the availability of Chinese investments and loans strengthens other countries' negotiation position by enlarging the range of options available to them, thereby creating room for manoeuvre. They are no longer dependent exclusively on Western funding. This, for example, applied to Italy in its negotiations with the EU Commission. Italy was the first G7 country to have signed to the BRI. However, the Chinese option assumes critical importance when it comes to peripheral states. Most have been shut out of private capital markets following the debt crisis of the 1980s. But for China, these countries would be dependent entirely on IFI lending. IFI credit ratings, often determined by US geopolitical interests, are then adopted by other potential lenders and, in the face of creditors' coordinated positions, may further reduce access to credit.[198]

195 Graeber (n 83) 372.

196 Michael Hudson in conversation with Bond (n 190).

197 Moyo et al., (n 39) 195.

198 Sam Moyo and Paris Yeros, 'Intervention: The Zimbabwe Question and the Two Lefts' (2015) 15(3) *Historical Materialism* 171 at 183.

Imperial rent: legacies of cultural taking

We conclude this section by looking at the role played by cultural and racial aggression in the project of taking by integration and transfer. Cultural taking is different in the sense that, on the whole, transfer flowed both ways. That is, from the colonisers to the colonised and then back to the new states through post-colonial adaptations. Still, cultural and racialised forms of taking do form part of the discussion in that they entail uncompensated losses of enduring consequences.

For the colonial powers to establish authority, cultural boundaries had to be dismantled. This necessitated hierarchical ordering and juridification of differences. 'Colonizing authorities understood just as readily that the structure of legal authority and the creation of legal hierarchies were inextricably intertwined'.[199] Differences were posited as absences, specifically the absence of European civilisational attributes. The imposition of extraterritoriality and rules of IL narrated as superior and universal provided the framework within which national identity and ways of life could be denigrated and made amenable to disappearance.

At the level of practices and strategy, Europeanised local elites were produced and co-opted. A class of people had to be created, urged British politician Lord Macaulay, who were 'Indian in blood and colour, but English in taste, in opinion, in morals, and in intellect'.[200] English was to replace Persian as the official language in the Moslem region of North India. British-style schools, colleges and universities 'were soon churning out faux-Englishmen of the kind Macaulay had hoped for'.[201] These purposely produced Englishmen, particularly Hindus who were generally favoured over Moslems, then participated in the administration of India. They were also co-opted as middlemen in the exportation of opium to China.[202] In 19th-century Africa, the costs implicated in direct colonial rule were reduced through a system of intermediaries. The authority of indigenous chiefs was harnessed to carry out tasks too risky for the colonial administration to undertake. A test of a good administrator, a manual warned, 'is the absence of disorder and the efficiency of chiefs and native courts'.[203] Such strategies were not altogether risk-free, as chiefs who had signed treaties discovered that they were not equal after all. However, on balance, an intermediary system which sought to incorporate the natives into the colonial administrative network was perceived as central to stability. In due course, these structures would shape a post-colonial state duality comprising formal institutions in alliance with the informal authority and markets of a 'shadow state'.[204]

In China, cultural and racial aggression found expression in accounts of the country as a place of stagnation and decline. Evolution was said to have been inhibited

199 Benton (n 116) 2.
200 Mishra (n 156) 35.
201 Mishra (n 156) 35.
202 Ibid 34–5.
203 William Reno, *Corruption and State Politics in Sierra Leone* (CUP 1995) 30.
204 Reno (n 203) 29–30 and generally.

by factors such as the 'Asiatic Mode of Production' and 'despotism'.[205] Oriental people were conceptualised as barbarians or children despite their antiquity. The absence of European civilisation was equated with savagery and backwardness.[206] This narrative of absences, coming as it did in the wake of military defeats and/or against a background of social and cultural fracturing, lent itself to internalisation by its objects. As we saw previously in the cases of Egypt and Türkiye, internalisation translated into subservience and policies of self-rescue in the form of unaffordable modernisation programs. The trauma experienced by China, hitherto a proud centre of the world economy and a source of inspiration to the leading figures of European enlightenment, was far in excess of the relatively modest foreign presence in its territory. With the repertoire of its technological, scientific, ethical and institutional contributions marginalised, its temporary weakness was now being depicted as an inherent condition, a permanent state of backwardness that was the antithesis of Western progress.[207]

It was by reference to this depiction that the country began to revisit its past and question its present. The search was on for the source of European power. Western ideas of progress, struggle and conquest of nature were hailed by Yan Fu and Liang Qiqiao, spokesmen for the Chinese intelligentsia at the end of the 19th century, as the key to harnessing individual energies and, through them, the attainment of economic growth.[208] To combat Western military might, the Qing government used translation bureaus and language schools to study Western science and technology. In the process, China's intellectuals also learnt about Western social and political institutions.[209] From the Christian egalitarianism of the Taipei Rebellion of 1850–1864 to the introduction of Marxism and Darwinism in the late 19th century, Western theories and ideologies were made the main protagonists in an iconoclastic project of new consciousness, self-strengthening and national regeneration.[210] 'As an intellectual from the developing world', reminisces Lin Yifu, 'I used to believe, like the monk in the classic Chinese epic novel *Journey to the West*, that the West had a holy sutra, which I needed only learn and apply to help my native country modernize and prosper'.[211] Earlier Asian observers noted, 'Individually, Europeans might be no more brave, innovative, sensitive or loyal than Asians, but as members

205 Timothy Brook, 'Capitalism and the Writing of Modern History in China' in Gregory Blue and Timothy Brook (eds), *China and Historical Capitalism: Genealogies of Sinological Knowledge* (Studies in Modern Capitalism Series, CUP 1999) 114, 117; Peter Moody, *Conservative Thought in Contemporary China* (Lexington Books 2007) 4; Jacque Hersh, 'The Eastern Will Not Subside: China's Long March Back to the Future?' in Li Xing (ed), *The Rise of China and the Capitalist World Order* (Ashgate 2010) 33.

206 Gregory Blue, 'China and Western Social Thought in the Modern Period' in Blue and Brook (n 205) 73; Anievas and Nisancioglu (n 14) 126.

207 Blue (n 206) 74, 77, 112; Brook (n 205) 114.

208 Maurice Meisner, *Mao's China and After: A History of the People's Republic of China* (3rd edn, The Free Press 1977) 13.

209 Brook (n 205) 119.

210 Meisner (n 208) 3, 4, 14, 17–19.

211 Lin (n 52) xiii.

of corporate groups, churches or governments, and as efficient users of scientific knowledge, they mustered more power than the wealthiest empire of Asia'.[212] This is not to detract from the resistance and revolts with which non-European people responded to the penetration, taking and reworking of their land, wealth, ideas and identity. Examples are the 1857 Indian mutiny, the 1899 Boxers Rebellion in China and the Boer wars in Africa (1899–1902) when Britain first introduced concentration camps into the European repertoire of oppression. Resistance also found expression in scholarly analysis and proclamations of moral abhorrence. We illustrate these by quoting from two pieces of writing selected for their topicality. One, dated 1836 and attributed to an unknown Chinese, opines on the rise of a civilisation of war:

> There is, probably, at the present no more infallible a criterion of the civilization and advancement of societies than the proficiency which each has attained in 'the murderous art', the perfection and variety of their implements for mutual destruction, and the skill with which they have learnt to use them.[213]

The second is a comment made by Swami Vivekananda, India's most famous end of 19th century Indian thinker on his encounter with the individualistic and materialistic civilisation of taking:

> Intoxicated by the heady wine of newly acquired power . . . dependent on material things, grabbing other people's land by hook or crook . . . the body their self, its appetites their only concern – such is the image of the western demon in Indian eyes.[214]

Conclusion

We may sum up the 19th century of formal colonialism as one of cross-border unequal exchanges secured by strategies of appropriation, discipline and control over colonised economies. Methodologies included direct political oversight exercised via administrative systems and manufactured local collaborative elites as well as a paraphernalia of IL, colonial states' laws applied extraterritorially, treaties, free trade, foreign investment, indebtedness and the perennial legitimising discourse of public good. Nineteenth-century structures of control over resources, extraction and value transfers persist. With the exception of China and a handful of other countries, the Global South has remained a periphery or at best a semi-periphery. In mainstream narratives it is depicted as a place rampant with developmental and

212 Mishra (n 156) 40.

213 Cited in Giovanni Arrighi, *Adam Smith in Beijing: Lineages of the Twenty-First Century* (Verso 2007) 4.

214 Cited in Mishra (n 156) 36.

governance absences and engaged in an endless pursuit of catching up.[215] Such depiction resonates with the narratives of 19th-century cultural denigration. It detracts from the significance of Global South contributions to the shaping of the post-colonial world, such as the non-aligned movement, revolutionary Cuba, 'Pink' South America, South Africa's apartheid struggle and China's path to development. The post-colonial state may have been fashioned by colonial legacies. Nonetheless, independence did entail a measure of control, standing to negotiate and, ultimately, the capacity to determine the country's own judicial and legislative arrangements. In particular, this is coming to the forefront as the unipolar moment of white domination is giving way to a multipolar world of colour and with it the space for new voices to be heard. Thus, the passage to present times may be characterised by what Hoogvelt calls 'continuity in change'.[216] That is, the vein of repetitiveness that runs through revisions, adaptations and innovations.

Perhaps the most striking feature of taking by transfer is its relative invisibility. Power is everywhere and nowhere. It is experienced but cannot be precisely located.[217] The guard's gaze is felt, though she herself has all but vanished from view. Coercion disappears behind a veil of what to all intents and purposes is a voluntary act on the part of an ostensibly sovereign state. The assimilation of corporate networks into networks of political power and IFIs has no formal expression or acknowledgement, leaving much room for denial. Wars too may become invisible, both in fact and in law. They may take the form of economic wars of attrition fought by means of currency manipulations, unilateral sanctions, foreclosure of access to the SWIFT system of international payments, appropriation of private assets as in the nationalisation of Gazprom's German subsidiary and the seizure and appropriation of central banks' reserves – arguably a breach of the IL doctrine of state immunity. Wars may also be secretive. In Ecuador in 2003, Perkins attempted to end a war which he had helped create. The fighting, he says, was virtually unknown beyond the place where it was fought.[218] In sum, the clarity of political coercion has been traded for the opaqueness of economic compulsions.[219] All states are formally sovereign. Yet, the world order into which they are integrated is prescriptive. It is intolerant of challenges and/or impediments to its market-based unitary wholeness.

Protection of property rights from taking forms an indispensable aspect of the informal regime of control by which the smooth operation of taking by transfer is secured. With MNEs acting as a network of arteries through which capital is transported, the capacity to shape national and transnational economic, political and legal regimes is essential if blockages are to be avoided. Speed and ease of capital migration requires not only freedom of movement, but also a say in the way

215 For a succinct introduction to the 'world-system analysis' which conceptualises the world under capitalist globalisation as made up of 'core', 'periphery' and 'semi-periphery' states see Immanuel Wallerstein, *World-System Analysis: An Introduction* (Duke University Press 2004).

216 Hoogvelt (n 5) xi.

217 Wood (n 12) 14.

218 Perkins (n 152) xvi.

219 Wood (n 12) 2–4.

state sovereignty is exercised upon capital's territorial penetration. This is achieved by actively shaping countries' ecopolitical and cultural landscapes with the aid of legal regimes which cast MNEs as a special judicial category deserving of greater protection.

Lenin, in his book about imperialism, quoted from a letter written as the 19th century was drawing to a close by Cecil Rhodes, a mining magnate, prime minister of the Cape colony and a main protagonist in the conduct of the infamous Boer Wars. In his letter Rhodes tells his journalist friend about a meeting of the unemployed in East London he attended. The speeches made at the meeting, he recounts, resonated with repeated cries for bread. The cries for bread persuaded Rhodes of the importance of imperialism as a solution to the UK's social problems. To avoid a bloody civil war, he wrote, 'we colonial statemen must acquire new lands to settle the surplus population, to provide new markets for the goods produced by them . . . The empire . . . is a bread and butter question. If you want to avoid civil war, you must become imperialists'.[220]

This view of imperialism as fundamental to Global North well-being is still with us. British prime minister Neville Chamberlain went on to advocate it as 'a true, wise and economical policy'.[221] Imperialist transfers, by ensuring bread and butter for the masses, also secured the stability and acquiescence necessary for the uninterrupted accumulation of historically unprecedented wealth by the ruling class. Thus, overseas taking facilitated and ensured uninterrupted domestic taking.

Yet, it seems a storm is approaching as the unipolar moment of the American Century is fighting extinction. It is being replaced by China-led multipolarity. New voices are being raised. Hitherto well-established imperialist methodologies are coming under threat as supply chains are malfunctioning and inflation is made worse by economic wars of attrition. The bread and butter question is raising its ugly head again as standards of living collapse, poverty and inequality intensify, dark clouds of a deep recession are gathering and increasingly overt oppression trigger resistance. It seems that, in the words attributed to Mao Zedong, China's revolutionary leader, 'There is great chaos under Heaven'.

Chaos, argues Giovanni Arrighi, signifies a period of transition when one hegemonic/systemic cycle of accumulation (SCA) ends and a new one rises. In a state of chaos, conflicts escalate beyond the possibility of countervailing. New rules and norms of behaviour are formed but without as yet replacing the old ones. Alternatively, the two get combined.[222] Preoccupation with finance and tolerance of debt – precursors to the end of an SCA – cause systemic chaos and breakdown. In turn, these prepare the ground for the rise of a new SCA. Arrighi identified this process in a series of four historical cycles. They bring to mind the second half of the saying attributed to Mao. When there is chaos under heaven, 'the situation

220 Lenin (n 191) 96–7.

221 Ibid 96.

222 Giovanni Arrighi, *The Long Twentieth Century: Money, Power and the Origins of Our Time* (Verso 2010) 31.

is excellent'. On this view, chaos is the ultimate precondition for change and an opportunity for the creation of a new order, this time with novel conceptions of taking, giving and receiving among humans as well as between them and other forms of life.

I began my exploration of the act of taking with land and to land I return as I conclude. From enclosures to contemporary land grabs, the uniqueness and significance of land has remained unchanged. The way it is perceived and treated defines social relations. It impacts on culture, identity, political economy, the prevalence of hunger and the way people treat each other and other forms of life. Thus, the grabbing of land has profound implications for the world we live in. It has become particularly topical with the massive spike in the global food prices in the 2020s. By May 2021, global food prices have risen by 40% compared with the same period in the previous year, hitting new heights in a decade. In March 2022 the Food Price Index of the UN Food and Agricultural Organisation has risen by 12.6% compared with February 2022 when it was the highest it has ever been since 1990.[223] The number of hungry people worldwide is reaching levels not seen in half a century. Land grabs for mining and the production of commodities, such as vegetable oils for biofuel and biodiesel, is one main cause for the growth in the number of hungry people.

Grabbing as used here refers to the commodified form of land. It may be defined as the multiple legal forms by which foreign corporations acquire for commercial purposes land that had previously been used communally by small-scale shareholders or was uncultivated. Excluded from it is taking by the state for distributive and collective purposes and, as in the cases of Zimbabwe and Section 25 of the South African constitution, taking so as to rectify historical denial of access to land.[224] There is, however, a caveat. With the introduction of neoliberalism into Africa, land distribution also entailed commodification and changes to tenure in line with the Western system of registered titles. Rather than increasing small farmers' participation, argues Moyo, the aim was to facilitate integration into globalised circuits of capital. This in turn strengthened the hands of national and foreign private investors and sovereign funds, particularly when it came to the current, third wave which combined land alienation with a scramble for energy resources.[225]

223 Food and Agriculture Organization of the United Nations, 'FAO Food Price Index Posts Significant Leap in March' 8 April 2022 <https://www.fao.org/newsroom/detail/fao-food-price-index-posts-significant-leap-in-march/en> accessed 17 April 2022.

224 Section 25(8) of the Constitution of South Africa 1996 elevates the 'taking of legislative and other measures to achieve land, water and related reforms, in order to redress the results of past racial discrimination' above all other provisions in that section. It is currently under review with a view to introduce an amendment enabling expropriation without compensation.

225 Moyo et al., (n 39) 198, 199.

7 Globalised taking

Land grabs

Introduction: new enclosures

The post-2008 surge in the phenomenon known as land grabbing is often referred to in the literature as 'new enclosures'.[1] Post-colonial taking of land is evoking images of the English enclosures and the Highland clearances in Scotland, Marx's poster child of original accumulation and his inspiration for the term 'land grabbing'. The narrative of 'new enclosures' condenses time and spaces to capture capitalism's structural continuity. However, argues Ince, this obscures differences. Twenty-first-century land grabs do not necessarily involve absolute dispossession or physical eviction. They may be confined to a process of commercialisation, or *in situ* displacement. Smallholders are compelled to enter a market governed by the coordinates of global value chains and shift from life-maintaining production to the production of surplus, from subsistence to accumulation. In consequence, they 'are displaced socioeconomically but not spatially'.[2] People remain where they are but their livelihood is rendered insecure by the decrease in entitlements. Another difference is the use of land's fungibility for purely speculative purposes. On the other side of this debate, Liz Alden Wily makes the point that past and present land scrambles share a denial of the legal force of customary rights to justify and enable the taking of land from the poor and powerless.[3] White and Borras focus on the changes to agrarian labour regimes occasioned by the taking of commonly held

1 See for example Ben White, Saturnino M. Borras Jr. et al., (eds), *The New Enclosures: Critical Perspectives on Corporate Land Deals* (Critical Agrarian Studies Routledge 2013); Maywa Montenegro de Wit, 'Stealing into the Wild: Conservation Science, Plant Breeding and the Making of New Seed Enclosures' (2017) 44 *The Journal of Peasants Studies* 169.

2 Onur Ulas Ince, 'Primitive Accumulation, New Enclosures, and Global Land Grab: A Theoretical Intervention' (2014) 79(1) *Rural Sociology* 126; for an overview of academic approaches, methodologies and issues involved in making sense of the phenomenon of land grabbing see Marc Edelman, Carlos Oya, and Saturino M. Borras Jr, 'Global Land Grabs: Historical Processes, Theoretical and Methodological Implications and Current Trajectories' (2013) 34(9) *Third World Quarterly* 1517.

3 Liz Alden Wily, 'Looking Back to See Forward: The Legal Niceties of Land Theft in Land Rushes' in White and Borras et al., (n 1) 133–58.

DOI: 10.4324/9781315386782-9

resources, 'their concentration, privatisation and transaction as corporate (owned or leased) property'.[4]

The taking implicated in post-colonial land grabbing is not only of the soil, but also of the wealth attached to it, such as water, metals and minerals. The act may be characterised by three main features. First, the uniqueness of land disappears under a veil of commodification and conversion into capital, including financialised capital. Second is the transference of control. When ownership is conveyed, so is the power associated with its bundle of rights. Third is privatisation. That is, the transition from community-based custodial relationship with land to one of individualised proprietorship. The impact goes beyond the starting point of sale or long-term leasing. Local inhabitants may be able to stay, but without the say they previously had in the way the land is held, managed and worked. Instead, they are incorporated into globalised circuits of capital with implications for how their labour is recruited and organised and its survival secured. Alternatively, they may be evicted from the countryside, but without necessarily being absorbed fully into other sectors of the economy, permanently urbanised or adequately compensated, if at all. Instead, they inflate the labour market, forming a reserve workforce which serves to push down wages.[5]

Actors comprise transnational capital and its TCC, as well as state officials, local capital and local elites operating in alliance alternatively, in competition with the TCC. Where historical methods of communal governance have been weakened by colonial legacies, customary authorities may also be drawn in by the prospects of communal and personal gains. In Africa, the 'second large wave of land alienation' was led by national capital with the support of foreign capital and advice from the World Bank. Land held under customary tenure was commodified and converted into private property, 'Non-traditional' crops and uses such as flower cultivation and tourism have been introduced.[6] The state may also be implicated when exercising its powers of eminent domain as part of the red carpet of incentives, concessions and legal reforms it rolls out to foreign investors.[7] The red carpet is legitimised by a narrative of poverty eradication, closing of the so-called developmental gap and overcoming the perils of scarcities. The narrative is constructed around national interest, quantitatively

4 Ben White, Saturnino M. Borras et al., 'The New Enclosures' in Ben White and Saturnino M. Borras et al., (n 1) 1–2.

5 Sam Moyo et al., 'Imperialism and Primitive Accumulation: Notes on the New Scramble for Africa' (2012) 1(2) *Agrarian South: Journal of Political Economy* 187.

6 The first wave was colonial land grabs which lasted till the 1960s when it was interrupted by developmentalism. Moyo et al., (n 5) 198–9.

7 There is disagreement in the literature on land grabs as to whether they include the taking of land for industrialisation and urbanisation projects. See for example A. Haroon Akram-Lodhi, 'Contextualising Land Grabbing: Contemporary Land Deals, the Global Subsistence Crisis and the World Food System' (2012) 33(2) *Canadian Journal of Development Studies* 119 at p. 126; Matias E. Margulis, Nora Mckeon et al., 'Land Grabbing and Global Governance: Critical Perspectives' (2013) 10(1) *Globalizations* 1 at 2; eminent domain refers to the power governments have under most national legal systems to take the land irrespective of the will of the landholder.

measured growth, improved exchange value and emphasis on technology and economies of scale. Public interest in economic welfare is equated with the accommodation of capital's needs and severed from externalised human and ecological loss.

To the dispossessed, taking-as-giving is posited as a new dawn of employment, modernity, improved social and economic infrastructure, compensation and resettlement programmes. The extent to which this new dawn actually materialises is debatable. At times, deals may be indeed intended to enhance food independence.[8] However, all too often, the evidence points to a trail of broken promises, greater vulnerability to hunger due to the loss of access to land on which subsistence food may be grown, greater pressure on land and resources, exploitation and social dislocation. In Sierra Leone, only 50 new jobs were created pursuant to a 50-year lease which gave a Swiss company 40,000 hectares of land for the cultivation and exportation to Europe of biofuel.[9] For the highlanders of Indonesia, observed Li, opportunities for ex-farmers to sell their labour for a wage proved hard to come by. Commercial tree crops require few workers, and alternative means of survival for surplus workers are scarce. State financial support is not forthcoming, and migration to other provinces is hindered by language differences and lack of personal connections. Moving to a nearby land is made impossible by the fact that such land has been enclosed as well.[10]

Li, having spent some five years (2010–2015) researching private palm oil plantations in the Indonesian province of West Kalimantan, describes the infrastructure of violence which permeates life in and around the plantations, not as an aberration, but as a newly created normality. Beneath their 'orderly, material grid of roads, palms, mills, and housing blocks, and behind their technical diagrams, account books, contracts, and job descriptions' lies 'a thoroughly entrenched, somewhat hidden, overwhelmingly predatory system for channelling and capturing plantations wealth'. Extra-economic means such as legislation and policing stand guard over the smooth and efficient transfer of value. They also guarantee state representatives' share in the immense financial gains to be made. 'The opportunities for rent seeking by state officials are "gigantic" '.[11] Extra-economic means

8 Saturnino M. Borras Jr and Jennifer C. Franco, 'Global Land Grabbing and Trajectories of Agrarian Change: A Preliminary Analysis' (2010) 12(1) *Journal of Agrarian Change* 34 <http://r1.ufrrj.br/geac/portal/wp-content/uploads/2012/11/BORRAS-e-FRANCO-Global-land-grabbing-and-trajectories-of-agrarian-change.pdf> accessed 6 November 2018.

9 The Economist, 'When Others Are Grabbing Their Land' (5 May 2011).

10 Tania Murray Li, *Land's End: Capitalist Relations on an Indigenous Frontier* (Duke University Press 2014) 2.

11 Rikke Brandt Broegaard, Thoumthone Vongvisouk, and Ole Merz, 'The Impact of Unimplemented Large Scale Land Development Deals' (*Frontiers*, 2022) <https://www.frontiersin.org/articles/10.3389/fsufs.2022.789809/full> accessed 17 August 2022 citing from Thomas Sikor and Christian Lund, 'Introduction: Access to Property: A Question of Power and Authority' in Thomas Sikor and Christian Lund (eds), *The Politics of Possession: Property, Authority and Access to Natural Resources* (Wiley Blackwell 2009) 15.

may intersect – openly or tacitly – with powers held by other actors such as MNEs, collaborative local elites, middlemen and the World Bank.[12]

Available data also suggests that land deals suffer from a high rate of failure and low level of implementation, prompting Cotula to question the extent to which they play a role in the alleviation of poverty.[13] Progress may be impeded by disputes, political changes, undercapitalisation and fluctuations in the availability of finance. The ProCana sugarcane project is one example. In 2007, the government of Mozambique entered into a 50-year-long renewable lease with Central Africa Mining and Exploration Company (CAMEC, a UK corporation) and ProCana, a Mozambican corporation. Pursuant to the lease, 30,000 hectares of land were assigned to sugarcane monoculture and ethanol production. Conflicts arose between the Ministry of Agriculture and the Ministry of Tourism which, by the time of the ProCana lease, had already promised the same land for use as a national park. The project was also opposed by local residents whose access to water was threatened by the irrigation plan. Two years later, when the local residents aligned themselves with the Ministry of Tourism, some key investors backed out. The government revoked the concession on grounds of non-compliance with contractual provisions. However, by that time, thousands of villagers had been expelled and at least one thousands hectares had already been cleared. A second attempt at carrying out the project with new investors failed by 2017.

From enclosures to new enclosures, at issue is a land reform in reverse: from the many to the few, from the common to the private. It mutated over time. Yet, at its core it remains a course of privatisation that is theorised, legitimised and enabled through the transformation of property relations. Land grabs are essentially a power-based process of 'control grabbing' entailing the construction of a renovated social, legal, material and political infrastructure.

Colonial legacies

The taking of land as a core feature of colonialism was observed previously. It accompanied colonial expansion at every step of its unfolding. The scale of taking was spectacular. By the 19th century, in the Atlantic, in the course of 47 years

12 Tania Murray Li, 'After the Land Grab: Infrastructural Violence and the "Mafia System" in Indonesia's Oil Palm Plantation Zone' (2018) 96 *Geoforum* 328 at 329, 334; for an analysis of the intersection between state and corporate power in the context of mining see Kristian Lasslett, *State Crime on the Margins of Empire: Rio Tinto, The War on Bougainville and Resistance to Mining* (Pluto Press 2014) and the class action brought in the US under the Alien Tort Statute (ATS) *Alexis Holyweek Sarei et al. v Rio Tinto PLC and Rio Tinto Limited* PLC 671 F.3D 736 (9th Cir. 2011); for claims against the World Bank see *Jam v International Financial Corporation* [2019] 586 US and *Joanna Doe Juan Doe v International Financial Corporation and IFC Asset Management Company, LLC* [2017].

13 Lorenzo Cotula, '"Land Grabbing" and International Investment Law: Towards a Global Reconfiguration of Property' in Andrea K. Bjorklund (ed), *Yearbook on International Investment Law & Policy 2014–2015* (OUP 2016) 184; for an analysis of the implications of unimplemented land projects see Broegaard, Vongvisouk and Merz (n 11).

between the promulgation of the 1887 Dawes Allotment Act and its reversal in 1934 (when the Indian Reorganisation Act was passed), Indians' land more than halved, diminishing from 138 to 52 million acres.[14] In Aotearoa, later to become New Zealand, with the aid of atrocities committed in breach of the treaty with the Māori nation, European settlers confiscated 400,000 acres of their land in the Te Urewera region. No compensation was paid and only 142 acres were returned.[15] Altogether, the New World contributed between 25 and 30 million 'ghost acres' of productive land to Britain alone – 'roughly double the size of Britain's own total arable land'.[16]

Legacies come with adaptations and variations reflective of changing conditions, systemic maturation and geopolitical shifts. Post-colonial land grabs have become globalised. They are interwoven into the matrix of transnational capital and mutate in response to its needs and crises. Their financialisation shores up 'foreign-sponsored rentierism'.[17] Dislocation of the dispossessed may not involve eviction and may be abstracted into a new regime of labour and production. Non-Western newcomers such as China, Saudi Arabia and Malaysia have joined in, albeit in smaller proportions. Yet, the new enclosures also mirror their colonial predecessors in their practice of eliminating divergence and their rationale of putting into productive use hitherto purportedly idle, underused and empty land. The frontier zones they create are 'improved' through processes of dispossession, privatisation and concentration, transfer of control, the formation of ownership and modifications to production methods and systems of tenure. At its core, grabbing is still 'the continuing capture of ordinary people's rights and assets by capital-led and class-creating social transformation'.[18] In the sphere of agriculture, large-scale, colonial-style plantations involving land concessions on which monoculture of industrial crops is practiced have been revived and expanded.[19] Grabs are 'less a new phenomenon than a significant surge'.[20]

Surges in land grabs are associated with land becoming lucrative investment. Typically, the price of food goes up and/or mining and energy enjoy a boom. The rush for land produced by the 2007–8 spike in the cost of food was further intensified by the 2009 EU Renewable Energy Directive (RED). European firms, prompted by the guaranteed market created by RED, turned their attention to the cultivation and processing of biofuels. In an iteration of colonial times, the

14 Eric Cheyfitz, 'Savage Law: The Plot Against American Indians in Johnson and Graham Lessee v M Intosh and the Pioneers' in Amy Kaplan and Donald E. Pease (eds), *Cultures of United States Imperialism* (New Americanists series Duke University Press 1993) 113.

15 David R. Boyd, *Rights of Nature: A Legal Revolution That Could Save the World* (ECW Press 2017) 147148.

16 Jason Hickel, *The Divide: A Brief Guide to Global Inequality and Its Solutions* (Penguin Random House 2018) 74.

17 Moyo et al., (n 5) 199.

18 Lily Alden Wily, 'Looking Back to See Forward: The Legal Niceties of Land Theft in Land Rushes' (2012) 39(3–4) *The Journal of Peasants Studies* 751.

19 Li (n 12) 328.

20 Wily (n 18) x.

quest for land took them out of Europe and into Africa, Asia and South America.[21] Focusing on transnational land deals, figures suggest that this quest peaked in the years 2009–11. Thereafter, for a while, fewer deals have been recorded. This is attributed, *inter alia*, to disappointing returns on investment and policy changes in some countries.[22] A recurrent surge is now expected as food and energy prices are hitting new heights and renewables create a greater market for mined commodities.

The pace and scale of contemporary land grabs is said to exceed that of the past.[23] However, they are difficult to measure. Many acquisitions are entered into in secret or remain at a speculative stage. Some are no more than Ponzi schemes reliant on the capture of sufficient numbers of investors to achieve increase in the value of shares. Other factors also contribute to a situation in which 'measuring land grabs' is 'like trying to pin a wave to a sand'.[24] Statistics are difficult to verify and quickly become outdated. The impact of transactions is not readily assessed and dispossession may have not as yet materialised. This is exacerbated by the absence of consensus about the definition of land grabs and a methodology for their counting.[25] The following figures may give an idea of the scale involved.[26] The World Bank estimates that 120m acres were taken in the decade between 2000 and 2010. Oxfam puts the figure at 560m acres, roughly the size of Western Europe.[27] In Indonesia, producer of 60% of global palm oil between 2007 and 2008, more than 10m hectares of rain forest and indigenous land were grabbed and 'improved' by transforming them into colonial type plantations; 60% of total Indonesian palm oil production takes places on these plantations. This is notwithstanding that palm oil can be produced successfully by smallholders. A mere 7% is under state ownership. The remaining 53% is privately owned. As of 2017, their net value reached US$10,000 per hectare.[28] In Tanzania, under the rubric of conservation and with the involvement of foreign multinationals such as the Boston-based Thomson Safaris and the UAE-based Ortello Business Corporation, domestic legislation and overt violence were applied to drive Massai people off their land so that it might be put to the productive use of safari tourism. The scale of evictions is such that it created 'a map of confinement that is as stifling and foreign to them [the Massai – my

21 Lorenzo Cotula, 'Land Grabbing in the Shadow of the Law: Legal Frameworks Regulating the Global Land Rush' in Rosemary Rayfuse and Nicole Weisfelt (eds), *The Challenge of Food Security: International Policy and Regulatory Frameworks* (Edward Elgar 2012) 209.

22 Cotula (n 21) 182–3.

23 Borras and Franco (n 8) 10–11.

24 Ibid 12.

25 White and Borras et al., (n 4) 2.

26 For a detailed account of the scale and geography of land grabs including quantity and location of land acquired as well as where investments come from see Lorenzo Cotula, 'The International Political Economy of the Global Land Rush: A Critical Appraisal of Trends, Scale, Geography and Drivers' in White and Borras et al., (n 1) 43.

27 Hickel (n 16) 234.

28 Li (n 12) 328, 329.

comment] as a zoo to a lion'.[29] In Myanmar, between 2010 and 2013, land earmarked for big projects increased by 170%. Its allocation for corporate development in the Rohingya's area first took place in 2012 and impacted 7,000 hectares. By 2017, this figure has increased dramatically to 1,268,077 hectares. It led Saskia Sassen to suspect that the international focus on religion and ethnicity as the underlying cause for the persecution and displacement of the Rohingya 'has overshadowed the vast land grabs that have affected millions, including the Rohingya'.[30] Since 2000, Peru tops the list of countries most impacted by land grabs. Deals for the purchase or use of more than 16 million hectares of land have been concluded, affecting some 12.6% of the country's landmass. The main driver is the boom in mining.[31]

Legal intersections

Domestic actors and institutions play their part in the taking of land for foreign investment purposes. They may encourage, incentivise and mediate such taking. However, it is their transnational counterparts which, more often than not, originate, design and drive the agenda.[32] In this neocolonial landscape, the role of the nation-state may be said to have transited from that of a principal to that of a broker and an intermediary. Nevertheless, it would be reductive to focus on transnational capital in isolation. What emerges is a complex landscape of entangled social relationships that stretch from the local to the global. It implicates people as far apart from each other as peasants and indigenous nations are from governments, World Bank officials, MNEs directors and fund managers residing in distant urban and financial hubs. At issue is the concept of property and competing claims advanced by multiple actors operating within a topography of power differentials.

In such a landscape, the rule of law is said to be the primary mechanism for replacing social violence and disorder with regularity, certainty and stability. Sites of authority and decision-making define the substance of rights and obligations and the procedures for their implementation. They both produce and deny capacities and spaces for contestations alternatively for dialogue. The World Bank highlights the importance of secure rights to stimulating growth and investment. It runs land

29 Anuradha Mittal and Elizabeth Fraser, *Losing the Serengeti: The Massai Land That Was to Run Forever* (The Oakland Institute 2018) 6 <https://www.oaklandinstitute.org/sites/oaklandinstitute.org/files/losing-the-serengeti.pdf> accessed 6 April 2022.

30 Saskia Sassen, 'Is Rohingya Persecution Caused by Business Interests Rather Than Religion?' (The Guardian, 4 January 2017) <https://www.theguardian.com/global-development-professionals-network/2017/jan/04/is-rohingya-persecution-caused-by-business-interests-rather-than-religion> accessed 6 April 2022; for further discussion of the surge in 'land grabs' see Cotula (n 21) 180–3.

31 Katharina Buchholz, 'The Countries Most Affected by Land Grabs' (*Statista*, August 2022) <https://www.statista.com/chart/19044/countries-most-affected-by-land-grabs/> accessed 17 August 2022.

32 For a view that focuses on domestic drivers and actors see for example Michael Levien, 'The Land Question: Special Economic Zones and the Political Economy of Dispossession in India' (2012) 39(3–4) *The Journal of Peasants Studies* 933; Shelly Feldman and Charles Geisler, 'Land Expropriation and Displacement in Bangladesh' (2012) 39(3–4) *The Journal of Peasants Studies* 971.

titling projects, including the setting up of a national land registry.[33] Yet, as can be seen further later, in the context of land grabs, the opposite may be true. In practice, large-scale deals feed on legal uncertainty and fuzziness. The World Bank observed that investors tend to target countries where rural land rights are insecure and enjoy weak legal recognition and protection.[34]

Contemporary land grabs engage an expansive legal architecture, including local land tenure systems, national land laws and IIAs. To these may be added trade, environmental and human rights instruments. Each has in its sight a different dimension of what is in reality a complex 'investment chain' permeated with interrelated contractual and proprietorship events: from purchases, concessions or long-term leases of land and resources to intellectual property rights in technology and products, to finance and the various aspects of design and implementation.[35] Yet, none of these legal disciplines is ring-fenced. As they intersect, property, labour and human–nature relations are reconfigured, creating pools of potential ruptures. For instance, national laws which govern the allocation of land to foreign investors and IIAs which shelter foreign investors' acquired rights may conflict. Simultaneously, IIAs shape and influence norms of domestic laws which then produce violent encounters at the community level.

The potential for violent encounters is particularly present where the bundle of rights associated with proprietorship is fractured so that the right to allocate and transfer land is centralised at the state level whilst the possessory right to use remains at the community level. This dissociation 'creates a misalignment in the distribution of cost and benefit . . . because those allocating the land are not those who bear the adverse consequences of allocation, particularly the loss of use rights'.[36] In the case of the Massai, the Rift Valley semi-nomadic pastoralists, a series of land and wildlife laws promulgated in Tanzania in the mid-20th century challenged their way of life and brought about their eviction from large areas of ancestral land. These included substitute tracts previously promised to them by way of concessions granted in exchange for their agreement to leave their original habitat voluntarily. Additional laws curbed their rights to graze cattle and engage in subsistence cultivation, leading to malnutrition and outbreaks of disease. Violent measures such as the burning and destruction of several communities were

33 See for example The World Bank, 'Why Secure Land Rights Matter' (2017) <http://www.worldbank.org/en/news/feature/2017/03/24/why-secure-land-rights-matter> accessed 6 April 2022; The World Bank, 'Rural Land Titling & Cadastre Development Project' (2019) <http://projects.worldbank.org/P035777/rural-land-titling-cadastre-development-project?lang=en> accessed 6 April 2022.

34 Tania Murray Li, 'What Is Land? Assembling a Resource for Global Investment' (14 July 2014) *Plenary Lecture, Transactions of the Institute of British Geographers* 598 <file:///Users/yonitpercival/Documents/publications%20and%20articles/property%20rights/What%20is%20land%3F%20%20Tania%20Li%20-%20Academia.edu.webarchive> accessed 11 October 2017; Klaus Deininger et al., *Rising Global Interest in Farmland: Can It Yield Sustainable and Equitable Benefits?* (The World Bank 2011).

35 Cotula (n 21) 188.

36 Ibid 200.

ordered by the government in August 2017. Thus, even before the conflict was further inflamed by the entry of foreign investment, the Massai's understanding of the land as belonging to them by virtue of their centuries-old symbiotic relationship with it was pitted against state-made law that declared all land to be public and under centralised control and management.[37]

Shortcomings in the treatment of customary landholders may present an opportunity for transnational capital. They create a space within which the state can be moved to counter resistance from below under cover of lawfulness. This space is secured by the threat of ISDS proceedings should the state resolve to respond to community demands and change course. For many years, the Guatemalan gold mine operated by the US mining company Kappes, Cassiday & Associates (KAC) was subject to opposition and peaceful resistance by local rural communities. On 23 May 2018 the Supreme Court of Guatemala held that the mining was unlawful by reason of KAC's failure to comply with the requirement of prior consultation. The court suspended KAC's licence and ordered operations to cease. KAC issued ICSID proceedings, claiming some US$350m in compensation for violation of the Dominican Republic-Central America-United States Free Trade Agreement (DR-CAFTA).[38] This type of conflict may also acquire a human rights dimension. The human right to property may collide with social, cultural and economic rights, including indigenous peoples' rights to their ancestral lands and the preservation of their way of life.[39]

Land law, IL and customary tenure

As between customary tenure, IL and municipal land law, customary tenure is the one most vulnerable to intervention. Its vulnerability is not easily explained either by rarity or by the absence of a concept of property. As to rarity, despite centuries-long assaults, customary tenure is estimated to cover over six billion hectares, potentially held by over two billion rural people. In Africa, it governs the way 90% of rural populations acquire, hold, use and transfer land.[40] Many do not feel the need to have their tenure officially registered and titled. Alternatively, these procedures are not easily accessible to them. In consequence, titled land occupies only a small percentage of total land and tends to concentrate in the hands of urban elites.[41] As to the concept of

37 Mittal and Fraser (n 29) generally. For an account of the legislation see 22–5.

38 *Daniel Kappes and Kappes Cassiday & Associates v Guatemala* ICSID Case No ARB/09/5.; see also for example *Pac Rim Cayman LLC v Republic of El Salvador* ICSID Case No. ARB/09/12; *Metalclad Corporation v The United Mexican States* ICSID Case No ARB(AF)/97/1.

39 'The United Nations Declaration on the Rights of Indigenous People' adopted by the General Assembly on 13 September 2017 <https://www.un.org/esa/socdev/unpfii/documents/DRIPS_en.pdf> accessed 6 April 2022.

40 Lily Alden Wily, 'Customary Tenure: Remaking Property for the 21st Century' in Michele Graziadei and Lionel Smith (eds), *Comparative Property Law: Global Perspectives* (Research Handbooks in Comparative Law Series Edward Elgar 2017) 1, 3.

41 Cotula (n 21) 213.

property, 'customary land interests have always had founding incidents of ownership amounting to property'.[42] Wily explains them as radical titles, collectively held and applied to a delineated geographical area and its resources.[43] Okoth-Ogendo argues that customary land interests amount to property because they confer 'a bundle of rights in a specified *res* vested in a verifiable body of entities recognised by a legal system'.[44] Ownership may be communal but is nevertheless private. That is to say, it is attached exclusively to a specific group (communities, lineages or families) operating as a corporate entity. Its members have clear rights and obligations pertaining to social and economic assets on which the group and individuals draw and which shape their political and spiritual life.[45] Yet, all too often, incidents of ownership are constructed as absences because of the fluidity and diversity of the way these assets are held, difficulties in translating norms and meanings into Western legal parlance, as well as the interests of powerful commercial actors.

Alden Lily defines customary systems as 'no more and no less than community based regimes for the ordering and sustaining of access and use of lands and resources, and thence delivering rights, and for which the community itself is the surety'.[46] The emphasis is on the words 'community based'. Norms may vary in line with changes in use and sustainability requirements. The meaning of ownership too may alter in response to fluctuations in socioeconomic conditions and land availability. However, the principle of communal governance is immutable. The jurisdiction to allocate land and determine how rights are held, upheld and applied is vested not in an individual or an external body, but in community members and their councils. Customary tenure's tenaciousness is said to be grounded in this conflation of collaboration, flexibility and bonds of identity, beliefs and culture with the land. This medley may also account for its efficiency and success in resource conservation. Even the World Bank acknowledged that, particularly in areas of low population density, formal title to land is not the most desirable or cost-effective way of securing land tenure and managing transfers. Rather, 'One alternative is to award property rights to communities which then decide on the most suitable tenure arrangements'.[47]

42 Alden Wily (n 40) 1.

43 Ibid 2. The concept of radical title, a product of colonial jurisdiction, is generally understood as a bare title which does not confer, at least not automatically, full beneficial ownership. See for example, Ulla Secher, 'The Meaning of Radical Title: The Pre-Mabo Authorities Explained' (2005) 11(3) *Australian Property Law Journal* 179.

44 H. W. O. Okoth-Ogendo, 'The Tragic African Commons: A Century of Expropriation, Suppression and Subversion' (2002) 12003 *University of Nairobi Law Journal* 107 at 109.

45 Okoth-Ogendo (n 44) 108.

46 Alden Wily (n 40) 4.

47 Klaus Deininger and Hans Bingwanger, 'The Evolution of the World Bank Land Policy: Principles, Experience and Future Challenges' (1999) 14(2) *The World Bank Research Observer* 247 at 269 cited in Alden Wily (n 40) 9; for a discussion of the relative advantages of private and common property rights see for example Elinor Ostrom and Charlotte Hess, 'Private and Common Property Rights' (2007) Indiana University Public and Environmental Affairs Research Paper No. 2008–11–01 <https://papers.ssrn.com/sol3/papers.cfm?abstract_id=1936062> accessed 6 April 2022.

The immutable principle of community-based governance comes under pressure at the intersection with centrally promulgated land laws. The rights it creates attract varying degrees, but overall limited legal recognition or protection. Registration which operates in the shadow of individual ownership perfected by centralised registration does not make for easy living. In Indonesia, 'government officials, village heads, army officers, customary chiefs, prominent villagers – grab land and claim ownership'.[48] Once the country's forests have been declared state land, the ability of the highlanders in the island of Sulawesi to continue their generations-old way of living and farming became contingent on official allocation by the Department of Forestry.[49] In the early 1990s, a handful of African states such as Tanzania, Namibia, Mozambique and Uganda passed legislation which brought customary systems into the legal fold. In the case of Tanzania, this took the form of a 1928 amendment to the country's primary land legislation. However, in the dual-track system of tenure created, customary land rights remained subordinate to rights granted by the state or vested in it. Views vary as to the real impact of a subsequent 1999 legislative overhaul which granted equitable status to customary tenure.[50] As to the Massai, many of the issues they face have remained unresolved, and conflicts between them, the government and foreign investors persist. Notably, the 2009 amendment to the Wildlife Conservation Act restricted the Massai's rights to graze and cultivate, with disastrous implications for their way of life, cultural heritage and their physical survival.[51]

These are but a handful of brief examples of what are long and complex processes of legislative reforms and adjudicative decisions that began in colonial times and continued post-independence. However, they serve to illustrate the vulnerability of communities-based systems in the face of competing claims. In the case of the Massai, such claims include not only those of commercial foreign capital, but also those of conservation lobbies. At least formally, the ultimate arbiter is the state exercising the rights of ownership vested in it, its monopoly over law-making, as well as its power of eminent domain. In Tanzania, the 1999 Village Land Act conferred on the president the power to transfer village land to other land categories, provided this was undertaken in the public interest. The definition of public interest includes 'investments of national interest'. Investments of national interest open the door to renewed mass clearances and evictions to make room for capital-led, large-scale agriculture and resource exploitation.[52] On the whole, says Alden Wily, state laws fail to recognise customary regimes' divergent concepts of land rights

48 Li (n 10) 14.
49 Ibid 14–15.
50 The United Republic of Tanzania, The Land Act 1999 S. 4(3) <http://extwprlegs1.fao.org/docs/pdf/tan23795.pdf> accessed 6 April 2022; The United Republic of Tanzania, Village Land Act No 5 of 1999 <http://extwprlegs1.fao.org/docs/pdf/tan53306.pdf> accessed 6 April 2022; Issa Shivji, 'The Land Acts 1999: A Cause for Celebration or a Celebration of a Cause?' keynote address, Workshop on Land Morogoro, 19–22 February 1999.
51 Mittal and Fraser (n 29) 21, 24.
52 Village Land Act S. 4(2)(1).

as lawful ownership and property formations. On the whole, they are treated as no more than a form of occupancy. As such, they are 'vulnerable to colonial type suspension or taking virtually at will'.[53] Okoth-Ogendo makes a similar point when he states that, post-independence, 'the policy and process of conversion to private property and use through state allocations, compulsory acquisition and other irregular purchases continued unabated'. This is aggravated by legislative gaps and inconsistencies, pressure to put grazing and foraging land to 'productive' use, low level of compensation and inadequate implementation associated with lack of political will, vested interests, administrative deficiencies and neocolonial penetration.

Mostly, there is no requirement to obtain local landholders' prior free and informed consent to the allocation of land to a foreign investor. Even where, as in Mozambique, local consultations are legally mandated, the law stops short of stipulating the need for a binding agreement.[54] In this respect, the November 2018 judgement handed down by the Gauteng High Court (Pretoria) in the matter of *Duduzile Baleni & Others v DMR* was hailed as a landmark decision. The case concerned an application made by the Australian company, Transworld Energy and Mineral Resources, to South Africa's Department of Minerals Resources (DMR) for a licence to mine in Xolobeni's land. The court held that the Xolobeni's prior consent had to be obtained. Consent was held to go beyond mere consultations and to include actual agreement. In its absence, customary communities may not be deprived of their land.[55] Yet, in both theory and practice the issue of consent is a complex one, giving rise to vexing questions of circumstances, consequences and promises relied on, as well as power differentials.

The arrival of foreign investors further complicates this already fraught relationship. Their entry into the domestic arena, says Cotula, makes statutory recognition of customary tenure all the more vital if the process of allocating land for commercial purposes is to be participatory, transparent and protective of third-parties rights.[56] Yet, where foreign capital avails itself of the protection afforded to it under the foreign investment protection regime, the state's hands may be tied. At the precise moment when the state is in pressing need of its powers and authority, it may find itself facing conflicting obligations and claims on the one hand and a reduced regulatory space on the other. Further, as noted earlier, land grabbing takes place within a wider context of transnationalised property relations. It forms an investment chain of which land and land rights form only one link. This link has particular features which make for even greater complexity.

First, land is an immoveable asset par excellence. It is fixed and cannot follow migratory capital as it crosses borders. This fixity finds expression in the *lex situs*

53 Alden Wily (n 40) 1.

54 Cotula (n 21) 215.

55 David Mckay, 'DMR Studying Historic High Court Ruling in Favour of Xolobeni Community' (22 November 2018) <https://www.business-humanrights.org/en/so-africa-court-orders-consultation-with-xolobeni-community-prior-to-granting-mining-permission-to-australian-company> accessed 6 April 2022.

56 Cotula (n 21) 180, 198.

principle which provides that the law governing dealings with land is that of the place where it is located. In consequence, cross-border transactions implicate information and coordination costs, as well as other legal intricacies associated with the *in rem* nature of property. Second, whereas the investment chain of which land grabs form part is transnational, land law is essentially a national construct. As such, it dovetails domestic sociopolitical specificities which may or may not correspond to the needs, expectations and concerns of transnationalised capital. Third, in the case of post-colonial states, legislation may reflect parallel spheres of formal and informal authority that have their social foundations in imperial designs and strategies.[57] With independence, the new states absorbed much of the legislation enacted by colonial administrators and the land-as-property' principles they had introduced. For example, in 19th-century Africa under British rule, English law was made the basis for colonial administration in all matters. By the turn of the century, a series of enactments legitimised the appropriation of land deemed unsettled and ungoverned by declaring it Crown land.[58] Thereafter, it was available for distribution along English proprietary principles, including registration and the requirement that a legally protected owner must be either a natural, or a juridical person, to the exclusion of communal ownership. Such legacies have remained imbricated in the new states' political economy. They continue to determine the way land is administered as between a centralised administration, local urban elites (for whom foreign investment may represent an opportunity for enrichment) and rural populations (for whom it may represent a threat of impoverishment). Frictions may arise around matters, such as the allocation of land, divergent understandings of development and the interpretation of customary legal systems. They may impact on the profitability of foreign investment, leaving the government between the devil of its obligations under the regime of investment protection and the deep blue sea of his obligations to its population.

Frictions nevertheless are not necessarily dramatic or visible. They may trigger insidious processes of ostensibly voluntary collaboration. It was not transnational capital which dislodged the Indonesian highlanders from their land. Theirs was a moment of seduction, an instance of self-rescue in the form of the planting of commercial tree crops. With it came the individuation of land rights, the disembedding of a way of life from its communal underpinnings and the production of winners and losers. For the winners, the planting of commercial trees was a dream come true. For the losers, it was a dream turned a nightmare upon discovery that there was nowhere for them to go except to a dead end.[59]

Land and foreign investment protection

Insofar as ISDS jurisdictional architecture turns on the existence of an investment, land, in and of itself, may not confer on a tribunal subject-matter jurisdiction.

57 See for example William Reno, *Corruption and State Politics in Sierra Leone* (CUP 1995) generally.
58 Okoth-Ogendo (n 44) 110–11.
59 Li (n 10) 3–5.

However, as in the case of the port treaties discussed earlier, dealings with land often form part of all manners of ventures and the foundation on which they rest. In June 2018, of the 676 cases registered in ICSID and its Additional Facility, sectors with manifest connection to land and its resources such as oil, gas mining, agriculture, fishing forestry and construction made up a total of 36% (24%, 4% and 8% respectively). By 2022, 22% of all cases related to the extractive and energy sectors and 24% concerned electric power and other sources of energy. Also prominent was the construction sector at 12%. Cases related to agriculture, fishing and forestry constituted 2%, making a total of 60%.[60] The volume of deals entered into, shortcomings in the drafting of contracts and treaties, popular pressures, inadvertent non-compliance, jurisdictional expansion and states' attempts to recapture sovereign control over its natural resources through legislative reforms conflate to augment exposure to the risk of a claim. In Tanzania, three new acts came into effect in July 20017 which appeared to give the government wide-ranging rights, including the right to renegotiate existing contracts, expunge unconscionable terms and increase royalty rates.[61] Multinational law firms were not far behind in advising their clients of the claims which may be available to them in consequence under both contract and treaty law.[62] *Agro EcoEnergy and Others v Tanzania*, the first case described as concerning land grab, was registered with ICSID in the second half of 2017.[63] Given that the taking of land tends to provoke opposition, the state may also be at risk of failing to accord the investor 'full protection and security' when dealing with organised contestations.[64]

The presence of investment provides a point of entry which then becomes even wider where lawfulness is no longer a prerequisite for protection. The definition of investment, the question of legality and the exclusion of local law from the applicable law came together in the ICSID case of *Bear Creek Mining Corp v Peru*. At issue was Peru's revocation of an administrative authorisation. The authorisation conferred on Bear Creek, a Canadian company headquartered in Vancouver, rights

60 ICSID, 'ICSID Releases New Caseload Statistics for the 2021 Fiscal Year' 4 August 2021 <https://icsid.worldbank.org/news-and-events/news-releases/icsid-releases-new-caseload-statistics-2022-fiscal-year> accessed 19 August 2022.

61 Natural Wealth and Resources Contracts (Review and Renegotiations of Unconscionable Terms) Act, The Natural Wealth and Resources (Permanent Sovereignty) Act, The Witten Laws (Miscellaneous Amendments) Acts.

62 See for example Allen and Overy, 'Briefing Note: New laws create potential for arbitration claims against Tanzania' (*Publications*, 5 September 2017) <http://www.allenovery.com/publications/en-gb/Pages/Briefing-note-New-laws-create-potential-for-arbitration-claims-against-Tanzania.aspx> accessed 6 April 2022.

63 *Agro EcoEnergy Tanzania Limited, Bagamoyo EcoEnergy Limited, EcoDevelopment in Europe AB, EcoEnergy Africa AB v United Republic of Tanzania*, ICSID Case No. Arb/17/33; the claim was brought under the Sweden-Tanzania BIT and arose out of a 2016 cancellation of a sugar cane and ethanol project on the ground that it would adversely impact a local wildlife sanctuary. At issue are 20,000 hectares of farmland and an alleged investment of US$52m.

64 *Pac Rim Cayman LLC v The Republic of El Salvador*, ICSID Case No ARB/09/12; *Bear Creek Mining Corporation v Republic of Peru*, ICSID Case No. ARB/14/21.

to operate the Santa Ana mine where significant silver ore deposits had been discovered. It was granted on the ground of 'public necessity'. When the authorisation was withdrawn, the claimant alleged breaches of the investment chapter in the Peru-Canada Free Trade Agreement (FTA). As to the applicable law, in its 2017 award, the tribunal relied on Article 837 of the FTA to exclude Peru's law. It held that the dispute was governed solely by the FTA and applicable rules of IL.[65] As to jurisdiction, the tribunal relied on the wide definition contained in Article 847 of the FTA to find that there was investment capable of conferring subject-matter jurisdiction. The definition included real estate and other property, tangible or intangible, as well as interests arising from the commitment to economic activity of capital. Contracts involving the presence of the investor's property in the country were held to be one such commitment.[66] Particularly significant in the context of investment arbitration practice was the tribunal's view on the question of illegality. As part of its jurisdictional challenge, Peru contended that the initial, 'public necessity' authorisation had been obtained in breach of Article 71 of its constitution and was therefore unlawful. Tribunals, Peru contended, lacked jurisdiction over claims derived from investments which violated domestic law and/or the IL principle of good faith. Bear Creek's investment contravened both. Thus, were the tribunal to accept jurisdiction, such acceptance would run contrary not only to the country's constitution, but also to the IL principle that a claimant may not benefit from its own wrongdoing.[67] In adjudicating this point, the tribunal confined itself to the plain language of the FTA to determine whether it stipulated that legality was a precondition for the finding of jurisdiction. It held that the treaty contained 'no jurisdictional requirement that the Claimant's investment be legally constituted under the laws of Peru'. It also concurred with Bear Creek that 'under international law the Tribunal may not import a requirement that limits its jurisdiction when such a limit is not specified by the parties . . . Therefore, the Tribunal does not consider that the alleged good faith is a further condition under the FTA for the jurisdiction of the Tribunal'.[68] The finding departs from previous awards in which illegality was held to deprive the investment at issue from treaty protection and thereby deprive the tribunal of jurisdiction to entertain the claim.[69]

Until *Bear Creek*, several investment treaty cases lent support to the proposition that compliance with the law of the land is a condition precedent for the tribunal's jurisdiction.[70] Broadly, three arguments are engaged: the wording of the treaty, general principles of good faith and the prohibition on benefiting from one's own

65 *Bear Creek v Peru*, Award paras 267–9 at 77–8.

66 *Bear Creek v Peru* Award paras 282–5 at 86–7.

67 *Bear Creek v Peru* Award para 299 at p. 92.

68 *Bear Creek v Peru* Award paras 318–24 at pp. 101–2.

69 Zachary Douglas, 'The Plea of Illegality in Investment Treaty Arbitration' (2014) 29(1) *ICSID Review* 155.

70 E.g. *Tokios Tokeles v Ukraine*, ICSID Case No. ARB/02/18, Decision on Jurisdiction (29 April 2004) para 86; *Phoenix Action Ltd v Czech Republic*, ICSID Case NO. ARB/06/5, Award (15 April 2009) paras 101–5.

wrongdoing. Also engaged is the respect to be accorded to the integrity of the host state's law.[71] These are to apply even in the absence of a treaty provision to this effect.[72] A plea of illegality may raise evidential difficulties exacerbated by gaps and 'shades of grey' in municipal legislation.[73] Zachary Douglas argues that, in any event, the illegality of the investment is not a jurisdictional issue. Rather, it goes to the admissibility of the claim.[74]

Other than the constitutional infringement pleaded in *Bear Creek*, circumstances which may support a claim of illegality include lack of consultation with local communities, circumvention of restrictions on foreign land ownership and insufficient compensation. They may also extend to the terms on which the land was alienated. One example is the widespread practice of low valuations and transactions at below market price. In one transaction in Mozambique, the annual land fee was a mere US$0.60 per hectare. This was against an estimated market value of US$9,800 per hectare.[75] In other cases, investors were exempt from paying land fees for either a few years or altogether.[76] Suppression of the price of alienation may amount to unlawful conduct with implications for the jurisdiction of the tribunal and/or the admissibility of the claim. It may also go to quantum. The question arises as to whether the below market price paid at the point of acquisition should be factored in when calculating compensation. Investment treaties which adopt the market value benchmark (most do as part of the Hull formula subject to drafting variations) tend to disallow adjustments to quantum in light of the circumstances surrounding the acquisition. It follows that where the tribunal adopts a mechanical approach to the application of the treaty, compensation will be based on market value with no account taken of the suppressed price paid at the outset.[77]

In sum, as Polanyi's 'great transformation' hurtles through the rural communities of the Global South and parts of Europe, it is mediated by governments, local officials, IFIs and transnational corporations. These actors speak the language of free markets. However, simultaneously, they also use the law to construct political regimes in which capital and its need may be nurtured. The law may also serve as a site of contestation and resistance. However, success is anecdotal. The jurisprudence available for contestation is short on enforceability. It comprises mostly soft

71 For a critical analysis of the proposition that that these arguments are capable of depriving the tribunal of jurisdiction see Douglas (n 69) generally.

72 Cotula (n 21) 208; *World Duty Free Company Limited v The Republic of Kenya*, ICSID Case No. ARB/00/7 (Award 25 September 2008) in which the tribunal dismissed the claims on the ground that contracts obtained by corruption (in this case bribery) were contrary to international public policy and could not be upheld.

73 Cotula (n 21) 208.

74 Douglas (n 69) generally.

75 Cotula (n 21) 207 referencing Klaus Deininger and others, *Rising Global Interest in Farmland: Can It Yield Sustainable and Equitable Benefits?* (Agriculture and Rural Development Series World Bank 2011) 40, 107–9.

76 Cotula (n 21) 207.

77 Ibid.

law and is littered with hurdles notable for their absence from foreign investors' path to protection.

Conclusion: land of frontiers

Paradoxically, the confinement inflicted on the Massai by the penetration of capitalist social relations is no more abhorrent to them than it is to capitalism itself. Indeed, the latter's nomadism may be said to be of greater scope, since that of the Massai is predicated on attachment to a particular land. Capital, on the other hand, is devoid of attachments. As observed by Marx, any limits to self-reproduction – be they regulatory or geographical – are anathema to it.

Seen from this perspective, capitalism may be described as a system of frontiers that are forever in a state of motion and advancement. A frontier is never a place of permanence. Rather, conquest and appropriation of a frontier's purported wilderness signal the birth of a new conquest and a new round of appropriation. Boundaries are barriers to be overcome and surpassed in the turbulence of what Marx identified and Schumpeter termed 'creative destruction'.[78] Thus, the boundary-barrier is not only a site of ruination, but also a place of investment and accumulation. It is impregnated with the promise of self-reproduction.[79] In the context of land, its taking is often the gateway, the boundary's first crossing point in capital's march towards the fracturing of non-capitalist social relations on which its expansion is contingent. Li termed the process she observed in Indonesia's interior highland an 'indigenous frontier'. It was characterised by the shifting of balance between communal collaboration and individualised detachment. Community governance was replaced with itemised people operating at a distance from each other.

Community governance was fluid. It was guided by practicalities, such as the protection of crop, desire to minimise conflicts and the presence or otherwise of a charismatic kin member acting as a leader. It was capable of extending to the planting of cash crop and the extraction of resources. It could also tolerate incorporation into external governance, including during colonial rule. In other words, it was not that prior to the penetration of capitalist relations there were no markets, or that cash was not coveted, or that crops were not switched, or that there were no periods of exclusion of others from a particular piece land, as in the case of a newly planted field. Nor was state regulation rejected out of hand. Yet, none of these constituted the core of the indigenous frontier. Central to it, and then lost with the introduction of capitalist relations, was autonomy. Autonomy was grounded first and foremost in shared access to common land. 'All highlanders who wanted to farm had free access to land, and they could survive on the food they grew for themselves. Their autonomy was slightly modified by state rule and taxation which were light and

78 For the term 'creative destruction' see n 46 above.

79 Karl Marx tr ed, *Grundrisse* (Penguin Books 1858 1975) 334; see also Joel Kovel, *The Enemy of Nature: The End of Capitalism or the End of the World?* (Zed Books London 2007) 41–7.

incomplete'.[80] Associated with such autonomy was not only the freedom to weave a rich tapestry of possible responses to changing seasons and circumstances, but also more generally the absence of the permanence and fixity which lie at the heart of the concept of land as an asset. Land could be cultivated and then left to lie fallow. It was not delimited by territorial boundaries. It was periodically individualised only so as to resume its collective character in due course. The forest was boundless and available for community members to clear, plant and then leave to allow time for regeneration. Conversely, the capitalist structures which came at the heels of the adoption of cacao tree crops signalled constancy. Land was enclosed and made irreversibly exclusive. Individualisation became permanent, as was competitive production whereby the enrichment of some became contingent on the pauperisation of others. In Hegel's words, 'Wealth and poverty increase simultaneously'.[81] In the context of Indonesia's highlanders, notes Li, 'The capacity of some highlanders to prosper depended upon the failure of their neighbours who fell into debt and were forced to sell their land'.[82] Thus, the indigenous frontier's transformation went beyond changes to the allocation and use of land to include also the implantation of new social structures and relations. Put in terms of Wood's and Brenner's observations about the uniqueness of capitalism, the market as an opportunity gave way to the market as a compulsion, a place through which all aspects of life must pass and where self-interest and best outcomes are realised through competition. From a society in which markets formed one of a host of routes to survival, the indigenous frontier transmuted into a market society.[83] Its winners are now defined by their capacity to produce exchange value and the opportunity to accumulate. Its losers are viewed as the victims of their own inefficiency. They are also a threat since, by their presence, they destabilise property values, both economically and culturally. Writing about mining in resource frontiers, Peluso makes the point that through 'violence, racialization and agrarian-environmental practice' land grabs create frontiers as well as conquer them. In these newly refashioned sites, some inhabitant are dispossessed but others are reproduced as landholders, key actors in a new political regime.[84]

The centrality of the 'frontier' to capitalist dynamism goes some way to explain why the discourse by which capitalist taking is enabled resonates with narratives of emptiness, idleness, waste, poverty, marginalisation and underutilisation. It also throws light on the staying power of these narratives, first encountered in connection with the formation and initial spread of capitalist property relations centuries

80 Li (n 10) 6–7.

81 Cited in Domenico Losurdo, *Hegel and the Freedom of Moderns* (Duke University Press 2004) 163.

82 Li (n 10) 8, 5–16, 85–90.

83 Robert Brenner, 'Agrarian Class Structure and Economic Development in Pre-Industrial Europe' in Trevor H. Alston and Charles H. E Philpin (eds), *The Brenner Debate: Agrarian Class Structure in Pre-Industrial Europe* (CUP 1985) 10–63; Ellen Meiksins Wood, *The Origin of Capitalism: a longer view* (Verso 2002) xxx.

84 Nancy Lee Peluso, 'Plantations and Mines: Resource Frontiers and the Politics of the Smallholder Slot' (2017) 44(4) *The Journal of Peasant Studies* 834 at 838–9 and generally.

ago. They survived the passage of time and continue into contemporary land grabs. Frontiers as zones of both vision and violence – yet unmapped, yet to be regulated – form the bedrock on which availability and access are imagined and taking is legitimised.[85] What is available and can be taken? That which is vacant and unused, the wilderness that sweeps through the social territory on the other side of Santos's dividing line where 'the lawless, the alegal, the nonlegal' are located.[86]

What constitutes vacancy? The answer, found in John Locke's theory of the origin and nature of property rights, has remained essentially the same. As in colonial times, existing uses are brushed aside and differences are constructed as absences. In other words, the term 'vacancy' is not intended as a statement that there is nobody there. The land declared empty may be in fact populated by a diversity of forms of life, including local producers of the human variety who use it for a host of acts productive of livelihood – from slash-and-burn to subsistence and semi-subsistence farming or nomadic herding. What makes it available is not the non-presence of life, but rather the nature of its presence – the perceived lack of improvement and therefore the absence of recognised ownership and claims to the land. From Alexis de Tocqueville's 19th-century legitimisation of President Jackson's policy of deporting the Indians to modern times, the presence of life in the frontier may be acknowledged. Yet, it is acknowledged only as a form of dispensable occupancy. The Indians of North America may have occupied their lands, argued de Tocqueville. However, in the absence of appropriation through labour, they did not possess it. They were there merely to await the arrival of civilised humans. The territory was in fact an 'empty cradle', a desert to be made to bloom upon the entry of white settlers and their commitment to battling 'the wilderness and savage life'.[87]

Indeed, a frontier it is not a frontier if there is nothing there, if it has no potential for novelty, self-reproduction and expansion of capital. A frontier must be able to sustain accumulation and growth. In what Anna Tsing termed 'economy of appearances', such potential may amount to no more than a spectacle of hidden treasures – illusory or intentionally fraudulent tales of value unrealised and resources yet to be discovered. Nevertheless, particularly in the context of an extractivist and financialised capitalism, economy of appearances suffices for the purpose of raising coveted funds.[88] At issue is therefore what Gavin Bridge refers to as 'bountiful emptiness'. These are coveted but unincorporated or lightly incorporated spaces that are simultaneously empty (of recognised claims) and full (of purportedly

85 Anna Lowenhaupt Tsing, 'Natural Resources and Capitalist Frontiers' (2003) 38(48) *Economic and Political Weekly* 5, 100.

86 Boaventura de Sousa Santos, 'Beyond Abyssal Thinking: From Global Lines to Ecologies of Knowledge' (2007) 30(1) *Revista Critica de Ciencias Sociais* 45 at p. 48. <http://www.boaventuradesousasantos.pt/media/pdfs/Beyond_Abyssal_Thinking_Review_2007.PDF> accessed 7 April 2022.

87 Losurdo (n 26, chapter 4) 229–33.

88 Anna Tsing, 'Inside the Economy of Appearances' in Ash Amin and Nigel Thrift (eds), *The Blackwell Cultural Economy Reader* (Blackwell Publishing 2004).

unclaimed resources and potential for exchange value generation), barren (unprofitably utilised) and lush (have the potential for profitable exploitation).[89] Cotula makes the point that in the context of agriculture, the narrative of 'marginal' masks the fact that investors often target the best land in terms of water availability, soil fertility and location.[90] Choice of location in semi-colonised China's system of port treaties was paramount. Similarly, in contemporary grabs, investors' choice of land is also guided by its commercial viability, proximity to markets and access to infrastructure so that the new value created may be transported to lucrative destinations elsewhere.

Emptiness and marginality are united with fertility and abundance by a discourse which acts as a 'grid for the perception and evaluation of things' and the manner of their disposal.[91] A different kind of conquest is at play. Both the collective and the individual self are colonised by new words, new meanings, practices and strategies. In Indonesia, prior to the introduction of cacao trees and the capitalist relations which came with them, the highlanders used a variety of words to convey their interaction with the forest and each other. Disparate terms were developed to describe and create the assemblage of social relations and materialities which made up the substance of their communal and natural world. Yet, there was no word for 'land'. It was only around 1990, with the transition to land as a commodity and a site of investment, that the term *lokasi* first made an appearance. Land-as-*lokasi* came to represent a new assemblage comprising processes of detachment and expansion: *lokasi* was a plot that was detached from collective and neighbouring plots. At the same time, the categories of those involved with the *lokasi* were enlarged to include neighbours and strangers bearing funds to purchase the plot. Notably, *lokasi* represented an Indonesian adaptation of the English word 'location'.[92]

Thus, the word selected to describe and create the assemblage of 'land-as-location' conveyed also the foreign origins of self-reform. That is, the Western narratives of modernisation and development, the promise of progress and betterment contained therein, and, directly or by implication, the assertion of Western superiority and corresponding depiction of the non-Western as residing in a state of chronic backwardness. Seen through this lens, the frontier's 'bountiful emptiness' fits into and forms part of what Escobar terms 'historically produced' regimes of representation along European benchmarks.[93] The European benchmark acts as the initiator and primary inspiration for unlocking the frontier's potential for bounty. By contrast, the non-European is constructed at best as a replica of the West

89 Gavin Bridges, 'Resource Triumphalism: Postindustrial Narratives of Primary Commodity Production' (2001) A 33 *Environment and Planning* 2149 at p. 2154.

90 Lorenzo Cotula, 'The International Political Economy of the Global Land Rush: A Critical Appraisal of Trends, Scale, Geography and Trends' in White, Saturmino et al., (n 4) 37.

91 Michel Foucault, 'Questions of Methods' in Graham Burchell, Colin Gordon, and Peter Miller (eds), *The Foucault Effect: Studies in Governmentality* (The University of Chicago Press 1991) 82.

92 Li (n 10) 590.

93 Escobar (n 132, chapter 6) 6–7.

(when developing), alternatively as part of the frontier's absences and desertification (when not developing). Either way, the non-European is open to intervention. Words such as overpopulation, poverty, illiteracy, inefficiency, corruption and no rule of law describe and create the Global South by reference to the North's material and institutional riches. Associated with these riches are economies of scale, technology and finance. In the field of agriculture, the narrative is of agglomerating farms to achieve the economy of scale necessary for implementation of the modern farming methods on which greater yield depends. To this end, the indigenous frontier's self-reform must be all embracing. In the words of a UN group of experts: 'Ancient philosophies have to be scrapped, old social institutions have to disintegrate; bonds of cast, creed and race have to burst; and large number of persons who cannot keep up with progress have to have their expectations of a comfortable life frustrated'.[94]

The frontier's transformation – who is in and who is out – involves the creation of new participants in the development apparatus. Peasants, women and the environment (e.g. sustainable development) are packaged discursively and mobilised for the big escape: from a world of tradition, poverty, oppression and inequality to a world of market-based modernity, freedom and equality.[95] Escobar observes a shift from green revolution imperialism to rural development populism. Under the World Bank's guidance and leadership, small farmers have been reconstructed as the rural poor burdened by low productivity. However, they have the labour, the land and 'at least some capital, which, if mobilized, could reduce poverty and improve the quality of life'.[96] In the Indian region of Vidarbha with its rocky terrain and dependency on rainfall, such mobilisation took the farmers to Monsanto's genetically modified cotton with its heavy reliance on water, pricey chemicals and the yearly purchase of patented seeds. As in the case of Indonesia's highlanders, the vision turned into a nightmare. Dead-end indebtedness led to over a quarter million suicides in the last 20 years or so.[97]

The same discourse also operates as a set of traffic lights for intervention by foreign investors, empire of capital's army of missionaries. On the websites of private funds – possibly land grabs' major protagonists – statistics of impending scarcity of land and food switch on a green light. Scarcity foreshadows rising prices and profitable opportunities. Underutilisation and inefficiency signal room for value creation. The red light of risk is also identified, classified into discrete political and economic categories, calculated and balanced against the profitability of investment in farmlands 'if you make the right moves'.[98] The political risk associated

94 United Nations, Department of Social and Economic Affairs [1951] cited in Escobar (n 132, chapter 6) 4.

95 Escobar (n 132, chapter 6) 154–63.

96 World Bank, *Rural Development: Sector Policy Paper* (World Bank 1975) 3 cited in Escobar (n 132, chapter 6) 161.

97 Nandan Saxena and Kavita Bahl, documentary *Cotton for My Shroud* (2011) <https://www.youtube.com/watch?v=jdlPD8Eccrw> accessed 6 April 2022.

98 Li (n 10) 598.

with sovereignty and social instability attendant on exclusion and dispossession may be minimised with the support of the World Bank. The general message is twofold: first, whatever you plan to do with the land, whether 'you plan to use it, hold it or flip it soon for speculation the graphs go sharply upwards'. Second, the accumulation of private profit goes hand in hand with the social function of improving the life of the undeveloped.[99] It is a win-win situation. Once again, the dispossessed is posited as the beneficiary of its own dispossession. Once again, the resulting inequality is taken to be a price worth paying, part of the constitution of things, a downside to be rectified, if necessary, by the same power which created it in the first instance.

The law can be and is harnessed to impose limits on land as property, recognise the multiplicity of forms which human interaction with the earth may take, occasionally protects divergence and may even applied to question the extent of the entitlement born out of improvement.[100] Yet, primarily, the law provides a vantage point from which the worldview and interests of those in possession of the means of production may be discerned. It allocates risk away from corporations at both national and international levels, adopting doctrinal turnabouts as and when necessary. Vagueness leaves room for jurisprudential expansion and blurs the line between the lawful and unlawful. The law thus creates routes by which those with the requisite power and means to exploit can travel undisturbed. All too often, the discourse of certainty, transparency, fairness and equality associated with the rule of law masks an underbelly of selective privileges and structural inequality. Options open to owners are foreclosed to the propertyless.

99 Ibid 596.

100 Baha Yigit Sayin et al., 'Land Law and Limits on the Right to Property: Historical, Comparative and International Analysis' (2017) 6(1) *European Property Law Journal*; Thomas Paine, for example, argued that improvement of land entitled the improver to appropriate only the additional value so created. Thomas Paine, *Agrarian Justice* (1797) <http://piketty.pse.ens.fr/files/Paine1795.pdf> accessed 14 July 2023; see also Elizabeth Anderson, ' Thomas Paine's "Agrarian Justice" and the Origins of Social Insurance' in Eric Schliesser (ed), Ten Neglected Classics of Philosophy (OUP 2016) 55–83.

Part two

Property rights and rights of nature

8 Rights or webs of interests?

Humans' ownership rights or custodians of the planet

Neoliberalism has at its heart a philosophy of individualism, based on a concept of ownership. A theory of 'rational choice' has been slowly transmuting into hyper-capitalism and excessive individualism, making the idea of 'mine' the fundamental ambition for living. Simultaneously, the neoliberal economic order has exacerbated 'mine' into a global crisis where humanity is threatened. To get unlimited growth, the neoliberalists construct a system of consumerism, extracting resources from the Earth without restraint. The inevitable result is a warming climate. One of the important tools of the neoliberal paradigm is an excessive focus on strong property rights. To extract resources from the earth, Western law allows property rights to be almost deified, ignoring the consequences.

The rule of law and legal contractual perceptions

Property rights are clearly embedded in legal culture, certainty in Western jurisdictions. With this comes the legal device called 'contract'. Interpreting contracts is itself fascinating. Contracts can be interpreted from a narrow or a broader perspective. Law can follow a strict principle of interpreting the words or the clauses from judgements or legislation, or judges could interrogate the ethical dimension of the problem to be solved. Commercial law tends to focus on the exact words and clauses without considering the importance of power relationships. Real justice needs full consideration of the clauses in law and the ethical context of the particular problem. This is shown from *Adam v Cape*,[1] where Slade J opined that no court could 'disregard the principle of *Salomon v Salomon* merely because it considers it just so to do'.[2] 'Justice' was irrelevant; the overarching principle was certainty. The case revealed that commercial law prefers certainty in contrast to an ethical consideration of the question to be solved and where ethical principles like justice and equality are valued.

1 [1990] BCLC 479.
2 Ibid 513.

DOI: 10.4324/9781315386782-11

In his seminal work on debt,[3] David Graeber shows that while societies use economic exchange to trade goods, this is not the full extent of their social order; morals are predicated not on selfishness but on reciprocation.[4] Through the neoliberal paradigm, some societies have lost the *ethical component* of *reciprocation* of contracts and the contractual model of companies, and this loss has led to increased human inequality and devastating damage to the planet, because the powerful will always win in a contractual relationship unless there is a countervailing actor. The powerful MNEs need some actors to counteract their power. The role of the state is to protect citizens against powerful adversaries, but the state has vacated this role to venerate GDP and unlimited growth. An ethical dimension of law is promoted by Voigt in *Rule of Law for Nature*.[5] Arguing that law should be 'reformulated to keep activity in harmony with the unchanging and universal law of nature',[6] nature should be a decider in all legal decisions or judgements, rather than economic tenets. However, the neoliberal paradigm is paramount in global finance.

The IMF believes one solution to this is 'fiscal redistribution: progressivity of income taxation'.[7] However, the limited understanding of contract and property rights means there will be powerful voices against any progressive changes. Any attempt to design a society is based on a constant fluctuation between actors, involving moral values, rational choice and pragmatism.[8] Legal discourse on ownership rights and property rights is vital, because there is constant tension between the extent of protection for property rights and what sort of property rights should be valued. The planet should be valued highly, but the overwhelming prominence of Western belief of strong property rights stops the possibility that nature will be properly valued. As an example, in the tax arena, the debate discourse is shrill. Many neoliberal commentators, especially the Libertarian Alliance, argue that all tax is theft because in a free market all services can be purchased, and government should not provide services to fund them. They argue that it is a fiction that the government provides services because they are in the public interest.[9]

3 David Graeber, *Debt: The First 5,000 Years* (Nook edn, Melville House 2014).

4 Ibid, 107.

5 Christina Voigt (ed), *Rule of Law for Nature: New Dimensions and Ideas in Environmental Law* (Cambridge University of Law 2013).

6 'Our Common Future' (1987) https://sustainabledevelopment.un.org/content/documents/5987our-common-future.pdf (accessed 15 March 2021).

7 International Monetary Fund (IMF), *Tacking Inequality* (2017) <https://www.imf.org/en/Publications/FM/Issues/2017/10/05/fiscal-monitor-october-2017#Summary> accessed 18 June 2020.

8 Michel Foucault, *Power/Knowledge* (Pantheon 2018); Rowan Williams, *Faith in the Public Square* (Bloomsbury 2012); Janet Dine and Andrew Fagan (eds), *Human Rights and Capitalism* (Edward Elgar 2007), especially Michael Blecher, 'Law in Movement: Paradoxontology, Law and Social Movements' in Janet Dine and Andrew Fagan (eds), *Corporations, Globalisation and the Law* (Edward Elgar 2006) 80–114; Tomas Sedlacek, *Economics and Good and Evil* (OUP 2011); Harvey Cox, *The Market as God* (HUP 2016).

9 Chris R. Tame, 'Taxation Is Theft' in *Political Notes* (Libertarian Alliance 1999) 44, <http://www.libertarian.co.uk/lapubs/polin/polin044.pdf> accessed 15 July 2017.

These tax arguments are key in the anti-environmentalist movements, chronicled by Rowell,[10] with the use of dominion theology (God gave man 'dominion' over the earth)[11] to justify the exploitation of natural resources: 'you can't really hurt the planet because God wouldn't allow that. God wouldn't have given man chain saws if he didn't think they were benign',[12] coupled with allegations that environmental regulation destroys jobs and interferes with private property rights. One of the aims of Alliance for America[13] is 'To restore and protect constitutional private property rights'. The 'Wise Use' movement helped construct Gingrich's now notorious 'contract with America'[14] which the National Resources Defense Council explained, 'threatens to undermine virtually every federal environmental law on the books, meaning dirtier air, dirtier water and more species pushed to the brink'.[15] Then came Trump. A *New York Times* analysis, based on research from Harvard Law School, Columbia Law School[16] and other sources, counts more than 80 environmental rules and regulations which were been abandoned by the Trump administration. President Biden has vowed to restore environmental protections; however, it is likely that it might take years.[17]

A conception of strong property ownership is coupled with a 'profound commitment to the notion that all citizens should have an equal right to participate in economic and social life, and that the state is more than a safety net of last resort: it is the fundamental vehicle for the delivery of this equality'.[18] However, these two competing aims hide profound tensions. To some extent, these attitudes were driven by different experiences vis-à-vis land ownership when notions of equality became important. In Europe, the density of the population meant that unless there was some redistribution, there was a danger of revolution.[19] In the US,

> When John Adams argued in 1776 that the acquisition of land should be made easy for every member of society in order to achieve equality and liberty, he

10 Andrew Rowell, *Green Backlash* (Routledge 1996).

11 Genesis 2:27–8: "so God created man in his own image, in the image of God created he him; male and female created he them. And God blessed them, and God said to them, Be fruitful and multiply, and replenish the earth, and subdue it: and have dominion over the fish of the sea, and over the fowl of the air, and over every living thing that moveth on the earth".

12 Chip Berlet, cited in Andrew Rowell, *Green Backlash* (Routledge 1996) 9.

13 The Alliance for America is an umbrella organisation for industry to increase property rights.

14 'Wise Use' and 'Contract with America' was the legislative agenda advocated for by the United States Republican Party in 1994.

15 National Resources Defense Council, *Breach of Faith* (1995), cited in Andrew Rowell, *Green Backlash* (Routledge 1996) 32.

16 Sabin Center for Climate Change Law, *Climate Deregulation Tracker* (Columbia Law School 2019) <http://columbiaclimatelaw.com/resources/climate-deregulation-tracker/> accessed 8 June 2019.

17 'Restoring Environmental Rules Rolled Back by Trump Could Take Years' (*New York Times*, 2021) <https://www.nytimes.com/2021/01/22/climate/biden-environment.html> accessed 20 March 2021.

18 Ibid 51.

19 C. Morrisson and W. Snyder, 'The Income Inequality of France in Historical Perspective' (2000) 4 *European Review of Economic History* 59–83.

> could disregard European concerns with how the state had to intervene to construct a just society: a continent lay before him waiting to be claimed.[20]

The European state thus had a real and vital role to play in constructing a fair society – a far cry from a minimalist role in protecting individual property rights.

The discourse of property rights is complex and controversial – and, from the perspective of the planet, crucial. Before humans significantly denatured nature, many scholars followed the erroneous path of deifying or glorifying humans. Locke himself assumed humans were superior creations and divided them into categories: savages or civilised men [*sic*].[21] The civilised were duty bound to improve nature, and he thought all value came from this concept; by labouring on the land and 'improving' it, all 'value' can be found. However, this concept of value has been challenged, and it is not clear what Locke meant; 'value' was, he wrote, 'For the provisions serving to the support of human life, produced by one acre of enclosed and cultivated land, are . . . ten times more than those which are yields by an acre of land an equal richness lying waste in common'.[22] Sedlacek[23] argues that some of the value discourse has been wrongly interpreted; that Locke and Novak were not suggesting a mechanical parcelling of land for gain, but rather an understanding of the mysteries of nature. Novak wrote about 'raw creation'[24] mixed with human effort to create the world:

> Man is established as the manager over the created world, he becomes responsible for leading creation to its full flourishing. As if through the raw (not completely reading) creation of the world, God connects man with the task of guarding and protecting the Garden of Eden, and thus man actually *co*creates the cultural landscape.[25]

This mythical concept is far from Marx's work on capitalism, but there are some common themes, and later in this text, these concepts will be linked to the ideas around the 'commons' and the Gaia philosophy.

From property rights to rights for nature, scientific methods disguise the domination idea

We have seen that the assumption of human superiority drives the argument for property rights, but this belief is also found in scientific thought. As an example, the 2002 UNEP report *Cultural and Spiritual Values of Biodiversity*[26] states that the

20 W. Hutton, *The World We're In* (Little Brown 2000) 61.

21 John Locke, *Two Treaties of Government* (Cambridge Text in the History of Political Thought 1988).

22 Ibid 304–5.

23 T. Sedlacek, *Economics of Good and Evil* (OUP 2011) 60.

24 Michael Novak, *The Catholic Ethic and the Spirit of Capitalism* (Free Press 1993).

25 Sedlacek (n 23) 60.

26 UNEP, *Cultural and Spiritual Values of Biodiversity* (Intermediate Technology Publications 2002) <https://wedocs.unep.org/bitstream/handle/20.500.11822/9190/Cultural_Spiritual_thebible.pdf?amp%3BisAllowed=&sequence=1> accessed 19 April 2020.

scientific method still sees nature as a collection of objects for human use to benefit from and exploit from nature. The report uses the banner of social 'objectivity' to mask the moral and ethical issues that emerge from a functionalist, anthropocentric philosophy and seldom embraces the values of local knowledge and traditions. The UNEP's work is predicated on domination by humans.

This idea is particularly important in the climate change crisis. Climate change is not only a scientific truth but also a construct that encompasses human beings' understanding of a number of specialities, including sociology, theology, science, politics and philosophy:

> Climate change . . . [is] a battleground between different philosophies and practices of science, between ways of knowing. 'Climate change as a scientific controversy' is a compelling discourse to which the media and other social actors are readily attracted. Although the controversy is allegedly about science, very often scientific disputes about climate change end up being as a proxy for much deeper conflicts between alternative visions of the future and competing centres of authority in society.[27]

Hulme lists a number of angles on this, including:

> *Climate change as justification* for commoditisation of the atmosphere and especially, for the commoditisation of the gas, carbon dioxide[28] . . . *Climate change as the inspiration for a global network* of new, or invigorated, social movements[29] . . . *Climate change as a threat to ethic, national and global security.*[30]

Using some aspects of James Lovelock's Gaia theory, this chapter proposes a distinct focus on the earth. Gaia theory, which concentrates on the planet, tells us that the earth's biosphere behaves as though it were a single organism.

> The Gaia hypothesis, also known as Gaia theory or Gaia principle, proposes that all organisms and their inorganic surroundings on Earth are closely integrated to form a single and self-regulating complex system, maintaining the conditions for life on the planet. The scientific investigation of the Gaia hypothesis focuses on observing how the biosphere and the evolution of life forms contribute to the stability of global temperature, ocean salinity, oxygen in the atmosphere and other factors of habitability in a preferred homeostasis.[31]

27 Mike Hulme, *Why We Disagree about Climate Change* (CUP 2009) xxvi. Emphasis in the original.
28 See Simon Dietz and Eric Neumayer, 'Economics and Governance of Sustainable Development' in *Governance Sustainability* (CUP 2009).
29 See Mathew Paterson, 'Global Governance for Sustainable Capitalism? The Political Economy of Global Environmental Governance' in *Governance Sustainability* (CUP 2009).
30 Mike Hulme, *Why We Disagree about Climate Change* (CUP 2009) xxvi. Emphasis in the original.
31 Harvard: <https://courses.seas.harvard.edu/climate/eli/Courses/EPS281r/Sources/Gaia/Gaia-hypothesis-wikipedia.pdf> accessed 15 June 2020.

While the Gaia hypothesis is not fully accepted in that the planet may not self-regulate, there is scientific consensus on the interrelationship between species and the biosphere.

Gaia

The original Gaia theory was controversial among scientists, who disputed many of the details.[32] However, Lovelock later improved his original idea, which only included organisms, to also include all of the components of the world as a regulator: 'if the regulator could be shown to be the whole Earth system made up from all of life, including the air, the ocean and the surface rocks, not just organisms alone'.[33] To test this idea, he tried to compose a model (with Andrew Watson) now known as 'Daisyworld'.[34] Although scientists have been more accepting of this concept, some of the details are still disputed. However, in 2001, a meeting of the European Geophysical Union signed a statement that read, 'The Earth System behaves as a single, self-regulating system comprised of physical, chemical, biological and human components'.[35] This was a seminal moment, but Lovelock's theory is more than a scientific hypothesis; it also has spiritual significance. He talks about the earth as 'alive': 'Until we all feel intuitively that the Earth is a living system, and know that we are a part of it, we will fail to react automatically for its and ultimately our own protection'.[36] Christopher Stone, the J. Thomas McCarthy Trustee Chair in law at the University of Southern California School of Law, agrees with Lovelock's position and adds from a scientific perspective, 'International scientific studies have shown irrefutably that the Earth as a whole is an organized system or most closely in interrelated and indeed interdependent activities. It is, in the broadest sense of the term an "organism" '.[37] Theologians have considered the spiritual significance of Gaia:

> The harsh reality of climate change challenges us to integrate what we understand of past events that shaped the planet's life-sustaining processes with an understanding of their present critical state, and with a heightened awareness of the role we play in the stabilisation or destabilisation of those processes.[38]

Studying the planet entails an understanding of the processes from the beginning of the world – the events that formed the earth, including the atmosphere. From this perspective, human life diminishes into a small framework; one that shows

32 Richard Dawkins, *The Extended Phenotype* (OUP 1999).

33 James Lovelock, *The Vanishing Face of Gaia* (Penguin 2010) 112.

34 Andrew J. Watson and James Lovelock, 'Biological Homeostasis of the Global Environment: The Parable of Daisyworld' (1983) 35B *Tellus* 284–9 <http://www.jameslovelock.org/biological-homeostasis-of-the-global-environment-the-parable-of-daisyworld/> accessed 19 June 2019.

35 Lovelock (n 33) 117.

36 Ibid 128. In Ancient Greece, Gaia was the goddess of the Earth.

37 C. Stone, *Should Trees Have Standing?* (OUP 2010) 28.

38 Anne Primavesi, *Gaia and Climate Change* (Routledge 2009) 6.

how insignificant humans were until we devastated the planet by unsustainably plundering the earth's resources: human activities are putting unprecedent stress on Earth's living system.[39]

The environmental emergency shows that the economic system of property rights must be reformed

The coming[40] climate change catastrophe poses a threat to the basis of our very existence.[41]

'There is a looming environmental crisis, which poses a threat to the basic of our very existence.'[42] The neoliberal paradigm aspires to continue unlimited growth, extracting resources from the planet without replenishing the earth. MNEs and their profit maximisation agendas are causing degradation of the earth, all for the sake of growth and GDP.[43] Trade, travel and consumption all require the burning of energy, which translates into expansion of GDP. Meanwhile, world temperatures are rising.

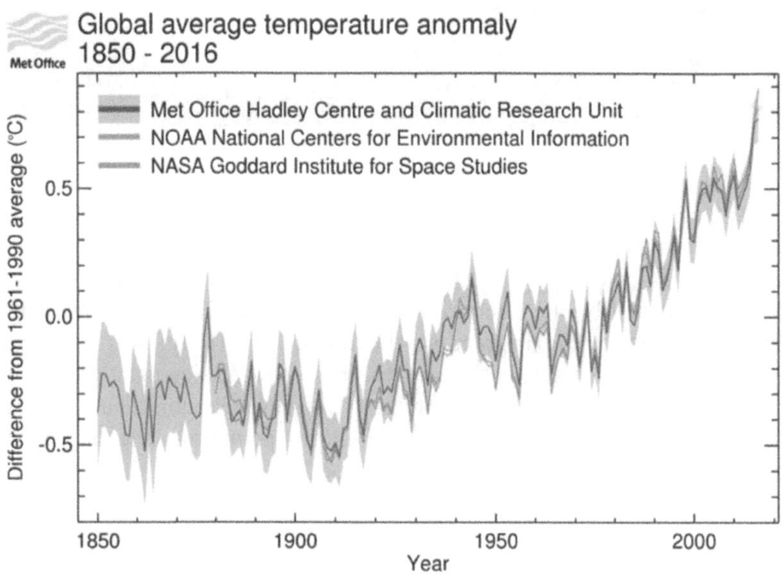

UK Metrological Office, 2020

All sectors are affected.

39 Ibid.

40 The sixth report of the IPCC shows that 'coming' is outdated. It is now; IPCC sixth report 2021 'Code Red for Humanity' <https://www.ipcc.ch/report/ar6/wg1/downloads/report/IPCC_AR6_WGI_Citation.pdf> accessed 8 December 2021.

41 Beate Sjafjell, *Towards a Sustainable European Company Law* (Wolters Klwer 2009) 3; Dieter Helm and Cameron Hepburn (eds), *The Economics and Politics of Climate Change* (OUP 2009).

42 Sjafjell (n 41) 3, Dieter Helm and Cameron Hepburn (eds), *The Economics and Politics of Climate Change* (OUP 2009).

43 Naomi Klein, *This Changes Everything; Capitalism vs the Climate* (Allan Lane 2014).

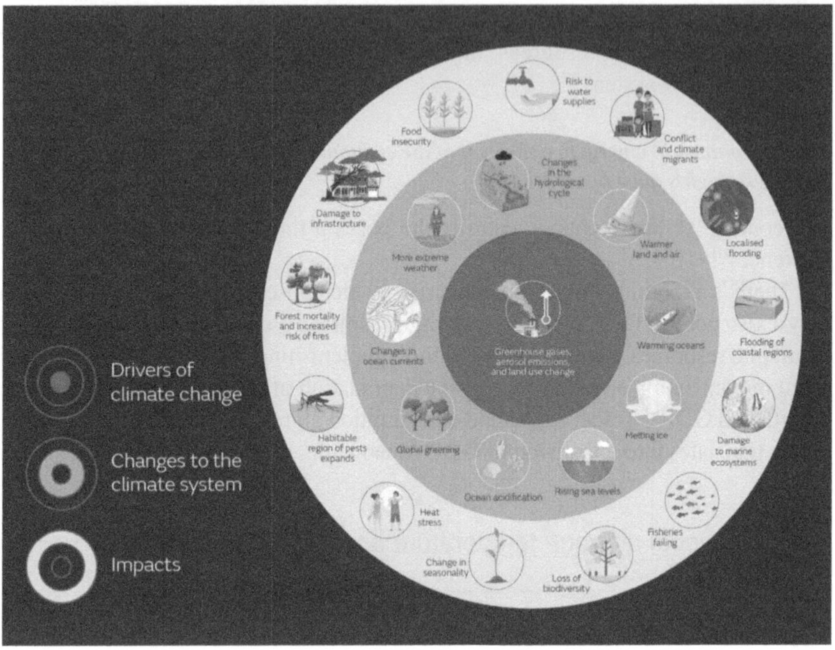

UK Metrological Office, 2020

This diagram shows the drivers of climate change (in the centre). The climate changes because of the increased production (the next layer) and the impacts of the emergency (the outer layer). Most of these are well known and have been meticulously researched by the Intergovernmental Panel on Climate Change (IPCC). However, one part of the diagram may be difficult to interpret; this is the 'global greening' effect. This refers to the fact that there is increasing plant growth in the northern high latitudes as the ice retreats.[44] Unfortunately, this small increase of greening in northern latitudes is offset by thawing permafrost releasing methane, which is a highly dangerous climate change gas.[45]

The human catastrophe

For humans climate change is a catastrophe. The IPCC reports, 'There is *high confidence* that neither adaptation nor mitigation alone can avoid all climate change impacts . . . Unmitigated climate change would, in the long term, be *likely* to

44 R. Myneni, C. Keeling, C. Tucker et al., 'Increased Plant Growth in the Northern High Latitudes from 1981 to 1991' (1997) 386 *Nature*, 698–702. https://doi.org/10.1038/386698a0.

45 Earth-Logs, 'Thawing Permafrost Release of Carbon and the Role of Iron' <https://earthlogs.org/2020/12/28/thawing-permafrost-release-of-carbon-and-the-role-of-iron/> accessed 29 January 2021.

exceed the capacity of natural, managed and human systems to adapt. Reliance on adaptation alone could eventually lead to a magnitude of climate change to which effective adaptation is not possible, or will only be available at very high social, environmental and economic costs'.[46] In 2021 the IPCC released their sixth report showing that there is unequivocal evidence that human influence has warmed the atmosphere, the oceans and the land:

A.1 It is unequivocal that human influence has warmed the atmosphere, ocean and land. Widespread and rapid changes in the atmosphere, ocean, cryosphere and biosphere have occurred.
A.2 The scale of recent changes across the climate system as a whole and the present state of many aspects of the climate system are unprecedented over many centuries to many thousands of years.
A.3 Human-induced climate change is already affecting many weather and climate extremes in every region across the globe. Evidence of observed changes in extremes such as heatwaves, heavy precipitation, droughts, and tropical cyclones, and, in particular, their attribution to human influence, has strengthened since the Fifth Assessment Report (AR5).
A.4 Improved knowledge of climate processes, paleoclimate evidence and the response of the climate system to increasing radiative forcing gives a best estimate of equilibrium climate sensitivity of 3°C, with a narrower range compared to AR5.[47]

António Guterres, the UN secretary-general, warned:[48] '[This report] is a code red for humanity. The alarm bells are deafening, and the evidence is irrefutable: greenhouse gas emissions from fossil fuel burning and deforestation are choking our planet and putting billions of people at immediate risk.'[49]

There has been for some time a pollution epidemic, but the climate change crisis has eclipsed this. Debate about corporate governance structures typically excludes issues of climate change and has shied away from the idea of internalising environmental costs such as carbon emissions and plastic waste.[50] In the meantime,

46 IPCC Core Writing Team, R. K. Pachauri and A. Reisinger (eds), *Climate Change 2007: Contribution of Working Groups I, II and III to the Fourth Assessment Report of the Intergovernmental Panel on Climate Change* (IPCC 2088) <http://www.ipcc.ch/pdf/assessment-report/ar4/syr/ar4_syr.pdf> accessed 16 October 2012.

47 <https://www.ipcc.ch/report/ar6/wg1/downloads/report/IPCC_AR6_WGI_Headline_Statements.pdf> accessed 28 August 2021.

48 <https://news.un.org/en/story/2021/04/1090382> accessed 28 August 2021.

49 *Guardian* <https://www.theguardian.com/science/2021/aug/09/humans-have-caused-unprecedented-and-irreversible-change-to-climate-scientists-warn>accessed 28 August 2021.

50 *Plastic Ocean: Art and Science, Responses of Marine Pollution*, Ingeborg Reichle, De Gruyter, 2021.

the loss of biodiversity is terrifying. In 2021, the UK government issued a report titled 'The Economics of Biodiversity: The Dasgupta Review.[51] The report shows that although many people have a high standard of living, this comes with a high cost for the environment, specifically in decreased biodiversity, and one reason for this is a flawed system of counting growth using GDP: 'As a measure of economic activity, GDP is indispensable in short-run macroeconomic analysis and management, but it is wholly unsuitable for appraising investment projects and identifying sustainable development. Nor was GDP intended by economists who fashioned it to be used for those two purposes. An economy could record a high rate of growth of GDP by depreciating its assets . . . in recent decades eroding natural capital has been precisely the means the world economy has deployed for enjoying what is routinely celebrated as "economic growth"'.[52] The founding father of economics wrote about the wealth of nations, not the GDP of nations. The idea of wealth that is developed in the Review is, not surprisingly, a lot richer than the one Adam Smith was able to fashion, but his identification of assets as the objects of interest was exactly right.

Market failure

The power of 'capital', specifically MNEs,[53] is so pervasive that even international law has been captured.[54] The neoliberal fixation of privatisation has allowed the 'market' to set its own regulations and even meddle with schemes, such as carbon trading, which are supposed to ameliorate climate change.

The Stern Review said that the negative effects of externalising greenhouse gases is 'the greatest and widest-ranging market failing ever seen.'[55] Using the *annual ceiling of 14.5 Gt* CO_2,

> if emissions were frozen at the *current level of 29 Gt* CO_2 we would need two planets to continue to survive. However, some countries are running a less sustainable account than others. With 15 percent of the world population, rich countries are using 90 percent of the sustainable budget. How many planets would we need if developing countries were to follow the example of these countries?[56]

51 <https://assets.publishing.service.gov.uk/government/uploads/system/uploads/attachment_data/file/957291/Dasgupta_Review_-_Full_Report.pdf> accessed 11 February 2021.

52 <https://assets.publishing.service.gov.uk/government/uploads/system/uploads/attachment_data/file/957291/Dasgupta_Review_-_Full_Report.pdf, forward> accessed 11 February 2021.

53 U. Beck, *Power in the Global Age* (Polity Press 2005).

54 Beck ibid and see Anna Grear, *Redirecting Human Rights* (Palgrave Macmillan 2010).

55 Stern, N, on the Economics of Climate Change: Executive Summary 2006 <www.sternreview.org.uk> accessed 16 October 2012, see also N. Stern, *The Economics of Climate Change: The Stern Review* (CUP 2007).

56 United Development Programme, *How Many Planets* <http://hdr.undp.org/en/statistics/data/climatechange/planets/> accessed 16 October 2012; Dieter Helm and Cameron Hepburn (eds), *The Economics and Politics of Climate Change* (OUP 2009).

Anthropogenic climate change is real: 'we have slowly, and at times reluctantly, realised that humanity has become an active agent in the reshaping of physical climates around the world, so our cultural, social, political and ethical practices are reinterpreting what climate change means.'[57] Principle 12 of the Rio Declaration requires states to cooperate to promote a supportive and open international economic system and demands, 'trade policy measures for environmental purposes should not constitute a means of arbitrary or unjustifiable discrimination or a disguised restriction on international trade'.[58] Agenda 21 of the Rio Declaration also says that international trade has been inequitable and this has been one reason for environmental degradation of the planet. It is a paradox that the Declaration also believed in the logic of trade liberalisation particularly because it would be good for the world. Elliott argues that one reason for the argument is a semantic one; the rhetoric of international trade does not allow 'protection' against nations. She says,

> Can environmental protection issues be accommodated within the logic of trade liberalisation? Can trade liberalisation contribute to overcoming environmental degradation or is it likely to contribute to further environmental degradation? Is it possible in trade liberalisation discourse, to distinguish between environmental protection and environmental protectionism? . . . These are important because 'trade rules and agreements are a major determinant of how natural resources are used, what pressures are placed on the environment and who benefits from the huge money flows . . . that cross borders with the exchange of goods . . . At a normative level, answers to these questions rest in part on different views about 'protection' – a 'pejorative term' for the trade community.[59]

Deregulatory, free market policies and environmental protection usually have conflicting aims, although some scholars hold that a market solution to the environmental emergency can be found. Paterson promotes a privatised market mechanism, arguing for a new paradigm known as 'global environmental governance'.

> While such governance is commonly seen in terms of a tragedy of the commons arising out of the anarchy of the interstate system, it is more fruitful to analyse these dynamics in relating to a conception of global capitalism. While efforts to govern global environmental problems started out as attempts to

57 Mike Hulme, *Why We Disagree about Climate Change* (CUP 2009) xxv.

58 UNCED 1992 *Report of the UN Conference on Environment and Development Annex 1, Rio Declaration and Development*, A/CONE. 151/26 (Vol. 1), 12 August.

59 L. Elliott, *The Global Politics of the Environment* (2nd edn, Palgrave Macmillan 2004), citing S. Postel and C. Flavin, 'Reshaping the Global Economy' in Lester R. Brown et al., (eds), *State of the World* (Norton & Co 1991); K. Berlin and T. Lang, 'Trade and the Environment' (2018) 16(4) *The Washington Quarterly*, Autumn, 35–51.

> regulate the side-effects of existing form of capitalism development, they have increasingly been organised to channel capitalism in novel directions.[60]

Indeed, climate change is a new sort of 'pure public commons', since no state or individual can fashion a solution. However, it is clear that interstate rivals can cooperate in treaties, accords and protocols.[61] However, Klein is scathing about the Paris Agreement,[62] writing about 'leaders' delivering 'passionate and moving speeches about the imperative to respect the Paris Climate Agreement and make the planet great again (France's Emmanuel Macron, Canada's Justin Trudeau, and so many others) but who then shower subsidies, handouts, and licences on the fossil fuel and agribusinesses giants driving ecological breakdown'.[63]

Very similar criticisms of the 2021 COP26[64] have been published. The scientists agree that the agreement has not decreased the threat of 2°C (or more).[65]

Paterson shows that global governance has been guided by the Washington Consensus and the fetishism of markets today and the obsession of growth.[66] Now privatisation has gone further, in a 'dynamic change where standards and regulations are obeyed not by governments but in market rules by the market for the market'.[67] So pervasive is the market[68] that governments worship the neoliberal discourse which believes that laws and regulations are injurious, and any solution that is needed must come from the market, which means that international law is becoming privatised. Paterson believes that market mechanisms are 'shaping business practice, potentially significantly. Should the variety of schemes to shape investment practice with regard to CO2 emissions – the Carbon Disclosure, Project, the Global Reporting Initiative, UNEP's Financial Industries Initiative, and so on – succeed in generating a norm which treats CO2-intensive firms as financial liabilities, then substantial change in investment in renewable energy can be expected'.

60 Paterson, Mathew, 'Global Governance for Sustainable Capitalism? The Political Economy of Global Environment Governance' in L. Adger, W. Neil, and Jordan Andrew (eds), *Governing Sustainability* (CUP 2009) 99.

61 Brown Katerina, 'Human Development and Environmental Governance: A Reality Check' in L. Adger and Jordan Andrew (eds), *Governing Sustainability* (CUP 2009); Mike Hulme *Why We Disagree About Climate Change* (CUP 2009).

62 UN, Paris Agreement <https://unfccc.int/process-and-meetings/the-paris-agreement/the-paris-agreement> accessed 25 March 2020.

63 Naomi Klein, *On Fire* (Allen Lane 2019) 7.

64 The UN Conference of the Parties (COP) the 26th session <https://ukcop26.org> accessed 8 December 2021.

65 Ehson Masood and Jeff Tollefson, 'Cop26 Hasn't Solved the Problem: Scientists React to UN Climate Change Deal' <https://www.nature.com/articles/d41586-021-03431-4> accessed 8 December 2021.

66 Paterson (n 60) 107.

67 Paterson cites instances like the International Organization for Standardization's 1400014000, the Forest Stewardship Councils, id page 109.

68 Harvey Cox, *The Market as God* (HUP 2016).

Even if the initiatives succeed to ameliorate climate change, the damage wreaked will be significant, since the companies involved will have *carte blanche* to set their own standards and corporate governance rules, 'privatisation not only entails firms attempting to self-regulate to organise and legitimate their growth'. The state will lose power and the only lever left will be to find 'environmental NGOs to fill the void left by declining regulation by states, through developing schemes to put pressures on firms to change practices'.[69]

It is unlikely these market solutions will work and effectively change the complacency shown toward climate change. Indeed, there is already an abundance of carbon trading markets,[70] but many commentators believe that financial emission markets are simply a way of making money, rather than ameliorating the problem of climate catastrophe.

> Alongside the development of proposals for emissions trading schemes at global and national level was a positive explosion of activity by financial markets actors . . . What explains this explosion of activity is that, while emissions trading can be understood in terms of economic efficiency, it very definitely operates through the creation of new markets in which firms can develop economic strategies and secondary markets. In fact, the future markets in this instance existed significantly before the real markets . . . Emissions trading as a project has been, and continues to be, propelled by realisation by powerful financial actors that here was a new commodity to be sold, new profits to be made.[71]

Similar projects are criticised in the same way, including the Joint Implementation and the Clean Development Mechanism.[72] This is clear evidence that the purely financial efficiency of companies will continue to generate profit for them, and growth will be enhanced at the price of an unhabitable planet. The inefficiency principle is clear in this instance.

Corporate governance mechanisms could affect the implementation of sustainable business; so far there are lamentably few effective strategies.[73] Although the sovereignty of states has been severely compromised recently, national governments have some power to act in regulating companies. There are growing international regulations to restrict emissions, but national corporate governance should also be

69 Paterson (n 60) 109–10.

70 Including the European Trading market, Australian, BP, etc. See S. Pulver, 'Making Sense of Corporate Environmentalism: An Environmental Contestation Approach to Analyzing the Causes and Consequences of the Climate Change Policy in the Oil Industry' (2007) 20 *Organisation and Environment* 1–40.

71 Paterson (n 60) 111–12.

72 Ibid.

73 P. Sands, *Principles of International Environmental Law* (CUP 2009); for a European perspective see Sjafell (n 41) especially on pages 227–8.

part of the picture if the planet is to be saved. This would entail embedding environmental policies into corporate governance, and the neoliberal model of corporate governance would have to be significantly changed. Later, some solutions will be assayed, but partly as a result of anti-scientific propaganda some 'solutions' are either diluted or abandoned.

9 Nature as a commodity

Humans value the environment as a commodity and try to own it

A neoliberal approach of sustainability; costing the environment

The foundation of this neoliberal economic approach is the desire to avoid the problem of externalities by turning 'the environment into a commodity which can be analysed just like other commodities'.[1] The motive may be to retain the economists' role as governmental advisers[2] or to seek genuine protection for the environment. It is clear that environmental resources have been hitherto free or undervalued, and the resources have been significantly overused.

In valuing the environment, it is argued that all aspects of the environment can be valued with a money yardstick.[3] This idea is supported by the view that human life is valued by the amount of resources a society will use to save it. Arguably this is unsound – it confuses the *resources available to achieve a certain aim* with the *value of what will be lost if the aim is not achieved* – but it is, nonetheless, often used. The World Bank coordinated efforts to set common measures, such as the value of ecosystems and their 'services' for humans – from relaxation to clean air and fertile land. This initiative is part a UN idea called 'The Economics of Ecosystem and Biodiversity'. The EU version of the initiative can be found in the EU's environmental documents.[4]

Neoliberal economists try to understand the economy using cost–benefit analysis, but the costs and benefits are very narrowly defined. A recent proliferation of economic models is vying to understand climate change and create the best framework. Hulme argues that one reason that there is disagreement about climate change is the plethora of philosophies around value. The neoliberal economists value the environment as a rational consumer, while ecological economists focus on environmental goods and services which are offered by the

1 P. Sands, *Principles of International Environmental Law* (CUP 2009).

2 Ibid 69.

3 D. Pearce, A. Markandya, and E. Barbier, *Blueprint for a Green Economy* (Earthscan 1989) 53.

4 EU <https://ec.europa.eu/environment/nature/biodiversity/economics/index_en.htm> accessed 18 June 2020.

DOI: 10.4324/9781315386782-12

climate and which are threatened by climate change.[5] There is no agreed global framework.

However, the dominant paradigm in Western capitalist societies today is neo-liberal economics. This system believes in an apparently simplistic attribution of value to environmental commodities, but sometimes 'mitigated by an attempt to factor into the equation not just "use" value but 'option value (the value of preserving something in case the consumer wishes to use it)'. Bequest value is the value of options for future generations. Existence value is the 'sentimental' value placed on the existence of whales and so on'.[6] Many scholars, including Jacobs, wish to reformulate a new valuation arrangement where the environment is more significant than money.

The intractable complications of valuation were at the heart of the Stern Review, which was an attempt to use economic analysis to find some policy recommendations for climate change. The review used cost–benefit analysis; however, it was predicated on questions such as risk and uncertainty and was therefore more nuanced than many economists expected[7] – although there are many disputes about the details.[8] Framing the climate change problem as a risk assessment, Professor Stern argued in 2021 that many economists have overvalued the risk for young people from the environmental emergency because many young people will die or be displaced as temperatures rise.[9] In an address Stern argued that investment to recover from the COVID pandemic is an opportunity to transform countries' economies to achieve net-zero greenhouse gas emissions using rapid technology change. This must be driven governmental regulation:

> the approaches to examining economic policy towards climate change that are standard in the economics literature have failed to grasp the nature and pace of the necessary economic transformation, and have biased results against strong ambition . . . that economic analyses of climate change should capture extreme risk; recognise that many relevant markets have important failures, that crucial markets may be absent, and that there are limits on the ability of government to correct these market failures or absences; embody rapid change in the structure of economies and technologies; examine rapid changes in individuals' beliefs and preferences;

5 Mike Hulme, *Why We Disagree about Climate Change* (CUP 2009) 112.

6 M. Jacobs, 'The Limits to Neoclassicism' in M. Redclift and T. Benton (eds), *Social Theory and the Global Environment* (Routledge 1994) 70.

7 Hulme (n 6) 125.

8 N. Stern, *The Economics of Climate Change* (CUP 2007) and see now <https://assets.publishing.service.gov.uk/government/uploads/system/uploads/attachment_data/file/957291/Dasgupta_Review_-_Full_Report.pdf> accessed 11 February.

9 'Climate Crisis: Economists 'Grossly Undervalue Young Lives', Warns Stern' <https://www.theguardian.com/environment/2021/oct/26/climate-crisis-economists-grossly-undervalue-young-lives-warns-stern> accessed 9 December 2021.

> and take into account the unequal distribution of risks and impacts, across and within generations.[10]

Hulme accepts that non-economic value of our world is incredibly hard to assess, and framing the problem as a risk assessment does not significantly facilitate the answers:

> For example, if a breeding site for a rare migratory bird species was lost in one country because of sea-level rise, but was then re-established in another country, how does one evaluate the monetary cost of this change in location? Does a loss of wildlife in one country offset the gain somewhere else? Or if snowy winters in a mid-latitude country no longer occur because of climate change, what would be (lost) monetary value of the experience of children playing in the snow? And with respect to the damage that might be caused by major disruption to some fracture of the climate system – such as an irreversible change in the south Asian monsoon – how does one incorporate the (presumably) large but unknown social costs associated with such a (presumably) unlikely outcome?[11]

These are intractable problems indeed – but there is more. If it is possible to adapt to climate change, there will also be costs.

In ethical parlance, there are extremely stark choices to be made – particularly in the field of intergenerational problems, where humans' lives will have to be balanced between each other.[12] Will a human life in a developing country have notionally less value than a human life in a developed country?[13]

Free will, property rights and an absence of Gaia philosophy

One theological stream shows how deluded humans are in believing that they can control nature. Freeman argues that the Franciscan 17th-century thinkers believed Christianity, as portrayed in the Gospels, was hostile to worldly wealth and power. The medieval ideas concerned ownership and control.[14] The Franciscans wished 'to submit themselves wholly to God by giving up all their worldly goods, including

10 N. Stern, 'A Time for Action on Climate Change and a Time for Change in Economics' <https://www.lse.ac.uk/granthaminstitute/publication/a-time-for-action-on-climate-change-and-a-time-for-change-in-economics/> accessed 10 December 2021.

11 Ibid 118.

12 And between animals; see Nicole Hassoun, 'Free Trade and the Environment' (2008) 22 *Public Affairs Quarterly* 4.

13 Samuel Fankhauser, Richard S. J. Tol, and David W. Pearce, 'Extensions and Alternatives to Climate Change Impact Valuation: On the Critique of IPCC Working Group III's Impact Estimates' (1998) *Environment and Development Economics* 3, 59–81.

14 Ibid.

control (*dominium*) of their own "property will" '.[15] These ideas were challenged by papacy and the Dominicans, who argued (conveniently) that it is impossible to live without at least food and drink, so the Franciscans' traditions were flawed. The Franciscans therefore posited a distinction between 'subjective' and 'objective' rights:

> Franciscans posited a radical disjunction between the individual subject and the world of things, in contrast with the philosophy of Aquinas, in which the individual was an integral part of the universal order. The roots of the liberal Western approach to human rights have been traced to this pre-capitalist debate.[16]

In 1328 Pope John XXII issued the bull *quia vir reprobus*, rejecting the Franciscan distinction between *ius* and *dominium*. The will of individuals was inviolable; their only duty was to use goods well. This instigated the slide to materialism, by dividing objects between good things and bad things.[17] At the same time during the Enlightenment[18] (from the late 17th century) in Europe, the concept of autonomy flourished, eventually turning into a philosophy of liberty and freedom for all humans, Earlier,

> Francisco de Vitoria suggested that liberty had an absolute value, even if it were not directed towards the good. It was better that the subject be able to direct himself towards his perceived good than that he should be directed towards a real good by an external agency. Right could therefore be equated with *dominium*, liberty and spirituality, or with nature as that faculty justifying action which was the result of each individual's inclination to its own good.[19]

As the human rights theory flourished, so did the Dominican theorists' ability to degrade the purity of the Franciscans' vow of poverty. They first did this by positing that since all humans had to drink and eat, the monks were wrong in their conception that all possessions were immoral; therefore, people were able to *choose* which possessions were moral or immoral, using the new power to own their *selves*.

Christian theology's acceptance that humans could have the right to possess and trade things subsequently enabled human choice; enjoying and disposing of things

15 Ibid.

16 Ibid.

17 The idea has been revived because of the climate change catastrophe. Many argue that we will need to revisit our concept of growth as a beneficial idea – and, with this, a different model of development. See David Pilling, *The Growth Delusion* (Bloomsbury 2018); Tim Jackson, *Prosperity Without Growth* (Earthscan 2011); Kate Raworth, *Doughnut Economics* (Random House 2017).

18 British Library, 'The Enlightenment' <https://www.bl.uk/restoration-18th-century-literature/articles/the-enlightenment> accessed 20 June 2020.

19 M. Freeman, 'Beyond Capitalism and Socialism' in J. Dine and A. Fagan (eds), *Human Rights and Capitalism* (Edward Elgar 2006) page 10.

was understood as rooted in the divine creation of human freedom. These ideas paved the foundation of rationality, leading to the Enlightenment thinkers and utilitarian theories. It is this concept of *entitlement* to own goods (including resources, like air, that are normally considered a natural occurrence and available to all) that neoliberal economists has corrupted, using aggressive utilitarian ideas. Once trading was liberated from divine norms, humans were free from inhibitions and able to possess goods and services without limits, fuelled by a discourse of rational choice. Human exceptionalism has been rife since Aristotle, who believed other animals and environmental features lacked souls and that humans were therefore able to exploit them. Liberty and consumerism, and human rights and property rights, are thus tightly bound up with Christian values. The fact that the values were degraded into aggressive capitalism and consumerism is just one way in which philosophies can degenerate into extremism, fuelling the belief that unlimited growth is the only way that humans can develop.

Expunging human exceptionalism: absolute property rights are an illusion

Gaia theory tries to imagine what the outcome for earth would be if humans served the earth rather than other humans. From anthropology, history and ongoing cultural practices it is clear that indigenous[20] humans replenished Gaia:[21] 'In the early years of Indian–White relations, Native people saw land as a shared resource rather than a commodity.'[22]

The Gaia ideas 'put [humans] in our proper place as part of the Earth system – not the owners, managers, commissars or people in charge'.[23] Although Lovelock has suggested interventions in planetary affairs, his important contribution is to understand that any human plan should be viewed with humility:

> The Earth has not evolved solely for our benefit and any changes we make to it are at our own risk. This way of thinking makes clear that we have no special human rights; we are merely one of the partner species in the great enterprise of Gaia.[24]

In contrast to human exceptionalism, the Tantric Buddhist concept of *tathāgatagarbha* teaches that the Buddha-nature can be found in other animals and some plants.[25] It is a doctrine that affirms that each sentient being has potential to be like Buddha. Dogen (1200–1253) taught that the entire earth had Buddha-nature.

20 <https://www.theguardian.com/environment/2021/mar/25/indigenous-peoples-by-far-the-best-guardians-of-forests-un-report> accessed 27 March 2021.

21 Jan Pettit, *Utes: The Mountain People* (Johnson Books 1990); Thomas King, *The Inconvenient Indian* (Anchor Canada 2012).

22 Thomas King, *The Inconvenient Indian* (Anchor Canada 2012) 161; and see S. Banner, *How the Indians Lost Their Land* (HUP 2007).

23 James Lovelock, *A Final Warning: The Vanishing Face of Gaia* (Penguin 2010) 6.

24 Ibid.

25 John S. Strong, *Buddhisms* (Oneworld 2015) 288.

The Gaia concept of a living earth can be tested against a number of propositions. Perhaps the most critical one is the discourse of property rights. The concept of property rights has placed huge tension on the planet by pretending that humans are able to own things; indeed, that humans *should* appropriate all of the resources of the planet, as a duty. Gaia theory reverses this understanding by arguing that humans have obligations to the earth and therefore have no property *rights* at all; only a duty to replenish any resources that humans use.

Can the Gaia theory deliver social justice?

Can a Gaian model deliver social justice through legal devices like the rights of nature? Will this resolve the distributional issues? This chapter argues that social and distributional issues can be solved by focusing on the protection of the earth. Humans must be served by Gaia rather than the wants of humans. If the earth is to be replenished, humans may not extract resources in an unlimited way, and any extraction must be done in harmony with each other. Why? Because if inequality is rife, conflict and arguments will increase the likeliness of imbalance between the planet and its biodiversity. Extracting too much will enrich the rich but is a dangerous path leading to dissent, conflict and denigration of the planet. Humans should serve Gaia cooperatively, which means social harmony is crucial. Instead of inventing a legal construct of rights to serve humans, humans must devise an order of property rights that includes *all* nature, including animals (including humans). All manifestations of the earth should be created with the intention of replenishing Gaia.

How could legal rights be formulated? To consider this, perhaps it is possible to utilise Boyd's thesis on the rights of nature, in which he shows the arrogance of the concepts that lie behind the property rights discourse. This arrogance must be taken down first and replaced with an inclusive design of the earth.[26]

> Our ongoing use and misuse of other animals, species, and nature is rooting in three entrenched and relating ideas. The first is anthropocentrism – the widespread human belief that we are separate, and superior to, the rest of the natural world . . . the second is that everything in nature, animate and inanimate, constitutes our property, which we have the right to use as we see fit. The third idea is that we can and should pursue limitless economic growth as the paramount objective of modern society.[27]

Einstein captured human exceptionalism well:

> A human being is a part of a whole, called by us the 'Universe'– a part limited in time and space. He experiences himself, his thoughts, and feelings, as something separated from the rest – a kind of optical delusion of his

26 David Boyd, *The Rights of Nature* (ECW Press 2017).
27 Ibid xxiii–xxiii.

> consciousness. This delusion is a kind of prison for us, restricting us to our personal desires and to affection for a few persons nearest us. Our task must be to free ourselves from this prison by widening our circles of compassion to embrace all living creatures and the whole of nature in its beauty.[28]

The extreme focus on humans is not universal. Writing in *The Guardian*, Julian Brave NoiseCat[29] says:

> While indigenous values, beliefs and practices are as diverse as indigenous people themselves, they find common roots in a relationship to land and water radically different from the notion of property. For indigenous people, land and water are regarded as sacred, living relatives, ancestors, places of origin or any combination of the above.[30]

The neoliberal concept of property rights and human exceptionalism is alien for many indigenous people. To indigenous people, humans are not sacred; rather, they are part of Gaia. Humans are custodians of the earth, and therefore owe duties to the land. Legally, this is difficult because of legal processes that are embedded in Western property rights, including appropriation and ownership. However, the apparent dichotomy between the two worldviews is not as stark as it seems; a more subtle grasp of the Western concept of property rights shows that the rhetoric around absolute ownership is a mirage.

Absolute property rights are an illusion

The rhetoric used in discussing property rights often ignores two aspects of property rights: one is the importance of always keeping in mind the insight that property rights are, in essence, rights against other people. This means that all property rights govern power relations between people. If property rights are seen as a person having rights over a thing, this ignores the fact that the rights actually lie against other persons, a right to exclude and so forth. This means that the role that property rights play in wealth distribution is ignored because the person-to-person relationship is clouded by the person-to-thing discussion. Thus,

> A theorist who supposes that ownership interests in objects may be justified, say, by a natural-rights argument, but then ignores questions of

28 Albert Einstein, 1950 letter, cited in David Boyd, *The Rights of Nature* (ECW Press 2017).

29 Julian Brave NoiseCat is director of Green New Deal Strategy for Data for Progress, a think tank, and narrative change director for the Natural History Museum, an artist and activist collective. He is also a correspondent for Real America with Jorge Ramos and contributing editor for *Canadian Geographic.*

30 Julian Brave NoiseCat, 'The Western Idea of Property Rights Is Flawed. Indigenous Peoples Have It Right' (*The Guardian*, 27 March 2017) <https://www.theguardian.com/commentisfree/2017/mar/27/western-idea-private-property-flawed-indigenous-peoples-have-it-right> accessed 4 July 2019.

> wealth-distribution, tells only half the story. The same is true, in the opposite direction of one who advocates a certain distribution of 'resources' but who neglects the question whether person-thing ownership relations are to form part of a property-institutional design.[31]

It is because rights over things can never be absolute but rather made up of a web of rights and responsibilities operating interpersonally that the debate resonates with issues of wealth distribution and power relations. If property ownership meant that I have absolute dominion over three beans and the right to use them as I wished, and you have similar rights over five beans, the property distribution debates would exist, but they would be a mere matter of counting. Do I deserve more beans than you? Because the reality of property relations is that I may exclude some (but not others) from use of an item and I may use that item only in non-harmful ways, the discussion of rights and duties becomes infinitely more complex and balanced. It is important, then, to understand what the nature of the bundle of rights called property rights actually consists of.

Harris argues that the Hohfeldian 'bundle of rights' concept, which emphasises rights against other persons rather than rights over things, can best be expressed on an 'ownership' spectrum, which enables an individual to have more or less exclusivity over the use of the property and more or less power to use it in designated ways. The concept of ownership is therefore seen as firmly rooted in social expectations, which have come to be embedded in legal rules. These include '(1) trespassory rules; (2) property-limitation rules; (3) expropriation rules; (4) appropriation rules. (There may be as well property-duty rules and property-privilege rules).'[32] This understanding means that attempting to infuse a particular side of the balance of interests with more weight, by claiming it is a 'property' right, is mere rhetoric designed to appeal to the conceptions underlying a particular society's view of the standing of 'property'. Of considerable interest in this context is Harris's examination of 'expansive' definitions of property, particularly economists' expansive use of 'property rights'. This is property right as including 'any right – whether Hohfeldian claim-right, privilege, power or immunity – concerning the use of a resource, where "resource" means all bodily and mental capacities of the right holder. In other words, all rights are property rights.'[33]

This expansion of the 'property rights' conception is, according to Harris, based on the conflation of owning and ownership. For Harris,

> it is one thing to say that a person is vested with ('owns') either a right or a bundle of rights; it is another to say that what he is vested with is that particular set of open-ended privileges and powers over a resource which counts as an ownership interest.[34]

31 Harris (n 33, chapter 5) 141.

32 James Harris, *Property and Justice* (Clarendon 1996) 141.

33 Ibid 146.

34 Harris (n 32) 147.

'Conventional' property (bank accounts, shares, etc.) is 'cashable rights', 'because expropriation and appropriation rules apply to them – they pass into a bankrupt's estate and they can be inherited. . . . Cashable rights are the subject of real markets'.[35] Such an understanding would exclude 'social rights', such as the right to use public spaces, which some have claimed as property rights. While Harris is not, in principle, opposed to this extended use of property, he does not see it as helpful:

> By all means let rights of all kinds be analysed in these terms. Calling all rights 'property rights' is, however, anything but an aid to clarity for the enterprises at hand since both the analyst and the reader must constantly remind themselves that they are not talking about 'property' as ordinarily understood.

More important, perhaps, is the insight that the use of 'property rights' is a rhetoric that will resonate with the reader according to the 'meaning' of property in a particular society:

> The plausibility of rhetorical expedients of this sort is difficult to assess. They depend on the way you suppose 'property' will ring in the ears of an addressee and on his willingness to fall in line with the terminological shift. Imagine the following dialogue:

EGALITARIAN:	For reasons of a, b and c, I maintain that everyone ought to have an enforceable right to work.
CONSERVATIVE:	For reasons of X, Y and Z, I disagree with you.
EGALITARIAN:	But you believe that property ought to be protected, don't you?
CONSERVATIVE:	I do.
EGALITARIAN:	Well the right to work is property.
CONSERVATIVE RESPONSE 1:	No it isn't.
CONSERVATIVE RESPONSE 2:	Why didn't you say that before? Of course, I now change my view to yours.[36]

The power of the property rights discourse cannot be underestimated, and legal processes are full of assumptions based on these positions. In the example, the right to work is put forward as a 'property right'. It would follow that in neoliberal speak it should be fiercely protected, and therefore can only be interfered with care and probably with compensation following. In a situation of a dispute between workers

35 Ibid 149.
36 Ibid 160.

and companies, it is likely to have the effect of a redistribution of wealth to poorer communities. If the workers have a *right to work*, the power balance between the shareholders (the 'owners' of the company) shifts. This semantic change between a right to work is the opposite of the rhetoric of shareholders owning the company.

We therefore need to closely examine the effects resulting from any expanded property rhetoric. As Harris notes:

> The concept-expanding arguments . . . concede, at least arguendo, that property as conventionally understood really deserves prestige and that the rights contended for have an importance which is merely parallel to conventional proprietary interests . . . [the arguments] make too much of property.[37]

It is clear that MNCs are one of the powerful actors in the global order. As such, to reach a proper understanding of what companies should be doing (and of better governance), it is vital to explode the 'shareholder-owner' myth. By doing so, it is possible to see the company as a freestanding structure and create mechanisms to reflect its responsibilities towards those it has power over due to its managers' exercise of property rights.[38]

As Harris points out, identifying a property right does not identify its parameters; it merely appeals to the importance of 'property'. The 'property concept' tells us nothing about the limitations to be imposed. Any recognition of property rights involves a bestowal of the right on one or more persons, a corresponding limitation of the rights of others and limitations on the owner's use of the right. Where the balance should be struck cannot be deduced from the 'nature' of the rights; rather, it needs to be considered as a distributional issue of social justice.

Spectrum of responsibilities: more power, more responsibility?

Focus on property rights tends to divert attention away from the duties and responsibilities associated with them. The exercise of ownership over anything brings both moral and legal responsibilities. If I own a poisonous snake, I have both a legal and a moral responsibility not to allow it to roam freely around a crowded shopping area. Rights over things give me rights against others (they may not steal my snake), but they also give me responsibilities towards others (I may not injure them by failing to confine my snake). Great attention has been paid to the 'spectrum' of *rights* that property ownership brings, but how is the spectrum of *responsibilities* structured? Again, it is important to bear in mind that just as these responsibilities are *towards* other persons, so are the rights *against* other persons.

The spectrum of ownership rights might be seen as a sliding scale; they give rights ranging from the nearly absolute (I am holding in my hand a bun, which

37 Harris (n 32) 161.

38 Although, as Paddy Ireland notes, this will be a difficult process. Paddy Ireland, 'Property and Contract in Contemporary Corporate Theory' (2004) *Legal Studies* 451.

I am about to eat, thus exercising my absolute right to prevent you eating it) to a contingent right to inherit an incorporeal hereditament, which will take a gaggle of lawyers to unravel and gives me very limited power over others. The spectrum of responsibilities may also resemble a sliding scale, with the heaviest responsibilities placed on owners whose property rights give them the greatest power over other people. Thus, the ownership of the snake brings with it the possibility of exercising lethal power over others – and, consequently, heavy responsibility. Where ownership of inanimate items is the issue, there is clearly a similar responsibility (for example, not to use my knife to stab someone). What about 'neutral' items, which have no immediately obvious harm potential? In those cases, scarcity and necessity factors must come into play; where items are both scarce and necessary for a dignified human existence, ownership of the power to exclude others must bear a concomitant responsibility not to unfairly wield that power. The inequality of power has been a continuous theme throughout this book. The following section argues that wherever great power is exercised over others by virtue of property rights, the consequent moral responsibilities are greater.

If there is to be any concept of individual property rights, these must be very limited, since the overriding responsibility for replenishing the earth trumps the right to property. Gaia cannot be served by wars or disruptions because of the amount of extraction necessary to promote wars and the inevitable disruption which increases inequality. Sharing and fair distribution between humans is key to a healthy planet. The inherent distributional implications contained within any concept of property ownership causes Harris to wrestle with the intractable question of the 'just' distribution of property. This may be a red herring, however; Harris himself points out that the major importance of unequal property distribution is the potential for domination. In a brief but compelling analysis, Richard Wilkinson shows how important inequality is. In *Mind the Gap*,[39] he demonstrates that 'inequality kills' and 'that income inequality affects health independently of average living standards, of the proportion of the population in absolute poverty, of expenditure on medical care, and of the prevalence of smoking'.[40] Further, inequality brings in its wake a significant increase in violence and social dislocation. It may well be that the extreme inequality of distribution causes unrest in society, not only because of simple envy of material possessions but also because of a system that perpetuates privilege and seeks to exclude the powerless from having a voice. Thus, an education system that continually perpetrates the rule of the moneyed classes may engender despair and exclusion in the remainder of the population.[41] Similarly, a world that refuses to permit the poorest to develop or have a say in how the planet's affairs are run will have the same effect.[42] This is now accepted as one of the prime

39 Richard Wilkinson, *Mind the Gap: Hierarchies, Health and Human Evolution* (Wiedenfield and Nicholson 2000).

40 Ibid 11; and see Thomas Picketty, *Capital* (HUP 2014).

41 Wilkinson (n 40).

42 Amartya Sen, *Development as Freedom* (OUP 1999).

indicators of poverty. Thus, justice may not require a mathematical 'slicing of the cake' to ensure equality of resources, beyond provision of basic needs, but it may well require checks on the use of power, which access to material things brings.

It can be seen, therefore, that problems are often caused not by the concept of property ownership itself but by the potential property ownership has to create unequal power relations. Thus, 'to concede a property relationship between one person and a thing, at any point along the property spectrum, is to negate the liberty of the rest of mankind to use the thing without the licence of the "owner" '.[43] The concept of property as power follows inexorably from the Hohfeldian/Honore/Harris understanding of property rights not as rights *over things* but as rights *against persons*. Inevitably, the property-as-power effect is exacerbated where there is huge inequality of property ownership:

> Theorists who deplore great inequality, in wealth-holdings and recommend measures to alleviate it often have in mind, not the social-psychological argument against wealth disparities . . . but rather inequality's resultant domination potential. It is not disparity in bank balances that matters. It is the influence over the lives of others which large property-holdings afford.[44]

So, property ownership brings power, and the greater the inequality of property ownership, the greater the domination potential. This is particularly true where the supply of particular goods is scarce:

> If the supply of objects like clothing, furniture and books is drastically restricted, those few who own them could dominate their fellows by the egocentric exercise of their ownership power to control use. On the other hand, where such chattels are widely available, the use-channelling and use-policing functions of ownership interests . . . as compared with costly and intrusive regimes of communal use, clearly outweigh such dangers of domination.[45]

These concepts are embedded in legal processes. How can these mechanisms be reformed in the light of the Gaia philosophy?

43 Harris (n 32) 264.
44 Ibid 265.
45 Ibid.

10 Property rights, animal rights and rights for nature

From property rights to animal rights and then rights for nature?

The prior chapter showed that property rights are a legal construct with significant consequences, not least that owners have the legal power to exclude others, therefore dominating them. In Western thought, based on a contractual model of bargaining, resources will be unequal, unless the poorer party has some protection. From that situation, this chapter will argue that not only should a poorer human party in a transaction have legal protection, for example, using a concept of good faith in contract, so too should animals be protected. Furthermore, this protection should be shorn of human exceptionalism, the idea that humans are different from other animals. For many years, jurisprudence recognised that non-human animals should be protected, but this patronising view has been challenged in some courts where the legal personality of non-human animals has been recognised. Non-human animals are normally considered as chattels, so indeed were slaves in the triangular slave trade.[1]

David Boyd's thesis is that human rights should be expanded to animal rights and rights for nature.[2] Legal concepts change slowly, and strong property rights can be eroded by the insight that ownership is a political tool to exclude poor parties. In this chapter, other radical ideas will be advocated and possibly normalised leading to a full reversal of Western thinking on property rights, especially the exceptionalism which allows the raping of the planet. Only then can the planet be healed using Gaian philosophy. There is now jurisprudence on animal rights, rights of nature and the legal personality of lakes, rivers and river basins. Slowly the law is accepting that humans must cooperate with nature. From considering rights of animals and crucially the legal personality of animals, some jurisprudence is recognising that some natural features should also have legal personality. One of the hurdles is, who will speak for the animal or the feature?

1 See the case *Zong* <https://www.blackpast.org/global-african-history/zong-massacre-1781/> accessed 10 February 2021.

2 See <https://igs.duke.edu/initiatives-global-asia-initiative-publications-and-presentations/"trans-species-listening-and> Edited by Jeffrey Nicolaisen, Ambika Aiyadurai, Prasenjit Duara accessed 14 February 2021.

DOI: 10.4324/9781315386782-13

The jurisprudence starts with the acceptance that animals should be protected in particular ways – for example, it is not acceptable to torture animals – so animals should also be protected by giving them rights. Boyd and Tom Regan agree and argue that humans use animals as a resource, and that this is unacceptable:

> The fundamental wrong is the system that allows us to view animals as *our resources,* here for *us* – to be eaten, or surgically manipulated, or exploited for sport or money. Once we accept this view of animals – as our resources – the rest is as predictable as it is regrettable.[3]

Discrimination

In Regan's book, *The Case for Animal Rights*,[4] he criticises Rawls's[5] 'contractualism' as a crude attempt to provide justice. Rawls argued that some clear discriminations like those against race and gender should be discarded during transactions to make sure that there will be no bias or prejudice. However, he is unable to say why some humans – those who are unable to contract – should be protected. This 'systematically denies that we have direct duties to those human beings who do not have a sense of justice – young children, for instance, and many mentally retarded humans.'[6] Regan argues that since most people accept that society has a duty to protect vulnerable humans because they are unable to contract, then there is no reason why animals should not have the same protection. Later in this chapter there are cases which explore the extent to which humans have a moral duty to protect animals and whether this protection should extend to other rights for nature, including rivers, estuaries and other features. However, it is important to interrogate the concept of value from a lens of neoliberalism driven by rational accumulation.

Neoliberalism is deficient because it misses the *inherent value* of individuals. Because the neoliberal paradigm only assesses the worth of objects in financial terms, 'Utilitarianism has no room for the equal rights of different individuals because it has no room for their equal inherent value or worth. What has value for the utilitarian is the satisfaction of an individual's interests, not the individual whose interests they are.'[7] Regan illustrates this deficiency by positing killing an aunt who is unpleasant and rich. Killing her will give many people benefits, so it

3 Tom Regan, 'A Case for Animal Rights' in M. W. Fox and L. D. Mickley (eds), *Advances in Animal Welfare Science* (The Humane Society of the United States 1986/87) 179 <https://animalstudiesrepository.org/cgi/viewcontent.cgi?article=1003&context=acwp_awap> accessed 31 July 2019, emphasis in the original.

4 Tom Regan, *The Case for Animal Rights* (Blackwell 2004).

5 John Rawls, *A Theory of Justice* (HUP 1971).

6 Tom Regan, 'A Case for Animal Rights' in M. W. Fox and L. D. Mickley (eds), *Advances in Animal Welfare Science* (The Humane Society of the United States 1986/87) 182 <https://animalstudiesrepository.org/cgi/viewcontent.cgi?article=1003&context=acwp_awap> accessed 31 July 2019.

7 Regan (n 4) 184.

passes the utilitarian test, but it is also morally repugnant. Regan's thesis is a moral argument; animals should be valued *for themselves*.

It is strange that this argument appears to still be controversial since this argument raged during Darwin's elucidation of evolution in *On the Origin of Species*, in 1859.[8] Although some people deny Darwin's theory, it is widely accepted and a foundation concept in science. Humans are animals.

In *The Rights of Nature*, Boyd shows how humans have increasingly recognised legal rights for animals. However, the legal issue is whether humans have a duty to protect animals, or whether animals themselves have rights. Scientific advances have shown that many animals are intelligent, and all animals are sentient. Peter Singer's philosophy work on animal ethics was seminal. In 1975 he published *Animal Liberation*.[9] As a result, from a legal perspective, there is a growing movement to accept animals as legal persons. In the Western world, legal doctrine accepts companies as legal persons, endowing them with significant rights; why not extend this to animals?

The fictive concept of companies is well understood. The essence of a company is that it has a legal personality distinct from the people who compose it. This means that even if the people running the company are continuously changing, the company itself retains its identity; the business need not be stopped and restarted with every change in its managers or members (shareholders).

It also leads to the 'agency challenge', which is one of the most intractable dilemmas in company law. Because a company is a fictive person, inevitably humans are needed to act for the company; therefore, they might protect themselves rather than the company's interests. In a company, these agents are called directors, and they have significant duties to the company (not to the shareholders). Any non-human right-bearing subject, whether it is another animal or an inanimate subject, will need to have custodians to protect them.

Legal rules to protect animals exist within an anthropocentric framework, but legal rules to protect inanimate features of the environment lack such a framework and are culturally alien to Western legal understandings. Legal rules are an example of why there is such a clash between indigenous and Western cultures – and why the Gaia project is so important for climate change and the future of the planet and humanity. Most indigenous cultures do not accept the overriding concept of anthropocentric models.[10] Chief Oren Lyon, Faithkeeper of the Onondaga tribe of the Haudenosaunee (Iroquois) Nation said:

> There is a hue and cry for human rights, they said, for all people, and the indigenous people said: What of the rights of the nature world? Where is the seat for

8 Charles Darwin, *On the Origin of Species (1859)* (Penguin 2019).

9 Peter Singer, *Animal Liberation* (HarperCollins 1975).

10 Chief Oren Lyon, Faithkeeper of the Onondaga tribe of the Haudenosaunee (Iroquois) Nation, 'There Can Be No Peace As Long As We Wage War Upon Our Mother, the Earth' speech at the UN Millennium World Peace Summit of Religious and Spiritual Leaders (15 August 2009) <http://www.thethird-eye.co.uk/a-message-from-the-indigenous-peoples-of-the-world/> accessed 5 August 2019.

> the buffalo or the eagle? Who is representing them at this forum? Who is speaking for the water of the Earth? Who is speaking for the trees and the forests? Who is speaking for the fish – for the whales, for the beavers, for our children?[11]

If Western legal cultures are to adapt to accepting indigenous cultural norms, the rights of animals or rivers must be protected by the personality of the feature, and any rights must be implemented by humans, and these custodians must have robust duties.

There has been a slow acceptance of animal rights and the concept of the legal personality of animals. As Boyd argues, 'over times, the boundaries of what is considered a legal person have evolved in concert with our values'.[12] Slaves – and even women! – are now persons.[13] Stone uses Darwin's concept of a long human development. He argues that, originally, humans could only care for themselves; then they could care for a limited group; then their 'sympathies became more tender and widely diffused, extending to men of races, to the imbecile, maimed, and other useless members of society, and finally to the lower animals'.[14] However, this comfortable illusion of human development-ism has been punctured by many scientific studies, which show that many non-human brains have complex networks and languages.[15] Unless all non-human animals are acknowledged as going through exactly the same process of development as humans, ideas of human development are incorrect.

The legal personality of animals, Gaia and the living planet

Recently, some courts have taken a jump from the idea that humans have extensive property rights and decided that not everything can be owned. Some non-human animals are *persons* and therefore cannot be owned. In 2016, an Argentine court decided a chimpanzee was not a thing but a person, and thus able to have rights. Judge Maria Alejandra Mouricio cited the Universal Declaration of Animal Rights, Argentina's constitution and Kant. She accepted that legal rights evolve over time, and that it is not currently acceptable to classify chimpanzees as 'things': 'This is not about granting them the same rights humans have, it is about accepting and understanding once and for all that they are living sentient beings, with legal personality'.[16] Kant said, 'We can judge the heart of a man by his treatment of animals'.[17] Although the judge's quote by Kant was apposite, the key legal issue

11 Ibid, cited in David Boyd, *The Rights of Nature* (ECW Press 2017) xxi.

12 Boyd (n 11) 48.

13 C. Stone, *Should Trees Have Standing* (OUP 2010).

14 Charles Darwin, *The Descent of Man* (Classics of World Literature 2003) 56.

15 Melanie Boly et al., 'Consciousness in Human and Non-Animals: Recent Advances and Future Directions' <https://www.frontiersin.org/articles/10.3389/fpsyg.2013.00625/full> accessed 22 March 2021.

16 Stephen Messenger, 'Zoo Chimp Freed in Historic Legal Case Takes First Steps onto Grass' (*The Dodo*, 4 July 2017) <https://www.thedodo.com/cecilia-chimp-sanctuary-rights-2348132702.html> accessed 5 August 2019.

17 Roger Scruton, *Kant* (OUP 1982, 2001).

was the personality of animals because you can protect animals from humans through regulations; accepting them as a living person, in the framework of an anthropocentric legal system, may be a further step.

Once this step is accepted, is there is huge jump to accepting natural features as legal persons with legal personality? The counterargument would be that yes, there is a huge jump, because animals are intelligent, can feel pain and are sentient. However, the Gaia theory is that all nature is sentient; as Lovelock has said, the planet is alive. However, the prevailing Western legal culture has been to stop any progressive changes in the jurisprudence of the rights of nature. However, in the US, the Endangered Species Act 1973 is a piece of environmental regulation which has fostered a large jurisprudence around it and that protects species other than humans to live, flourish and not be eliminated from the earth. The act has made significant strides in protecting animals and plant species; they do not have legal personality, but some animals are protected by becoming *plaintiffs* or *claimants*, which indicates that they have legal standing in law. For example, in *Northern Spotted Owl v Hodel*, the case is entitled 'Northern Spotted Owl'; the owl therefore appears as the claimant. In the case, the issue was a judicial review, and the judgement told the United States Fish & Wildlife Service to review the evidence that the owl is not endangered, arguing that the evidence was not properly reviewed. Another instance was *Psittirostra bailleui (Palila)*, an endangered species, *Sierra Club, a Non-Profit Corporation, National Audubon Society, a Non-Profit Association, Hawaii Audubon Society, a Non-Profit Association, and Alan C. Ziegler, Plaintiffs, v. Hawaii Department of Land and Natural Resources, and Susumu Ono, in his capacity as Chairman of the Hawaii Board of Land and Natural Resources, Defendants.*[18] Here, the standing of the bird was not argued.[19] Later, in the long and contentious legal process in the Ninth Circuit,[20] Circuit Judge O'Scannlain said, 'the bird (*Loxioides bailleui*), a member of the Hawaiian honeycreeper family, also has legal status and wings its way into federal court as a plaintiff in its own right.' Other cases have followed,[21] but other US cases have rejected the concept of the standing of non-human plaintiffs, including in *Cetacean Community v Bush*.[22] The court decided that earlier cases stating that non-human claimants could have standing were dicta, and therefore not a precedent: 'A statement

18 471 F. Supp. 985 (1979).

19 Jack R. Nelson, '*Palia v Hawaii Department of Land and Natural Resources*: State Governments Fall Prey to the Endangered Species Act of 1973' (1982) *Ecology Law Quarterly* 10.

20 *Palila v Hawaii Department of Land & Natural Resources* (9th Cir. 1988) 852 F. 2d 1106.

21 See David Boyd, *The Rights of Nature* (ECW Press 2017) 76–7.

22 386 F. 3d 1169 (9th Cir. 2004), 'The court acknowledges two cases in which courts conferred ESA standing upon an animal plaintiff' See *Marbled Murrelet v Pacific Lumber Co.* (N.D. Cal. 1995) 880 F. Supp. 343; *Loggerhead Turtle v County Council of Volusia County, Florida* (M.D. Fla. 1995) 896 F. Supp. 1170. However, both cases relied upon *Palila v Hawaii Dep't of Land & Natural Resources* (9th Cir. 1988) 852 F.2d 1106, 1107, in which the Ninth Circuit stated: 'As an endangered species under the Endangered Species Act . . . the bird *(Loxioides bailleui)*, a member of the Hawaiian honeycreeper family, also has legal status and wings its way into federal court as a plaintiff in its own right'. As other courts have recognised, however, this statement is dicta, and does not constitute precedent binding upon this court. See *Hawksbill Sea Turtle v Federal Emergency Management Agency* (3d Cir. 1997) 126 F.3d 461, 466 n. 2; *Coho Salmon,* 30 F.Supp.2d at 1239 n. 2.

is dictum when it is made during the course of delivering a judicial opinion, but . . . is unnecessary to the decision in the case and [is] therefore not precedential'. However, the judge accepted that

> It is obvious that an animal cannot function as a plaintiff in the same manner as a juridically competent human being. But we see no reason why . . . Congress [could authorise] a suit in the name of an animal, any more than it prevents suits brought in the name of artificial persons such as corporations, partnerships or trusts, and even ships, or of juridically incompetent persons such as infants, juveniles, and mental incompetents.[23]

Although this case is a blow to rights-of-nature activists and the standing of non-human claimants, it seems to mean that if there are no competent humans who can claim for the harm under specific statutes, the court could accept a non-human claimant. Some argue that this case stops any possibility of non-humans becoming claimants (unless Congress has specifically authorised a suit allowing the personality of animals),[24] but the judgement was not so restricted, and it includes an unusual situation that is not covered by legislation. Since there are dicta stating that non-humans can have personality, the issue may be decided by the Supreme Court.

Less known examples of using the rights of nature are also interesting, often in municipalities. Although these ordinances do not designate legal persons, the community are enabled to protect it. The Community Environmental Legal Defence Fund was founded in the 1990s to promote more democratic control over their local environmental decision-making which had been eroded by the power of MNEs.[25] The Fund drafted ordinances that included rights for nature so that citizens could exercise these rights to protect nature features.

> For an example, the City of Pittsburgh passed such an ordinance aimed at preventing natural gas fracking within the city's boundaries. It banned such fracking, removed certain rights of corporations, and included rights for nature, including rights for the river through the city.
>
> (b) Rights of Natural Communities. Natural communities and ecosystems, including, but not limited to, wetlands, streams, rivers, aquifers, and other water systems, possess inalienable and fundamental rights to exist and flourish within the City of Pittsburgh. Residents of the City shall possess legal

23 *Cetacean Community v Bush,* 1176.

24 M. Armstrong, '*Cetacean Community v Bush*: The False Hope of Animal Rights Lingers' (2005–06) 12 *Hastings W-Nw J. Env'l L. Pol'y* 185; Cass Sunstein and Martha Nussaum, *Animal Rights* (OUP 2005).

25 Catherine Iorn Magallanes, 'From Rights to Responsibilities Using Personhood and Guardianship for Rivers?' in *Responsibility: Law and Governance for Well with the Earth, B Martin, L Te Aho, M Humphries-Eil* (Routledge 2019) and City of Pittsburgh, The Pittsburgh Code, Title Six, Art. 1, Ch. 618.3(b); <www.harmonywithnatureun.org/content/documents/203Ordinance-Pittsburgh-.pdf>. This was passed by the Pittsburgh City Council in November 2010 as part of a ban on fracking within the city.

standing to enforce those rights on behalf of those natural communities and ecosystems.[26]

Similar ordinances have been enacted in other areas, including in California where Santa Monica passed an ordinance[27] decreeing,

> Natural communities and ecosystems possess fundamental and inalienable rights to exist and flourish in the City Of Santa Monica. To effectuate those rights on behalf of the environment, residents of the City may bring actions to protect these natural communities and ecosystems, defined as: groundwater aquifers, atmospheric systems, marine waters, and native species within the boundaries of the City.[28]

These examples show that humans should protect the environment, however it does not extend to a legal concept of the personality of features.

It is therefore important to find the fundamental reason for suggesting a change of position on animal or non-human legal personality. Stone is correct to realise that the philosophical point is *valuation*. In recent Western culture, in the neoliberal world valuing means valuing by economic means, often by valuing it with GDP.[29] However, it is possible that this mindset will change because of the climate change emergency, in which continuous growth is impossible. A concept of mindless growth must be replaced with a concept of human flourishing and the human duty to the planet, but unfortunately 'there will be resistance to giving the thing 'rights' until it can be seen and valued for itself'.[30] A number of international agreements recognise the value of animals and the environment. The UN World Charter accepts that '[e]very form of life is unique, warranting respect regardless of its worth to humans',[31] and the UN Convention on Biodiversity has strengthened this perception; in its preamble, the Convention states: '*Conscious* of the intrinsic value of biological diversity and of the ecological, genetic, social, economic, scientific, educational, cultural, recreational and aesthetic values of biological diversity and its components'.[32]

In *Laudato Si'*, Pope Francis said:

> 32. The earth's resources are also being plundered because of short-sighted approaches to the economy, commerce and production. The loss of forests and woodlands entails the loss of species which may constitute extremely important

26 Magallanes (n 25) page 3.

27 City of Santa Monica, Santa Monica Municipal Code, Ch 4.75 ('Sustainability Rights Ordinance'), 4.75.040(b). <www.harmonywithnatureun.org>.

28 Ibid.

29 <https://assets.publishing.service.gov.uk/government/uploads/system/uploads/attachment_data/file/957291/Dasgupta_Review_-_Full_Report.pdf> accessed 11 February 2021, see chapter 6.

30 C. Stone, *Should Trees Have Standing* (OUP 2010) 2.

31 UN General Assembly, A/RES/37/7, 1982.

32 UN Convention on Biodiversity (1992) <https://www.cbd.int/doc/legal/cbd-en.pdf> accessed 12 August 2019.

> resources in the future, not only for food but also for curing disease and other uses. Different species contain genes which could be key resources in years ahead for meeting human needs and regulating environmental problems.
>
> 33. It is not enough, however, to think of different species merely as potential 'resources' to be exploited, while overlooking the fact that they have value in themselves. Each year sees the disappearance of thousands of plant and animal species which we will never know, which our children will never see, because they have been lost for ever. The great majority become extinct for reasons related to human activity. Because of us, thousands of species will no longer give glory to God by their very existence, nor convey their message to us. We have no such right.[33]

Although it is clearly important for humans to recognise that ecosystems are valuable in themselves, embedding the ethical concept of the value of ecosystems into our current mechanisms is difficult, partly because it would leave humans more vulnerable. Only by withdrawing from anthropocentric thinking can it be possible to look at our earth and value it for itself rather than as a resource for exploitation by humans. For example, if a lake is considered as a legal person rather than a 'resource' for humans, the lake becomes the focus of interest, allowing it to be properly protected rather than just a tool for exploitation by humans.

The jurisprudence of rights and legal personality of rivers, lakes and features

A new concept of property rights which will include natural features as legal persons is challenging, and there are a number of obstacles, not least finding a legal mechanism to enforce the rights. However, accepting that natural features are valuable is the first step.

> By making the lake itself the focus of . . . [damage], and 'incorporating' it so to speak, the legal system can effectively . . . urge before the court injuries not presently cognizable – the death of eagles and the inedible crabs, the suffering of the sea lions, the loss from the face of the earth of species of commercially valueless birds, the disappearance of a wilderness area.[34]

Stone recognises the complexity of valuing such interests. He posits a 'replenishing' approach, but he accepts that his ideas on reparations are not fully clarified, and he argues that it is impossible to have a

> total 'freeze' . . . on the environmental status quo. Nature is a continuous theatre in which things and species (eventually man) are destined to enter and

33 Pope Francis, 'On Care for Our Common Home' (2015) <http://w2.vatican.va/content/dam/francesco/pdf/encyclicals/documents/papa-francesco_20150524_enciclica-laudato-si_en.pdf> accessed 12 August 2019.

34 Stone (n 30) 14.

exit. In the meantime, coexistence of man and his environment means that *each*[35] is going to have to compromise for the better of both.[36]

The nature of rights: absolute guarantees or compromises

Earlier in this chapter, the nature of property rights was explained, including the strong link between human rights and property rights in the Western world. It is time to consider what legal foundations could be found to embed a concept of rights for nature.

The concept of rights itself is problematic since many 'rights' are not absolute or guaranteed. However, as Harris has shown, although property rights are not absolute, the boundary between many rights are strongly contested, so this means that the boundaries for a new concept of a right for nature will be also controversial. Is it sensible to invent a construct which will be labelled a 'right' with the language connotations that has been found when any right has been debated? Characterising a new construct of rights and the personality of features might be divisive, pitting different rights against each other, which will entail division. It is likely that any concept promoting a right for nature will be part of a Western legal framework which is against the grain of the Gaia philosophy. Virginia Marshall argues that applying legal personhood for natural features is 'counterintuitive from an Aboriginal perspective, and essentially counterproductive'.[37] This is particularly true when water is involved.

> Water landscapes hold meaning and purpose under Aboriginal laws. The inherent relationships of Aboriginal peoples with water are evidenced by Aboriginal creation stories, with Aboriginal identity defined through Aboriginal ontologies (Aboriginal normative values and beliefs, laws and knowledge). From an Aboriginal perspective, water is inseparable from the land; in many Aboriginal creation stories (not myths) water came first, then the land. Water is sacred and underpins Aboriginal kinship connection in birth, life and death. These traits are exemplified in Aboriginal obligations to maintain waterholes, ensure fire management (burning) practices, and monitor the health of all things within traditional boundaries and care for country. Aboriginal communities continue to seek to exercise their inherent rights and obligations as sovereign peoples, in spite of continual efforts in contemporary Australia to undermine Aboriginal property relationships, ownership of resources and ancient knowledge.[38]

Where there are different cultural and legal sensitivities it is sensible to go slowly to make sure that a new concept is accepted and understood by all stakeholders in a

35 Emphasis in the original.

36 Stone (n 30) 17.

37 Virginia Marshall, 'Overturning Aqua Nullius: An Aboriginal Perspective on Personhood' in *Conferring Legal Personality on the World's Rivers: A Brief Intellectual Assessment*, Texas A & M University School of Law, Research Paper No. 19–30 <https://ssrn.com/abstract=3431344>.

38 Marshall (n 37).

community. This is problematic particularly when some communities are inspired by spiritual knowledge. The people might be passionate about a deity or many gods, but it might also include engrained economic 'truths'. Undoing paradigms are very hard. Although human brains have plasticity and are therefore flexible,[39] many humans become distressed if their viewpoints are challenged. When Western people arrived in Australia, the authorities decreed that the land belonged to nobody. The doctrine of *terra nullius* has now been debunked. In 1992 the majority of Australia's High Court[40] determined that the doctrine of *terra nullius* was not based on truth. The Aboriginal peoples had settled laws, ancient traditions, customs and practices. However, the governments in Australia have continued to regard indigenous First Peoples as just another stakeholder or a special interest group in community decisions.[41] Marshall argues that since Aboriginal peoples in Australia have the oldest living cultures in the world, Aboriginal water rights require legal recognition as property rights and that water access and water infrastructure are integral to successful economic enterprise in Aboriginal communities. Aboriginal peoples' social, cultural and economic certainty rests on their right to control and manage customary water. Marshall argues that in Australia, 'lawyers and policy drafters deconstruct Aboriginal laws and practices and reconstruct them into Western legal concepts'.[42] She strongly contends that Aboriginal values, narratives and spiritual beliefs should be formally incorporated in Australian law. That would entail acknowledging that Western legal jurisprudence on property rights should recede and be replaced by a concept of a 'web of interests' to explain how everything is interconnected.[43] Marshall believes that this concept resembles Aboriginal beliefs and laws. It is also very similar to the Gaia philosophy. There are two interrelated problems that should be explored: one is delving into the new idea of the 'web of interests'. The second one is whether a *right* for nature is dangerous because it might endorse an absolutist concept of property rights. The concept of rights has been partly explored in this section; however, some scholars have linked rights to an expanded perception of a social interaction between of objects and human relationships. Arnold tries to find a metaphor to express the importance of the interconnections between humans, the environment and objects, suggesting that a web of interests 'can better accommodate integration of human-human relationship, human right-object relationship and the particular characteristics of the objects to defining the nature of the legal in it'.[44] Rejecting the 'bundle of rights' theories as inadequate, Arnold accepts that Hohfeld recognised that

39 Catherine Malabou, *What Should We Do with Our Brain?* (Perspectives in Continental Philosophy, Fordham University Press 2008).

40 *Mabo v Queensland 1992 (no. 2) 175 CLR 1.*

41 Virginia Marshall, *Overturning Aqua Nullius* (Aboriginal Studies Press 2017).

42 Marshall (n 41) page 6.

43 Craig (Tony) Anthony, 'The Reconstruction of Property: Property as a Web of Interests' (2002) 26 *Harvard International Law Review* 281–4.

44 Ibid page 282.

property rights are rights against *persons* and how people can own objects. From this viewpoint, property rights in a Western world are therefore inevitably divisive and androcentric. However, if this position can be extended, property rights can be 'defined as legal relationship among people concerning valued resources'.[45] In that way, intangible values can be included in property rights, including equality, expression, security and dignity,[46] including a right to work.[47] Arnold hopes that the value of objects are reassessed so that a web of interests could be so wide to include all interests, and therefore reach all interests and promote all interconnections. A wider definition of social relationships involving valued objects requires that the value of those should be carefully considered because, as Harris argues, property rights are fluid, and therefore the language of rights is not settled. To understand the interconnections, Arnold calls for contextualism. Objects shape human relationships; they are not void of purpose in human social relationships. Such contextualism includes whether the object can be occupied; whether it is natural or human-made; whether it is destructible; whether it is renewable; the cultural meaning of the object and the importance for the natural environment.[48] By ignoring the human-object relationship properly, property rights have become estranged from social reality. This creates two sorts of alienation. One is the inevitable fact that humans are different from objects. Arnold argues that this alienation can be ameliorated by developing 'socially appropriate . . . [personal enrichment] relationship, which allow the individual to become a whole person in the context of society and the physical world'.[49] More damaging is the other alienation where 'social, political, and economic forces that destroy or debase the person's healthy relationship with things . . . typically by commodifying things and, in turn commodifying people (i.e. their labor, their identity and their value). Dominant property concepts in society can such alienation'.[50]

It is clear that property rights can be viewed from two opposite positions, mirroring the divide between the Western legal concepts of rights and Aboriginal perceptions. The Iwi peoples in New Zealand regard the Whanganui River as their ancestor and believe that the people are inseparable from the river, and therefore they have responsibilities to protect and manage the river. 'It is this belief that has given rise to the Whanganui proverb, "Ko au te awa, Ko te awa ko au" (I am the river and the river is me)'.[51] The concept of a right for nature could be aligned with the Gaia theory, or alternatively it could be a trap turning rights into a Western legal perception of dominating nature.

45 Ibid page 291.
46 Ibid.
47 See the earlier argument on 'absolute property rights'.
48 Anthony (n 43) page 296.
49 Ibid, page 298.
50 Ibid.
51 Magallanes (n 25).

Marshall has found, 'The culture of the common law has imposed a conceptual grid over both space and time which divides, parcels, registered, and bounds people and places in a way that is often inconsistent with Indigenous participation and environmental integrity'.

With this caveat sounding loudly, the next chapter explores the ways that objects could be protected by human custodians.

11 Standing, remedies and custodians

Standing, remedies and custodians

To illustrate the complexity of these legal mechanisms, this chapter will analyse three legal cases in detail and then consider the situation in New Zealand. The first case concerns a theme park in the US; the second focuses on the Vilcabamba River in Ecuador; and the third on the Atrato River in Colombia. After covering these case studies and the analysis of the New Zealand solutions, the chapter will explore a mechanism to find compromises between indigenous thinking on nature and Western legal environmental rights, arguing that states should devolve some powers to natural features where the people in the area would become custodians of the feature and have a duty to the feature. The most obvious example of a duty for a feature is found in New Zealand where the Whanganui River is revered, and this chapter will build on the experiences there to suggest that a more equitable and sustainable world can be found. Environmental activists have used various legal mechanisms, including legislation, treaties, court cases and constitutional processes in the US, New Zealand, Colombia, India, Ecuador and Bolivia;[1] some of these mechanisms will be examined later to bolster the suggested plan, but in this chapter the details of these three cases illustrate the difficulties involved and the effectiveness of this theory of rights of nature in practice.

Sierra Club v Morton (1972)[2] came about when Walt Disney proposed building an extensive skiing development in the Mineral King Valley in the Sequoia National Forest. The Sierra Club – an environmental pressure group with 'a special interest in the conservation and sound maintenance of the national parks, game refuges, and forests of the country'[3] – sued Walt Disney, arguing that the

1 Gregorio Mesa Cuadros, 'The Rivers as Subjects of Rights: Analysis of Comparative Law in the Cases of the Atrato, Whanganui, Vilcabamba, Ganges and Yamuna Rivers' in Gregorio Mesa Cuadros (ed) *Environmental Standard and Environmental Rights in Post-Peace Agreements: Some Case Studies* (Unijus 2019) 25–51; David Boyd, *The Rights of Nature* (ECW Press 2017); Jane Gleeson-White, 'It's Only Natural: The Push to Give Rivers, Mountains and Forests Legal Rights' (*The Guardian* 2018) <https://www.theguardian.com/australia-news/2018/apr/01/its-only-natural-the-push-to-give-rivers-mountains-and-forests-legal-rights> accessed 14 August 2019.

2 *Sierra Club v Morton* (1972) 405 US 727.

3 Ibid.

DOI: 10.4324/9781315386782-14

'development' would change the nature of the wilderness. The resort was to include a new highway, power lines, hotels, restaurants, swimming pools, car parks and ski infrastructure. The Supreme Court dismissed the claimant's arguments – not on the substance of the suit (it was clear that the environment would be significantly changed) but on the ability of the claimant's standing. The Sierra Club relied on '§ 10 of the Administrative Procedure Act, which accords judicial review to a "person suffering legal wrong because of agency action, or [who is] adversely affected or aggrieved by agency action within the meaning of a relevant statute."[4]

The petitioner did not allege that the challenged development would affect the Club or its members in their activities but maintained that the project would adversely change the area's aesthetics and ecology. The District Court granted a preliminary injunction. The Supreme Court decided:

> A person has standing to seek judicial review under the Administrative Procedure Act only if he can show that he himself has suffered or will suffer injury, whether economic or otherwise. In this case, where petitioner asserted no individualized harm to itself or its members, it lacked standing to maintain the action.[5]

The legal procedures governing legal disputes in the US are strict; judges are anxious to limit the number of disputes, so they wish to stop irrelevant claims. Because US (and UK) law is designed to settle particular arguments between individuals, public interests are irrelevant. In US tort law, to achieve standing in a case, a person must show:

1) through breach of a duty owed by a defendant
2) a plaintiff has suffered an 'injury in fact', that is, a legally recognized harm that is both
   (a) concrete and particularized, and
   (b) 'actual and imminent', not 'conjectural' or 'hypothetical'
3) the injury is fairly traceable to the challenged action of the defendant (causation); and
4) it has to be 'likely' as opposed to merely 'speculative' and the injury will be redressed by a favourable decision (redressability).[6]

Since these procedures limit persons' ability to sue for environmental harm (unless there is clear damage for the claimant), the area could not sue, even though it would

4 Ibid.
5 Ibid 728.
6 C. Stone, *Should Trees Have Standing* (OUP 2010) 36, citing Justice Antonin Scalia's jurisprudence.

be damaged. However, this case has become a *cause célèbre* because, in a dissent, Justice William O. Douglas argued there should be a rule

> that allowed environmental issues to be litigated before federal agencies or federal courts in the name of the inanimate object about to be despoiled, or invaded by roads and bulldozers and where injury is the subject of public outrage. Contemporary public concern for protecting nature's ecological equilibrium should lead to the conferral of standing upon environmental objects to sue for their own preservation . . . This suit would therefore be more properly labeled as *Mineral Kings v Morton*.[7]

This dissent, and Stone's article (now subsumed in *Should Trees Have Standing*), started a debate on how to include animals and other non-human claimants in legal processes. Some of this had been rehearsed earlier, in the US and the UK; but, although a number of cases have argued for standing for non-human claimants, the courts were not convinced.

However, in *Animal Legal Defence Fund v Glickman*,[8] while there was no huge reversal of the lack of standing for inanimate claimants, Justice Scalia's strict rule that a claim cannot proceed unless claimants prove 'a legally recognized harm that is both (a) concrete and particularized, and (b) "actual and imminent", not "conjectural" or "hypothetical"' was relaxed. It was recognised that the test of 'injury' can be less stringent, allowing a claimant to have standing because individual claimants allegedly suffered 'aesthetic and recreational injuries' while witnessing the physical and emotional conditions of captive primates.[9] This is a long way from getting non-human claimants into court; a softening of the rigid procedural rules on standing may be on the way, but sadly, the relaxation is usually on the basis of potential injury to one or more human. As such, the law is completely androcentric. If there are humans able to protect the environment (as in the *Mineral King* case, in which the Sierra Club redrafted its complaint to allege that their members' interests would have been damaged), standing is possible.[10] In 1973, the Supreme Court allowed an incorporated group of law students to challenge the government decision to change freight rates without filing an impact statement on the environment. The court agreed the students had standing, but they lost on the merits.[11] Relaxing the restrictions on standing is possible but uncertain. In the meantime, Stone made a valid and powerful point: although humans are able to protect non-humans in the courts,

> the 'persons' who were *really* harmed – who deserved, at any rate, a day in court – were the mice and monkeys [and other non-human claimants] . . .

7 *Sierra Club v Morton* (1972) 405 US 727, 742–3.

8 US District Court for the District of Columbia (D.D.C. 1996) 943 F. Supp. 44.

9 Ibid.

10 Stone (n 6).

11 *United States v Students Challenging Regulatory Agency Procedures* (1973) 412 US 669–90.

> Why shouldn't such suits be brought in the name of the animals, given that the object of judicial focus is their welfare?[12]

Further procedural hurdles face any claimants trying to protect the environment, and judges are not on the same page regarding the stringency of Scalia's tests. In *Lujan v Defenders of Wildlife*,[13] the judges disagreed on the facts:

> Justice John Paul . . . took strong exception to Scalia both on 'imminence and redressability' . . . On imminence, Steven demanded no more than that demonstration that the plaintiff's interests was 'genuine'. For Scalia, Steven's proposal would engage the Court in an unworkable task, distinguishing the genuine from the nongenuine.[14]

It is clear that jurisprudence is not settled, of course – the Trump administration was hostile to environmental suits, particularly on climate change issues. Any suit to limit greenhouse gases would have had extraterritorial challenges, not least a challenge 'based upon sovereign immunity'. Any of Scalia's tests might not provide a hurdle, since Scalia suggested that if a complaint were justified on *procedural* grounds, the plaintiff would have a low hurdle to jump to achieve standing.[15] However, using a procedural test provides a less successful outcome; because the plaintiff will not achieve resolution of the issue,[16] the only outcome would be the relevant agency being ordered to put right the procedures. The agency may simply allege that, at the end of the amending procedure, the environment is not damaged. Further legal litigation might be necessary, since environmental impact statements can be easily disputed, and the costs of continuing litigation might be significant.[17] Any company involved can also settle, meaning there would be no precedential effect on the law.

A second case involves the Vilcabamba River. The claimants, who were property owners in Ecuador, complained that their property's adjacent river had been damaged by development; specifically, by the building of a road. The suit contended that the project should immediately stop because the 'development' was dumping debris in the river. The claimants argued that the natural course of the river should be restored, and the rocks, dirt, gravel and vegetation deposited in the river be removed. Eventually (after an appeal), the Provincial Court of Loja[18] upheld the constitutional right of the river. The judge stated, 'It is the duty of constitution judges to immediately guard and give effect to the constitutional rights of

12 Stone (n 6) 175. Emphasis in the original.

13 404 US 555 (1992).

14 Stone (n 6) 42.

15 *Lujan v Defenders of Wildlife*, 504 US at note 7.

16 See the South African case, *Mining and Environmental Justice Network Community of South Africa v Minister of Environmental Affairs*, Case No. 50779/2017.

17 *Border Power Plant Working Group v Dep't of Energy* (s.D. Cal 2006) 467 F. Supp. 2d 1040.

18 Richard Frederick Wheeler y Eleanor Geer Huddle c/ Gobierno Provincial de Loja, juicio 11121–2011–0010 (30 March 2011).

nature, doing what is necessary to avoid contamination or remedy it'. The court added that injuries to nature are 'generational injuries', in that they will impact future generations.[19] This precedent has fuelled a number of initiatives,[20] and the Ecuadorian example has been replicated in New Zealand, India and Colombia:

> The Ecuador constitution was crucial in the case of the Vilcabamba River. In 2008, Ecuador became the first country to secure the rights of nature – *Pachamama* – in its constitution, Bolivia enacted the Law of Mother Earth three years later, and in Ecuador became the first country to secure the rights of nature.[21]

Sadly, there is no evidence that the court's ruling has been implemented.[22] Enforcing the rights of nature is problematic, as Whittemore argues.[23] In 2008, Ecuador became the first nation to give rights to nature when it ratified constitutional amendments (new articles 71–74) granting the environment the inalienable right to exist, persist and be respected; however, a raft of challenging hurdles need to be overcome to enforce these rights, including 'legal barriers, such as Ecuador's lack of a standing doctrine and a history of judicial corruption and dysfunction'. Whittemore argues, 'Ecuador should grant lifetime tenure to its constitutional court judges, codify a standing doctrine, create an independent enforcement body, and create an independent environmental tribunal with criminal contempt power'.[24]

The jurisprudence hurdles are also evident in New Zealand and India. Both countries have recognised the intrinsic rights of rivers, beyond their use for humans. Both recognise rivers as having spiritual, physical and metaphysical characteristics, but enforcing the rights is not easy in either country. Clearly, then, the standing issue is only the start of the question, not the full answer.

The third case involves the Atrato River in Colombia, although it was about more than the river itself; the case also affected the river basin and all of the interests in the area.[25] This case was

> an *acción de tutela* by disadvantaged ethnic communities before the constitutional court to protect the fundamental rights to life, health, water, food security, a healthy environment, the culture and the territory of the active ethnic

19 Boyd (n 1) 163.

20 Ashish Kothari, Mari Margil, and Shrishtee Bajpai, 'Now Rivers Have the Same Legal Status as People, We Must Uphold Their Rights' (*The Guardian*, 21 April 2017) <https://www.theguardian.com/global-development-professionals-network/2017/apr/21/rivers-legal-human-rights-ganges-whanganui> accessed 17 August 2019.

21 Ibid.

22 Ibid.

23 Mary Elizabeth Whittemore, 'The Problem of Enforcing Nature's Rights under Ecuador's Constitution: Why the 2008 Environmental Amendments Have No Bite' (2011) 20 *Pacific Rim Law & Policy Journal Association* 3, 659.

24 Ibid.

25 *Center for Social Justice Studies et al. v Presidency of the Republic et al.* (10 November 2016) Judgment T-622/16 Constitutional Court of Colombia (trans. Thomas Swan, Erin Daly and James R. May, *Dignity Rights Project*, Delaware Law School 2019).

> communities, and to address the health, socio-environmental, ecological and humanitarian crisis in the Atrato River Basin, its tributaries and surrounding territories.[26]

With the caveat that it is difficult to translate legal language from a different jurisdiction, an *acción de tutela* involves a sort of custodianship for the area, which is enormous;

> The district of Chocó, where the facts of the present protection action have developed, has an area of 46,530 km^2 (28,913.40 mi^2), which is equivalent to 4.07% of the total area of Colombia . . . It is inhabited by multiple racial groups, with a population of approximately 500,000 inhabitants, of which 87% of the population is Afro-descendant, 10% indigenous and 3% mestizo. 96 percent of the continental surface is constituted by collective territories of 600 black communities grouped into 70 larger community councils with 2,915,339 titled hectares and 120 indigenous reserves.

One of the questions in this case was the concept of

> bio-cultural rights, in their simplest definition, [which] refer to the rights that ethnic communities have to administer and exercise sovereign autonomous authority over their territories – according to their own laws, customs – and the natural resources that make up their habitat. Their culture, traditions, and way of life are developed based on the special relationship they have with the environment and biodiversity. In effect, these rights result from the recognition of the deep and intrinsic connection that exists between nature, its resources, and the culture of the ethnic and indigenous communities that inhabit them, all of which are interdependent with each other and cannot be understood in isolation.[27]

The region is rich in gold and wood and is considered to have the highest fertility for agriculture in Colombia, so it was clear that there would be conflicting priorities. The basin is home to many Afro-Colombian and indigenous communities, who have inhabited them ancestrally, as well as communities descended from migrants from different regions of the country. Among the communities are artisanal mining, agriculture, hunting and fishing, with which they ensured for centuries a total supply of their food needs.

There is also a thriving extraction industry, with few regulations. The indigenous people argued the basin should be protected from intensive, large-scale mining and logging:

> These methods include heavy machinery, such as dredgers and backhoes, and highly toxic substances, such as mercury, in the Atrato River (Chocó), its

26 Ibid, translator's note.
27 Ibid.

> basins, swamps, wetlands and tributaries. The methods have been intensifying for several years and are having harmful and irreversible consequences on the environment, thereby affecting the fundamental rights of ethnic communities and the natural balance of the territories they inhabit . . . Specifically, through the use of heavy machinery, such as suction dredgers, also called by the locals 'dragons,' hydraulic elevators and backhoes, these destroy the riverbed and perform indiscriminate dumping of mercury and other substances.[28]
>
> The communities argued that the river water was consumed directly, and that the dangerous substances found therein were a direct threat to their health, agriculture, and culture. The court found that problems affecting the Indigenous people included their difficulties accessing legal mechanisms, as well as their remoteness, poverty and diverse cultures and languages. To overcome these hurdles, the court accepted that the rigid procedural rules should become more flexible, allowing people easy access to representatives so that the court can protect their rights.[29]

The judgement said:

> It must be remembered that the plaintiffs are black communities . . . These communities have historically occupied territories that have been recognized as being under common ownership according to their practices, uses, and traditional customs . . . To that extent, the protection of a healthy environment of which these communities are holders, is closely linked with the protection of the territory. A healthy environment goes beyond simple biological diversity; it is a necessary condition for the effective enjoyment of the right to territory. In this sense, it is understood that having a healthy environment is a necessary condition to guarantee other fundamental rights of ethnic communities, such as: collective identity and cultural integrity.[30]

For these reasons, although an individual could sue to protect their human rights, an *acción de tutela* was necessary to protect the community from a loss of cultural diversity and identity. The court recognised that biocultural rights were crucial to remove the Western property rights framework and the only way that this could happen if the area was designated as an indigenous enclave where indigenous law was enforced. This is a key point and the reason behind the custodian ruling, because one reason for the indigenous populations' inability to stop degradation is MNEs' ability to use 'divide and rule' tactics between individuals. If this tactic is removed and does not therefore work, the environment is more likely to be protected. Using a community action can help not only humans and animals but also natural features like rivers.

28 Ibid paras 2.1–2.2.

29 Ibid para 3.2.

30 Ibid.

The Colombian Constitution recognises the 'social rule of law' (SRL), which includes special protection for the weakest and an active role for the authorities:

> In relation to equal justice, it has been estimated that the allocation of the economic resources of a society should tend to privilege the less favored sectors. This principle serves as the basis for the design and implementation of a tax regime, rules of budget preparation, the hierarchy of spending, and the setting of priorities in the provision of public services.[31]

However, the judgement recognises that the authorities must accept that the SRL cannot be delivered without cooperation between the layers of government – a weakness that MNEs will exploit, and one that returns to the question of whose interest is paramount: the animals', the river's or the humans'? If you are a trustee, director or a guardian, how can you balance these interests? The Colombian Constitution is a homocentric document:

> One of the main concerns of the 1991 Constituent in constructing the SRL formulation was focused on the most adequate, modern and efficient way to protect the environment, as a whole . . . At the same time, this model seeks to achieve the ends mentioned, by allowing human beings – the foundation of every constitutional construction since the origins of modern constitutionalism – to live and interact within a healthy environment unthreatened by the extractive activity of the state.[32]

The Gaia concept and accepting the rights of nature are just the first steps towards stopping destroying the planet. The competing interests are the most intractable, especially if the neoliberal economic model continues:

> The conceptual evolution of law in recognition of the importance of 'mother earth', and its multiple components in the strategy of sustainable development have been the result of a complex and difficult process that still generates controversy when trying to reconcile at the same time three elements: economic growth, social welfare and protection of the environment in the understanding that this conjugation allows the possibility of sustainable use of resources in the present and in the future.[33]

The Colombian Constitution tries to solve the Gordian knot by using the concept of biocultural rights. In doing this in the Atrato judgment, a huge area has been removed from the jurisdiction of Western property rights and can pave a way to eliminate some the worst inequality, not only for humans but also for the earth.

31 Ibid para 4.9.
32 Ibid para 5.1.
33 Ibid para 5.3.

The Atrato judgement rules that the interests between nature and humans must be based on a profound unity between both. It also accepts that the neoliberal economic model is unethical and accepts the idea that rights for nature might resolve clashing interests. The Supreme Court of Colombia said that the

> Atrato River, its basin and tributaries as an entity subject to rights of protection, conservation, maintenance and restoration by the State and ethnic communities . . . will order the national government to exercise legal guardianship and representation of the rights of the river (through the institution designated by the President of the Republic, which could be the Ministry of the Environment) together with the ethnic communities that inhabit the basin of the Atrato River in Chocó; in this way, the Atrato River and its basin – henceforth – will be represented by a member of the plaintiff communities and a delegate of the Colombian Government, who will be the guardians of the river.[34]

The Court ordered the government to review and cooperate with the ethnic communities via governmental departments. The implementation of the decision will be complex and difficult because of the special interests involved – including the MNEs, which are very powerful and may use bribes to corrupt officials. However, the court accepted that environmental NGOs and universities should be involved, which might help with proper implementation. To deal with all of the interests will need much research, finding out the details and talking between many experts. Some scholars have been able to design a similar project involving a river basin; one example is the work done by the Centre for Energy, Petroleum, Minerals Law and Policy, University of Dundee. Their work has been detailed and sensitive and involved full consultation with the people; if this can be replicated frequently there is some positive hope for increased biodiversity and the planet.[35]

New Zealand: The Whangaui River

In contrast with the Atrato guardianship, where the government will be the guardian of the river with consultation with stakeholders, a different solution for the guardianship of the Whangaui River was found in New Zealand. The river is a legal entity and has legal personality and all of the rights, powers, duties and liabilities, but the guardianship of the river is vested in the Maori tribes or *iwi*, rather than the government.[36] An agreement between the government and the Maori was settled. It came from many battles between the sovereign government of New Zealand and

34 Ibid 169.

35 See work by Dundee University's scholars, including the project "Uncovering the Environment: The Use of Public Access to Environmental Information": J. Mendel, C. Reid, V. Roben, and A. Rafael Macatangay, *Conciliation for Marine Transboundary Energy Resources* (Centre for Energy, Petroleum, Minerals Law and Policy, University of Dundee 2020). Ongoing project (2020).

36 Section 14 of the Te Awa Tupua (Whangaui River Claims Settlement) Act 2017.

the Maori tribes. The Treaty of Waitangi was signed on the 6th of February 1840 between the British Crown and Māori chiefs. The treaty promised to protect Māori culture and at the same time giving the Crown the right to govern New Zealand. The Crown asserted both legal and actual control the river. The *iwi* disputed the ownership or control over the river and argued that they were still the 'rightful *kaitiaki* or guardians of the river and of its *mauri* (life force)'. They argued that the Crown had usurped their guardianship and assumed ownership of the river and undertook gravel extraction and water diversions for hydroelectric power schemes.[37] This conflicts with the spiritual cosmology since the diversion of the water violated the spirits of the river. The 2017 agreement between the government and the *iwi* upheld the spiritual relationship with the river. In section 13 it says,

> Te Awa Tupua is an indivisible and living whole, comprising the Whanganui River from the mountains to the sea, incorporating all of its physical and metaphysical elements . . . The iwi and hapu of the Whangaunui River have an inalienable connection with and responsibility to Te Awa Tupua and health and well-being.[38]

Section 41 vests the title in the riverbed in the river itself. Magallanes argues that this is against the Maori's beliefs and culture, specifically the sacredness of the river because the riverbed is split from the water in the river. However, the whole of the catchment including the water are included for management purposes, and therefore the solution is a compromise between the iwi cultural sensitivities and Western legal concepts of title and ownership, showing that these compromises are possible.[39]

Te Awa Tupua (Whangaui River Claims Settlement) Act 2017, section 18 implements the legal personality of the river by appointing two persons 'of high standards', one appointed by the Crown and one appointed by all tribes who have interests in the river. These persons have the duty to the river and are the custodians or guardians (*kaitiaki)* of the river. Arguably this is stronger than the arrangements for the Atrato where the government became the guardian for the river assisted by the tribes, NGOs and academics. In the settlement in New Zealand, the tribes have more legal influence than the tribes in Supreme Court in Colombia judgement, although in the New Zealand settlement, there is a lack of evidence on the ground about how the guardianship has been executed. This office of guardianships, called Te Pou Tupua, must promote and protect the health and well-being of Te Awa Tupua and speak on behalf of the river.[40] To implement the guardianship the legislation

37 Catherine Magallanes, 'From Rights to Responsibilities Using Legal Personhood and Guardianship for Rivers' in *ResponsAbility: Law and Governance for Living Well with the Earth*, B Martin, LTe Aho, M Humphries-Kil (Routledge 2019) page 7.

38 Section 13 of the Te Awa Tupua (Whangaui River Claims Settlement) Act 2017.

39 Magallanes (n 37) page 8.

40 Section 19 of the Te Awa Tupua (Whangaui River Claims Settlement) Act 2017.

provides for a 'whole of River Strategy'[41] and establishes a 'river Fund' of NZD $30 million to support the health and well-being of the river.[42] Magallanes argues that the legal personality of the river and the appointment of guardians,

> [a]s a means of settling indigenous grievances, is an attempt to uphold justice through upholding indigenous human rights and community rights. The creation of legal personality, owning title to its own riverbed, with guardians to protect its interests, and an emphasis on intrinsic value, all represent a significant step for environmental protection.[43]

Further interest for those who advocate legal personality for natural features came from jurisprudence in India where a local resident, Mohammed Salim, petitioned the High Court in 2014, asking it to direct the government of Uttarakhand to remove illegal construction along the banks of the Ganges River. He also alleged that the state government of Uttarakhand and Uttar Pradesh were not cooperating with federal government efforts to set up a panel to protect the Ganges. He also sought a direction that the central government better manage land and water resources in the area. The Ganges is critical to 400 million people who rely on it for water, fish, navigation and electricity; for these reasons it is revered and sacred to Hindus. However, it is heavily polluted.[44]

Much of the argument in the case was focused on the Indian Constitution, which is federal. The court ruled that the 'Constitution of India has created a federation but a bias in favour of the centre. Within the sphere allotted to the States, they are supreme'.[45] Several months later the matter came before the High Court, which expressed its displeasure that no action had been taken to implement its directions. The Court noted, 'The extraordinary situation has arisen since Rivers Ganga and Yamuna are losing their very existence. This situation requires extraordinary measures to be taken to preserve and conserve Rivers Ganga and Yamuna.'[46]

To that end, the High Court declared,

> the Rivers Ganga and Yamuna, all their tributaries, streams, every natural water flowing with flow continuously or intermittently of these rivers, are declared as juristic/legal persons/living entities having the status of a legal

41 Section 36 of the Te Awa Tupua (Whangaui River Claims Settlement) Act 2017.

42 Section 57 of the Te Awa Tupua (Whangaui River Claims Settlement) Act 2017.

43 Magallanes (n 37) page 9.

44 <https://www.nytimes.com/2019/12/23/health/ganges-drug-resistant-bacteria.html> accessed 10 September 2021.

45 Mohammed Salim v State of Uttarakhand, Writ Petition No 126 of 2014 High Court Uttarakhand <https://www.casemine.com/judgement/in/5b1a21874a932631a5a08d3f> accessed 10 September 2021.

46 <https://www.elaw.org/salim-v-state-uttarakhand-writ-petition-pil-no126-2014-december-5-2016-and-march-20-2017> para 10.

person with all corresponding rights, duties and liabilities of a living person in order to preserve and conserve river Ganga and Yamuna.[47]

In describing the concept of a juristic person, the Court explained,

like any other natural person is in law also conferred with rights and obligations and is dealt with in accordance with law. In other words, the entity acts like a natural person but only through a designated person, as their Lordships have held in the judgments cited hereinabove, that for a bigger thrust of socio-political-scientific development, evolution of a fictional personality to be a juristic person becomes inevitable. This may be any entity, living inanimate, objects or things. It may be a religious institution or any such useful unit which may impel the Courts to recognise it.[48]

The High Court appointed two officials from the state of Uttarakhand to serve as persons *in loco parentis* for the two rivers, with the obligation to uphold the health and well-being of the rivers.[49]

Unfortunately, the Supreme Court of India reversed the High Court decision and the river has lost its legal personality. 'However, even before the dust on celebratory editorials had settled, the Supreme Court abruptly stayed the order in July'. A petition from the Uttarakhand government raised an issue, which had potentially steep financial consequences for the State: could flood victims sue the Ganga and Yamuna's legal guardians for compensation? Indiscriminate damming in the upper reaches of the Ganga was held primarily responsible for the devastating flash floods of 2013, and authorities were wary of what the 'living persons' formulation, if stretched to its legal limit, might entail. The Supreme Court did not hesitate and stripped both rivers of the 'living persons' designation. The Ganga and Yamuna returned to being merely rivers after 109 days as 'living persons'.[50]

The Supreme Court of India agreed with the State that the High Court had exceeded its jurisdictional remit because the river passes through Nepal, Uttar Pradesh, Bihar, Jharkhand and West Bengal, as well as Bangladesh. The guardians would have a duty to protect the river extraterritorially, always a sensitivity where there are issues of sovereignty of states and even where there is a united federal state. Magallanes argues that the guardians of the river 'could still be directed to clean up the river and activities occurring on it within their jurisdiction'.[51] However, this would be an inimical duty for the guardians because they would be unable to fully protect the river in other jurisdictions. This is why the New Zealand approach taken in the Te Awa Tupua (Whangaui River Claims Settlement) Act 2017 was a

47 Ibid para 19.
48 Ibid para 16.
49 Ibid paras 19–20.
50 <https://blogs.lse.ac.uk/southasia/2017/11/01/law-alone-cant-protect-our-rivers-and-their-rights/> accessed 10 September 2021.
51 Magallanes (n 37) page 14.

broad strategy, where legislation and local authorities are bound to recognise the river as a person and where any person exercising functions under 25 named statutes 'must recognise' and 'provide for' the Te Awa Tupua status as a legal person, and for Tupua te Kawa. Three statutes are singled out for differential treatment: the Heritage New Zealand Pouhere Taonga Act 2014 (NZ), the Public Works Act 1981 (NZ) and the RMA. Any person exercising powers under these three acts must 'have particular regard to' the Te Awa Tupua status and Tupua te Kawa. '[R]ecognise and provide for' has been interpreted by the courts as being stronger than the phrase 'have particular regard to'. Therefore, this means that there is a lesser standard required of decision-makers under these three Acts.[52] The strategy is therefore legally complex and involves a range of authorities, including the guardians of the river. One of the guardians' functions is to enter into relationships with Crown agencies and local authorities and powers in relation to the granting of consents relating to the river. In this duty the guardians are assisted by an advisory group of three, two of them are Maori. The legal framework is further enhanced by the Te Awa Tupua Strategy (Te Heke Ngahuru) to implement issues relating to the river and recommend actions to be taken.

> Because the purpose of Te Kōpuka is intended to be collaborative, the group will be relatively large, comprising up to 17 members, one appointed by the trustees (of Ngā Tāngata Tiaki o Whanganui) and up to five members appointed by the iwi with interests in the Whanganui River.[53]

The settlement provides that it 'compels local government relationships agreements'. Although this seems to be a strong rule, O'Bryan argues,

> it only mandates engagement, rather than an outcome in the form of an agreement, stating 'Te Pou Tupua will engage with relevant local authorities for the purpose of entering into a relationship' which they 'may agree to record . . . in a relationship document.[54]

The settlement also preserves existing customary rights and titles.[55] Although there are deficiencies in the settlement, it seems to be a radical attempt to resolve two completely inimical legal frameworks by compromise:

> The recognition of the Whanganui River as a legal entity, in combination with various elements of the rest of the settlement, is an innovative development in river management by Māori . . . It is undeniably Māori in its terms;

52 Katie O'Bryan, 'Giving a Voice to the River and the Role of Indigenous People: The Whanganui River Settlement and River Management in Victoria' (2017) 20 *Australian Indigenous Law Review* 55.

53 Ibid page 56.

54 Ibid page 61

55 Te Awa Tupua Act section 46(2)(b).

> it guarantees standing to access the courts to protect the River's values, those values being unquestionably Māori in orientation. It ensures that the River's values are considered in any decisions which will affect the River or its catchment; it provides for significant Māori representation on the strategy group; it promotes relationships with local authorities; it enhances the ability for heritage protection; it opens the door for the River itself to become a consent authority.[56]

Although New Zealand's strategy seems to be a significant step for the environment and a blow on Western strong property rights, the settlement did not deal with extraterritoriality and the sovereignty of different jurisdictions, which was the issue in India. Can the New Zealandian, Colombian, Ecuadorian and the legal personality of features be adapted to allow a comprehensive settlement of interests in many areas or in all areas?

The case studies have opened several avenues which could lead to a Gaian radical shift on property rights. They are;

- The personality of features/rights for Nature
- Biocultural rights
- The fundamental importance of river and water

Custodians and citizen assemblies?

The early jurisprudence on the neoliberal concept of absolute or strong property rights and chattel ownership has shifted. From the Hohfeldian/Honore/Harris understanding of property rights not as rights *over things* but as rights *against persons*, the courts have sometimes accepted that some non-human sentient animals can have legal personality and therefore have rights, including that humans could have liability if the animal was damaged. The animal would have rights against the relevant human/s. Humans cannot own the animal in a simplistic ownership relationship; rather the animal must have human custodians. From there, some tentative jurisprudence has gone further to include natural features, particularly lakes, rivers and river basins, leading to the previous discussion on whether a right for nature is wise because using a language of 'rights' has property ownership neoliberal connotations. This section tries to bypass the argument about whether it means that 'rights' are guarantees and suggests some solutions on the new concepts of the legal personalities of animals and features, specifically whether it can be a necessary foundation of legal personality leading to a new understanding between humans and nature. Legal personality is an old construct in corporate governance, but the new jurisprudence could improve it and open a dialogue to develop the new idea of the personality of features. Therefore, this part of the chapter considers a set of measures which is consonant to the Gaia philosophy and puts forward some

56 O'Bryan (n 52) page 68.

detailed legal mechanism proposals to advance the theory. In the Vilcabamba River and Rivers Ganga and Yamuna case studies, no concrete steps to implement the judgements happened. In the case of the Atarto River and its basin, the Supreme Court ruled that the national government was to be the guardian of Atarto with a number of stakeholders and accepting help by NGOs and universities. The case showed how many diverse interests were involved, and these interests are unlikely to be easily settled. The claimants will have some input, but the government will be torn between the plaintiff's interests (their culture, traditions and way of life are developed based on the special relationship they have with the environment and biodiversity) and companies and MNEs who want to mine gold and mercury and cut wood for profit. Here the concept of biocultural rights are crucial.

Biocultural rights

In the Supreme Court of Colombia this concept was examined;

> bio-cultural rights, in their simplest definition, [which] refer to the rights that ethnic communities have to administer and exercise sovereign autonomous authority over their territories – according to their own laws, customs – and the natural resources that make up their habitat. Their culture, traditions, and way of life are developed based on the special relationship they have with the environment and biodiversity. In effect, these rights result from the recognition of the deep and intrinsic connection that exists between nature, its resources, and the culture of the ethnic and indigenous communities that inhabit them, all of which are interdependent with each other and cannot be understood in isolation.[57]

Western property rights focus on monetary values (GDP) rather than spiritual or ethical values, so that when a US/UK company model of companies are proposed or implemented, the stakeholders' interests are valued in money terms rather than their security, well-being or flourishing. The guardians of the Atarto River will not be able to value the stakeholder's using monetary values; the spiritual aspect must be significantly weighed and valued. This is also true in New Zealand, in the Whangaui River area where a stakeholder society appears to be happening. In the Whangaui River Claims Settlement Act 2017, the drafters tried to inject the spiritual essence of the scheme. Whether this can be sustained is not clear. Unfortunately, there is a delicate balance between a raft of regulations and a spiritual purpose. The latter can be lost when regulations are drafted and when wrangling about definitions and boundaries becomes fractious. In all of the examples different interests will have to be settled, and the pressure from the neoliberal establishment (MNEs and IFIs) will be intense. The human custodians/directors will need to have a commitment to understand the *purpose* of their duties. In neoliberal economics,

57 Ibid.

the purpose of the company is shareholder profit (and, in recent times, profit maximisation), and the agency 'problem' arises when managers are corrupted by money or status – as happened in ENRON and many other commercial scandals.[58] Where the custodians of a river basin have multiple interests to consider, devising a set of duties for them is extremely complex. In the Atrato case, the judgement was complicated and involved a set of actors: the claimants, the government, governmental agencies and disparate communities. This is true in the Whangaui River settlement. In the Atrato judgement, the court hoped the actors would agree policies. In New Zealand a complicated structure was put into place including a guardian for the river, but the agency theory shows that when a new powerful actor comes into a position where they can fraudulently shift the purposes of the legal person to a profit maximisation, the temptation to do so is strong. It is for this reason that it is crucial to enact detailed regulation but also to continue the overriding purpose to protect the river, otherwise the system will be corrupted. All involved must abide with Gaia principles and a focus on a substantive drafting regulation and a clear understanding of the rule of law which not only incorporates nature into law decisions but is the paramount decider in drafting law.[59]

The Atrato River and the New Zealand cases had a particular resonance in that they focused on rivers.

58 B. Mclean and P. Elkind, *The Smartest Guys in the Room* (Penguin 2003); ENRON was a company which used a neoliberal model of corporate governance to become very powerful but eventually became riddled with conflicts of interests and fell into fraud and became insolvent in 2001.

59 Christina Voigt (ed), *Rule of Law for Nature: New Dimensions and Ideas in Environmental Law* (Cambridge University of Law 2013).

12 Delineating boundaries

A different way of delineating boundaries

The fundamental importance of rivers and water

Water if essential for life on this planet, so if the planet is to heal, water and river basins are an obvious starting point. Some territorial boundaries are arbitrary, sometimes done for ruling populations who are diverse and do not have a similar culture. The colonising powers did not set their boundaries with an intention to make sure that there were harmonious relations with different people and nature.

The Atrato River and the New Zealand case studies show that biocultural rights should eclipse narrow financial and political interests and focus on the health of the area. The same is true for political boundaries. This means that sovereignty of the state or province could be diminished as against the integrity of the river basin or river boundary. In the Ganga and Yamuna judgement, the Supreme Court of India ruled that the political boundaries were sacrosanct, but arguably the court was wrong. The environmental emergency is so severe that norms should be reordered. Perhaps a new geographical pattern of river basins should be envisaged, and the custodians of those basins would have duties only to the rivers, lakes or basins. This would break the accepted pattern of boundaries which was often established by colonising powers. When the new pattern of boundaries is established, environmental concerns will be supreme rather than the destructive extractive configuration of primacy of shareholder and profit maximisation.

International stakeholder governance solution?

To ease the tensions between the stakeholders and to help the custodians, this section suggests that an international stakeholder governance solution (ISG) could be devised. All stakeholders in this ISG will have the overriding duty to protect the river basins and therefore the earth. Gaia philosophy argues that the earth is a living entity; jurisprudence could use the legal personality of the earth to appoint guardians or custodians to protect its rights. Those appointed would have a duty to use the earth's resources, and they must replenish the earth and deliver a 'Green New

DOI: 10.4324/9781315386782-15

Figure 12.1 British Museum print

Deal'[1] for ameliorating the effects of climate change and the lack of biodiversity. There are many versions of a Green New Deal, but arguably all of them will follow the primacy of the earth. However, if any of them can be more than a pipe dream, law and regulation must be a key part of implementing it.[2]

Although it is unlikely that the earth will attain legal personality soon, the Atarto basin case and the New Zealand settlement can lead to research pilots in particular areas where there is significant sensitivity between humans and nature. The Atarto River and Whangaui River cases could be a template for an eventual ISG. In the Atarto case, the Supreme Court ordered that the river was to be protected by the government forming a stakeholder guardianship cooperation between the ethnic communities that inhabit the basin of the Atrato River in Chocó. Implementing this guardianship will be very difficult, but it might be that this case can illuminate several intractable complications from stakeholder corporate governance to environmental sustainability. It is clear that in linking the Colombian government and

1 Naomi Klein, *On Fire: The Burning Case for a Green New Deal* (Allen Lane 2019); Ann Pettifor, *The Case for the Green New Deal,* Verso 2019; Greta Thunberg, *No One Is Too Small to Make a Difference* (Allen Lane 2019).

2 Christina Voigt (ed), *Rule of Law for Nature: New Dimensions and Ideas in Environmental Law* (Cambridge University of Law 2013).

the ethnic communities together in joint guardianship there will be tensions. This part of this chapter suggests an approach which could resolve these frictions. The regulations in the Whangaui River settlement could follow a pyramid formation which would show the stakeholders at the bottom. All participants would have an overriding duty to protect the earth. In an ISG, all people in this area would be able to participate and debate their interests. The stakeholders will be legal persons. If there is a contentious debate about who are legal persons, a river, an infant, a prisoner and so on, a citizen's assembly should be convened to decide who is able to be a stakeholder. If there is a further argument about who is a citizen and therefore able to participate with the citizen assembly, all legal persons who have been designated a legal person during five years before the assembly would be able to participate, and if there were 'public interest groups' who argue that other legal persons have been excluded wrongly, they would also be proportionally[3] included. The term public interest groups (PIGs) was coined by Ayers and Braithwaite during an Australian review of regulating companies.[4] Based on economic analysis as well as empirical research, they carried out research among pharmaceutical companies, coal mining companies, Australian regulatory agencies and nursing homes and found that a highly punitive regime engenders a subculture of resistance and therefore inhibits self-regulation. In essence, the regulator is seen as the enemy. Further, a solely punitive regime 'engendered a game of regulatory cat and mouse whereby firms defy the spirit of the law by exploiting loopholes and the state writes more and more specific laws to cover the loopholes'.[5] Ayres and Braithwaite argue that, added to this climate of resentment, the inefficiency and uncertainty of enforcing punitive regulations makes it clear that a cooperative standpoint should be the starting position. The Colombian government cannot, therefore, use strict regulations to enforce environmental or social behaviour on businesses. Rather, they should cooperate with all stakeholders, including the businesses who should design a system of 'enforced self-regulation'. The stakeholders would propose its own environmental and social norms. Ayres and Braithwaite's insights show that this sort of regulation is arguably cheaper and more efficient than 'outside' regulation, in that it achieves greater depth within group and engenders more cooperation.[6] Adapting Ayres and Braithwaite's regulatory design of regulation, to the stakeholders, involves 'tripartism'. This strategy involves the empowerment of PIGs, which will inject more democratic involvement since it would be an 'opportunity for participation by stakeholders in decisions over matters that affect their lives'.[7] Ayres and Braithwaite's model also accepts that a 'benign big gun' would be needed – a regulator who cooperates with the stakeholders but has power to enforce the duty to the earth. Their vision of a benign big gun (in the Atarto case the government

3 In proportion to the number of stakeholders.
4 I. Ayres and J. Braithwaite, *Responsive Regulation* (OUP 1992).
5 Ibid page 26.
6 Ibid page 103.
7 Ibid 82 and see Chapter 5.

and in New Zealand the Te Pou Tupua) which the regulators have at its command is a pyramid of sanctions. The pyramid is used by deploying a 'tit for tat' approach of regulation. This involves encouraging cooperation, but if it is not forthcoming using a lower-level sanction. If cooperation is then forthcoming, a full cooperative model is re-established. If no cooperation is forthcoming, the regulator moves up the pyramid to a heavier penalty. In this way, the cooperation between the stakeholders would be enhanced. However, if the tensions spill over, using a citizen assembly could be a method of settling the matter. These are now examples of deliberative polling or citizen assemblies. In 2017 citizens of Mongolia gathered in Ulaanbaatar at the Government Palace to deliberate on six possible constitutional amendments.[8] Forms of deliberative democracy is becoming more popular to address issues, including waste management in Brazil and environmental disaster management in Uganda.[9] A citizen assembly worked well in Ireland,[10] even though the issue involved was abortion, which has been politically toxic there. In 'Defibrillating Democracy', Wilson and Mellier argue that citizen assemblies have the potential to restart democracy.[11] They also argue that they tend to generate policies far more ambitious than those politicians come up with alone. Often citizen assemblies consist of gathering people (often 100–150) who are selected to be a true snapshot of the area based on demographic criteria such as gender, age, income and education level.[12] The citizens are selected by lot, and it is necessary to ensure that everyone participating gets support by paying attendance fees, providing childcare and providing the necessary accessibility for persons who are disabled. Often the assemblies convene for two or three weekends to focus on a controversial issue and come up with a set of recommendations. In the case of the Atrato guardianship and in New Zealand the Te Pou Tupua, the citizen assembly could recommend the membership of the guardians. Once the members of the guardians are settled, the citizen assembly might recommend that each of the joint guardians and all of the stakeholders in the area should design their own norms with the cooperation of the big gun.

If the tensions between the stakeholders spill over, another citizen assembly should be called to deal with the particular issue.

This next chapter will focus on business, companies and MNEs and adapting to a Gaia philosophy – this is the next challenge. In a river basin there will be commercial enterprises but no profit maximisation.

8 <https://cdd.stanford.edu/2017/mongolias-first-national-deliberative-poll-on-constitutional-amendments/>

9 <https://osf.io/preprints/socarxiv/discover?q=citizens%20assemblies> accessed 27 March 2021.

10 Caroline Bannock, 'Transparency and Fairness: Irish Readers on Why the Citizens' Assembly Worked' (2019) <https://www.theguardian.com/commentisfree/2019/jan/22/irish-readers-citizens-assembly-worked-brexit> accessed 09 September 2020.

11 R. Wilson and C. Mellier, 'Defibrillating Democracy' (*New Internationalist*, March 2021).

12 <https://www.involve.org.uk> accessed 27 March 2021.

13 Corporate governance

The Atrato and Whangaui River cases

Corporate governance system building on the Atrato and Whangaui River cases

What is clear from the previous discussion is that any businesses involved with the Atrato basin or similar areas must consider its corporate governance structure in order to cooperate with all stakeholders in the area. A neoliberal shareholder, free market, contractual model cannot fit into a Gaia philosophy. Rather, it is necessary to consider all of the interests of all stakeholders. Businesses in this area must instead become custodians of the earth, and all custodians/stakeholders should have access to debate and deliberate. They will need to have a code of ethics to guide them in their work. Extreme individualism has led to the degradation of the planet and has produced detrimental results for both communities and individuals, as the property rights debate shows. In commercial law, the concept of a fair contract or bargain has been abused to mask any natural imbalance between powerful and weaker parties in the bargain. Individualism posits that it is the right of each individual to pursue a life plan and, short of the harm principle, to be free from interference. In the Atarto and Whangaui River cases, the old neoliberal discourse must not distort the decisions between the companies who wish to extract metals and fell trees. If their corporate governance systems were to turn around from profit maximisation to protecting the environment, the earth would be hugely benefited.

The legal personality of a river basin and that of a company have similar characteristics, specifically their legal personalities and the fact that a company needs a management system because it is legal fiction.

In the Atarto and Whangaui River cases, the businesses in the area will have to adapt to the corporate governance systems recognising that the legal person (river) is the dominant interest in the area. The businesses will be managed by the directors and will owe their duties to the welfare of the area. Unless the contractual model of companies or businesses are adapted, there will be a conflict of interest between the river and the duty to business or shareholders (the agency problem), because a legal person (the river) cannot act without custodians. However, if the businesses shares an ethic of caring for the area and the human managers/custodians share the same goal, the agency 'problem' is resolved.

DOI: 10.4324/9781315386782-16

For many years corporate governance scholars have debated the concept of a stakeholder model,[1] without a breakthrough, partly because of the pre-eminence of the 'owners' of the company, since the shareholders are the only people who can sue directors. Stakeholders other than shareholders have no power to bring a claim against the directors in company law. If UK directors' duties could be amended to include all stakeholders in an area, like the Atrato and Whangaui River cases, it could be template for sustainable growth. Section 172 of the Company Law 2006 would be reformed to make sure that all stakeholders could have a real impact on the company, rather than a minimal effect of changing policies. This section focuses on a stakeholder model of corporate governance, since shareholder primacy cannot deliver on the goals of Gaia.

The Atrato and New Zealand case studies exemplify a stakeholder model theory. The court and the regulations tried to balance all interests involved, raising a challenging question: where/who are the priorities? Even if the Gaia principle is adhered to (that is, that the primacy of the earth trumps other interests), we need specifics. Where is the balance between beavers and trees, or fish and birds – and, crucially, where do humans fit in? In an 'Atarto River basin' or 'Whangaui River' case it would be necessary to design sustainable enterprises and therefore a corporate governance framework, since this is the only way that any commercial activities could be consonant with the Gaia philosophy.

Stakeholder theory and balancing interests

Some stakeholder theories[2] extend their attention to all actors they consider to be stakeholders.[3] Other scholars argue that stakeholders are defined as 'those groups without whose support the organisation could cease to exist'.[4] This includes both internal stakeholders (employees and shareholders) and external stakeholders (not only suppliers, creditors and customers but also the nearby community). In this sense, corporate governance is 'the process by which corporations are made responsive to the rights and wishes of stakeholders'.[5]

The roots of stakeholder theory can be traced to the realisation that corporations have evolved into vast entities, whose activities and policies have an enormously far-reaching effect on the livelihoods of many in close proximity to them, or even loosely associated with them. Originally, stakeholder theory emphasises the importance of stakeholders to the company and its profitability. The company is still viewed as a profit-making mechanism, but this time its constituents are not

1 See chapter 2.

2 T. Donaldson and L. Preston, 'The Stakeholder Theory of the Corporation: Concepts, Evidence, Implications' (1995) 20 *Academy of Management Review* 65.

3 Max Clarkson, 'A Stakeholder Framework for Analysing and Evaluating Corporate Social Performance' (1995) 20 *Academy of Management Review* 92, 112.

4 R. E. Freeman, *Strategic Management: A Stakeholder Approach* (Pitman 1984) 31.

5 A. Demb and F. F. Neubauer, 'The Corporate Board: Confronting the Paradoxes' (1992) 25 *Long Range Planning* 3, 9.

viewed as irrelevant actors who co-exist alongside the shareholders while failing to form a part of the corporate strategy; rather, they are seen as active contributors to enhancing the company's profits, and their highly skilled labour, supplies, reliability or availability in times of insolvency is recognised as a necessary component of the corporate profitability strategy. Therefore, if the company is to take better advantage of the aforementioned skills and services, it should also be prepared to include those actors as essential elements of its decision-making – including taking into account their interests and special considerations. 'Business is about putting together a deal so that suppliers, customers, employees, communities, managers and shareholders all win continuously over time'.[6]

This realisation births a moral argument that emphasises the obligations of the corporation (as an entity) towards, on the one hand, its constituents (widely defined to include the stakeholders); and, on the other, towards the community – not only the community in which it operates but also the community through which it acts as the channel of government policy implementation or the environment. The existence of the corporation 'as an entity separate from the individuals who compose it meant that it could be conceived as a person imbued with a sense of social responsibility'.[7] As such, an element of morality or 'conscience' is inherent to this theory. The latter, according to Berle,[8] could lead to the corporation unfolding a list of priorities that would include targets other than profit maximisation. Berle does not view conscience as a theoretical construction; rather, the ultimate aim was to build his theory into its institutions, so that it gives rise to rights and obligations. Conscience would also render certain expressions of corporate power as contrary to the values of the community as a whole.[9]

One criticism of this theory is that a management with such a multi-purpose agenda will focus on achieving the necessary balance between (sometimes conflicting) interests, instead of on what should be the primary focus of the company (profitability), thus undermining the company's fortunes.

However, even the broad interpretation of the stakeholder theory is anthropocentrism. The focus of the activities of business needs to be redirected to protecting the earth.

The difficulties of prioritising interests are made easier if the overwhelming aim is to protect the earth. Anything extracted from the planet and any damage (including any externalities, including CO_2) must be replenished or reparations must be visited on the company.

6 Edward R. Freeman, Andrew Wicks, and Bidhan Parmar, 'Stakeholder Theory and the Corporate Objective Revisited' (2004) 15 *Organisation Science* 364, 365.

7 Merrick Dodd, 'For Whom Are Corporate Managers Trustees?' (1932) 45 *Harvard Law Review* 1161.

8 Adolf Berle, *The Twentieth Century Capitalist Revolution* (Macmillan 1955) 89.

9 Adolf Berle, *Power Without Property* (Harcourt Brace 1959) 90.

Can you have a 'sustainable enterprise'?

Oslo University's SMART project analysed obstacles to sustainability in the EU and proposed interesting answers. Favouring Kate Raworth's concept of doughnut economics, they argue that a sustainable company is possible and that a circular economy can ameliorate climate change.[10] Raworth argues that economists have been using the wrong model because there are missing parts of Samuelson's diagram of the economy.[11]

Samuelson's vision of the economy was a 'circular flow' and was based on water flowing through plumbed pipes.

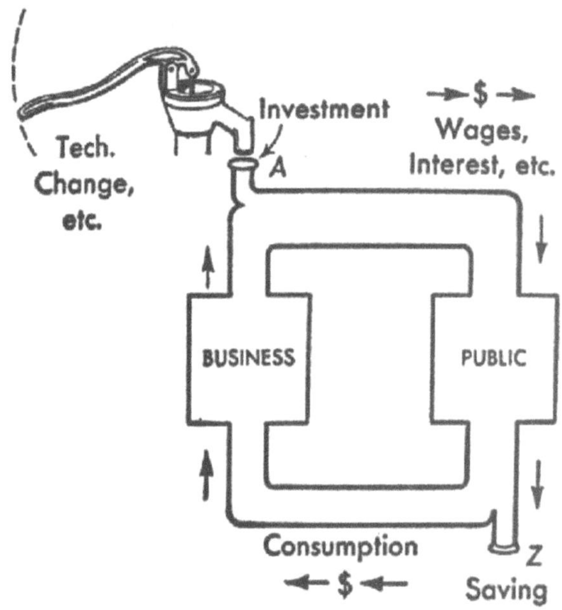

This diagram shows the macroeconomy:

Centre stage is the market relationship between households and business. Households supply their labour and capital in return from wages and profits, and then spend that income buying goods and services from firms. It is this interdependence of production and consumption that creates income's circular flow.[12]

10 Beate Bjaflell project leader, Sustainable Market Actors for Responsible Trade <https://www.smart.uio.no 2016–2020> accessed 04 April 2020.
11 P. Samuelson, *Economics: An Introductory Analysis* (McGraw-Hill 1948).
12 Kate Raworth, *Doughnut Economics* (Random House 2017) 63.

However, this diagram excludes some externalities, including energy which is so crucial, as we have realised as the climate emergency continues. Materials are also missing, including land. John Sterman rightly says, 'The most important assumptions of a model are not in the equations, but what's not in them; not in the documentation, but unstated; not in the variables on the computer screen, but in the blank spaces around them'.[13] Raworth depicts the neoliberal model as a play with characters, two of whom are the earth and power; 'EARTH, which is inexhaustible – so take all you want . . . POWER, which is irrelevant – so don't mention it'.[14]

Raworth's brilliant encapsulation of the neoliberal discourse shows how the model lacks empathy for people and the environment. So, she designed another model which she names 'the embedded economy'.[15]

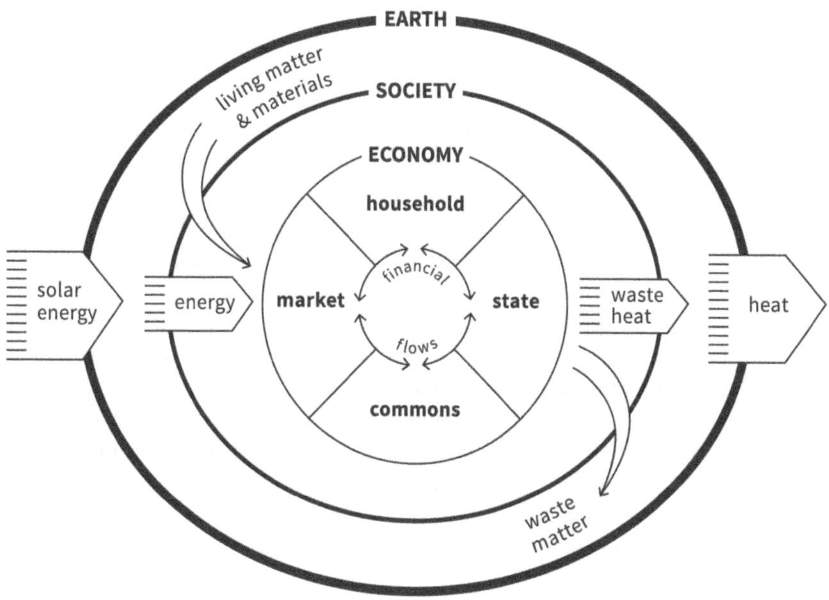

This diagram shows, first, the importance of the source of all of our wealth, the sun and the earth, something that is often lost in economic discourse. Samuelson's diagram excluded energy and materials found in the earth. This is why economic modelling is so dangerous, since crucial inputs are excluded, as Sterman noted. Second, Raworth's diagram includes *waste* to better capture the externalities that are lacking in the neoliberal model of the economy. Raworth's new philosophy

13 J. D. Sterman, 'All Models Are Wrong: Reflections on Becoming a System Scientist' (2002) 18(4) *System Dynamics Review* 513, cited in Raworth, *Doughnut Economics* 66.

14 Raworth (n 12) 68–70.

15 Ibid 71.

is explained briefly by the argument that the purpose of economics is to 'create a thriving balance' between the earth and humans. Her cast of actors are very unlike the neoliberal actors;

Cast in order of appearance:

EARTH, which is life-giving – so respect its boundaries
SOCIETY, which is foundational – so nurture its connections
THE ECONOMY, which is diverse – so support all of its systems
THE HOUSEHOLD, which is core – so value its contribution
THE MARKET, which is powerful – so embedding it wisely
THE COMMONS, which are creative – so unleash their potential
THE STATE, which is essential – so make it accountable
FINANCE, which is in service – so make it serve society
BUSINESS, which is innovative – so give it purpose
TRADE, which is double-edged – so make it fair
POWER, which is pervasive – so check its abuse[16]

In an Atarto basin or Whangaui River case, all of the actors/stakeholders would be found, discussing the best way to deploy resources and always remembering the guiding principle of sustainability.

Raworth has encapsulated many of the points found in this text in a simple diagram, the 'doughnut', showing some of the damage that humans have wreaked on the planet.

The doughnut shows the boundaries of acceptable living (in deep green). The red zone shows a circle around the circumference – these are ways that humans have broken beyond the boundary of planetary sustainability, the ecological ceiling, for example climate change or biodiversity loss. In the middle of the diagram is the way that the social foundation has been broken down, the shortfall of acceptable living in an appropriate society. Around the doughnut shortfalls are the examples of societal indicators – social equity, political voice, education, health and so on. The diagram shows clearly how humanity has wounded the earth.

The SMART project

The University of Oslo's SMART project tries to flesh out some of the points Raworth visits, focusing on corporate actors.

Concentrating on the details of EU's sustainability initiatives, the final report of the project says,

> Achieving sustainability is possible. The adoption of the UN Sustainable Development Goals (SDGs) in 2015 and the Paris Agreement in the same

16 Ibid 72.

year created a new impetus for the debate on how to do so. With an emerging recognition of the serious risks of continuing with unsustainability, there is currently unprecedented support for change.[17]

The SMART project aims to change how business operates, how products are produced and consumed and how finance can create value in a sustainable way.

The project argues that the linear economy should turn into a circular economy dealing with waste and energy. This links with Raworth's vision where all components of society are considered and is the opposite of Samuelson's diagram where waste and other externalities are not recognised.

The SMART project focused on business and specifically on corporate governance. On businesses, the emphasis is on boards: 'We propose to redefine the purpose of business and the duties of the board, to ensure that sustainable value creation is integrated throughout the business. This enables business to move away from linear, unsustainable business models of overconsumption'.[18]

To enforce businesses to act responsibly (defined by the planetary boundaries), audits and due diligence mechanisms were proposed.

Although the SMART project has produced concrete legal proposals, in the corporate governance section, their solutions are perhaps not radical enough to address the environmental emergency and inequality tragedy. The project is using company structures that have been part of the neoliberal paradigm for many years. More reporting will not change the fundamental philosophical roots of individualism, profit, competition and strong property rights. If each sustainable company tries to assess the viability of a product against the planetary boundary, what is to stop another company from breaking the boundary? It is not clear whether the SMART ideas of sustainable *products* extend to making sure that any extraction must be immediately remedied. Certainly, this is the crucial point of the circular economy, but reporting mechanisms and audits tend to slip away into vagueness. Strong regulation on all extraction could be a robust remedy following Gaia principles.

There needs to be a complete rethink about corporate structures before social responsibility becomes an embedded reality within companies.

This means that as well as jurisdictional complexities and the comparative economic power imbalance (some MNCs may be considerably more powerful than the regulating host state), philosophical and structural problems must be considered. As the SMART project found, many of the MNCs based in the US or UK are driven by the concept of maximising shareholder value, and the project coined a term 'sustainable value creation'.[19] The excellent work of the SMART project has given

17 Beate Sjåfjell, University of Oslo, Jukka Mähönen, University of Oslo, Mark Taylor, University of Oslo, Eléonore Maitre-Ekern, University of Oslo, Maja van der Velden, University of Oslo, Tonia Novitz, University of Bristol, Clair Gammage, University of Bristol, Jay Cullen, University of York Marta Andhov, University of Copenhagen, Roberto Caranta, University of Turin <https://www.smart.uio.no, 2020> accessed 08 April 2020.

18 Ibid.

19 J. Dine, *The Governance of Corporate Groups* (CUP 2000), esp. ch 1.

momentum and detail to consider more radical solutions. The SMART project did not suggest smaller companies, although they considered benefit corporations (US and Canada), community interest companies (CICs) (UK) and other initiatives in the EU.[20] However, for a sustainable environment for the planet, it might be sensible to consider smaller companies rather than MNEs, although the COVID-19 pandemic shows that some MNEs can be beneficial. To determine which large enterprises are beneficial is, of course, problematic; however, those small numbers who have constructive aims should be tightly regulated and certainly not following a corporate governance model of profit maximisation. Smaller enterprises are less likely to damage the environment and can be more easily regulated.

Changing or minimising companies

The SMART project did consider different models of companies, but they did not suggest a wholesale reform; for example, replacing limited liability companies with CICs or benefit corporations. The project did not take a radical step like this because these sorts of companies are not part of mainstream commercial entities. This is a pity because if the earth is to be healed, it is sensible to get rid of MNEs' profit maximisation and replace it with different sorts of enterprises. The SMART project tried to ameliorate the structures of companies by strict audit and reporting regulations. Unfortunately, a culture change is necessary, and unless shareholder primacy and profit maximisation are eliminated, even strong regulations will not provide a necessary shock to transform corporate governance. CICs cannot profit maximise, as the next section will show. A compromise might be possible if companies will share beneficial innovations. The AstraZeneca COVID vaccine's arrangements for providing vaccinations in poorer counties are not yet clear, but it might start a new chapter of corporate social responsibility.[21] This initiative is welcome and should be studied, but it is too early to hope that profit maximisation will disappear easily.

The legal mechanisms of incorporation of companies are simple.[22] Each company has legal personality and usually limited liability. Under its original interpretation, limited liability only covered shareholders who were natural persons, as a company could not become a shareholder in another company.[23] In the USA until the end of the 19th century, a company could not acquire shares in another company, save the cases where this was explicitly authorised by statute.[24] 'This changed in the US in the 1890s when the state of New Jersey introduced new

20 Sjåfjell (n 18).

21 Peter Beaument, 'Oxford AstraZenca Vaccine to Sold to Developing Countries at Cost Price' (*Guardian*, 23 November 2020) <https://www.theguardian.com/global-development/2020/nov/23/oxford-astrazeneca-results-covid-vaccine-developing-countries> accessed 15 February 2021.

22 Blumberg Philip, 'Accountability of Multinational Corporations: The Barriers Presented by Concepts of Corporate Judicial Entity' (2001) 24 *Hastings International and Comparative Law Review* 207 and see Dine (n 19).

23 Navarro Lezcano Maria Jose, *Piercing the Corporate Veil in Latin America Jurisprudence, A Comparison with the Anglo-American Method* (Routledge 2016) 16.

24 See: *Louis K. Liggett Co. v Lee*, 288 US 517, 556. 1933.

legislation[25] that allowed a company to form a subsidiary and to own its shares'.[26] After companies in the US were allowed to become shareholders of other companies, 'the doctrine of limited liability began applying to parent corporations, as shareholders, for acts of their subsidiaries'.[27] As companies incorporated subsidiaries, multinational enterprises thrived. This is the simple legal device which protects enormous MNEs. There are other methods of inventing powerful commercial entities, like franchises, but they are contract based. They can use contracts to hide their power by decoupling their supply chains, but they cannot easily play jurisdictional arbitrage games. For example, the easy way to avoid a state's tax regulations is to move assets into another subsidiary. Sadly, there are many more devices,[28] and there is a race between the state authorities and the commercial lawyers. However, the purpose of this fight is to limit unnecessary growth and useless consuming and to repurpose GDP and truly value the planet.

If MNEs become dangerous for the environment of society, it is possible to make them smaller. *Legally* this is simple. Politically it would be dynamite.[29] The special interests of the powerful are involved, and the economic consensus is that profit maximisation and trickle-down 'ethics' are acceptable.

Community interest companies, benefit corporations and restraining limited liability

Is it possible to turn limited liability companies into entities that benefit humans and the planet? The French language accepts that companies are 'societies'. Perhaps the state should outlaw profit maximisation companies and constrain company limited liability. The invention of limited liability was a risk-shifting mechanism, so conceivably this legal device should itself be limited for the benefit of the planet and human equality.

One small initiative might give some reason for optimism. In 2004, the Community Interest (Audit Investigation and Community Enterprise) Act was passed. This provides for a new type of company, the community interest company (CIC). The CIC is regulated by the Office of the Regulator of Community Interest Companies.[30] A CIC is a limited company with special additional features, created for the use of people who want to conduct a business or other activity for community benefit

25 New Jersey Act, 4 April 1888, ch 269 s1 (1888 N.J. Laws 385).

26 H. Butler, 'Nineteenth Century Jurisdictional Competition in the Granting of Corporate Privileges' (1985) 24 *Journal of Legal Studies* 161.

27 Gwynne Skinner, 'Rethinking Limited Liability of Parent Corporations for Foreign Subsidiaries' (2015) 72(1769) *Violations of International Human Rights Law, Washington and Lee Law Review* 1773.

28 J. Dine and M. Koutsias, 'The Three Shades of Tax Avoidance of Corporate: Groups Company Law, Ethics and the Multiplicity of Jurisdictions Involved' (2019) 30(1) *European Business Law Review*.

29 However, there are calls to limit some MNEs like Google, Facebook and Amazon because they are evidently a threat for governments and democracy; <https://www.washingtonpost.com/technology/2020/07/29/apple-google-facebook-amazon-congress-hearing/> accessed 27 March 2021.

30 <https://www.gov.uk/government/organisations/office-of-the-regulator-of-community-interest-companies>, UK Government website, Department for Business, Innovation and Skills, accessed 24 March 2014.

and not purely for private advantage, like profit maximisation. CICs are not part of mainstream business – limited liability companies are the normal template for businesses. However, if businesses should be sustainable and abide by a concept of planetary boundaries, all enterprises should be CICs because it limits profits and changes the purpose of the entity from a profit goal to a community objective.

The pieces of legislation that set up CICs are the Community Interest (Audit Investigation and Community Enterprise) Act; the Community Interest Company Regulations 2005; and the Companies Act 2006 (Commencement No Consequential Amendments, Transition Provision and Savings) Order 2007. The idea was to have a form of enterprise that can provide some social purpose but is not a charity. In the UK, charities are very tightly regulated and must be established and run exclusively for charitable purposes, so this was to be a compromise solution between a profit-centred company and a charity. CICs can be established for any lawful purpose (other than political causes) as long as their activities are carried on for the benefit of the community. CICs can be limited by guarantee or shares; if the company is limited by guarantee, the administrators will be known as 'trustees'. The guarantee is normally set at £10 each; each trustee has one vote. No dividend can be paid. A CIC also can be limited by shares; the shareholders will each own shares, any amount of shares, and the articles define the structure of the company and the voting control. A dividend may be paid. The option of limitation by shares is better for a business enterprise, while the guarantee option is probably better for managing getting money from funding bodies. When the CIC is registered the different options (guarantee or shares) are closed. They cannot convert from a share option to a guarantee option or vice versa. The Community Interest (Audit Investigation and Community Enterprise) Act, section 35, specified that 'a company satisfies the community interest test if a reasonable person might consider that its activity are being carried on for the benefit of the community'. At the end of 2013 there were over 8,500 CICs.[31]

Every CIC must:

- meet the Community Interest Test;
- file an annual CIC report with its accounts;
- keep the community in touch with its activities;
- only use its assets and profits for the community specified (or pass them to another body with similar features), known as the asset lock.

CICs which are limited by shares are also limited by a cap on dividends. CICs must be registered at Companies House in the same way as a normal company with the same incorporation documents but supplemented by a Community Interest Statement.[32]

31 Ibid: <https://www.gov.uk/government/organisations/office-of-the-regulator-of-community-interest-companies>.

32 <https://assets.publishing.service.gov.uk/government/uploads/system/uploads/attachment_data/file/626088/cic-12-1333-community-interest-companies-guidance-chapter-1-introduction.pdf> accessed 08 May 2023.

All directors of the CIC have an additional obligation to prepare an annual community interest company report, which will be placed on public record. The purpose of the report is to demonstrate that the CIC is still satisfying the community interest test and that it is continuing to carry out activities which benefit the community.[33] The 2013 report says that the regulator is a 'light touch' regulator. Unfortunately, there is a lack of research on CICs and the effectiveness of the regulations, so assessing their benefit is difficult. There is a complaints system. Section 42 of the Companies (Audit, Investigations and Community Enterprise) Act 2004 ('the Act') allows the regulator to investigate the affairs of any CIC, and Schedule 7 provides the necessary investigatory powers. An investigation will not happen unless the regulator believes that there is a

> genuine and serious concern that circumstances may exist which would justify the use of her other supervisory powers, and considers that it is necessary to investigate in order to maintain confidence in community interest companies. In addition, the Regulator will also only investigate where this is a proportionate response. It is expected, therefore, that the Regulator's power to investigate will only be used on rare occasions.[34]

Some CICs are substantial: for example, Realise Futures CIC has £16.7million assets, creating more than 100 new jobs. It provides advice, training, skills development and paid employment for people who are disabled or disadvantaged.[35] It is sad that this initiative is necessary since the original purpose of the company was to have a vehicle to support society. The shareholder primacy doctrine has distorted the purpose of the limited liability company, turning it into a profit maximisation vehicle for the rich and powerful. Perhaps all companies should be transformed into CICs. CICs limited by shares with a strong regulator and a cap on dividends[36]

33 <https://www.gov.uk/government/organisations/office-of-the-regulator-of-community-interest-companies>, UK Government website, Department for Business, Innovation and Skills, accessed 24 March 2014.

34 IBID <https://www.gov.uk/government/organisations/office-of-the-regulator-of-community-interest-companies>.

35 Ibid.

36 The Community Interest Company Regulations 2005 Section 17 provides:

> (1) A relevant company may declare a dividend to its members only –
>
> (a) to the extent that its memorandum and articles permit it to do so;
> (b) if an ordinary or special resolution of the company's members has approved the declaration of the dividend; and
> (c) if the declaration of the dividend does not cause –
>
> (i) the total amount of dividend declared on any of the company's shares for the financial year for which it is declared to exceed the maximum dividend per share for that financial year; or
> (ii) the total amount of all the dividends declared on shares in the relevant company for the financial year for which it is declared to exceed the maximum aggregate dividend for that financial year, see http://www.legislation.gov.uk/uksi/2005/1788/contents/made.

might provide an answer to the dilemma in which societies are apparently locked in a pattern of more and more growth, which is unsustainable for the planet. There are similar entities in the EU and the US, where there is an increasing use of benefit corporations.[37]

A further legal reform could be to curb limited liability. The doctrine of *Salomon v Salomon*[38] and *Adam v Cape*[39] has fetishised corporate personality and limited liability into a way that opposes justice. Recently, in the UK and the EU some courts have accepted a tort route to ameliorate the injustice.[40] However, a mixed stakeholder model of small enterprises and benefit corporations could significantly limit environmental damage.

On 10 December 2013 the Regulator published a report on a consultation on the caps on interest and dividends; Department for Business, Innovation and Skills, 'Changes to the Dividend and Interest Caps for Community Interest Companies' (2013) <https://www.gov.uk/government/uploads/system/uploads/attachment_data/file/264664/CIC-13-1333-community-interest-companies-response-on-the-cic-consultation.pdf>.

37 Benefitcorp.net, <https://benefitcorp.net/what-is-a-benefit-corporation> accessed 17 February 2021.

38 [1897] AC 442.

39 [1990] BCLC 479.

40 *Vedanta Resources PLC and another v Lungowe and others*, 10 April 2019, [2019] UKSC 20; *Okpabi and others v Royal Dutch Shell and another*, 12 February 2021, [2021] UKSC 3 Court of Appeal The Hague 29 January 2021, ECLI:NL:GHDHA:2021:132 (Oguru/Shell). *Milieudefensie et al. v Royal Dutch Shell*, ECLI:NL:RBDHA:2021:5339, Judgement (Dist. Ct. The Hague May 26, 2021) (Neth.).

14 Conclusion

This text has emphasised that neoliberalism has at its heart a philosophy of individualism, based on a concept of ownership and property rights. The idea of 'mine' has been paramount. The neoliberal economic order has exacerbated 'mine' into a global crisis where humanity is threatened. The immediate effect of climate change is obvious, but subtle changes in our brains are also happening.[1] A neoliberal brain believes that competition is vital, because this is the only way that your identity can be satisfied; a mental crisis has ensued where each person tries to be perfect and proves it by consuming more. A neoliberal brain also means that societies must have unlimited growth. To have unlimited growth, aggressive capitalist societies construct a system of consumerism, extracting resources from the earth without restraint. To oppose individualism, this chapter explored the Gaia philosophy which believes that the earth is alive. Now, international scientific studies have shown irrefutably that the earth as a whole is an organised system with interrelated and indeed interdependent activities. It is, in the broadest sense of the term, an 'organism'.

The coming climate change catastrophe poses a threat to the basis of our very existence. In chapter 8 the science was explained, and the chapter described the strategy of the climate change deniers. This chapter shows how different experts think: economists think very differently from the environmental lobby; macroeconomists believe unlimited growth is crucial to achieve the material gains pushed by their neoliberal ideology, while environmentalists believe the planet's sustainability requires targeted growth and more redistribution.[2] Legislators and lawyers are locked in a power struggle between powerful interests. One key actor in this struggle are the MNEs. MNEs and unlimited growth is a key concept on 'mine', property rights and unlimited growth. In fact, this chapter shows that absolute property rights are an illusion, a language trick. Morally, if an actor has property rights,

1 Catherine Malabou, *What Should We Do with Our Brain?* (Perspective in Continental Philosophy 2008).

2 M. Sandel, *What Money Can't Buy* (Allan Lane 2012); R. Skidekshy and E. Skidelsky, *How Much Is Enough* (Allan Lane 2012); and see Janet Dine and M. Koutias, *The Nature of Corporate Governance: The Significance of National Cultural Identity* (Edward Elgar 2013).

DOI: 10.4324/9781315386782-17

she should have a moral duty to bear more responsibility because property rights are not 'things' but rights against *persons*. So, property ownership brings power, and the greater the inequality of property ownership, the greater the domination potential.

The Gaia philosophy accepts that humans have full responsibility for the planet. So, arguing from the human responsibility for vulnerable humans because the powerful have property rights, those who have property should care for the vulnerable humans. This duty should extend then to other animal species and then the whole of the planet. Legally, this can be achieved by designating areas as a legal person, eventually designating the planet as a legal person. To do this, the person will need custodians or trustees and, when interests clash and entities try to extract anything from the earth, the custodians must replenish the damage. To find suitable custodians, a system of citizen assemblies should be created to deliberate on the sustainability of the planet and humans' impact in particular areas and eventually in the world. The custodians will need a governance structure; this will be a stakeholder model, not an individualist with the purpose of healing the planet. Chapters 11–13 also suggest a range of solutions for either healing the damage done by extractive activities or ameliorating it. Repealing laws which allow MNEs is a radical solution; legally it can be done easily but the political reverberation would be vast.

A further idea is curbing limited liability, since the risk-shifting mechanisms used in the 1880s are not appropriate now since the world is in a climate change emergency. Alternatively, other entities such as benefit corporations, cooperatives and community interest companies could be used to replace profit-maximising companies. However, it is clear that humanity needs to reorganise their economies now.

Any reform must accept that humans have a duty to the planet and make them custodians, so that the purpose of any legal mechanisms, including proposals for rights for nature and different models of commercial arrangements, must be focused on this obligation.

Index